STONEWALL

THE REAL STORY
OF THE WATERGATE PROSECUTION

BY **Richard Ben-Veniste**

AND **George Frampton, Jr.**

SIMON AND SCHUSTER

New York

Copyright © 1977 by Richard Ben-Veniste and George T. Frampton, Jr.
All rights reserved
including the right of reproduction
in whole or in part in any form
Published by Simon and Schuster
A Division of Gulf & Western Corporation
Simon & Schuster Building
Rockefeller Center
1230 Avenue of the Americas
New York, New York 10020

Designed by Irving Perkins
Manufactured in the United States of America

1   2   3   4   5   6   7   8   9   10

Library of Congress Cataloging in Publication Data

Ben-Veniste, Richard.
   Stonewall.

   1. Watergate Affair, 1972–   I. Frampton, George, joint author.   II. Title.
E860.B43   364.1'32'0973   76–56340

ISBN 0-671-22463-8

To the men and women
who served on the staff
of the Watergate Special Prosecution Force,
1973–1975

Contents

"I don't give a shit what happens. I want you all to stonewall it, let them plead the Fifth Amendment, cover-up or anything else, if it'll save it—save the plan. That's the whole point."

—Richard Nixon, March 22, 1973,
in a conversation with John Mitchell

Introduction

IN THE EARLY-MORNING HOURS of June 17, 1972, five rubber-gloved agents of Richard M. Nixon's reelection committee (CRP), including its "security coordinator," James W. McCord, Jr., were surprised by plainclothes Washington, D.C., police in the Democratic National Committee headquarters at the plush Watergate office building. In the burglars' possession the scruffily attired police officers found wire-tapping equipment, cameras for photographing documents, and thir-teen one-hundred-dollar bills.

The arrests triggered the most high-reaching conspiracy to obstruct justice in history—a concerted effort by the most powerful men in government, including the President, to cover up the facts behind the break-in and to sidetrack the criminal investigation being con-ducted by the United States Attorney's office and the Federal Bureau of Investigation.

For ten months, the cover-up succeeded. In November its principal goal was achieved: Richard Nixon was elected to his second term as President by a record-shattering margin of votes, carrying every state but one. In January and February of 1973, the five Watergate burglars and two other men identified as their leaders—CRP's bizarre chief lawyer, G. Gordon Liddy, and a mysterious former White House con-sultant and CIA agent named E. Howard Hunt, Jr.—were convicted in federal court on wiretapping and conspiracy charges. The prose-cutors told the jury that Liddy and Hunt alone had masterminded the espionage scheme.

Then, in April of 1973, the cover-up collapsed.

In a letter to Judge John J. Sirica, who had presided over the bur-glars' trial, McCord announced that higher-ups at CRP and the White House had been involved in Watergate. Counsel to the President John W. Dean III and former CRP deputy chief Jeb Stuart Magruder

11

rushed to the federal prosecutors to tell their stories. Suddenly the newspapers were full of reports implicating the President's closest aides and advisers in a massive scheme to suppress the true origins of Watergate.

At the end of April the President was forced to announce the resignations of White House chief of staff H. R. (Bob) Haldeman, domestic czar John D. Ehrlichman, John Dean, and Attorney General Richard G. Kleindienst, who had nominally headed the federal investigation into Watergate since June of 1972. The President stressed his faith in the innocence of Haldeman and Ehrlichman, calling them among the "finest public servants" it had been his privilege to know. Of Dean he said nothing.

The resignations opened the way for a unique experiment: appointment of a Special Prosecutor to take over the criminal investigation into Watergate and prosecute the accused. Nominally attached to the Department of Justice, the Special Prosecutor would act in the name of the federal government but would in fact operate independently of the Nixon Administration—virtually as an autonomous regulatory agency. A constitutional part of the Executive, the Special Prosecutor and his staff would at the same time be the Chief Executive's adversaries.

Most of those who played an active role in the Special Prosecutor's investigation and prosecution of Watergate were young people in their late twenties and early thirties. To the task they brought an unusual degree of professionalism, energy, idealism, and openness to self-criticism and—when the pressure of the work mounted—a certain degree of irreverence.

This book is an account of this unique experiment from their point of view.

CHAPTER **1** **The First Special Prosecutor**

JOHN DEAN'S CALL came as Richard Ben-Veniste was hastily recorking a recently opened bottle of Soave Bolla. The remains of a half-eaten dinner lay on the table. It had not begun as a very festive Saturday night. In the last few minutes, things had gotten a lot worse.

As usual, Dean's voice betrayed no emotion. "Rick," he said, "I guess you've heard what's happened."

Moments before, Ben-Veniste had watched a breathless Carl Stern of NBC, live from the White House lawn, stun the nation with the news that President Richard Nixon had fired Watergate Special Prosecutor Archibald Cox, abolished his office, and dispatched agents of the Federal Bureau of Investigation to seize his files. Attorney General Elliot L. Richardson and his deputy, William D. Ruckelshaus, Stern reported, had resigned in protest.

"Well, what are you guys going to do?" Dean insisted. "I've got a lot invested in the outcome of this."

Only the day before Dean had finally yielded to prosecutorial pressure and entered a plea of guilty to conspiring to obstruct justice in the Watergate case.

"John, I don't know what's going to happen. I'll call you tomorrow and let you know how things are shaking down."

There was no point in describing to Dean Ben-Veniste's helpless outrage. Sure Dean had a lot riding on the outcome, but so did the prosecutors—and the American people.

In less than ten minutes Ben-Veniste was in the lobby of a private office building at Fourteenth and K Streets in downtown Washington that housed the offices of the Watergate Special Prosecution Force. In front of the elevator he met George Frampton. Over the past four

13

months the two had worked together on the Special Prosecutor's investigation of the Watergate break-in and cover-up.

Frampton had left the building earlier that evening. He had expected some response during the afternoon to Cox's nationally televised defiance of the President's ultimatum to desist from seeking White House tapes. But none had come. Nothing official ever happens in Washington on a Saturday night.

Like Frampton and Ben-Veniste, the rest of the staff rushed instinctively to the office when they heard what had happened, as if to find strength in mere numbers and in shared adversity. Intellectually, they had accepted by that afternoon the fact that their boss might be sacked. But not emotionally. The resignations of Richardson and Ruckelshaus heightened the atmosphere of helplessness, trauma, even fear. That the President was willing to sacrifice these two men as well as Cox in order to stop the Watergate investigation from reaching him showed how desperate he had become, how much *he* felt was at stake. Knowing that, there was no telling how much further the President might go to render Cox's staff harmless and to make certain that the investigation could not be continued.

Over the months, the elaborate security arrangements at the Special Prosecutor's office—an impressive array of alarms and other gizmos, coupled with around-the-clock protection by armed, uniformed officers of the Federal Protective Service—had given Cox's staff a sense of psychological as well as physical security. Only those with plastic access badges, color coded, with the wearer's picture embossed upon them, were permitted entry beyond the unmarked door. Inside was an oasis of order and calm, a sanctuary from the currents and shoals of Watergate Washington, the hurly-burly of the federal courthouse, the constant onslaught of the media. The emotional shock of finding the office invaded by outsiders, this violation of territorial imperative, fell on many of the staff as an even heavier blow than the initial news of Cox's firing.

Ben-Veniste and Frampton had devoted most of their waking hours in the past months to documenting a massive abuse of executive authority. Yet it was the physical occupation of their offices on that Saturday night in October 1973, more than any other single event, that brought home to them personally the tremendous power available to a President of the United States, and the contrasting frailty of the legal restraints in our system that are designed to check the usurpation of that power.

WHEN THE WATERGATE cover-up was exposed in April of 1973, and the finger of suspicion pointed at President Nixon's closest aides and advisers, there was no historical precedent for a federal criminal investigation independent of the executive branch. Prosecutors in the Justice Department and United States Attorneys throughout the country (who are themselves Presidential appointees) are all answerable to the Attorney General; he in turn serves at the pleasure of the President, the nation's "chief law enforcement officer."

Institutionally speaking, the Watergate Special Prosecutor too was a creature of the President and his Attorney General. But in spirit and in fact the post was not of their making. It was forced upon them by a combination of congressional pressure for a thorough inquiry into the burgeoning Watergate scandal and of President Nixon's weakened political position.

In a nationally televised speech on April 30, 1973, the President announced the resignations of his highest White House aides, who had been linked with Watergate, and told the nation that he would now turn to Defense Secretary Elliot Richardson to assume the job of Attorney General and become titular head of the Watergate criminal investigation. Almost as an afterthought, the President mentioned that Richardson could, if he chose, appoint a "special supervising prosecutor" within the Justice Department to take day-to-day responsibilities for the case off Richardson's shoulders.

If Nixon hoped that Richardson's public reputation for integrity and lack of previous involvement in Watergate would head off pressure for an independent investigation truly outside the range of White House control, he was sadly mistaken. Both the House of Representatives and the Senate quickly voted bipartisan resolutions calling on the President to nominate an individual of the "highest character and integrity" from outside the executive branch to serve as a Special Prosecutor. The resolutions urged that the Special Prosecutor be given concrete guarantees of independence from the White House and that his nomination be submitted to the Senate for confirmation. Republican Senator Charles H. Percy sponsored the Senate measure; indicative of the gap between Percy's idea of an independent Special Prosecutor and the "supervising prosecutor" mentioned in the President's speech were reports that Nixon had vented his spleen against Percy by declaring to advisers that "that son of a bitch" would "never become President" while Nixon was alive.

There were rumblings, too, from members of the Senate Judiciary Committee that Richardson's nomination might be held hostage to appointment of a Special Prosecutor. Several senators hinted diplomatically that they "expected" that Richardson would soon give the committee an advance commitment to appoint an independent man to take over the case.

Richardson got the message. On May 7, he announced that he would indeed appoint a Special Prosecutor, and he offered the committee the opportunity to pass on his choice—in effect, to confirm the appointment informally—prior to approving Richardson's own nomination. At the opening of his confirmation hearings two days later Richardson reiterated his willingness to appoint an individual who would command congressional and public respect.

Unfortunately, Richardson was less forthcoming about concrete guarantees to insulate the Watergate investigation from direct or indirect White House influence. His solemn pledge that there would be an "arm's length" relationship between the Justice Department and the White House with respect to the Watergate case (the President, Richardson claimed, did not even want to be kept informed of the progress of the investigation) did not impress the committee. Nor were the senators happy with Richardson's declaration that the Attorney General would retain "ultimate authority" for the probe. It was too late to settle for assurances that Richardson and his nominee would be "honorable men"—that good faith and good character alone would suffice to convince the public that the investigation would get to the bottom of Watergate.

External pressures on Richardson also mounted. His first four candidates for the Special Prosecutor post turned him down, charging that the position as Richardson conceived it did not offer sufficient autonomy. The president of the American Bar Association criticized Richardson's unwillingness to assure his Special Prosecutor a completely free hand, urging that if necessary a special federal agency should be established to handle the investigation and any subsequent prosecutions.

With its power to veto Richardson's nomination as Attorney General, the committee had him (and indirectly the President) between a rock and a hard place. Successful installation of Richardson at Justice and a publicly satisfactory resolution of responsibility for the Watergate criminal investigation were essential ingredients in the President's plan to shore up shattered public confidence in his Administration after the revelation of the cover-up.*

In short order Richardson gave in. On May 17 he issued a proposed charter defining the authority of the Watergate Special Prosecutor he would appoint. In it, Richardson promised not to "countermand or interfere with" the prosecutor's "decisions or actions" or to remove him from office "except for extraordinary improprieties." The same day, he telephoned his former constitutional-law professor at Harvard, Archibald Cox, and offered Cox the job. Following further negotiations between the two about the terms of the charter drafted by Richardson, Cox agreed; his appointment was announced by Richardson the next day.

When Cox and Richardson appeared before the Senate Judiciary Committee together on May 21, Cox expressed satisfaction with the text of the charter. The Special Prosecutor and a staff of his choosing would assume jurisdiction over a wide range of possible crimes: not only the Watergate bugging and cover-up, but all "allegations involving the President, members of the White House staff, or Presidential appointees," and other offenses related to the 1972 Presidential campaign. The Watergate Special Prosecution Force would be endowed with the customary law enforcement powers of the executive branch— the authority to conduct grand-jury investigations, issue subpoenas, immunize witnesses, and institute prosecutions. The new Force would also get some unusual powers, reflecting its special independent status: the Special Prosecutor could go to court to contest White House refusals to produce evidence—something no Attorney General had ever done—and he was guaranteed access to evidence "from any source."

As the charter was written, Cox told the committee, the only authority Richardson retained was "to give me hell if I don't do the job."

---

* The President's grand shuffle also included replacement of Haldeman as White House chief of staff by Army Vice-Chief of Staff Alexander Haig, appointment of Environmental Protection Administration head William Ruckelshaus to replace the disgraced L. Patrick Gray III as director of the FBI, movement of the new director of Central Intelligence, James R. Schlesinger, to Defense, appointment of career CIA man William E. Colby to take over that agency, and designation of two lawyers, Leonard Garment and J. Fred Buzhardt, to handle the White House interests in Watergate.

Richardson agreed. He would retain, in effect, only the "residual" authority to provide support for the Force, to delegate some matters to Cox, and, of course, to fire him—but only for "extraordinary improprieties."

The committee's vote and full Senate confirmation of Richardson and Cox came two days later. On May 25 both professor and former student were sworn in. On May 31 Richardson formally issued the charter of the Watergate Special Prosecution Force as part of a legally binding federal regulation.

THE ABSENCE OF any precedent for an independent federal prosecutorial unit removed from Presidential control was an accident of legal and political history. In the Constitution, the Framers chose not to adopt the British system in which criminal prosecutions were (and still are) often instituted by private citizens. Instead, they placed the power to enforce federal law squarely in the hands of the Executive. The President alone was charged with the responsibility to "take care that the laws be faithfully executed," and was given the power to appoint (subject to senatorial confirmation) and to remove subordinate law enforcement officials.

Evidently the Founding Fathers did not anticipate the specter of the Chief Executive's intimates, or indeed the President himself, becoming the subject of an ordinary criminal investigation instituted by a subordinate. They adopted the remedy of impeachment for the extreme case of Presidential corruption or usurpation of constitutional authority. But what if a President were accused of criminal misconduct that did not give rise to congressional proceedings to remove him? Or a trusted Presidential adviser were implicated in criminal activity, in circumstances suggesting that the President was reluctant to see the matter thoroughly aired? Perhaps the Founders were confident that in such cases our system of checks and balances would see to it that the President fulfilled his constitutional duty to enforce the law no matter how difficult his conflict of loyalties.

If so, their confidence was rewarded for nearly two hundred years. Historically, in scandals involving the executive branch, the nation relied upon the investigatory powers of Congress to dig out the facts and upon the ordinary prosecutorial authority of the Attorney General to bring the culprits to justice. Even in the infamous Teapot Dome scandal—sometimes cited as precedent for appointment of a federal special prosecutor—the two special counsel appointed by President Coolidge remained under his direct authority and complete control. The suspects in the Teapot Dome case were Cabinet officers whom Coolidge had inherited from his predecessor, Warren G. Harding—including the holdover Attorney General—not Coolidge himself.*

Not until 1973, when the Watergate cover-up came to light, had any sitting President ever been a potential subject of an ongoing federal criminal investigation. Nor had any mechanism ever existed for insulating such an investigation from ultimate Presidential control. Most constitutional scholars agree that Congress could in the past have enacted legislation authorizing a special prosecutor to be appointed in such situations by judges of the federal courts. A judicially appointed Watergate prosecutor would, of course, have been even more protected from Presidential manipulation than was Archibald Cox. But the matter was not free from constitutional doubt, and in any event Congress had never acted. Indeed, later efforts to pass such legislation, in the fall of 1973, came to naught.

* In the Teapot Dome scandal, as in Watergate, President Coolidge was compelled by congressional pressure to appoint two "special counsel," one from each political party. Their principal task, however, was not criminal investigation. They were charged to bring suit on the government's behalf to rescind leases of valuable government-owned oil lands made by Secretary of the Interior Albert B. Fall, a Harding appointee, to two of Fall's cronies. Coolidge himself was never personally implicated in the corruption surrounding the leases, which had been made while he was Vice President under Harding. It was Fall and other Harding Cabinet members who were suspected of having improperly enriched themselves. The use of special counsel was a device permitting Coolidge to supersede his own Attorney General—a Harding holdover and a friend of Fall's who had become suspect—without actually having to fire the man. Coolidge's special counsel were the President's agents, directly answerable to him, rather than employees of the Justice Department. Only after winning lawsuits to declare the oil leases invalid for fraud did the special counsel turn to instituting criminal prosecutions against Fall and his cronies. Even then, the criminal side of their work alone spanned more than four years and resulted in more acquittals than convictions!

The first criminal charges brought against Fall and the first of the lessees, Edward L. Doheny, for conspiracy to defraud the government resulted, after a three-week trial in 1926, in both being acquitted. Nearly a year later Fall and his other crony Harry F. Sinclair were tried for conspiring together in connection with the other oil lease, but a mistrial was declared when it was discovered that Sinclair had hired Burns guards to surveil the jury. This gambit earned Sinclair a conviction for contempt of court and a six-month jail sentence. But when Sinclair was retried on the conspiracy charge alone (Fall had allegedly become too ill to stand trial), he was acquitted. Finally Fall was convicted in 1929 on a single charge of accepting a bribe from Doheny. He was sentenced to a year in jail and a $100,000 fine. Doheny, tried in the fall of 1930 for bribing Fall, was again acquitted. In all, Coolidge's special counsel litigated two civil suits, two contempt cases and eight criminal trials over a period of six and a half years. Coolidge's own actions were never called into question during the criminal investigation and the trials.

Ironically, in 1951 then-Senator Richard Nixon introduced a bill that would have permitted federal grand jurors to seek outside assistance in extraordinary cases from special attorneys who would be empowered to investigate on their own initiative. The bill did not pass.

The few well-known special prosecutors prior to Watergate had been in the state rather than federal criminal-justice system. Undoubtedly the most famous was the Republican "boy wonder" of New York, Thomas E. Dewey. As an assistant U.S. Attorney in New York, Dewey gained a widespread public reputation for crusading against the corruption that flourished under New York City's Democratic-controlled Tammany Hall political regime. In 1935, after Dewey had returned to private law practice, a courageous New York State grand jury convened by the Tammany district attorney ousted the DA and his associates from the grand jury's deliberations and publicly demanded that a special prosecutor be appointed to root out corruption in the city. Pressure from the voters and the organized bar mounted on Governor Herbert H. Lehman, also a Democrat, to take his Democratic DA off the case and select Dewey to oversee the probe instead. Virtually by public acclaim, the ardent thirty-two-year-old Republican was thus designated—by a Democratic DA, on orders of the Democratic Governor—to investigate New York City's corrupt Democratic political machine.

Technically, Dewey's legal guarantees of independence were far less formal than those of Archibald Cox. Dewey was simply appointed a deputy assistant DA for Manhattan and, theoretically, served under the man whom the grand jury had rejected. Cox's independence, at least, was to be based on a written charter approved by the Senate as a moral condition of Elliot Richardson's confirmation and incorporated in a legally binding federal regulation—although the regulation could be withdrawn by the President and the Attorney General. Nonetheless, Dewey compiled a remarkable record battling corruption, organized vice and racketeering without interference from his superiors. As Cox was to do nearly forty years later, Dewey relied heavily on the reality of independence that sprang from deep-seated public support for a truly independent investigation.

In 1935 it would have been inconceivable to suggest that because of overzealousness Dewey might be fired by the Governor or his own boss, the Tammany DA. So, too, in May of 1973, no one seriously considered it possible that Richard Nixon, having acquiesced in the creation of the Watergate Special Prosecution Force to shore up his Administration from the erosion of Watergate, might soon cast aside the pledges he had made to Congress and the public and seek to do away with his own Special Prosecutor.

IN CONTRAST TO DEWEY, Archibald Cox was a man who had done his government lawyering as a Democrat before being appointed by a Republican Attorney General, on the "instructions" of a Republican President, to investigate Republican political corruption. Cox was an unlikely choice, too, in light of his role as a member of John F. Kennedy's "brain trust" in the 1960 campaign against Nixon, and his service under Robert F. Kennedy in the Justice Department. However, it was not Cox's politics but something more profound in his character that Richard Nixon miscalculated.

The Williston professor at Harvard Law School sometimes seemed almost a reincarnation of one of those ancient giants of jurisprudence into which the school strives mightily to breathe eternal life. Yankee, scholar-aristocrat (with emphasis on the former), sometime government servant, man of moral rectitude, Cox was the possessor of impeccable credentials and unusual talents.

His academic career had been distinguished: St. Paul's School, Harvard Law School, *Harvard Law Review*, law clerk to the famous Judge Learned Hand, and professor of law at Harvard in his early thirties. His first specialty, and one that continued to be regarded as his province within the law school, was labor law. But to the legal community at large and especially in Washington, Cox was thought of primarily as a constitutional scholar. After advising Kennedy during the 1960 campaign, Cox became Solicitor General of the United States, the President's lawyer in the Supreme Court. The tall, erect New Englander with the unfashionably close-cropped steel-gray hair cut a fine figure in traditional morning coat and tails, arguing the government's most important constitutional cases before the Court. Cox himself insisted on the sartorial tradition when he appeared before the Supreme Court in argument. To his mind, it emphasized the solemnity of the occasion, the significance of the Court's role, the majesty of the law. Yet in everyday life Cox favored bow ties and suits that emphasized a tweedy and professorial demeanor. The contrast was only one of a number that made up the man.

In informal discussions, as in court, Cox could be a brilliant oral advocate. Yet the consensus among Harvard Law students had long been that in the classroom he was a stiff and somewhat boring teacher. Although staff meetings at which he presided tended to drag on for hours, his writing was, to the contrary, incisive, brief and to the point. The same law students who avoided his classes seized on his law review articles. Some of the scholarly pieces he had written were gems: clear, penetrating, with a fine economy of style.

Arrogant, some said of him, and there was truth to it if only because of his milieu: self-righteousness and intellectual smugness have always been the dark side of the great Harvard legal tradition. Anecdotes of Cox's unyielding manner in arguing cases before the Supreme Court were legion. Yet, one of Cox's strengths as Special Prosecutor would be his openness to different points of view, his willingness to be challenged by younger staffers and to debate and even to change his mind —especially his eagerness to learn about the craft of prosecuting from those who he recognized knew more about it than he did.

Cox's predominant characteristic, one sometimes mistaken for arrogance, was his overwhelming sense of the importance of distinguishing right from wrong. Cox believed deeply in the necessity for rules and order in the life of society as in the life of the mind. He believed in the preeminence of law. His style and demeanor were professorial, but his passion was for principle. When he perceived an important principle, legal or moral, to be at stake, he was unbending. His tenacity on matters of principle might have seemed odd for an experienced labor arbitrator, inured to the process of resolving disputes by turning to the particular disagreement involved and trying to fashion a fair solution. Fairness, for Archibald Cox, was a major principle in itself and one about which he could be very stubborn.

Few recalled that in 1952, after serving for a few months as head of the Wage Stabilization Board, Cox resigned in protest when President Truman overrode the board's decision to lower from $1.90 an hour to $1.50 an hour the wage increase John L. Lewis had negotiated with the coal industry for his coal miners. Forty cents an hour was a matter of principle, and a matter of principle was worth resigning over.

It was Cox's passion for order that won him praise in many quarters (but poor marks from students and their sympathizers) for the role he played as an "independent" outside mediator in campus disturbances at Columbia University in New York City and later at Harvard. Students complained that Cox's most determined efforts at impartiality were undermined by the strength of his adherence to the principle of campus order as a value above all others. He simply couldn't "relate" to the student side of the controversy, some said.

A forbidding portrait, this, of a stern, dry Yankee lawyer with strong feelings about justice, order and the proper functioning of institutions. Yet Cox was a man who visibly worried about taking himself too seriously—a trait almost unknown these days in public life—and he had an uncanny ability to puncture a natural tendency toward professorial pomposity at just the right moment with a self-deprecating word or phrase.

Before his swearing-in Cox had asked two colleagues on the Harvard Law School faculty to lend him a hand setting up his office, giving the Special Prosecution Force an instant staff of three. One, Jim Vorenberg, forty-five, was a specialist in the study of the criminal-justice system. In 1964 he had been appointed the first chief of the Office of Criminal Justice—a new policy-planning organ set up by Attorney General Robert Kennedy in the Justice Department—and later he had served two years as executive director of President Johnson's Commission on Law Enforcement and Criminal Justice, which systematically canvassed American law enforcement practices and made comprehensive recommendations for reform. Within a few days a third member, Tom McBride, joined the staff. A onetime assistant DA from New York, McBride too was more of a criminal-justice professional than a prosecutor, having worked in policy-planning at Justice and as staff director of the Washington-based Police Foundation.

Confusion reigned for the first several weeks of the infant Force's lifetime. Cox and his assistants were temporarily squeezed into an obscure three-room suite in the cavernous Justice Department Building. Cox himself, together with a single locked file cabinet containing Justice Department summaries of some of the grand-jury testimony in the Watergate case, occupied one of the smaller rooms. The rest of the staff had to make do with two secretarial desks and a couple of straight chairs in the main office of the suite. As new lawyers joined the Force, each was allotted a small segment of the mantelpiece over the suite's fireplace to serve as mailbox, desk and a place to put sandwiches brought for lunch.

Cox had bigger plans—plans for dozens of attorneys and even more support personnel. But he had decided that for symbolic as well as logistical reasons the Force's permanent offices should be located away from the Justice Department Building. Space was quickly found in a private twelve-story office building at 1425 K Street in downtown Washington. A large part of the building was already rented by the State Department's Passport Agency and thus protected by government security systems.

WHILE THE NEW OFFICES were being readied for use and job applications that had flooded Cox's now bustling suite were being reviewed, Cox devoted his personal attention not to the Watergate cover-up investigation but primarily to administrative and organization problems, such as his relationship with various parts of the Justice Department. But there was one key problem in the case itself he could not avoid facing immediately: how to handle the three federal prosecutors eight blocks down Pennsylvania Avenue at the U.S. Courthouse who had been conducting the Watergate criminal investigation since June of 1972.

The three—Earl J. Silbert, principal assistant U.S. Attorney for the District of Columbia, Seymour Glanzer, chief of federal fraud prosecutions in the District, and Donald E. Campbell—had moved quickly when the cover-up fell apart in April to assemble strong cases against high-ranking officials of the Committee to Re-Elect the President (CRP) and of the White House. Believing that they themselves had been instrumental in "breaking" the case, they were surprised and angered at newspaper allegations charging that they might have been integrally involved in the cover-up itself. Appointment of a Special Prosecutor to supersede them was the last straw.

On the eve of Cox's swearing-in, the *New York Times* had reported that the Silbert team was on the verge of resigning in protest. At the same time, the U.S. Attorney "announced" that his assistants had made major breakthroughs in the case, and defended their work at length for quotation by the media. Cox was livid. He viewed the prosecutors' press conference and the threat of resignations as an attempt to coerce him into agreeing to keep them on the investigation—a commitment he could not make, since one of his first tasks would be to investigate their role, if any, in the cover-up. Cox also saw the news stories as confirmation that at least some of the confidential information that had been appearing in the press over the last month came from the prosecutors themselves, a situation Cox was determined to stop cold.

Premature departure of the original prosecutors would shatter the momentum of the investigation, leave a vacuum in the case for months while Cox struggled to get his own operation on its feet, and possibly result in important leads being abandoned or lost. For Cox was a prosecutor with no office, little staff, few files, only a minimal knowledge of the case, no contacts with the potential witnesses, and no prosecutorial experience. For the time being, then, Cox had no choice but to keep the Silbert team happy and rely on them for day-to-day supervision of the investigation.

The task of convincing Silbert and his associates to remain on the case temporarily without endorsing their past efforts was one tailor-made for Cox's talents. In a meeting with the assistant U.S. Attorneys, Cox invoked professional and legal principles the prosecutors could not ignore. In no uncertain terms, Cox told the three that professional ethics and their responsibility as government employees absolutely required them to stay on the job and effect a smooth transition. For the moment, they agreed.

Lacking an able prosecutor on his staff to keep a watchful eye on the Silbert team and give him an assessment of their past performance while he was engaged in organizational tasks, Cox telephoned James F. Neal, in Nashville, on May 25. It was a fortunate decision. Neal, forty-three, was, like Cox and Vorenberg, a sometime law professor— he lectured on trial practice at Vanderbilt University School of Law— but the background and experience he brought to his students was a world away from that of Cambridge, Massachusetts. A native of Nashville, an ex–Marine officer, a former football player at the University of Wyoming and a law graduate of Vanderbilt, Neal had twice prosecuted James Hoffa for Robert Kennedy's Justice Department and then been appointed United States Attorney in Nashville. A self-styled country boy and a registered Democrat who had chosen Richard Nixon over George McGovern in 1972, Neal enjoyed a thriving two-man law practice in partnership with a friend and colleague who had succeeded him as U.S. Attorney. The practice depended in large part on white-collar criminal defense work but included a number of interesting civil clients, including country singer Johnny Cash.

Neal was reluctant to drop his new practice and commit himself to Cox indefinitely. But when Cox pressed, Neal agreed to come to Washington and help out "for a few days." As Neal put it, "You know, when I was in the Justice Department and knew Cox, I mean, he was way up there, and I was way down here. I was thirty-two years old or something, and he was Solicitor General of the United States. I guess the excitement of the Watergate case, the interest of it, was my 'pinch of greed.' But I knew it would be a big mess, just like the Hoffa case, coming in with all those congressional committees already under way, and having to work hard just to catch up. When it came down to it, I just didn't feel I could turn Archie down if he felt he needed me."

As Neal talked to Cox on the telephone that day, he could swivel in his chair and see hanging on his office wall a panoramic photograph from the early sixties, taken in the Attorney General's office. It depicted Robert Kennedy and a dozen aides conferring on the Hoffa case. The photo, snapped from behind Kennedy's shoulder, shows the Attorney General's sleeves rolled up, his suit jacket thrown in a clump onto the big desk in front of him. Among those clustered around were Neal, Nicholas de B. Katzenbach and Ramsey Clark (both later Attorneys General), Herbert J. (Jack) Miller (who would later represent private citizen Richard Nixon in the Watergate matter), and Archie Cox.

ON MAY 29, Neal arrived in Washington to assume the role of Cox's liaison with the Silbert team. Every day, Neal camped out at the U.S. Courthouse: meeting with the prosecutors, reading grand-jury testimony, sitting in on witness interviews, talking to Silbert and Glanzer, "trying to catch up." And reporting to Cox. Cox told him, "Look, without my knowing it those fellows might be making some decisions over there that are going to stop me, or at least cut off some of my options. I have to be informed about that ahead of time, so I can do something about it."

The "few days" would stretch to weeks, then months, as Neal, virtually commuting some weeks between Nashville and Washington, eventually took over the investigation from Silbert. Neal's office diary for 1973 tells the tale: scrawled across the page for May 29, in large capital letters, is the word "WATERGATE." For the rest of the summer and fall, the book is blank.

On June 1, George Frampton began work as an assistant special prosecutor. Frampton, twenty-nine, had received his law degree from Harvard in 1969. He was still undecided about his legal career, despite such varying experiences as doing legal-services work for the poor in New York City as a VISTA volunteer attorney and serving as a law clerk to Supreme Court Justice Harry Blackmun. Since December 1972 Frampton had been working as a staff attorney at a public-interest law firm in Washington, the Center for Law and Social Policy. When Jim Vorenberg telephoned Frampton about a job in late May, Frampton had to stop off en route to his interview to break out a suit and tie, items that were not *de rigueur* at the Center. Frampton had been following Watergate closely in the newspapers. He decided that working on the case was bound to be more interesting than his current legal project: compelling the government to decide whether a proposed Central American highway to be built partly with American funds might hasten transmission of hoof-and-mouth disease to the continental U.S.

Frampton accompanied Neal each day to Earl Silbert's office. His assignment was to learn everything he could about the material the original prosecutors had accumulated and to make a rough inventory of their files: grand-jury testimony, subpoenaed hotel and telephone records, thousands and thousands of FBI reports. File cabinet after file cabinet, jammed into Earl Silbert's office, overflowed with the chaotic paperwork generated during the investigation.

At the end of each afternoon, Neal and Frampton trudged back to Cox's suite at the Justice Department. Neal remembered that room well. It was the place where he had started to work when he came into the Justice Department in January of 1961 as a prosecutor and special assistant to Robert Kennedy. Then, as now, there was a feeling of getting on the train in midride: in 1961 the room had been piled high with transcripts of hearings on racketeering and organized crime before the McClellan investigating committee and other committees. Watergate gave Neal the same feeling, the frenzied scramble to get on top of the case, to compress a year of work into a few weeks.

In those first days of the Special Prosecution Force, though, there was an added dimension of anxiety in the work: the feeling of not knowing whom to trust, where to turn for help. Nobody on the fledgling staff knew quite what to think, whom to believe, what was safe. Who had participated in the cover-up? The Criminal Division of the Justice Department, the FBI, and the CIA as well as the original prosecutors were all potentially suspect—yet the new prosecutors had to deal with all these people every day in getting the investigation off the ground, and to depend heavily on the Criminal Division for support.

Every evening during the first week or two Cox, Vorenberg, Neal, McBride, Frampton and one or two others sneaked down Pennsylvania Avenue at dinnertime like a band of outlaws to a dark, depressing little grill for steak sandwiches. Cox would have his one Old Grand-Dad and water and wearily question his staff about the day's events in a low voice, always pausing when a waiter came near. After dinner, the little band marched back to Justice through the murky heat for another few hours of work.

Cox's TINY BUT GROWING ARMY moved to its permanent barracks on the ninth floor of 1425 K Street, N.W., in mid-June, when a sufficient number of security devices had been installed for the area to be deemed "safe." Safety was one thing the staff would not lack. The security system boasted not only round-the-clock protection by armed three-man teams of the Justice Department's Federal Protective Service, stationed at the one unmarked door to the office, but devices in all exterior walls to prevent penetration by "spike-mikes," alarms on every window, curtains of a specially made metallic-fiber fabric to resist long-range electronic snooping, and ultrasonic sensors in every room that would respond to any movement, however silent.

Frampton inspected the offices during the first week of June and was surprised to find technicians placing tape on the windows of the Special Prosecutor's office which looked out over K Street onto McPherson Park across the street. The sealed picture window was part of a sheer façade that rose nine stories from street level. Frampton inquired if this was another special electronic device. "Nope," chuckled one of the technicians, "just a regular burglar alarm that goes off if somebody climbs in the window. It's to protect you fellows in case Batman comes flying across the park." The snoopers in the walls were especially disconcerting: anyone who tried to hammer a picture hook into his office wall soon found that he had triggered alarm central.

The elaborate security system was the product of a bureaucratic gambit. Jim Vorenberg, concerned that time would be lost wrangling about specific security precautions at the new offices when Justice bureaucrats asked Cox exactly what he required in the way of security there, simply told them that he wanted the same security the FBI had for the areas surrounding the FBI director's office and he didn't care what devices were used to achieve it. Later he would shrug and say, "Well, better too much than too little."

Inside, almost all papers of any consequence were kept in "file safes" with big combination locks on the front. The only problem was that the locks were so sensitive that many staff members were incapable of opening their own safes, even with the correct combination. Attorneys and secretaries who had the deft touch necessary to twist the little dials in just the right fashion were usually much in demand from 8 to 9 A.M.

Only staff members of the Force were permitted to roam around inside the offices by themselves. They were required when entering the front door to trade their ID cards for green access badges, that were required to be worn on chains around their necks in the office at all times. Witnesses and other visitors got temporary red-colored badges and were required to be accompanied at every moment by a "green-badge." A few nonstaff people such as the FBI agents working on the case were permitted blue badges; they had to be accompanied past the checkpoint at the front door by a permanent staff member, but, once inside, they would not be challenged.*

It did not take long to realize the fundamental truth that "security" breaches are usually the result of human, not mechanical, lapses. The staff had been told that trash, like everything else, was "secure." After all, each office was locked in the evening when the occupant left, the FPS officers patrolled the hallways, and officers accompanied the people who collected the trash on their nightly rounds (the cleaning personnel, like the staff, all had received top-secret security clearances). Staff members thus routinely threw marked-up drafts of memoranda and like material into their wastebaskets. Not until one such draft was quoted verbatim on the front page of the *Washington Post* did an

---

* Thomas E. Dewey's operation in New York forty years before offered some remarkable parallels to that of the Watergate Force. Offered space in public city buildings, Dewey set up his quarters instead on the fourteenth floor of the private Woolworth Building—partly for security and partly to be located where cooperating witnesses could slip in and out of the many entrances and exits without being identified. A twenty-four-hour special police guard was mounted on the offices, which were almost hermetically sealed off. Special locks were placed on all filing cabinets. The offices were full of cubbyholes equipped with partitions to prevent one staff member from seeing the confidential informers of another. A special, untappable telephone cable was installed direct from the Woolworth Building to the telephone company's central office. Ironically, former Dewey aides credit a good deal of the legendary prosecutor's success to widespread use of his own wiretapping.

investigation disclose that the contents of these wastebaskets were nightly bagged up and set out in the basement of the building near a back curb for commercial trash collection. If only Ronald L. Ziegler, Nixon's press secretary, had been in such an authoritative position to accuse the *Post* of "gutter journalism." As a result of this embarrassing episode, a burn-bag system was initiated. Sensitive trash was placed into bright-colored fertilizer bags distributed to each office. The contents of these bags were then shredded into tiny remnants in an enormous, frightening-looking machine in the central file room—producing top-secret confetti.

The offices were periodically "swept" for electronic bugs. Among the office's hardware collection was a futuristic rolling console of oscilloscopes designed specifically for this purpose which looked like a cross between a vacuum cleaner and Lyndon B. Johnson's three-network TV hookup. Cox was also the recipient of an automatic tape recorder that was supposed to record all of his personal telephone calls —not surreptitiously, of course. Someone had convinced Cox that no Special Prosecutor should be without the capability to make a verbatim record of all contacts with outsiders. The machine, pursuant to Federal Communications Commission regulations, was designed to utter periodic little beeps to warn the listener that he was being recorded. This had a predictable effect on those who expected to engage in a confidential communication with the Special Prosecutor.

In fact Cox never managed to record more than a handful of calls, because he could never get his device to work properly, despite the help of a number of staff attorneys, his indefatigable secretary, Florence Campbell, and several puzzled technicians. When it was pointed out to Cox that even if he *could* get the machine to work, the parallel with the Watergate bugging was unfortunate and would not be lost on the public if the practice became common knowledge—and that nobody would ever tell a damn thing anyway with the ridiculous beeping going on—Cox briefly considered and then ordered the balky thing taken away.

The elaborate antibugging precautions became the subject of a few good pranks when Assistant Special Prosecutor Carl Feldbaum got hold of a small but nasty-looking piece of electronic equipment of indeterminate origin suspended by an electric wire from a large alligator clip. When a staff attorney was out of his office, Feldbaum would slip in and attach the alligator clip to the attorney's telephone cord where the cord disappeared under the desk, or clip it on the back of the office draperies. A little later, Feldbaum or one of his confederates would "accidentally" notice the device while chatting with the innocent attorney in the victim's office. "Say, how long has this been here?" The device would then be rushed to the security desk to be sent off for "examination" in the FBI lab, leaving the gullible staffer wondering whether he had been implicated in a catastrophic breach of security.

WITH THE FORCE INSTALLED in permanent quarters, Cox turned his full attention to deciding whether to retain the Silbert group or recruit an entirely new staff for the cover-up investigation. The decision was not as easy as it appeared. Cox appreciated more than did the public the importance of continuity and momentum in a criminal investigation. He also knew that there was no evidence to support charges that the original prosecutors had been part of the cover-up or had been importuned by their superiors in the Justice Department and the White House. In fact, it appeared that they had done a competent, if uninspired, job during the early part of the investigation—employing all the customary prosecutorial techniques—and had performed well in "shaking the trees" when the cover-up collapsed in the spring of 1973. There were those who argued that Silbert had originally been overzealous in his advocacy of the theory that Liddy and McCord were off on a lark of their own, but at the time there had been no hard evidence to the contrary.*

In the end, what convinced Cox was his belief that public confidence in the thoroughness of the investigation required that it be placed entirely in the hands of his own people. Cox had already instructed Silbert to move all his files to 1425 K Street, and during June Jim Neal increasingly began to make decisions in the case. At the end of the month, the original prosecutors' resignations were formally announced and accepted in a polite public exchange of letters. Cox's letter was carefully couched to make it clear he thought they had done a creditable job, without taking him too far out on a limb; he

---

* By May of 1973, Silbert and Glanzer were openly hostile toward the Nixon aides they realized had victimized them during the cover-up. In fact, Frampton learned that during the spring, when they discovered that their superior at the Justice Department, Assistant Attorney General Henry E. Petersen, was still passing along details of the fast-breaking investigation to President Nixon, Silbert and Glanzer blew their tops and demanded that Petersen desist. When Petersen refused, the prosecutors cut the Justice Department off altogether from information about their activities, thus making themselves for a time de facto special prosecutors.

was still afraid that if he gave the Silbert team a ringing endorsement and something unexpected later turned up, he might look foolish.

The Silbert team took their separation from the case as gracefully as could be expected under the circumstances. They had done little to hide their bitterness (they reacted to Cox's manifest suspicion of them by referring to him as "the Purfessor," thus highlighting his ignorance of the practical world of prosecuting). But they had graciously cooperated with Neal—whom they respected because he spoke their language—and with Frampton and others in turning over the reins of the case to its new masters.

RICHARD BEN-VENISTE was thirty years old when, in late June, he received a telephone call from Jim Vorenberg asking if he would be interested in discussing a job with the Special Prosecution Force. After Columbia Law School and a Ford Fellowship in advanced trial advocacy at Northwestern, Ben-Veniste had jumped at an offer from Robert Morgenthau, United States Attorney for the Southern District of New York (primarily Manhattan and the Bronx) to join Morgenthau's staff. Specializing in the trial of organized crime and labor racketeering cases, Ben-Veniste soon inherited a major case involving corruption in the office of Democratic Speaker of the House John W. McCormack that had resulted in indictments of McCormack's chief aide, Martin Sweig, and political fixer Nathan Voloshen. Later, as chief of the six-lawyer anticorruption section in the U.S. Attorney's office, Ben-Veniste had won convictions against corrupt Democrats and Republicans.

Vorenberg had heard of Ben-Veniste's record, but he had one reservation—word had it that Ben-Veniste was hard-nosed and cocky in court. Ben-Veniste replied that it was tough to hold your own against experienced lawyers twice your age without getting that kind of reputation.

An interview was quickly set up in Washington. Ben-Veniste met Cox in the Special Prosecutor's spartan K Street office. Not a single picture hung on the stark white walls. Professor Cox, rail thin and wearing a suit which was probably out of fashion when purchased, cut a foreboding figure. After going over Ben-Veniste's resumé, Cox grilled the young lawyer on fine points of criminal conflict of interest and bribery law—frequently referring to himself as the wrongdoer in his hypotheticals, much to Ben-Veniste's discomfiture.

Cox passed Ben-Veniste on to Jim Neal. Despite Neal's Nashville drawl, they had much in common. While Neal had prosecuted Hoffa, Ben-Veniste had won a kickback conviction against Hoffa's de-facto successor as head of the Teamsters' Pension Fund. The two discussed the Watergate cover-up case and the need for timely and sure-footed action. Neal explained that his own ability to continue as full-time head of the investigation was in doubt. He needed someone to assist him with a view toward taking over much of the responsibilities of the investigation at some time in the near future. If Neal returned to participate in major Watergate trials, he promised he would share the trial responsibilities with Ben-Veniste equally. That was all the inducement that was needed. On the Fourth of July weekend, Ben-Veniste hurriedly packed a suitcase and came to Washington to begin full-time work, moving into the Statler Hilton on Sixteenth Street while he looked for other lodgings.

The "Watergate Task Force" now numbered four: Neal, Ben-Veniste, Frampton and Gerald Goldman. Goldman, twenty-eight, had been a year ahead of Frampton at Harvard Law School and on the *Harvard Law Review*. After three years of military service in the Coast Guard, assigned as an attorney to the general counsel of the Department of Transportation, Goldman had clerked for Supreme Court Justice William J. Brennan and then entered private practice.

Next to join the investigation was Jill Wine Volner, thirty, who after graduating from Columbia Law School had worked for five years as a prosecutor in the Justice Department—first in the Organized Crime and Racketeering Section of the Criminal Division, then in the Management and Labor Section specializing in labor racketeering cases. Volner was the first woman prosecutor of organized crime in the department's history.

Soon afterward, Peter Rient, thirty-five, former chief appellate attorney in the U.S. Attorney's office in New York, joined the task force. Rient had been working on revisions in the federal criminal code in Washington when he was detailed to Cox in late May. Though formally made part of the cover-up investigation staff in order to serve as "law man" for the group, Rient soon became involved like the rest of the staff in the day-to-day investigatory chores. In July, Lawrence Iason, twenty-eight, a New York University Law School graduate and former law clerk to Judge Clement F. Haynsworth of the U.S. Court of Appeals in Richmond, Virginia, became the seventh member of the prosecutive team. Later, Judy Denny, twenty-seven, a recent graduate of George Washington Law School, would be assigned full time to the Watergate case during the cover-up trial.

These eight people, average age thirty-one, would be primarily responsible for the investigation and prosecution of the most sensational political scandal in the nation's history.

AROUND OUR LITTLE prosecutorial group a whole office was growing up. Cox's jurisdiction did not end with the Watergate bugging and cover-up. The sweeping jurisdictional grant on which he had insisted included responsibility for a staggeringly wide range of matters. Borrowing on Jim Vorenberg's experience with the President's Crime Commission, Cox decided to organize the office in a series of task forces, each covering a major area. Our team, the Watergate Task Force, would be responsible for the investigation and prosecutions of the Watergate or "main" case. Other task forces were established to look into the activities of the White House "Plumbers" unit (including the break-in of Daniel Ellsberg's psychiatrist's office and other abuses in the name of "national security"); charges that International Telephone and Telegraph (ITT) had received favorable antitrust treatment in exchange for campaign contributions; the dirty-tricks activities of Donald H. Segretti and others acting on behalf of the White House and CRP; and allegations that campaign-financing and reporting laws had been violated in generating secret Nixon slush funds. In effect, the Watergate Special Prosecution Force would be organized a little bit like a traditional prosecutor's office, with each task force pursuing its own "case," and a little bit like an investigatory commission.

As Deputy Special Prosecutor—the man who would coordinate all these task forces—Cox chose Henry Ruth, forty-two, director of New York City's Criminal Justice Coordinating Council, the agency that directs law enforcement planning there and disperses federal and state law enforcement grant funds. Like Vorenberg and McBride, Ruth was a criminal-justice professional. His experience spanned government (he had once headed the Justice Department's "think tank," the National Institute of Law Enforcement and Criminal Justice) and academia (he had been a professor at Pennsylvania Law School).

Cox also decided that a small group of lawyers should be hired to provide extensive background legal research for all the task forces. As head of this group Cox hired Phillip Lacovara, thirty, a brilliant young lawyer who had been serving as a top assistant to Solicitor

General Robert H. Bork. After graduating at the head of his class from Columbia Law School, Lacovara had worked in the Solicitor General's office, a Wall Street law firm, and as special counsel to New York City's police commissioner. Among his proudest credentials were his seven children. The legal issues with which Lacovara's group would soon be faced would be even more novel than anyone had expected.

In hiring attorneys to head up and staff the other task forces besides ours, Cox relied in part on the hundreds of applications that had come flooding in, and in part on the "old-boy network." The job had to be done fast, and Cox was adamant about hiring only the most able, reliable people. At the same time Cox initiated a systematic round of inquiries with friends, former colleagues, judges and well-known practicing lawyers to elicit the names of able experienced trial lawyers. There would soon come a time when investigations would be concluded and trials begun. Some people in the office, he realized, had damn well better know which way to face in a courtroom.

On paper, Cox's army was predominantly Eastern-oriented and heavily Ivy League. Many of the seasoned prosecutors, for instance, came from the U.S. Attorney's office in the Southern District of New York. Most staffers' resumés reflected a high percentage of government service compared to private law practice. But the apparent similarity in the staff's backgrounds contrasted with a surprising diversity of experience, outlooks and values among the Force's thirty-odd lawyers.

There were, for example, the criminal-justice professionals, those whose vocation had been the study and administration of law enforcement systems. Some had been prosecutors, but their principal experience was with program planning. These staff members were inclined to regard the problems fundamental to an institution's success as procedural and organizational, problems that could best be solved through deft manipulation of bureaucracies. They placed a high premium on institutional values and were acutely aware of the Force's need to maintain its credibility with the public. Thus they were especially conscious of the effect various decisions would have on the overall public impression of the office and were keen to adopt regularized procedures to govern our investigations. Above all, they were cautious and wary of making mistakes.

Finally, the criminal-justice professionals were more partial than the rest of the staff to paperwork—a burden that ordinarily is minimized in prosecuting but seemed more important in our work because of the need to make a historical record of our investigations. In fact, the attorneys with a criminal-justice-system administrative background sometimes had a tendency to regard a problem as having been "solved" once a written memorandum dealing with it was drawn up, approved, and disseminated to the rest of the staff.

In contrast to the criminal-justice professionals were the trial prosecutors. By and large, prosecuting is a young person's game: the majority of prosecutors begin trying criminal cases within a year or two after graduating from law school and stay with it only four or five years. Then they often move on—to assume supervisory positions in prosecutorial agencies, or to become defense attorneys, or to take positions with private law firms doing civil litigation. Most of the prosecutors on the Special Prosecution Force were around thirty or not much older, but already had substantial trial experience.

The experienced prosecutors tended to be more pragmatic than the criminal-justice professionals, more interested in realpolitik. They were preoccupied with the tactics and techniques demanded by concrete problems in their investigations rather than with fashioning general guidelines to meet hypothetical problems. Personally, the prosecutor types were more aggressive, impatient with delay and red tape, unaccustomed to memo-writing. Most of all, they were trial-oriented: they realized that every major decision made during an investigation is reflected at trial, that the criminal investigator's mistakes come back to haunt him. The dirty linen of an investigation usually gets hung out in the courtroom. So they evaluated a proposed course of action not by abstract standards but by the ramifications it would have for convicting prospective defendants.

The experienced prosecutors were especially concerned about Archibald Cox's lack of prosecutorial experience: they knew that the principal suspects in the Watergate case were represented by skilled defense lawyers, and they wanted to be sure these experts were not going to pull the wool over the professor's eyes.

ONE OF THE FIRST policy questions faced by the Special Prosecution Force illustrated the different modes of thinking brought to bear on our work by these two groups of staffers. The issue was whether task force prosecutors should make written summaries for the files of all their office interviews with witnesses. In late June an official policy memo, inspired by the criminal-justice professionals, was issued giving such instructions to all members of the staff. Not only did this course seem necessary to guard against loss of memory on the part of the interviewers, but the generation of written records would also begin to build a solid information base. The write-ups would be especially useful where two different task forces had overlapping interests.

By federal statute, when a government witness testifies at trial the defendants are entitled to receive copies of his grand-jury testimony and all prior recorded "statements" he has made to prosecutors. The experienced prosecutors warned Cox that in ordinary cases criminal investigators are extremely wary about making written records of what a witness says in informal interviews for precisely this reason. Written memoranda of interviews, even handwritten notes, might well fall within the provisions of the "Jencks Act" (so called after the name of a 1957 Supreme Court decision first enunciating the principle).*

The experienced prosecutors pointed out that by instituting an across-the-board policy of writing up witness interviews, and thus generating unnecessary Jencks material, the Special Prosecution Force would be cutting its own throat. Clearly, the law did not *require* a prosecutor to write a memo every time he spoke to a potential witness. Balky witnesses whose status was uncertain might be debriefed many times before they divulged the full extent of their knowledge. If the prosecution then decided to use them as witnesses, they would be subject to cross-examination at trial about their prior conflicting statements. In fact, three different prosecutors might record a witness's account in their notes in different ways. The prosecutors urged flexibility. In many instances, the task forces might want to wait to record a witness's account until he came before the grand jury—where testimony is taken under oath in response to formal interrogation and customarily recorded verbatim by a stenographer.

But Cox was not persuaded by the tactical arguments. He decided that the unusual responsibilities placed on the office required an internal record of the thoroughness of its investigations that would stand up to later scrutiny. The Force would simply have to live with

---

* Staff discussion at the time was based on the assumption that most written memoranda of witness interviews would have to be turned over to the defense under the Jencks Act at any trials. In fact, all of them were turned over well in advance of the Watergate cover-up trial. Subsequently, however, the Supreme Court ruled that only prosecutors' write-ups that are reviewed and "endorsed" in some way by the witness——such as by his initialing them—constitute the kinds of "statements" that must be given to the defense for use at trial.

whatever trial-related disadvantages were involved in the making of that record.

The younger attorneys with little or no criminal-trial experience constituted a third loose grouping of staffers within the office: young lawyers with exceptional law school records who had worked on their schools' law reviews (the legal publications staffed and published by the law students with the highest grades and the best writing ability) and then gone on to be law clerks for federal judges, many of them on the Supreme Court. Most of these bright young generalists were well acquainted with the latest legal developments in criminal and constitutional law, but from an academic bent. Most had had some experience in private practice or civil litigation but had had no intimate contact with prosecuting. They staffed the various task forces and Phil Lacovara's legal-research group.

The young generalists on the task forces were responsible for much of the preparation and investigation of the various cases in the office—assembling information, interviewing witnesses, and conducting grand-jury investigations under the supervision of the experienced prosecutors. They, like Cox, were getting a crash course in prosecuting—the ultimate in on-the-job training—while providing the meticulous attention to detail that many superb trial lawyers, by nature, are too impatient to indulge in themselves. At the same time, they tended to ask a lot of challenging questions about "customary" prosecutorial procedures that ordinarily do not get asked in the typical United States Attorney's office.

Jim Neal, older and eminently experienced, was, like Cox, in a category of his own. On the surface, Neal displayed the instincts and attitudes of the quintessential prosecutor. Impatient with paperwork, uninterested in general guidelines, he had a short attention span for anything he regarded as peripheral to the guts of the case—namely, that small core of evidence he could use most effectively at trial to convince a jury of the defendants' guilt. His first investigative priority was to do everything possible to protect and build up this little core of evidence, while looking ahead to protect or overcome the prosecution's potential weaknesses at trial.

Neal was at his best haggling with a prospective witness and his counsel to persuade them to cooperate, and, when he succeeded, sitting down to find out just what the witness could say on the stand, what legally admissible testimony he could give. The witness and his attorney would be ushered into Jim's office, where Neal and a couple of other Watergate Task Force attorneys would be waiting. Pushing his chair back, Jim would loosen his tie, unbuckle his belt in true Southern fashion, light up the first of a string of enormous Jamaican cigars (which he half smoked and half chewed to death), and "get down to it" for hours and hours on end as the room gradually filled with dense, choking smoke. The other attorneys participating in the session, and the poor witness, would stumble out at intervals to breathe. Sometimes we wondered just who was being smoked out in these marathons. Other members of the task force conducting their own interviews down the hall would occasionally hear Neal's broad Tennessee drawl rise almost to an exasperated shout from behind the closed door of his office as the afternoon wore on: "I don't care what your *impressions* of the conversation were; damn it, that's not evidence. All we want to know is, as best you can recollect, what did he say to you and what did you say to him."

Despite appearances, however, Neal shared with the criminal-justice professionals a good measure of caution and institutional protectiveness. He had been in some pretty tough criminal battles on both sides of the fence—prosecuting and defending. As a longtime defense lawyer, experienced in the plight of defendants vis-à-vis the federal government, he was alert to issues relating to the overall fairness of the investigation and of our procedures. Besides, from experience he knew the importance of proceeding slowly and carefully in the investigation, making sure every important step was justified so that no attack from the targets of the investigations or from the White House reasonably could be sustained.

To ASSIST THE LEGAL STAFF, Cox moved quickly to establish several support groups within the office. The first was an information section to summarize, analyze and store the vast amounts of grand-jury testimony and other evidence. To many in the office the lure of technology—the computer—as an answer to this problem was irresistible. The Watergate Task Force and some of the other experienced prosecutors in the office protested that a computer retrieval system was not going to be helpful for investigation or trial preparation in Watergate. The main problems facing us could be solved only by experienced lawyers working personally with potential witnesses. But the Senate committee investigating Watergate—Senator Sam Ervin's Select Committee on Presidential Campaign Activities—was fast putting summaries of all its testimony on coded computer cards. If everyone else was going to computers, wouldn't the Special Prosecution Force be remiss if it failed to follow suit? The prospect of getting access to the Ervin Committee's computer tapes, thus assuring *our* computer of an instant "data base," carried the day. As predicted, the computer project would bear little fruit for the Watergate Task Force, despite the money sunk into it and the reams of noxious-smelling printout that came spilling out. It would be the research analysts in the information section, under the long-suffering direction of Sally Willis and Ann Goetchus, not the computer, that would prove the section's worth.

Shortly after moving to K Street, Cox hired a highly respected Pulitzer Prize–winning national political reporter for the *Washington Star,* Jim Doyle, to serve as his press secretary. Since reporters were not allowed in our offices and there was no nearby press room, Doyle and his assistants often handled hundreds of telephone calls a day. Some of the attorneys initially questioned the need for such a person, accustomed as they were to the rule that prosecutors' only comment on cases is what they have to say in court. Many were fearful that establishment of a permanent liaison with the press would legitimize unnecessary press-prosecutor contacts, leading to leaks. But the legal staff soon came to appreciate the importance of Doyle's role. For one thing, he kept reporters off the prosecutors' backs. Reporters soon adapted to the policy that prosecutors would make no comment—on or off the record—about any aspects of the investigations and that only Cox, Doyle and task force heads should even talk to the press. And Doyle put out the word that there just weren't going to be any leaks from the Watergate Special Prosecution Force.

Reporters often nagged Doyle and task force prosecutors for confirmation of investigative leads they were pursuing on their own. Sometimes Doyle could confirm that the office was "investigating" a particular charge, but beyond that the office would seldom have any comment, never with respect to specific allegations. The one exception was an occasional willingness to give reporters off-the-record "negative guidance" designed to deter publication of unreliable rumors circulating in the media that were refuted by evidence in our possession. The technique had to be used sparingly, though, lest a pattern develop where reporters treated refusal to give negative guidance as roundabout confirmation of their allegations.

Like any bureaucracy, large or small, the Special Prosecution Force would not have been complete without its own administrative office. Ours was an office with a difference: it was staffed with about a dozen deaf students from the Model School for the Deaf, a special high school connected with Washington's Gallaudet College. Among other things the students delivered mail, ran errands, and operated the Xerox machines. Our administrative officer, Dan Mann, and his reliable assistant, Dan Rosenblatt, could communicate with the students by sign language; the task force attorneys had to rely principally on the students' excellent lip-reading abilities.

By early July the Watergate Special Prosecution Force numbered nearly twenty full-time attorneys and a total staff of well over thirty; by the end of the summer the number of attorneys would climb to thirty-eight, with a total staff of over eighty.

It wasn't long before the Nixon White House began to get apprehensive about Cox's growing little army. The new Special Prosecutor, it appeared, not only was serious about getting to the bottom of Watergate but was putting out tentacles in a lot of other directions too. Cox's office wasn't going to be as easily contained as the original probe. White House propagandists put out the word: Cox had assembled a staff of left-wing Democratic zealots jealous of the President's electoral victories, ideologically biased against his policies, and personally determined to "get" him.

The White House never abandoned this line—we would hear it till the end of Richard Nixon's tenure in office—but the charges wouldn't stick. The staff of the Force was selected on a strictly nonpartisan basis, solely on professional ability and experience. Cox sought out the best lawyers he could find for the work that had to be done. Neither political affiliation nor ideological beliefs ever came into the selection process; in fact, the staff was composed almost exclusively of attorneys who were neither active nor identifiable politically.

There were a few exceptions. The chief of the Plumbers Task Force, Bill Merrill, a former federal prosecutor and practicing lawyer from Detroit, had once run for Congress in his home district as a Democrat. On the other hand, Phil Lacovara had served as campus chairman of Students for Goldwater in 1964. Frampton and Vorenberg had been associated briefly with the McGovern-Shriver campaign in 1972. On the other side of the political spectrum, Joe Connolly, formerly a practicing lawyer in Philadelphia and now head of the ITT Task Force, was the son of a longtime Republican congressman from the Philadelphia area and proudly identified himself as a Republican.

Other task force leaders and top aides to Cox had no politics at all. Henry Ruth and Jim Neal had both served in the Justice Department under Democratic Presidents, but that didn't make them "Democrats" any more than the service of Ben-Veniste, Volner and others under a Republican U.S. Attorney in New York and a Republican Attorney General in Washington made *them* Republicans. Jim Doyle, queried by a reporter about Ben-Veniste's political affiliation, answered that Ben-Veniste had voted in court against corrupt politicians from both parties. Jim Neal's Nashville associates would have had a good chuckle at the notion of Neal as a "left-wing zealot."

The staff was proud of its professionalism and keenly aware that the public would tolerate no less than a thorough, competent, lawyerlike job completely free from any partisanship. To slip from the high path of political color blindness meant jeopardizing the success of the investigation and our own reputations in the bargain. Whatever feelings individual prosecutors had about the policies and the personalities of the Nixon Administration, pro or con, had to be suppressed in the performance of our duties. As the summer wore on and the hostility of the White House toward the office and toward our investigations became more and more manifest, that standard would become a hard one to live up to for many of us on the Watergate Task Force. That we managed to do so in spite of White House provocation put the lie to the Administration's whispering campaign.

THE DIFFERENT TASK FORCES worked together in remarkably synergistic fashion. Archie Cox's leadership, of course, was a major factor. In many ways things hadn't changed much from the days when Jim Neal was thirty-two and Solicitor General Cox was "way up there": the older men still looked up to Cox in the same way as did the younger attorneys. Cox, in turn, inspired enthusiasm in the staff by making each lawyer feel that he needed the best that man or woman could give him in order to help him meet the challenge of Watergate.

The open process of decision-making embraced by the Special Prosecutor also kept morale high. Whenever a task force had a serious problem, those concerned could always sit down and talk it out with Cox. The office was run on a town-meeting basis. Every Thursday afternoon task-force heads would meet with Cox and others in the "front office"—Ruth, Lacovara, and assistants Peter Kreindler and Carl Feldbaum—for regular planning sessions. The meetings seldom resulted in firm decisions being reached. In fact, they sometimes dragged on interminably, coming to resemble seminars more than staff meetings. However, they had definite value. The meetings kept everyone informed and helped resolve scheduling and tactical conflicts between task forces. Most important, they served to pinpoint future problems, both strategic and legal, and provided a forum for hashing them out.

Then, of course, there was the sense of destiny, of unprecedented responsibility that unified the staff and prompted it to work together with a mutual respect and good humor that would have been rare in any other circumstances. In the minds of those Cox had recruited, there was something "special" about the Force that transcended its special legal status.

The Watergate Task Force, by mid-July, had established a base of information, tentatively divided up the case into "areas" of expertise (the bugging, the hush money, perjury, destruction of documents, etc.), and sketched out the outlines of the investigation. Our goal was to return indictments by mid-autumn, a task that would require us to interview every potential witness, however minor, personally and exhaustively, either in the office or before the grand jury, or both. With two lawyers participating in each interview, we could schedule six to eight interviews a day, but that required preparing for the following day during the evenings. But any way the schedule was divided up, we were confronted with an enormous amount of work.

The keen rapport and sense of teamwork that quickly developed among the seven lawyers on the Watergate Task Force itself undoubtedly was due in part to this burden of work. Our natural camaraderie was heightened, too, by a shared feeling of isolation. We were engulfed in work with which everyone else in Washington was fascinated, but we could talk about it only with one another. Jill Volner's problem was especially acute because her husband, Ian, was a lawyer who represented media and publishing interests. Volner was afraid that if any leaks surfaced in the press she might be unfairly blamed for disclosing confidential information to him that he subsequently leaked to his clients. Consequently, the Volners made it a firm rule to discuss nothing whatsoever about the case with each other.

Beyond all this, the special nature of the case for the Watergate Task Force derived from more than the challenge of an especially tough investigation. We saw our work in symbolic terms, as a test of the criminal-justice process. The success or failure of our efforts would, we believed, have a grave impact on the public's future respect for the legal system and its confidence in the rule of law.

We knew, of course, that we were in for a struggle, especially when the Nixon White House opened its attacks on the office. But in June and July of 1973 we had only an inkling of how powerful would be the forces eventually arrayed against us: the historic prestige and power of the Executive; the grinding effect of public inertia and sometimes even cynicism; and in time our own doubt and fatigue. In the first months of the Special Prosecution Force, all of this was still on the horizon.

CHAPTER **2** **The Script and the Players**

THE CASE THAT THE Watergate Task Force inherited from the original prosecutors was more than a mass of information—facts, leads to evidence, unanswered questions. It was also a pattern of commitments, intentions and ongoing relationships with potential witnesses and defendants, a prosecution in the making. Our job was to pick up all the different threads of this incomplete fabric, both factual and tactical, and weave them together effectively.

The original prosecutors had by June of 1973, when we entered the case, traced the origins of the bugging to the hiring in late 1971 of G. Gordon Liddy, an alumnus of the White House Plumbers unit, as general counsel to the Committee to Re-Elect the President (CRP). Liddy, a former FBI agent turned local prosecutor from upper New York State, was an ultra-right-wing gun fanatic who had used political connections to wangle a job at the Treasury Department before coming to the White House.

In addition to his legal duties, Liddy was told to develop an "intelligence plan" for CRP. To assist him, Liddy promptly recruited his former associate in the Plumbers unit, E. Howard Hunt, Jr., with whom Liddy had engineered an unsuccessful raid earlier that fall on Daniel Ellsberg's psychiatrist's office in Beverly Hills to get information the White House could use to smear Ellsberg in the Pentagon Papers case.

Twice in early 1972 Liddy presented his intelligence plan to then Attorney General John N. Mitchell (who was planning to assume the top position at CRP within a few months but was already making important campaign decisions), acting CRP head Jeb Stuart Magruder and White House counsel John W. Dean III in meetings at the Attorney General's Justice Department office. With multicolored charts

Liddy unveiled a series of proposals involving code words, illegal electronic bugging and surveillance, a chase plane, illegal trespassing, kidnapping, prostitutes and blackmail. The cost estimated by Liddy was an even million dollars. The overall name: "Gemstone." But twice Mitchell turned him down—too expensive—and told him to come back with something more reasonable in cost.

After the second meeting, Dean described the Liddy plan to White House chief of staff H. R. (Bob) Haldeman. Dean suggested that the White House ought to keep its distance from this business; Haldeman agreed. But in the meantime Hunt had introduced Liddy to Hunt's friend and White House mentor Charles W. Colson so that Liddy could make a pitch for White House help. As a result, Colson telephoned Magruder and urged him to get moving on the plan. Right here, the Watergate Task Force was presented a difficult evidentiary problem: Colson claimed that Liddy had been vague in describing the plan and had never mentioned illegal activities. Magruder's recollection of the phone call he had received from Colson was inconclusive. And Liddy was telling us nothing.

Liddy's final budget, with a reduced price tag of $250,000, was resubmitted to Mitchell in late March of 1972 by Magruder and Frederick C. LaRue, a close friend and CRP aide of Mitchell's, at a meeting in Key Biscayne, Florida. According to Magruder, Mitchell gave the go-ahead. LaRue was less sure: he recalled that Mitchell wanted to postpone any decision—leaving us with a serious conflict in testimony to puzzle out. In any event, the plan did go quickly ahead. Liddy received some $200,000 in cash from a secret CRP slush fund of unreported campaign contributions. Hunt and Liddy recruited former CIA security man James W. McCord, Jr., and then the burglary team, four men from the Cuban emigré community in Miami. And on Memorial Day weekend of 1972 McCord and the Miamians entered the Democratic National Committee headquarters at Watergate undetected, installed wiretaps, photographed documents and slipped away undetected. Liddy began to type up highlights of information received from the bugs on bold stationery headed "Gemstone" and gave the memos to Magruder.

When Magruder showed him what Liddy had wrought, John Mitchell was not pleased. The material was junk. Besides, one of the bugs—the one on the phone of Democratic National Committee Chairman Lawrence F. O'Brien—was not functioning. Mitchell chewed Liddy out. Liddy said he would "take care of" the problem.

Magruder said he had transmitted Liddy's budgets and showed some of the Gemstone memos to Gordon Strachan, a young lawyer from Mitchell's New York law firm who was serving as Haldeman's political aide and liaison with CRP. Here again we were faced with a conflict in testimony: Strachan denied having any knowledge of the bugging. If Strachan *had* received incriminating information from Magruder, there was a presumption based on his usual office routine that he would have brought it to Haldeman's attention; Haldeman, through Strachan, liked to keep a tight rein on CRP. In our minds Strachan was a critical link because his denials served not only to protect himself but to protect his boss and his boss's boss, the President, from being implicated in prior knowledge of the bugging.

Liddy's attempt to "take care of" the malfunctioning bug resulted in McCord and the four Miamians being caught red-handed in the Watergate at about 2 A.M. on Saturday, June 17. Led off to jail, all five men gave false names backed up by phony ID cards they had in their possession. Hunt and Liddy, who were monitoring the operation from nearby, fled. In the hours after the break-in, as Hunt and Liddy scrambled to cut the links between themselves and the arrested men, the word went out across the United States notifying White House and CRP officials of what had happened.

One of the first tasks undertaken by the Watergate Task Force was to go back to the beginning and interview the burglars themselves. Hunt and the "Cubans," as they were generically called—Bernard L. Barker, Virgilio R. Gonzalez, Eugenio R. Martinez and Frank A. Sturgis (given name Frank Fiorini)—were all in jail serving their sentences and were brought to our offices in the custody of federal marshals. Actually, Barker and Sturgis were American born, but all four men had been active in anti-Castro activities. It was natural that they should have been recruited by Hunt, who was a hero in Miami's Cuban community for his role in the Bay of Pigs fiasco. As one of the ranking CIA officers involved, Hunt had borne the code name "Eduardo," which was what the Cubans still called him.

In appearance Hunt was the antithesis of the James Bond superspy prototype. While Bond was tall, tan, fit and sartorially elegant, Hunt was sallow, short and showed the beginnings of a middle-aged tummy. His bright-colored wool socks drooped and never matched his drab suits. His slacks always ended a couple of inches above his shoe tops.

Bond enjoyed the finest five-star cuisine and the best wine; Hunt was plagued by an ulcer. Where Bond had to fight beautiful women off his back, Hunt was ridiculed in print by a young free-lance writer from Boston over a maladroit pass he made at her during the period when he was out on bail. Ben-Veniste quickly developed a special dislike for Hunt, who was taken to dressing up his lies about the involvement of higher-ups in Watergate with considerable cant and foppery. Time and again Ben-Veniste hammered at Hunt, pointing out the inconsistencies in his story and ridiculing Hunt's lightweight explanations.

The Cubans presented a different case. We were sympathetic to the fact that they were the low men on the totem pole. They had been used by more powerful figures in this drama; their anti-Castro zeal had been exploited to involve them in crimes for which they should have had no motive. Nonetheless, we felt they were still holding back information about the cover-up—probably out of the same misguided loyalty that had originally enmeshed them in Watergate.

Bernard Barker's nickname with the other Cubans was "Macho." He had fled from Havana with his family after Castro's takeover. In Miami he had become active in the Cuban movement to unseat the Castro regime. Hunt, ensconced in the White House, called upon "Macho" first with minor assignments such as roughing up anti–Vietnam War protesters, or punching out some demonstrators at the funeral of J. Edgar Hoover. Then came the break-in of the Beverly Hills office of Daniel Ellsberg's psychiatrist, Dr. Lewis Fielding. When Eduardo called for a team to hit the Democratic headquarters at Watergate, Macho needed no time to make up his mind.

In person, Barker, short and stocky with thick black-horn-rimmed glasses, could be menacing or charming, depending on his mood. He was clearly the most voluble of the Cubans and, with the best command of English, was generally regarded as their spokesman. He gruffly viewed himself as being plagued by a daughter he regarded as a brainwashed liberal because she pleaded with him to give up his loyalty to the Nixon Administration and tell what he knew. Yet tears came to his eyes when he described how the same young daughter had been terrified by machine-gun-toting Castro soldiers who were searching his Havana home for him.

Martinez, nicknamed "Musculo" in deference to his physique, was from all accounts a true hero in the cause he espoused. On numerous occasions he had braved the elements to make the Miami–Cuba circuit, captaining small boats to evacuate refugees from the night-blackened beaches of his former homeland. Barker and Hunt had explained to him that he could not honorably refuse the modest requests of their allies in Washington.

Gonzalez gave the impression of being totally at a loss to understand the events swirling about him. He was recruited to join the team because he was allegedly a locksmith by trade; judging by his later success as a burglar, he was probably the only locksmith they knew.

Sturgis was a soldier of fortune, fighting first for Batista, then for Castro, then against Castro. Underneath the glitter of the term "soldier of fortune" Sturgis was just plain no good. After serving his Watergate prison term he was convicted of moving hot cars between the United States and Mexico.

With the incredible seriousness of the issues at hand also came the inevitable gallows humor. It seemed that no one could get through an account of one of the Cubans' exploits without wondering whether it had been choreographed by Woody Allen. In their first attempt at cracking Fort Watergate, the ragtag band posed as top sales executives having a sumptuous dinner meeting at the Watergate Hotel, complete with bogus promotional visual aides, planning to secrete themselves in the banquet room and then make their way to DNC headquarters upstairs. Gonzalez, who had some trouble understanding English, had not entirely grasped the nature of their mission. He stared intently at the movie screen, hoping to gain some insight about the task ahead of them from the flickering travelogue which outlined development opportunities in Arizona, while Hunt puffed confidently on an after-dinner cigar and warmed a glass of Five Star Hennessy. This elaborate charade proved in the end to be ill-conceived, as the team members, who had secreted themselves in the room, learned to their consternation that when the waiters had left for the night, they had locked them in. Not even the skilled hand of Gonzalez the locksmith could extricate them from this unexpected incarceration. Early the next morning, the rumpled "executives" ignominiously filed out of the banquet room. The scoreboard read Watergate 1, Burglars 0.

The team had had similar troubles on the West Coast. Their marching orders had been to try to gain entry to Dr. Fielding's office inconspicuously and photograph the Ellsberg file. Their ruse to leave the door unlatched was thwarted by a cleaning woman, and the lock again proved too intricate for Gonzalez. Always he seemed to be lacking the appropriate tool. Demonstrating an unfortunate predilection toward flexibility in strategy, the team swung from picklock to crowbar.

Barker described the manner by which he methodically searched the office for the all-important Ellsberg file. After finding stock certificates, reams of material relating to financial reports, balance sheets, investment opportunities, bank statements and the like, Barker got the queasy feeling that the team had somehow miscalculated and broken into a stockbroker's office, not a psychiatrist's.

On the night of their arrest in June 1972, the burglary team, through a Herculean effort by Gonzalez, gained entry to the DNC headquarters at the Watergate. They were equipped with walkie-talkies purchased by McCord. A confederate posted across the street was supposed to warn the team inside via walkie-talkie of any approaching danger. When the police arrived the confederate tried to warn the team, but there was no response—Barker had decided to conserve the walkie-talkie batteries by turning them off. And McCord had left adhesive tape visible on the lock of an entrance door even after it had once been removed by a building guard.

THE BUGGING ITSELF evidently had been a CRP operation. The evidence we inherited from the original prosecutors demonstrated that the massive cover-up that began on June 17 when the burglars were arrested had been masterminded jointly by CRP and the White House. Each did what was necessary, as the cover-up unfolded, to hold up its side of the endeavor. The object: to convince investigators that the bugging had been conceived and executed by McCord, Hunt and Liddy on their own, without the knowledge or sponsorship of anyone else at CRP or the White House.

On the same night that the Watergate burglars were seized by police in Washington, the CRP brass—Mitchell, Magruder, LaRue, Robert C. Mardian and others—were on a campaign trip in southern California. According to Magruder, Mitchell's first action when he learned of the arrests was to instruct Mardian to telephone Liddy in Washington. Mitchell wanted Liddy to contact then-Attorney General Richard G. Kleindienst and arrange for Kleindienst's help in getting McCord out of jail before McCord's true identity (and his link to CRP) was discovered.

Mitchell's alleged instruction was typical of the nagging problems with which we were confronted in our investigation of the cover-up. Liddy had indeed received marching orders from California on June 17 and had rushed out to see Kleindienst at the Burning Tree Country Club, where Kleindienst was playing golf. But neither Kleindienst nor CRP press aide Powell Moore, who accompanied Liddy on the trip, had ever volunteered information about the episode during the original Watergate investigation; if they had, the investigation's course might have been far different. When called in by Silbert in the spring of 1973, Kleindienst (who had since resigned as Attorney General) acknowledged Liddy's visit to Burning Tree but said that Liddy had come there only to "inform" Kleindienst of McCord's arrest—a story that made no sense to us at all.

Early in our investigation we sought out Moore and Kleindienst for further questioning. Only after we interviewed them repeatedly did they acknowledge that they had not been candid about the Burning Tree incident: Liddy had in fact represented on that day that he was acting for Mitchell, and had in fact mentioned springing the burglars from jail. The former Attorney General of the United States told us he had hidden the truth about Liddy's statements when interviewed by Silbert because he believed Liddy was "puffing" when he said he was acting pursuant to instructions from Mitchell. Incredibly, Kleindienst saw no harm in revising the evidence to fit what he said he believed to be the truth—or at least a "truth" more favorable to his close friend John Mitchell.

When CRP officials in California learned that McCord's true identity had been discovered, they quickly put out a false press release characterizing McCord as a sometime "consultant" to CRP with many other clients and claiming that CRP knew nothing of the activities that had led to his arrest and had no connection with them. The cover-up had been launched.

Within days, to make sure that the link between the bugging and the CRP hierarchy was severed, all incriminating documents that could establish that link were destroyed. Liddy shredded all his files, together with hotel soap wrappers (he kept the soap) that he had saved from his pre–June 17 travels; he was afraid that his movements could be traced through them. He even shredded leftover cash unused in the Watergate operation. Mitchell, at a meeting attended by Dean, Magruder, LaRue and Mardian, instructed Magruder to take his Gemstone documents and "have a good fire." Strachan reported to

Dean that, on Haldeman's instructions, he too had destroyed sensitive material in the White House. And at the urging of Colson and Presidential domestic-affairs adviser John D. Ehrlichman, Dean ordered a raid on Howard Hunt's White House safe and brought its contents to Ehrlichman. Ehrlichman suggested that Dean "deep-six" them, but when Dean demurred they were instead turned over to L. Patrick Gray III, acting FBI director, with instructions that they were politically embarrassing and should "never see the light of day." Gray later destroyed them.*

When the conspirators at CRP realized that federal prosecutors were probably going to uncover the involvement of Hunt and Liddy (who had not been arrested) they formulated a strategy of "containment." Liddy and Hunt, they maintained, were off on a lark of their own. Because so many employees at CRP knew that Liddy had received large sums of money in cash, however, a cover story had to be developed to explain the purpose of the nearly $200,000 funneled to him for his intelligence plan. Investigators were told that the money was supposed to have been used for security at the upcoming Republican convention and for "surrogate" candidates campaigning around the country on behalf of President Nixon. Magruder repeated this story to the FBI and the grand jury. Mitchell, for his part, denied knowing *anything* about what Liddy had been doing at CRP. Mitchell and Ehrlichman also helped perpetuate the cover-up by telling FBI agents that they knew nothing at all about the Watergate bugging other than what they had read in the newspapers.

Meantime John Dean was able to get FBI files and confidential information about the progress of the federal investigation from Acting FBI Director Gray and from Assistant Attorney General Henry E. Petersen, head of the Justice Department's Criminal Division. Dean told them he needed the information because he was conducting an investigation for the President. In fact Dean was passing the information to Haldeman, Ehrlichman and high officials at CRP, enabling them to stay one step ahead of investigators.

How many people had actively participated in feeding the false

---

* The safe contained material relating to a number of discreet projects Hunt had undertaken for the White House, chiefly for Charles Colson, including in addition to the Ellsberg break-in an attempt to alter secret State Department cables from 1963 to create the impression that President Kennedy had been responsible for the assassination of President Ngo Dinh Diem of South Vietnam. The bogus cables were to be leaked to the media.

cover story to investigators? Mitchell, LaRue, Magruder and Dean all knew that the story was false. Dean said he kept Haldeman and Ehrlichman advised. What about Robert Mardian—a Mitchell confidant and political coordinator at CRP—and Kenneth W. Parkinson and Paul O'Brien, two Washington lawyers retained as counsel to CRP after the break-in when the Democrats filed a civil suit against CRP charging the Republicans with responsibility for the Watergate bugging? Magruder testified that he had told Parkinson the true story of Watergate on one occasion and that Parkinson had subsequently helped him prepare a statement more along the lines of the cover story.

As for Mardian, he had heard the story of Watergate from Liddy himself at a bizarre meeting at LaRue's apartment several days after June 17, 1972. Liddy, after turning up the radio to frustrate possible electronic surveillance, tried to give Mardian a one-dollar bill in order to secure a lawyer-client privilege with him. Liddy then proceeded to describe not only the background of Watergate but also some of the other things done by Hunt, Liddy and the Plumbers on behalf of the White House in 1970 and 1971. When Mardian later reported these other escapades to Mitchell, Mitchell dubbed them the "White House horrors." Liddy also warned Mardian that financial "commitments" had been made to the Watergate burglars in case anything went wrong. The containment strategy was bound to fail if the burglars talked. The burglars were demanding that the "commitments" made to them be honored. Above all, they had to be kept quiet. So within two weeks of June 17 a massive, covert operation was launched to accumulate large amounts of cash and distribute it secretly to the burglars, Hunt, and Liddy. In the next eight months over $400,000 in cash was used to make these surreptitious payments.

Herbert W. Kalmbach, the President's personal California attorney and longtime Nixon fund raiser, arranged the first deliveries at the request of John Dean (but not till Dean had gotten the OK from Haldeman and Ehrlichman). Kalmbach called on Anthony (Tony) Ulasewicz, the former New York police investigator whom the White House previously had used for discreet political inquiries, to contact the burglars and deliver the cash. Kalmbach obtained most of the money from secret CRP coffers through LaRue. Ulasewicz used code words to govern the operation: Hunt was "the writer," the money was the "script," and the other burglars were "the players." Ulasewicz and Kalmbach communicated only by pay phone and used code names for each other as well—"Mr. Bradford" and "Mr. Rivers." Money for the burglars or their lawyers was left in "dead drops": on top of a phone booth in the lobby of the building where Hunt's lawyer, William O. Bittman, had offices; in luggage lockers at National Airport; and on a shelf in the lobby of a Howard Johnson's motel.

In the fall of 1972 Kalmbach got nervous and bowed out of the money operation. Fred LaRue was forced to take over. The burglars were making more strident demands, but the money had run out. At Mitchell's urging Dean received Haldeman's permission for CRP to use a secret $350,000 White House cash fund being held under Haldeman's control. Haldeman had his assistant Strachan deliver the cache to LaRue in two installments, and the money—much of it going to William Bittman for the benefit of Hunt—kept flowing.

Finally, in mid-March 1973, Hunt threatened that if he did not receive $120,000 within a few days he might "reconsider" his options and tell about the "seamy things" he had done for Ehrlichman and the White House. Dean learned of the threat and informed Ehrlichman, Haldeman and the President. On Mitchell's go-ahead, LaRue made a final payment of $75,000 to Hunt on the evening of March 21.

The hush-money aspect of the case was going to be most effective before a jury, but it was not without its problems. The main drawback was the lack of firm evidence of a quid pro quo—a specific agreement or understanding that the money was being provided in exchange for silence. Of course, the inference was obvious: the most powerful people in the country had not undertaken to make secret payments of over $400,000 in cash to a bunch of third-rate burglars simply out of untainted altruism. But hard evidence to support this inference would certainly strengthen our case.

There were some indications of quid pro quo that we could use before a jury. Ehrlichman had told Kalmbach that paying the burglars "had to be done" and that if the payments weren't kept secret "they'll have our heads in their laps." We also had a tape recording of a conversation between Hunt and Charles Colson, taped by Colson in November of 1972, in which Hunt warned that Watergate could fall apart for lack of money, that the burglars were "protecting" those responsible and that this was a "two-way street." Hunt's final demand for money in March 1973 (the "seamy-things" episode) also made the quid pro quo overt.

However, most of the communications about the burglars' "commitments" had been maddeningly vague. Typically, demands for money had been initiated through Hunt's lawyer Bittman, then a partner at the Washington law firm of Hogan and Hartson. The messages from Bittman were transmitted by one or the other of the CRP lawyers, Parkinson or O'Brien, up to Dean, Mitchell and LaRue. Of the three lawyers, only Bittman had actually handled any money. Parkinson and O'Brien denied knowing that the burglars were being covertly paid off, and Bittman—despite repeated and skeptical questioning by the task force—consistently disclaimed any knowledge that the money was designed to buy Hunt's silence.*

The Silbert team, stymied in their efforts to find hard evidence linking anyone higher than Liddy to the bugging, had successfully prosecuted the seven burglars on the theory that Liddy was the "leader of the conspiracy, the money man, the boss" and that the burglars were off on a lark of their own without CRP sanction. Then, a few days before the convicted men were scheduled to be sentenced on March 23, 1973, James McCord wrote a letter to Judge John J. Sirica (who had vocally expressed doubt during the burglars' trial that the whole truth had yet come out) stating that political pressure had been applied to the burglars to keep silent, that perjury had been committed at the trial, and that others besides the burglars who were involved in Watergate had not yet been publicly identified. Within days of the sentencing, the prosecutors, as they had long planned to do, acquired court orders immunizing Hunt, Liddy and McCord and subpoenaed them to testify before the grand jury to reveal what they knew about higher-ups.

In a series of grand-jury appearances during March and April 1973 Hunt had maintained (falsely) that he knew nothing of Liddy's superiors. Liddy chose jail (for contempt of court) rather than tell the grand jury anything. The prosecutors nevertheless concealed Liddy's

---

* Although we did not learn about it until nearly a year later, when Hunt finally began to tell us the truth about the cover-up, there *was* a document that laid out with pristine clarity the quid pro quo understanding about the money payments. It was a memorandum Hunt said he gave to Bittman in November 1972 for transmittal to Kenneth Parkinson and to others at the White House and CRP. The memo unequivocally established that the burglars would keep silent as long as the payments continued. The memo did not surface until the cover-up trial; it turned out then that Bittman had had a copy in his possession during our entire investigation and, despite our repeated requests for all the information he possessed, had never mentioned it or turned it over to us.

intransigence by ceremoniously leading him into the grand-jury chambers and, when he refused to testify, letting him cool his heels for hours in a hidden anteroom, shielded from public view. The press saw only that Liddy was ushered into the jury chambers and, some hours later, ushered out, giving rise to speculation that he was singing choice arias to the jurors. At the same time the Ervin Committee was gearing up for imminent hearings, and the first person it wanted to talk to was McCord. Newspaper stories began to hint that McCord and others would implicate Dean, Magruder and possibly Mitchell in the bugging. It was the fear of what McCord, Hunt and Liddy might say that prompted Dean and Magruder secretly to approach the federal prosecutors in the first week of April to offer their cooperation, thus triggering the collapse of the cover-up.

With information provided by Dean and Magruder, the Silbert team had moved swiftly to interview and put before the grand jury the most important witnesses. Kalmbach, Ulasewicz, Mardian, Paul O'Brien and Charles Colson were all called or came in. The prosecutors got an important bonus when Fred LaRue agreed to cooperate. Scores of requests went out for FBI action. Haldeman, Ehrlichman and Mitchell were all interrogated before the grand jury.

Based on the evidence gathered by the Silbert team in their investigation since April, the outlines of the cover-up were clear. We now had to take that information and put together a prosecutable case.

THE NEED TO "MAKE" OUR CASE at trial meant that our task as prosecutors was considerably more difficult than that of the Ervin Committee, which in June had already begun its series of televised hearings. The object of a congressional investigation is simply to unearth the facts—the more the better. From whom the facts are obtained, how, and in what sequence of events is usually of secondary importance. If there is conflicting testimony, if witnesses change their stories, if at a hearing legislators get an opportunity to cross-examine and berate cooperative as well as hostile witnesses, so much the better. It shows that the committee is on the ball, its investigation has struck pay dirt.

For us, things weren't quite this easy. The criminal prosecutor—notwithstanding the oft-repeated maxim that the government "always wins" in a criminal case because justice is done regardless of the outcome—is usually judged not by how many facts he brings out but by whether he obtains convictions. Every major decision reached during a criminal investigation—what leads to pursue, whom to interview when, how to approach those who have information, how to resolve conflicts in testimony, whose credibility to rely on, whom to select as witnesses—has an impact on the course of trials that occur months later. The prosecutor's investigatory problem is twofold: not just to find out who did it, but in the course of finding out to choreograph successful prosecutions of the guilty.

Most white-collar cases are "made" on the testimony of insiders—participants in the crime—together with whatever corroboration is possible from physical and circumstantial evidence. During his investigation, the prosecutor must have something to induce insiders to come forward and tell what they know. Then, after he has pieced together the facts, he still must have witnesses who will take the stand at trial on behalf of the government. Some of those responsible have to be used by the prosecution in order to convict the others. The public often seems not to appreciate that except in the rarest case everybody who is culpably involved cannot be a defendant. Inevitably, the prosecutor faces a series of very hard choices.

The trouble is, these choices often have to be made *early* in the investigation, while it is still unraveling—without the benefit of full information. Having to make important choices that affect the overall direction of the case *before* the facts are fully developed is one of the greatest problems in prosecuting cases like Watergate.

Of course, good judgment alone cannot make an investigation successful. The heart of any case like Watergate is just plain hard work: attention to detail, persistence in building up the facts from divergent sources, meticulous preparation for every interrogation—and a healthy measure of good luck. Guilt or innocence in the political-corruption case often hinges on very small differences in testimony, on fine interpretations of motive and intent. Thus skillful use of corroborating evidence, no matter how trivial in the overall scheme of the case, is also essential. Nowhere is this problem more acute than when the targets of an investigation are already familiar with the testimony that will be given against them and can construct a defense to meet it—sometimes even before the prosecutors have heard from their accusers. During the cover-up, lawyers for CRP had participated in prosecutors' interviews with individual CRP employees, providing the architects of the cover-up with progress reports on the investigation. Then the Ervin Committee decided to call cooperative witnesses Magruder and Dean *before* it called the likes of Haldeman and Ehrlichman. The future defendants were provided a golden opportunity to tailor their versions to the testimony of others.

In the typical public-corruption case it is often difficult for the prosecution to produce live witnesses at trial whose testimony will be believed by the jury. Invariably the defendant in such a case is (or was) a high public official. He comes into the courtroom a pillar of the community, a man who has proved that at one time he commanded the trust and respect of the public. In contrast, the prosecution witnesses will already have acknowledged their participation in corrupt or criminal activity. The inherent credibility problems involved in using insider witnesses thus places a premium on the way those witnesses are developed and handled during the investigation and pre-trial period.

Persuading those who may have been criminally involved to cooperate with the prosecution despite their potential vulnerability to criminal charges is an art that requires experience, good instincts and not a little insight into human motivation. In essence, the prosecutor's object is to get more for less: to get useful information (and the witness's trial testimony) without losing his prosecutive options—his leverage over the witness. The witness's object ordinarily is to win assurances of how he will be treated by the prosecutors *before* he must risk incriminating himself by disclosing his and others' involvement. Once the prosecutor decides to extend some kind of assurances about the disposition of the witness's case, he must consider carefully their nature and scope. If the assurances are too narrow, he may lose the witness's full cooperation; if they are too broad, he may foreclose his option to prosecute.

The prosecutorial technique used in this exercise that is most familiar to the public is "immunity." In fact that word has a broad range of meaning and uses in prosecuting.

In a new statute enacted in 1970 at the urging of the Nixon-Mitchell Justice Department, Congress for the first time gave federal prosecutors the power to compel a witness who had refused on Fifth Amendment grounds to testify before a grand jury to answer the jury's questions by giving him "testimonial immunity." Under the new law, a court order obtained by prosecutors guarantees the witness that neither his compelled testimony nor any other evidence or leads derived from it can be used against him in a subsequent prosecution.

However, the government can still prosecute a witness who has received statutory "testimonial" immunity if it can show that *all* its evidence against him was obtained completely independently of the disclosures he was forced to make under the immunity order.

Howard Hunt, James McCord and the five Watergate burglars had all received formal court-ordered grants of testimonial immunity after they were sentenced in March of 1973 for the Watergate bugging. John Dean's counsel initially sought statutory immunity from the Silbert team for his client, but in the end did not obtain it.

It surprises many people to learn that, aside from the complicated mechanism for granting immunity by court order under the immunity statutes, a prosecutor, by making a simple oral promise to a witness or his lawyer, can confer *informal* testimonial immunity that is just as binding on the government as a formal court decree. The availability of informal immunity as an investigatory technique gives the prosecutor added flexibility in pursuing valuable information, but the careful prosecutor knows that it must be used sparingly. With little forethought, a prosecutor can easily foreclose the possibility of subsequently prosecuting a suspect who has engaged in substantial criminal activity.

Before agreeing to accord a witness any kind of immunity, formal or informal, a prosecutor can evaluate what the witness is likely to say in a number of ways. Sometimes the witness's attorney will make an "offer of proof," a hypothetical statement of what his client will say if granted testimonial immunity. The attorney's statement isn't really hypothetical at all. Everyone understands that the attorney is describing what his client really knows. But the client is protected: under such an arrangement what his lawyer says cannot later be used against the client if negotiations break down. A prosecutor is not permitted to cross-examine a defendant at trial by asking whether it is a fact that his attorney once admitted the defendant's criminal involvement "hypothetically" during negotiations with the prosecutors.

Sometimes the witness himself will make his own "hypothetical" statement by agreeing to be interviewed by prosecutors "off the record." Defense lawyers sometimes like to use this procedure when seeking to convince prosecutors that a client would make a good trial witness against others and therefore should not be indicted: let them hear the story from the witness's own mouth. Unless expressly specified, an "off-the-record" interview does not bar prosecutors from using a witness's disclosures as leads to develop additional evidence against him; thus it is less protective of the witness than informal testimonial immunity. The Silbert team had used this technique in April and May of 1973 to decide whether to grant John Dean formal, statutory immunity.

Prior evaluation of a witness's testimony is important because the prosecutor has to be cautious of buying a pig in a poke. Once accorded immunity, a witness may confess his own guilt (thus making it difficult to prosecute him for what he has admitted) but claim, falsely, that he knows nothing about criminal conduct by others.

If the prosecutor decides that a particular individual's culpability is minimal relative to that of others and that his testimony would be useful at trial, he may exercise prosecutorial discretion and extend a conditional assurance of "witness status"—pledging that the individual will be a witness in the case rather than a defendant *if* he has been and continues to be completely candid. (If the prosecutor later finds out the witness has been lying, the deal is off and the witness will probably be prosecuted.) The Silbert team had given such assurances to a number of persons in the Watergate investigation, and we were bound by these assurances in structuring our prosecution.

Sometimes, of course, persons involved in criminal conduct will cooperate without any preconditions, throwing themselves on the prosecutor's mercy. Before Cox was appointed, Fred LaRue and Herbert Kalmbach had both voluntarily testified about their involvement in the cover-up without seeking any prior assurances from the Silbert team.

When a prosecutor determines that a potential witness was deeply involved in criminality, he will usually abandon consideration of immunity or witness status and inform the potential witness that he is being viewed as a defendant. This does not mean the prosecutor has given up hope of getting the individual's testimony at trial; rather, he has now entered the realm of plea bargaining. The prosecutor is still offering something in exchange for testimony: an opportunity for the potential defendant to reduce his total exposure by pleading guilty to a reduced charge or fewer charges than he might face if indicted. The Silbert team had taken this tack with Jeb Magruder, Fred LaRue and John Dean. Frequently a bargain is struck regarding the prosecutor's recommendation to the sentencing judge of an appropriate sentence, but in our investigation no such assurance was ever given.

Assurances of immunity, witness status or leniency invariably have a substantial impact on a witness's credibility at trial—sometimes fatal. Defense counsel can be counted upon to bring out any promises a witness has received from the prosecutors and to argue that it is these assurances and the witness's desire to save his own neck, rather than any devotion to the truth, that have motivated him to incriminate others.

Like many important prosecutorial decisions made during a criminal investigation, the decision to extend assurances to a potential witness is invisible to the public when made. Only at trial do such decisions surface. Only then, when it is too late to correct mistakes, does the prosecutor's skill and judgment (or lack of them) become apparent.

As it turned out, in our investigation the Watergate Task Force did not extend new assurances of immunity to any government trial witness—though we did accept guilty pleas from five major figures in the cover-up and participated in negotiations resulting in the plea of a sixth (Herbert Kalmbach) to violations not directly related to the cover-up. In part, this record was due to our reluctance to make any commitments to anyone with potential criminal liability. Besides, the original prosecutors had already initiated most of the government's relationships with potential witnesses where appropriate—either assurances of witness status or demands for guilty pleas.

LONG BEFORE COX's APPOINTMENT, the original prosecutors had cut a deal with Jeb Magruder and his attorneys. Magruder would plead guilty in the Watergate case to one felony charge relating to his participation in both the planning of the bugging and the cover-up, and would testify as a government witness. In exchange, the government would agree not to charge Magruder with additional counts arising out of Watergate and would bring Magruder's cooperation to the attention of his sentencing judge.

The Watergate Task Force told Magruder's attorney that we would honor the deal (as indeed we were equitably bound to do as the succeeding representatives of the government) and in fact that we were eager to consummate it. But as time went on Magruder seemed reluctant to go through with his bargain. There was one excuse after another about the timing; then Magruder announced that he had arranged for a last-minute European fling.

A star witness, whom the original prosecutors had gotten up to the gate, was now reluctant to enter the corral. Jim Neal decided that we needed a bell cow to bring Magruder in. So he imposed on a long-standing friendship from Justice Department days with Fred Vinson, who was now representing Fred LaRue.

LaRue hadn't had a lawyer when he first approached Earl Silbert to bare his soul; the prosecutors had had to help him chase down legal counsel. Unlike Magruder, LaRue's principal interest in coming in hadn't been to get the best break for himself but just to own up to what he'd done because he believed it was the right thing to do. Consequently, there had been no concrete arrangement about what would happen to LaRue. Since LaRue had not asked for any immunity but had admitted voluntarily to the prosecutors his considerable involvement in criminal acts, he was obviously a target for prosecution; and since he was totally vulnerable, it seemed likely he would be willing to plead rather than fight.

Neal was frank with Vinson. "Fred, we desperately need to get this fellow Magruder in here, but I just don't think he's going to go through with it. I don't think he'll ever be the *first* one to plead. We need something to bring him in. Getting your man to plead first is our best bet. Would he be willing to plead to one felony count?"

After consulting with his client, Vinson told Neal that LaRue would be willing to enter into the plea bargain on condition that Neal inform the sentencing judge how important it had been to the prosecutors to have LaRue come in first. Vinson wanted to be assured that his client's willingness to put his neck on the block first would be taken into consideration when the time came for imposition of punishment. Neal agreed. LaRue also wanted something else: a guarantee that sentencing be postponed until *after* he had testified at the main Watergate trial or trials. Neal and Vinson went to see Judge John Sirica, before whom (as Chief Judge of the United States District Court) LaRue would enter his plea. The judge agreed to defer sentencing.

On June 28, while John Dean was testifying before national television cameras at the Ervin Committee, LaRue entered a plea of guilty before Judge Sirica to one count of conspiracy to obstruct justice in the Watergate cover-up.

After LaRue bit the bullet, Magruder still kept finding reasons not to go through with his plea. But he knew and we knew that, for all practical purposes, the gate had shut behind him. In mid-July, work began on the language of the charges to which Magruder would plead, and the deal was "reaffirmed." The actual entry of Magruder's plea did not come until August 16.

THE PROSECUTION'S WILLINGNESS to accept one-count pleas of guilty from Jeb Magruder and Fred LaRue as a resolution of their total Watergate culpability was generally understood and accepted by the public. Magruder's theoretical vulnerability to criminal charges was far greater. He had perjured himself in two appearances before the Watergate grand jury and again at the Watergate burglars' trial. But he also was the only key figure in the planning of the break-in and early development of the cover-up at CRP whom the government was likely to obtain as a trial witness; in addition, he was the bedrock of the case against his former boss, John Mitchell. The prosecution needed Magruder badly. The five-year maximum sentence to which Magruder became vulnerable under his plea was probably near the top range of the sentence he would actually receive as a cooperating government witness even if he had pleaded guilty to three or four felonies (making him liable to a maximum fifteen-to-twenty-year sentence). As for LaRue, he provided the all-important corroborative evidence that cinched the case against Mitchell, and his involvement, while extensive, had not been that of an initiator.

The Watergate Task Force's willingness to entertain the same deal for John Dean—i.e., a one-count felony plea—while not publicly announced during the summer of 1973, had been communicated to Dean's lawyer and was well known to the attorneys for other major figures in the investigation. Dean, of course, was an even more important potential government witness than Magruder. Dean's testimony before the Ervin Committee that electrified the country went far beyond what Dean had told the Silbert team in his meetings with them, in both scope and detail. Dean's most dramatic revelation, of course, was his account of the conversations he had had with President Nixon about the cover-up in March and April of 1973, and of the maneuvering within the White House as the cover-up collapsed. Most of this was brand-new information for the prosecution. Of greater immediate importance was the fact that Dean was the only witness with substantial testimony to give against both Haldeman and Ehrlichman.

Dean had a lot of chips with which to bargain, and he knew it.

Moreover, while active as an initiator and expediter in the cover-up, Dean—unlike Magruder—had apparently not been involved in approving the bugging plan, nor had he lied under oath during the investigation. This had to be taken into account in assessing the minimum measure of blood it would be just to demand of Dean in any plea bargain.

Nevertheless, counsel for some of the potential defendants were not pleased with the outstanding offer to Dean. Frank Strickler, co-counsel for Haldeman with the feisty John J. Wilson, assailed Neal. "It's just outrageous that you'd take a one-count plea from that guy," Strickler complained. "Here he is, the architect of the cover-up, the fellow who made it work, who did more than anyone else to insure its success, and you're prepared to let him off with a single felony count?"

But Neal quickly stopped the complaining. "Frank," he told Strickler, "there isn't any deal I'll make for Dean that I won't make for Haldeman too. I'm telling you, if you bring Haldeman in and he's willing to tell what he knows about this business I'll recommend one count to Archie same as I did for Dean. I might get overruled, but I think it's a good deal and I'll fight for it."

Strickler muttered his reply. Haldeman's lawyers were not interested in that kind of deal.

Neal broached the same subject to John Mitchell's lawyer, William Hundley, an old friend from Justice Department days and once head of the department's Organized Crime and Racketeering Section. But efforts to secure a plea from Mitchell were unsuccessful. Despite a number of clandestine meetings—including a hastily arranged meeting of Archie Cox, Neal and Hundley in the basement of the U.S. Supreme Court—it appeared that Mitchell really had no interest in coming in except as part of a package deal—in other words, simultaneous pleas by himself, Haldeman and Ehrlichman. Mitchell apparently regarded such a possibility as being "in the national interest," presumably because it would obviate the need for any major Watergate trial and perhaps create public pressure on us to "wind up" our investigation rather than pursue further the role of President Nixon in the cover-up. Mitchell's idea of what was in the "public interest" differed sharply from our own.

THE MANNER in which Herbert L. (Bart) Porter's Watergate involvement was handled by our task force points up some of the competing philosophical issues present in plea bargaining. Porter, thirty-two-year-old scheduling official at CRP, had been persuaded by Jeb Magruder that he, Porter, could show his Nixon team colors by corroborating Magruder's false cover story about CRP cash given to Gordon Liddy. In so doing, Porter had lied to FBI agents and committed perjury in sworn testimony before the grand jury and at the trial of the Watergate burglars. When Magruder confessed to the prosecutors, Porter was among the first to be implicated.

No one had suggested that Porter had known about the entire cover-up; rather, Magruder had convinced him that he was protecting CRP from embarrassment over loose handling of campaign funds. But it was incontrovertible that the young Californian had done wrong in placing Magruder's pitch for loyalty above his obligation to tell the truth under oath. Porter himself not only showed contrition and remorse at his behavior (more so than most others far more deeply involved in Watergate), but without any request for immunity or special consideration confessed his seduction by Magruder and his attendant perjuries before a national television audience at the Ervin Committee hearings.

None of us was terribly eager to prosecute Porter. After all, there was bigger game to be hunted; Porter seemed almost pathetic by comparison. Porter's relatively slight involvement, his relative youth and his relatively contrite posture made him an unattractive target for a major prosecution. But, Ben-Veniste asked, how could we in good conscience *decline* to prosecute? Were we in the business of separating the crimes involved in Watergate from the rest of the criminal-justice system? Was it just that a young man who had received the benefits of a fine education and family life as well as career opportunities few Americans even dreamed of should be spared because his crimes were *relatively* far less serious than crimes committed by his former superiors? Could we turn our backs on the fact that every day young men and women with none of Porter's advantages in life were being sentenced to long terms of imprisonment for *relatively* minor crimes?

Porter, we decided, must be prosecuted or plead guilty. But plead guilty to what charge? One count of perjury? Such a conviction would potentially subject Porter to five years in prison—the same maximum facing Magruder, LaRue and (if he decided to accept our one-count offer) John Dean. How could we demand that Porter, whose criminal involvement was negligible compared to these men, subject himself to the same punishment? On the other hand, there was nothing *less* than one count to offer, and no misdemeanor charge (providing for a maximum of a year in jail) was appropriate to what Porter had done.

The chances are that Porter might never have been prosecuted at all if he had had something the prosecutors badly needed, but he was not so lucky. He had no useful testimony to give against anyone else which he might have used to bargain with, and he had not even come forward with his own confession until implicated by Magruder.

In the end, we reached an agreement to accept a plea from Porter to one count of making a false statement to FBI agents. The charge was a five-year felony, but we chose it to signal that we believed Porter's involvement in the cover-up to have been minimal compared to that of those charged with conspiracy, something we also pointed out to Porter's sentencing judge. Some of the relative unfairness in this result was mitigated by Porter's relatively short sentence: he served only about one month in a federal prison in California, emerging (he later told us) with a great deal of insight into the events that occasioned his incarceration. In fact, Porter felt in the end that Watergate had rescued him from a life of blindly clambering up the corporate ladder—a lifestyle that no longer had any attraction for him.

Porter's case sparked more than the usual amount of discussion within the Watergate Task Force about the broader issues of plea bargaining, and about relative versus absolute justice. The pressures that compel plea bargaining in the typical prosecutor's office—crowded dockets, heavy backlogs, overworked lawyers, defendants in jail awaiting trial—were not present in Watergate. However, there were other pressures to plea bargain present in our case: the need for insider witnesses, and public pressure to resolve responsibility for Watergate abuses in a short period of time.

Porter forced us to face the hard fact that there are many factors that enter into plea bargaining that may seem philosophically "unjust": the value of the potential defendant's testimony to the prosecutors; his history of cooperation; his personal demeanor (i.e., whether he will be a jury-pleasing trial witness); and the ability and aggressiveness of his lawyers. The more the witness has to offer in the way of information that implicates others, the better deal he is going to get. Sometimes it was difficult for the young generalists on the task force to accept with equanimity the consequences of "leverage." But that is the kind of factor that inevitably must be taken into account by experienced prosecutors striving to do "justice in the large" by assuring convictions of those most responsible for the crimes under investigation.

ANOTHER SUBJECT of much philosophical debate within the task force was the development of internal office procedures to safeguard the rights of those with whom we would come into contact during the investigation. In our system, the prosecutor possesses extraordinarily broad discretion—discretion that is largely unreviewable and is ordinarily exercised in secret. The prosecutor alone may initiate an investigation, determine its course, decide whom to call as witnesses, define the crimes to be charged, dispose of cases through plea bargaining and (with the grand jury's concurrence) decide whom to indict.

In addition, through the grand jury the prosecutor wields awesome power over individual rights that can result in disruption, harassment and serious injury to innocent people if it is misused. The operation of the grand jury, in fact, has spurred as much heated debate in legal circles recently as any other facet of the criminal-justice system. While many of the leading judicial decisions over the past two decades have operated to benefit criminal suspects, the courts consistently have reaffirmed and expanded the power of the grand jury. Originally conceived as a protective buffer to insulate citizens from arbitrary or malicious criminal prosecution, the grand jury has unquestionably become more and more a rubber stamp for the prosecutor, and its powers in certain political and socially controversial cases have been misused by the government.

Grand-jury proceedings are required to be conducted under the most stringent veil of secrecy. Courtroom rules of evidence are inapplicable, and a witness may not be accompanied by his attorney during the interrogation (though in a few recent state cases courts have experimented with permitting the witness to have counsel inside the jury room). The prosecutor can inquire into any matter that is "related to" the investigation. Production of evidence such as handwriting, voice exemplars, fingerprints and corporate records can be compelled by grand-jury subpoena, even though a prosecutor or a policeman would otherwise have to obtain a judicial search warrant showing "probable cause" under the Fourth Amendment to seize such material. As for the decision whether to indict, the grand jury rarely comes into contact with anyone but the prosecutors for any extended period of time, and is reliant on the prosecutor for presentation of evidence; if in the end a grand jury refuses to indict a suspect, the prosecutor may resubmit the matter to another grand jury.

On the other hand the federal grand jury provides the single most important vehicle for the investigation of white-collar crime.* It provides the prosecutor with invaluable and otherwise unavailable tools for uncovering sophisticated wrongdoing, not the least of which is nationwide subpoena power. If the grand jury were abolished, a great deal of financial fraud, organized crime and political corruption would go undetected, not to mention unpunished.

Naturally, there are legal and ethical restraints that limit the exercise of prosecutorial power and discretion. Because the prosecutor is both an advocate for the government within the criminal-justice system and an administrator *of* that system, he is charged with weighty public responsibilities: he is supposed to "do impartial justice," to protect the innocent, and to guard the rights of the accused as well as to convict the guilty. Often, however, recognized ethical rules turn out in application to be distressingly vague, and the standard of conduct they prescribe is a loose one. As much as we may dislike to admit it, the principal guarantee the public has today that prosecutorial power will not be abused lies in little more than the personal integrity and professionalism of individual men and women who serve as prosecutors.

The Special Prosecution Force was endowed with an unusual degree of prosecutorial power and autonomy. Because of that extraordinary power and of our acute need to maintain public support in face of intense media scrutiny, the attorneys on the Force decided that it was not sufficient for us simply to adopt the customary procedures employed by most other prosecutors to protect individual rights. Unusual efforts would be required to make certain that our work was characterized by scrupulous fairness. The symbolic goal of the Watergate Task Force to demonstrate the integrity of the criminal-justice system could scarcely be accomplished if those responsible for abuses of executive power were brought to account only through further abuses of power.

Consequently, at every stage we attempted to build into the conduct

---

* The grand jury is a particularly potent investigative tool in cases involving alleged misconduct by public officials. Unlike other "targets" of criminal investigations, public officials and political figures often prefer to waive their rights and testify before the grand jury when subpoenaed, rather than risk the stigma of having taken the Fifth Amendment. False statements made to a grand jury may be used at a witness's subsequent trial as evidence to help prove his guilt or the basis for perjury charges.

of the Watergate cover-up investigation the most stringent safeguards available to insure that the rights of those involved would not be infringed, even though some of these procedures were tactically detrimental to the prosecution. The practice of writing up every office interview was one such procedure. Another was our policy of notifying subjects of the investigation that, if they chose, they could appear before the grand jury and make any statement or presentation they wished to make to the jurors. When targets of the investigation appeared before the jury they were carefully warned of their rights to remain silent, to have an attorney present outside the jury room, and to leave the room to consult with him—even though the Supreme Court later held that such warnings are not legally required.

Realizing that there was a potential for unfairness inherent in exploiting the possible reluctance of some targets of the investigation publicly to take the Fifth, a policy was instituted to minimize their embarrassment and avoid any prejudice in the minds of the grand jurors from seeing a potential defendant stand up and refuse to answer questions. Subjects of the investigation were informed that it would not be necessary for anyone who intended to take the Fifth before the grand jury actually to appear before that body formally and do so—it would be sufficient for the individual's attorney to notify us in writing that he would choose that course, and he would not then be subpoenaed.

Although there is no legal or ethical obligation on the prosecutor to present *exculpatory* evidence to the grand jury, we made it our policy in the cover-up case to do so. We also advised subjects that we would be happy to place before the grand jurors any evidence the subjects or their lawyers called to our attention that they believed to be favorable to them.

In the ordinary criminal case there are few safeguards for the accused at the charging stage, given the prosecutor's domination of the grand jury. The requirement that an indictment be based on "probable cause," for example, is in truth almost a meaningless limitation. Probable cause can be based on tainted evidence, secondary evidence, hearsay or circumstantial evidence. When it came time to recommend indictments to the grand jury, the Watergate Task Force decided that each prospective defendant and his counsel would be invited to meet with the Special Prosecutor and the task force for a discussion of his case. It was inevitable in these sessions that we would reveal a great deal of valuable information about our evidence and our strategy to the prospective defendant, but this was a price we believed it was worth paying to make sure that we had taken into consideration every argument against indictment.

Finally, in making prosecutive decisions we agreed to adopt a higher standard than the constitutionally mandated one of probable cause. We would not recommend indictment unless we were convinced that a conviction at trial was probable.

While these and other measures adopted by the task force involved tactical costs, we believed the measures were essential to convince the public that we had leaned over backward to avoid infringement of any rights, that from start to finish our investigation was characterized by an extra measure of fairness.

ONE OF THE MOST PLEASANT ASPECTS of the Watergate Task Force's investigation was our work with the Watergate grand jury, twenty-three nonlawyers—selected from the same voter registration lists as trial jurors—who had been hearing testimony since a few days after the June 17, 1972, break-in and had voted the original indictment naming Liddy, Hunt, McCord and the Cubans. Collectively, the jurors knew more about Watergate than anyone outside of government. They had good reason to feel that the special prosecutors were the new kids on the block. Our first meetings with the grand jury involved some acclimation on both sides. Would they resent us for usurping the roles of the original prosecutors who had been working with them on and off for nearly a year?

In short order the jury and the task force satisfied themselves about each other's dedication, and our relations generally became good. The grand jurors, true to their oaths, had unfailingly kept secret (and would continue to do so) the most exclusive and shocking information any grand jury had ever heard. Yet when the indictments were returned in the cover-up case sources close to President Nixon would begin an open campaign to discredit them on the grounds of the jury's alleged racial prejudice.

In fact the grand jury was composed of seventeen blacks and six whites randomly selected from the District of Columbia voter registration rolls. Their foreman, Vladimir Pregelj, a distinguished-looking and animated Yugoslav refugee and naturalized American citizen, held a master's degree in economics and served as an economic analyst on the Library of Congress research staff. Those not employed by the government found it most difficult to hold down a job with the prospect of being away from it as many as three or four days a week in connection with their obligations as jurors. Even those holding government jobs were reportedly bypassed for advancement because of their justifiable absenteeism. For the days the grand jury was called into session, each juror received twenty dollars.

While the grand jury displayed none of the malice attributed to it by the Nixon group, neither was it in awe, after a year's investigation, of the executive staff or of Presidential trappings. Indeed, a few members of the jury occasionally thumbed through their newspapers in boredom during the course of especially uninteresting testimony. No doubt this practice had sprung up in the days when scheduling delays and eleventh-hour debriefings left the jury alone to amuse itself for long stretches of time.

The grand jury's often blasé posture had a particularly disquieting effect on some of the junior White House staffers summoned to give testimony—the bright-eyed and bushy-tailed aides to Haldeman, Ehrlichman and other White House biggies. We could imagine the mortification of the former head of the interfraternity council flashing his most winning Ipana smile only to be met by a score of unimpressed faces and two copies of the *Washington Post*.

The grand jurors were nobody's fools, and demonstrated as much in the questions they asked to supplement our interrogation of witnesses. What many lacked in formal education they made up for in common sense mixed with a healthy dose of pragmatic skepticism. Being asked to swallow some highly implausible explanations during their term of service had substantially raised their threshold of gullibility. The jurors believed strongly that they had an independent interest in the outcome of the investigation, and they didn't let us forget it. A number of jurors regularly provided us with lists of witnesses they wanted to hear. Others passed suggestions through the foreman. Without question the Watergate grand jury was not going to be anyone's rubber stamp.

IN MANY RESPECTS the most puzzling aspect of our case was the role that top CIA officials had played in the cover-up. In the days following the Watergate arrests the White House and CRP learned that the FBI had traced money found on the Watergate burglars to a Mexican bank. If the FBI went any further, it would discover that the bank had been used to launder CRP campaign contributions, anonymously turning checks into cash—and thus discover an official link between the CRP hierarchy and the burglars. John Dean swiftly notified Haldeman and Ehrlichman of this development.

On June 23, 1972, CIA Director Richard M. Helms and his newly appointed deputy, General Vernon A. Walters, were summoned to a White House meeting with Haldeman and Ehrlichman. (Walters, a longtime Nixon associate, had served as personal interpreter for Nixon on a number of overseas trips.) Helms disclaimed any CIA interest in Watergate. But Haldeman complained that the FBI's Watergate investigation was getting to a lot of important people and might get worse. The White House chief of staff then turned to Walters and specifically instructed him to meet with L. Patrick Gray, acting director of the FBI. Walters was to tell Gray that CIA interests might be prejudiced if the FBI pressed ahead with its investigation of the Mexican money chain. Walters got the distinct impression that these instructions were coming straight from the President.

Somewhat reluctantly, Walters carried out Haldeman's instructions. As a result, Gray delayed FBI interviews in Mexico for nearly two weeks and top officials at CRP got some breathing space to develop their cover-up strategy. However, Gray was growing restive under Walters' restrictions. Gray's inherited FBI brass, the survivors of some vicious past bureaucratic infighting, told their new director that he better have a damn good reason for terminating such a significant investigative lead. "Make the CIA put it in writing," they counseled. So Gray asked Walters for a written memorandum officially stating that CIA interests were at stake.

The canny FBI high command had hit the nail on the head. Walters balked. At a meeting in the FBI director's office, Gray and Walters concluded that they were being manipulated by "those kids" at the White House and resolved they would both resign before they would let themselves be further importuned.

At about the same time, John Dean approached Walters on several occasions to see if the CIA would provide hush money for the burglars. Each time, Walters refused. Walters made memoranda for his files on his meetings with Dean and briefed Director Helms. But neither of them ever told anyone about the meetings, or about the White House attempt to block the FBI's investigation in Mexico, until after the cover-up collapsed in April of 1973.

One of our first duties was to determine whether the CIA had actively participated in the cover-up. This proved a substantial challenge. Unlike ordinary citizens and government officials who recognize moral and legal obligations to provide information to a criminal investigation pursuant to the legal process, we found that by instinct and professional training the natural reaction of CIA officials was to *withhold* information: bury it, obfuscate it, deny that it existed, or just plain lose it. Attempts to get documents from them were inevitably Kafkaesque.

To take an example, we soon discovered that throughout the cover-up McCord—a former CIA official and once head of the Agency's office of physical security—had been writing cryptic letters to an old friend of his who was still in the Agency. The friend had taken them straight to Director Helms. Helms made all the proper bureaucratic moves, calling in his general counsel for a lengthy discussion of the Agency's legal and ethical responsibilities in the matter. The letters were then relegated to the bottom drawer of a file safe, and no one was any the wiser. Most of McCord's letters warned of "pressures" from the White House to throw responsibility for Watergate off onto the CIA.

Every month or two the Agency would provide us with a few more documents relevant to Watergate. Each time this happened we would be told that we now had the "entire file," everything conceivably relevant to the case. But there was always more to come. It wasn't till very late in the investigation that we discovered hidden away in a mass of CIA documents just provided to the Plumbers Task Force a record of an interview of Robert F. Bennett, president of the public-relations company where Hunt had worked as a consultant at the time of the Watergate arrests. The firm, Robert Mullen and Company, had long assisted the CIA in placing operatives abroad under cover. Bennett, a friend of Colson's and a well-connected Republican, apparently had been told a fair amount about Hunt's involvement in the Watergate bugging within a few days of June 17, and he had passed along his information to his "case officer," who routed it directly to Helms. Like the McCord letter, the Bennett interview had never surfaced during the original investigation.

There was simply no satisfactory explanation or justification for the CIA's failure to notify prosecutors of the approaches made by the White House for help in stopping the FBI investigation and for cooperation in providing money to the burglars, of McCord's letters and of the Bennett interview. Certainly disclosure of White House approaches could have had a radical impact on the direction of the original Watergate investigation. Disclosure of McCord's letters would at the least have aroused the prosecutors' suspicions. There was no question that the CIA was imprudently protective of the Nixon Administration in its handling of the Watergate matter and that it unnecessarily weakened its position in the eyes of the public.

However, aside from Walters' approach to Gray, we concluded that the Agency had had no detailed information about the cover-up and had taken no affirmative steps to assist in it. Rather, possessed of a few clues that would have been highly useful to criminal investigators, the CIA chose to shrink away from Watergate altogether like the exotic plant that enfolds its leaves at sunset, lest any contact whatsoever risk tainting the Agency with suspicion that it had had some role in the planning or execution of the bugging itself. Natural CIA instincts for secrecy combined with the historical watchword "Protect the Agency" to produce an attitude of mute separation from everything that occurred.

The CIA's actions most often appeared to reflect a mixture of paranoia and confusion—actual or contrived—based on a policy of compartmentalization and "need to know" within the Agency. A typical example was the Pennington affair.

Early in our investigation we received a tip that right after the Watergate break-in, while James McCord was still in jail, a former CIA agent named Pennington had been sent by the Agency to break into McCord's home and destroy incriminating evidence linking the CIA to the bugging. The CIA denied this allegation. We thereupon demanded a description from the Agency of any present or former employee named Pennington who might fit this description. As we would later discover, the Agency knew exactly whom we were talking about: Lee R. Pennington, Jr., a retired FBI man who was on the CIA payroll for a few hundred dollars a month to clip newspaper and magazine articles from right-wing publications, and who was a social friend of McCord's. Moreover, Pennington had made a report of his activities in connection with McCord to the Agency. Nonetheless, a lower-ranking CIA officer decided that it would be a good idea to give us the name of *another* CIA employee who had recently resigned from the Agency whose name was also Pennington (different first name). His superiors all approved this plan on the ground, apparently, that we had asked only by last name and the ersatz Pennington fit the bill just as well as the real one. We promptly interviewed the Pennington whose name they supplied and he, of course, denied everything.

In February 1974, many months later, a new batch of CIA documents disclosed that one of the lower-ranking official's colleagues had finally decided to blow the whistle on this caper. Accordingly, the documents disclosed the existence of the real Lee R. Pennington, whom we hastened to call into the office for interrogation. Pennington's physical appearance alone was enough to corroborate his denial that he had been engaged in a second-story operation for the CIA. It was apparent that had the CIA chosen a cat burglar to penetrate McCord's home they would never have chosen this particular gentleman. Even if his spirit had been willing, he was in his late seventies and commensurately slow-moving. Lee R. Pennington, Jr., admitted that soon after the Watergate arrests he had been called by his friend Mrs. McCord for assistance in burning some of McCord's personal papers relating to his former CIA service. He had certainly not engaged in a break-in. Pennington had obligingly dropped by and helped burn all the papers that were sitting around in McCord's den, but the plan hit a snag when Mrs. McCord decided to burn sheaves of used carbon paper. As a result, billows of black smoke emanated from the McCord chimney that June day and the entire living room was coated with carbon soot. Pennington understood that it had to be repainted later.

As far as Pennington knew, nothing that was burned related to the Watergate bugging; he didn't even think any of it related to CIA. Later, when Pennington turned over his month's worth of clippings to his CIA case officer he had also related his visit to McCord's house. Nevertheless, the CIA adopted the attitude of "better safe than sorry," deciding to keep *l'affaire* Pennington from the Watergate Special Prosecution Force.

THE QUESTION OF whether to charge Haldeman (and Ehrlichman) with an obstruction of justice for their part in using the CIA as a weapon against the FBI investigation was from the beginning a ticklish one. Both gave a different version of the June 23 meeting than did Helms and Walters: Haldeman and Ehrlichman recollected that Haldeman had simply asked Walters to remind Gray of the long-standing jurisdictional agreement between the FBI and the CIA under which the FBI will take care not to expose CIA methods or agents in other countries. Moreover, both Haldeman and Ehrlichman adverted to genuine national security or CIA interests that might be involved. They claimed that these interests were known only to the President. The President had supported this line of defense in a statement in May 1973, when he said that he was genuinely concerned about national-security ramifications of the FBI's action. Without access to the President or Presidential documents, and given the position staked out by Haldeman and Ehrlichman, we were reluctant to open up the possibility of some kind of "national-security" defense by including these events in our eventual indictment. Not long into our investigation another good reason to avoid this episode unexpectedly popped up: the mysterious June 28 memo.

In midsummer Neal and Frampton interviewed Richard Helms, then Nixon's ambassador to Iran, in our offices. A charming and informal man, Helms put on an impressive display of apparent candor and sympathy. He explained frankly the tradition of protecting the Agency from political entanglement and cited that motive as the reason he had been reluctant to cough up information about Watergate. As for the White House approaches, Helms admitted that he knew perfectly well that the Agency was being importuned but said that he felt well out of it to extract the Agency from these pressures and retire gracefully to the sidelines, where the Agency could get on about its own business. Helms assured Neal that there were no real CIA interests involved in Mexico, that it was obvious to him at the time that this was a political gambit by the Nixon palace guard.

Not too long after Helms returned to Teheran a new batch of documents from old CIA files brought with it a nasty surprise. According to one document, five days after the June 23, 1972, White House meeting Helms had written a memorandum to his deputy, General Walters, saying that the CIA would "adhere to" its request to the FBI to "desist from expanding this investigation into other areas which may well, eventually, run afoul of our operations." The original of the memo, initialed by Helms, had been found in Helms's personal files. And it would provide an excellent cornerstone for a White House defense that because there were legitimate CIA interests at stake there had been no improper attempt to obstruct justice. The memo expressed an opinion that was 180 degrees around from the opinion Helms told us he actually held at the time. What made the memo even more peculiar was that General Walters claimed that he *never received it*.

The task force was extremely suspicious about this strange document. Helms was again flown back from Iran. Ben-Veniste and Frampton quizzed Helms about the memo, pointing out to him that it seemed to say just the opposite of what he had claimed he was thinking at the time. Helms was sorry, but he just couldn't explain it. The memo was unfortunately phrased. True, it was hard to reconcile what he wrote with his state of mind; what could he say? Helms was sure that the memo was delivered to Walters. He couldn't understand why the original reposed in Helms's own files.

Was it possible that Helms had written this memo in the spring of 1973, backdated it, and placed it in his own file for the specific purpose of providing corroboration for the White House line? Rigorous investigation failed to produce an answer to this question, or to the true patronage of the memo. The task force had typewriter and paper analyses run on the original of the memo, interviewed the secretary who typed it, checked Helms's initials on it, and ascertained the normal distribution channel for a memo such as this from the director of the CIA to his deputy. All to no avail in getting any additional insights. It seemed farfetched to suppose that Helms might be blackmailed by the White House. But such speculation was not eased by a later Nixon tape on which the President commented that the White House had "protected Helms from a lot of things." Not till later disclosures about the intelligence community's abuses in other fields did the full import of the President's statement fit into place.

AT THE OUTSET of our investigation there were similar suspicions about the role the FBI had played in the cover-up, given L. Patrick Gray's involvement in destroying documents from Howard Hunt's White House safe and in passing FBI reports to John Dean. One of Cox's first acts had been to ask the new acting director of the FBI, William D. Ruckelshaus, in whom he had confidence, for a full internal report on FBI actions, including copies of all internal FBI memos on the Watergate case.

The report, and the task force's investigation, produced no evidence that any FBI official other than Gray had had reason to know about the cover-up. And any lingering doubt certainly did not provide a basis for doubting the integrity or diligence of the many agents throughout the country who had done the real legwork in the initial Watergate investigation. In truth, the FBI is too big and too much of a bureaucracy for a major investigation to be impeded by corrupting an entire phalanx of line agents.

Accordingly, Cox decided that the Special Prosecution Force would use the resources of the Bureau rather than hire its own independent staff of investigators. Most of the important interviewing in the case would in any event be conducted by the prosecuting attorneys on the task force. The Bureau provided assistance in checking leads, corroborating witnesses' stories, and gathering physical evidence throughout the country speedily and reliably. In order to avoid risking high-level Bureau interference, and to save time, Cox arranged with Ruckelshaus that Watergate Task Force prosecutors could make investigative requests directly to field agents working on the case and get reports directly back from them, without the paperwork having to go through the entire FBI headquarters bureaucracy. Cox also won Ruckelshaus' assurance that the Attorney General and the Justice Department would not be made privy to this information.

For the Watergate Task Force, the relationship was an ideal one. When we wanted a minor witness in California interviewed, or we wanted to serve a grand-jury subpoena for records of a hotel in Florida, someone would call Angelo Lano, the chief case agent, or one of his colleagues working on the case at the Washington field office. Within twenty-four to forty-eight hours, Lano could usually give us the results of the interview; a written memorandum of it (called a "302") or Xerox copies of the subpoenaed records would be along a day or so later. Lano and some other agents had worked with Silbert on the Watergate investigation from the outset, so they knew the case inside out.

As THE TASK FORCE worked through the summer to interview and evaluate personally the various major figures who had been involved in Watergate and who were potential government trial witnesses, there were many who proved in one way or another enigmatic to us. L. Patrick Gray, for instance, was a believable man, a sympathetic man, though he often seemed to be on a crusade to rehabilitate himself, to set "the record straight" on everything in which he had been involved.

Like Herbert Kalmbach, he inspired more sympathy than outrage. Both men obviously had been crushed by the Watergate collapse, their most cherished illusions shattered—as though they could not believe just how they had become enmeshed in such activities.

Kenneth Parkinson, with whom Neal and Volner spent innumerable hours, was also a puzzle. Parkinson seemed to be such a genuinely straight, even prim person—how could he have been so naïve, as he claimed to have been, about what was going on around him? Parkinson's demeanor contrasted sharply with that of William Bittman, Howard Hunt's attorney, who loudly and aggressively claimed his actions had been proper. Bittman and the younger members of the task force, particularly Ben-Veniste, clashed repeatedly during the course of our investigation.

One witness who did not provoke sympathetic feelings was Jeb Magruder. Magruder was basically a manipulator. That's how he rose in business and politics and that's how he got into Watergate. While Magruder had confessed his guilt and even written a book that exposed with some insight the personal weaknesses that landed him in the Watergate mess, he had not eschewed his manipulative tendencies. Time after time Magruder sought to cajole us into doing favors for him, such as recommending short furloughs from jail.

Magruder had won the special scorn of Gordon Liddy. Liddy was a fierce enthusiast of the principle of mind over matter—the supremacy of the will. On one occasion in 1972 at a West Coast restaurant Liddy's dinner companions took notice of the peculiar smell of burning flesh. Looking over toward Liddy, they discovered that the former G-man was sitting impassively with the palm of his hand in the flame of a candle—demonstrating to his companions that mental tenacity could overcome even the strongest pain. Some of those we talked to in our investigation could pinpoint dates by recalling whether a certain event occurred before or after the time Liddy started going around CRP with a large bandage on his hand. Other "Liddy stories" abounded, including Egil "Bud" Krogh's account of Liddy's excitement at watching old Nazi propaganda films which he had arranged to have screened in the White House basement while on duty with the Plumbers unit.

Jim Neal made several dogged but fruitless attempts to get Liddy to open up. Neal had been to see Liddy in the D.C. jail very early in the investigation and had apparently impressed Liddy with his sincerity: Liddy told his lawyer that if he ever decided to talk, it would be to

Neal. Later in the summer Neal and Frampton made another lengthy appeal to Liddy in our offices. Neal pitched Liddy to cooperate, not in order to "do justice" (Neal knew that wouldn't appeal to Liddy's peculiar sense of justice) but because Neal personally didn't feel comfortable with the idea that the whole truth about Watergate wasn't out, that Liddy hadn't had *his* opportunity to set the record straight. Liddy wasn't tempted. He reviewed his global opposition to "copping out" and told us without rancor that he regarded what the prosecutors were doing as the most subversive thing to happen in the country during this century.

Despite his many eccentricities, Liddy was a most genial character in his dealings with the task force. The saver of hotel soap bars and shredder of currency seemed genuinely hurt that he had been characterized as violence prone, and he had a special bone to pick with Magruder in this respect. Magruder had testified publicly that Liddy once threatened to kill him with his bare hands. For our benefit, Liddy quickly set the record straight about this incident, complaining that Magruder had been too literal. Apparently Magruder was unhappy with some work Liddy had done and criticized it to Liddy's face in a hallway at CRP one day, in the presence of others. True to his syrupy style, Magruder was resting his arm patronizingly on Liddy's shoulder the whole time he was telling him how lousy his work had been. As Liddy recounted it, he gently lifted Magruder's arm off his shoulder and said to him, "If you ever put your arm on me again, I'm going to break it off your shoulder and beat you to death with it."

As inscrutable in his own way as Gordon Liddy was Fred LaRue. An independently wealthy and influential Mississippi Republican, LaRue had developed a tight mutual personal and political affinity with John Mitchell and in January 1972 went to CRP as a sort of special personal assistant to Mitchell. LaRue's was an extraordinarily shy and retiring personality. Though a remarkable look-alike for Robert Mardian (we sometimes joked about the possibility that we might have to have a lineup at trial so that some witnesses could be sure which was which), he was as phlegmatic as Mardian was excitable. In interviews he would let whole minutes go by without a sound, just puffing on his pipe and staring into space while pondering the answer to a question. When he did answer, he was often frustratingly vague. The testimony of LaRue, Magruder and Mitchell about their meeting at Key Biscayne on March 30, 1972, where the Gemstone budget was finally approved, was a classic in prosecutorial dilemmas: each of the three "witnesses" claimed that the other two did all the talking at the meeting. We reckoned that must have been one of the quietest campaign meetings in history.

In contrast to this unusual cast of characters, Tony Ulasewicz was a refreshing breath of air. Tony was probably the only Watergate figure who was truly streetwise, and he was also a skilled raconteur. His account of how *he*, a former New York City cop, had had to point out to Kalmbach, lawyer for the President of the United States, the obvious impropriety of what they were doing in the hush-money scheme was an especially poignant tale.

Ulasewicz also recounted to Frampton and Ben-Veniste how he had tested various investigators for "leak-proofness" in the spring of 1973. Ulasewicz had planted a number of different wild and original stories with separate staff members of the Ervin Committee and with the original prosecutors. Then he sat back to see which ones would appear in the newspapers, knowing that he could identify the leaker since each of the stories he had told was either utterly untrue or known only to him. One of the stories involved his investigation for the White House of a film called *Millhouse*, a cinematic endeavor regarded by the President as being without redeeming social value. Ulasewicz began his investigation, so he told an Ervin Committee investigator, by viewing the offending film one afternoon at a third-rate movie house in a seedy district of mid-Manhattan. On his arrival, he said, he found only two other patrons in the theater, so it was more than suspicious when one of the other two men in the audience quickly shifted his seat next to Tony's. Without much ado, the burly investigator revealed both his displeasure and his "law enforcement" background. The would-be Romeo, Ulasewicz confided to his Watergate interrogator, must have lost years off his life span. Sure enough, this story (and one or two others) quickly surfaced in the press, and Ulasewicz had marked his men.

By MID-AUGUST the Watergate Task Force had drawn up a comprehensive list of all those potential witnesses who remained to be interviewed or taken before the grand jury, a process that would continue through September. Lengthy interrogations of H. R. Haldeman and John Ehrlichman in the grand-jury room provided the task force with the first close look at two of the three men who would in all likelihood be our principal defendants. The contrast between the two was strik-ing and set a pattern that would continue when we met them again at trial. Haldeman was unfailingly cordial, if aloof. He seemed to under-stand what we were doing and why we were doing it, even if he didn't like it one damn bit. In contrast, Ehrlichman put forth a consistently arrogant, bitter, mean visage; he enjoyed bantering with the prose-cutors as long as he could get in the last word, one that was invariably acid-tinged.

Our investigation had fallen nicely into a pattern as we chipped away steadily at the mass of things that had to be done before indict-ments could be recommended to the grand jury. There were only two things missing, two big things that fell together outside the daily and weekly routine.

One was John Dean. Without Dean as a government witness the cases against Haldeman and Ehrlichman at trial would be weak in-deed. The task force was still at arm's length with Dean. We had offered to accept a plea to one felony count from him, but so far there had been no answer.

The other missing element was Richard Nixon. That we had not pursued his case was a story in itself, a story that told a great deal about the nature of the Special Prosecution Force and the people who were working on it.

CHAPTER **3** **The Case Against Richard Nixon: "If you shoot at a king..."**

WHAT JOHN DEAN told the Ervin Committee about his Watergate meetings with President Nixon electrified the country and focused its attention on the question of the President's personal involvement in the cover-up. At the Special Prosecutor's office, however, no active investigation of the President was set into motion. Indeed, our posture vis-à-vis Richard Nixon was characterized by extreme caution and deference. While the summer-long Ervin Committee probe zeroed in on the President's personal role—in the words of the committee's vice-chairman, Senator Howard H. Baker, Jr., of Tennessee, "What did he know and when did he know it?"—the prosecutors worked away steadily to build solid cases not against the President but against his aides.

There were a number of reasons for our cautious approach. In the first place, when Archibald Cox took over the Watergate criminal investigation in late May with "full authority for investigating and prosecuting . . . allegations involving the President" there was no hard evidence of any criminal conduct on the part of Richard Nixon. True, new disclosures in the spring of 1973 brought Watergate right to the door of the Oval Office. There was the apparent involvement of the President's closest advisers in the Ellsberg psychiatrist break-in, the Administration wiretaps on Nixon aides and newsmen without resort to judicial authority, and the vast domestic spy program (the "Huston plan") developed back in 1970. Yet evidence that Nixon himself had been party to the Watergate cover-up, campaign spying, or funding abuses, was circumstantial at best. The President denied it vehemently. And the activities he admitted knowing about he claimed were justified by "national security."

Dean's Senate testimony provided the first direct allegations that the President had personally participated in the Watergate cover-up. If corroborated, that testimony would prove that the President had adopted a self-serving and corrupt attitude toward the criminal investigation of Watergate; that his primary interest had been to protect his reelection and his closest aides; and that he had lied to the American people about his actions and motives. Yet in our estimation Dean's testimony fell short of meeting the standard of proof necessary under federal criminal law to demonstrate that the President had obstructed justice or participated in a criminal conspiracy.

Proof of obstruction of justice would require evidence that Nixon had personally taken some affirmative action to further the cover-up. Dean did not allege that the President personally ordered payment of hush money or encouraged anyone to commit perjury. He could provide only circumstantial evidence (which, in turn, was based on hearsay) that the President had approved an offer of executive clemency to Howard Hunt to keep Hunt quiet. Moreover, while federal conspiracy law allows the prosecution to bring in a wide variety of acts and statements in support of criminal culpability, it has limitations as well. The cover-up was surely a criminal conspiracy. The issue was whether the President had become a "member" of that conspiracy. As first-year law students learn, a person who discovers an ongoing criminal conspiracy and does nothing to blow the whistle on it still does not become criminally liable. Something more is required than just looking the other way. The individual must "cast his lot" with the conspirators and help promote the illegal venture.

The President's failure to report what he learned in March and April of 1973 to investigators may have constituted "misprision of felony," an archaic offense incorporated in the federal criminal code but seldom charged in modern times. It was certainly reprehensible conduct for any citizen and particularly for the President of the United States—the country's chief law enforcement officer. It might even be grounds for impeachment. But standing alone it could not support indictment.

A prosecutor, unlike a newspaper or a congressional committee, cannot make a case from secondhand accounts and inference alone. Even in the investigative stage he must evaluate the facts available to him in the framework of a future trial where there will be strict limitations on what will be accepted as evidence. Hearsay, supposition, the actions of an accused's associates—the bulk of the Ervin Committee's evidence—is not proof in court. The prosecutor needs live witnesses who were present during conversations and can relate to a jury what was said by whom, or else documents that stand in the stead of human recollection.

Even with the limited testimony Dean could theoretically provide against the President, he was far from being in the position of a potential government trial witness. Dean had refused to cooperate with the original prosecutors unless they granted him immunity. He had maintained that position with us. He had already claimed his Fifth Amendment privilege rather than testify before the grand jury. We had firmly refused to consider granting Dean immunity, so we were not able to interview him, test his recollection or elicit additional information he might possess. In short, it was a standoff. Until we immunized him (or proceeded in a two-step process to prosecute and convict him, and then compel his cooperation through an immunity grant), we were left to study the Ervin Committee record. This in itself was not very helpful, since Dean had not been adequately cross-examined by the committee—his interrogation by the committee members and staff hardly went beyond his prepared statement.

The task of corroborating Dean, even if we secured his cooperation, would be difficult. There were tactics and legal doctrines uniquely available to Richard Nixon, as President, to shield his wrongdoing. He had availed himself of each of them. Throughout the cover-up he had carefully isolated himself from all but a few trusted cohorts: Haldeman, Ehrlichman and on one or two occasions John Mitchell. Thus he had "plausible deniability" for almost everything that had happened. And his aides had set their course to defend themselves and their boss to the end, admitting nothing.

Added to this difficulty was the historic respect accorded Presidential claims of executive privilege and "national security." In the past, federal prosecutors in ordinary criminal cases had rarely, if ever, attempted to penetrate the wall of secrecy surrounding White House deliberations or to look behind claims of national security to decide whether they were legitimate or simply politically self-serving. From the beginning, the President had shown himself capable of wide-ranging, indiscriminate use of these two shields to block our attempts to obtain documentary evidence from the White House and elicit testimony from those close to him.

In addition to the lack of hard evidence, there were a number of other reasons for our cautious approach to investigating the President, both institutional and personal: the customary doctrines of prosecutorial restraint, intensified in the case of a sitting President; the symbolic character of the Presidency in our political system; the personality and values of Archibold Cox; and the lack of any productive investigative line.

Among the ethical restraints that limit the prosecutor's considerable power and discretion even in the run-of-the-mill criminal case are those relating to the management of a criminal investigation. The prosecutor is not supposed to go off on "fishing expeditions" or launch a grand-jury probe just because he believes some area may be ripe for discovery of criminal activity. Each major step in a grand-jury investigation should be based on information giving rise to a reasonable belief in possible criminal conduct; and it should be designed to obtain specific evidence that might reasonably be pertinent to such criminal activity.

These ethical considerations applied with even greater strength to our investigation than to the ordinary criminal case. The Special Prosecution Force had been endowed with extraordinary power and autonomy in order to prevent interference by the White House or a Nixon-appointed Attorney General. Linked to this unusual power was a corresponding extra duty of care in exercising it. Just as we had opted for more than the customary prosecutorial procedures to guarantee fairness to witnesses, something more than customary restraint was called for in deciding where to focus our investigatory efforts. We wanted to be certain that every step in our investigation was justified by a reasonable expectation of finding evidence relating to a possible crime.

Ironically, the same mandate that endowed us with so much power left us in a situation where the investigation could not succeed without continued public support. While directly accountable to nobody in government, we were dependent on the credibility we maintained with the public—on the confidence we could instill that a thorough investigation could and would be carried out. Dependence on public confidence added to the importance of proceeding cautiously and fairly. The public had a right to expect that the job would be done without cutting corners. More to the point, it could be anticipated that any investigation of someone who thought he was being unjustifiably pursued would quickly be publicized, and might arouse suspicion of our office if we could not defend our action. There was nothing we feared more that might erode our credibility than controversy about the fairness of our overall investigatory efforts.

In the case of the President all these pressures became more acute. A large segment of the public believed President Nixon had been unfairly maligned by the Eastern liberal press, which they saw acting in concert with his political opponents. Despite Watergate and press reports about campaign sabotage, Nixon had been reelected to a second term in 1972 by a record majority. As the Watergate cover-up came crashing down around him, he traded upon his political mandate and the media access that accompanied it. The White House line portrayed Watergate as a desperate, overblown attempt by Nixon's political enemies to take revenge for the drubbing they had received at the President's hands in November. The President's accusers, principally John Dean, were subjected to a vicious and orchestrated campaign of character assassination that sought to label them turncoats who had falsely implicated Mr. Nixon in order to save their own skins. The White House was selling "Watergate as vendetta" full time, and a lot of people were buying it.

Moreover, the office of the Presidency has historically enjoyed a very deep-seated respect from Americans of all political persuasions. One commentator has likened the Presidency to the "totem" of the American tribe. Certainly media preoccupation in recent years with the personal life and habits of the President, rather than decrease the awe with which most Americans regard the office, seems to have intensified its mythic character. For better or worse, the Presidency has become the symbol for our political system.

A sitting President had never before been criminally investigated. We were interested in answering a number of questions about Richard Nixon, the President: What had he done, what had he said to whom? Instead we kept running into a symbol—the Presidency. Nixon knew well how to blur and confuse the two to his advantage. Relying on public relations, he played to the patriotic sympathies of the entire body politic as well as the partisan sympathies of his political supporters.

The White House was inordinately sensitive to any suggestion that the Special Prosecutor's office might be investigating the President himself. "The case of the San Clemente mortgage" illustrates how

White House touchiness and extraordinary media attention combined to make us ever more cautious.

In midsummer the *Los Angeles Times* published a number of reports relating to President Nixon's personal financial dealings in acquiring his San Clemente estate. Other papers picked up the story, focusing national attention on it. We knew nothing of this. Our office had no basis at that point to justify an investigation of Nixon's personal finances. We were intrigued to see what new disclosures each day's *Times* would bring, but formally opening an investigation was deemed premature at that point. However, Archie Cox worried that some reporter might ask him a question about the subject. He wanted to be briefed on what the newspapers were saying so that, if asked, he could at least have an informed "no comment" on the subject.

Cox asked his executive assistant, Peter Kreindler, to summarize the news stories for him. The trouble was, our office didn't have a complete set of them. So Kreindler set out to get the *Los Angeles Times* press clips for the previous week. Where, Kreindler asked Jim Doyle, our public-information officer, could he get them? There was some discussion about getting clips from libraries or other sources, but that was too cumbersome. Well, Doyle suggested, why not just call up this fellow whom Doyle knew at the *Los Angeles Times* and get the clips directly from him? That seemed to be a sensible and efficient way to proceed, so Kreindler duly made a telephone call and arranged to acquire the clips.

Two days later, the *Los Angeles Times* reported in a prominent page-one headline that it had learned the Watergate Special Prosecutor was conducting a criminal investigation into President Nixon's San Clemente real-estate finances. The President hit the ceiling. Alexander Haig phoned Attorney General Elliot Richardson to find out what the hell was going on and to express outrage that Cox was getting into this area. Richardson phoned Cox. The Attorney General told him the President was demanding that our office make a public statement to the effect that the story was unfounded. Cox assured the Attorney General it was all a misunderstanding. The Special Prosecutor agreed to deny the story.

During July and August, Nixon (through Richardson) stepped up the pressure on Cox to confine himself to a narrow interpretation of his charter—one that would keep us far from the Oval Office. Eventually, the President's efforts would culminate in the firing of Cox in the Saturday Night Massacre.*

In early June Cox let the Watergate Task Force know that he personally would "handle" anything related to possible criminality by President Nixon. Archie's background, his experience, and his personal view of the Presidency undoubtedly reinforced the institutional restraints holding us back from a full-scale investigation of the President. Cox's governmental experience, including his service as President Kennedy's Solicitor General, had taken place in an atmosphere that entailed deference to the President as an individual. Moreover, Cox the constitutional lawyer and Harvard law professor was steeped in an intellectual tradition that stressed achievement of a proper balance between competing governmental institutions. Cox saw the possibility of a criminal investigation of the President as an institutional rather than a prosecutive problem. In this, he was guided by the institutional deference to the head of the executive branch that has come to be, for better or worse, a central theme in American constitutional law.

Somewhat to Cox's chagrin, he was readily identifiable as a "liberal" Democrat who had served in the Kennedy Administration and had ties to the Kennedy family. It could not have escaped the President's notice that Senator Edward M. Kennedy and members of his family, wreathed in smiles, personally attended Cox's swearing-in as Special Prosecutor. As the tapes later confirmed, Richard Nixon's antipathy for the Kennedys and his neurotic preoccupation with them was unbounded. Cox was aware of the label he bore and determined not to let it affect, or appear to affect, his performance. In practice, this meant he consciously attempted to bend over backward in order to avoid giving the appearance that he was "going after" Richard Nixon. In the tense, oversensitive atmosphere of Watergate Washington, any move by Cox to "investigate" the President directly would have triggered a wrangle with significant political overtones and highlighted Cox's supposed political affiliation.

Jim Neal, a man with his own Kennedy identification, shared many of Cox's personal and institutional views about the Presidency. Neal's Southern roots reflected a reverent attitude toward the Presidency. In Tennessee the public was less inclined than in New York or Washington to believe the worst about Richard Nixon.

* See Chapter 6.

Despite his reluctance to push ahead with an active investigation, Cox would have to be totally informed of what evidence *did* exist tending to implicate the President. In July Cox asked Jim Vorenberg to assemble a comprehensive study laying out all the evidence available to our office concerning President Nixon. Vorenberg in turn asked Frampton to prepare the Watergate portion of this report and to coordinate and evaluate similar information from the other task forces. Strict instructions were given that the existence of this project should not be made known to anyone in the office except those with a "need to know" (an instruction honored in the breach). Completed copies were not to be disseminated but locked away in Cox's safe.

The resulting memorandum was a decidedly non-explosive document. It concluded that there was meaningful information to suggest possible criminal conduct by Mr. Nixon only in the Watergate cover-up area, that the evidence in that area was entirely circumstantial except for Dean's testimony, that Dean's most telling points could not be corroborated at that time, and that his account in any event fell short of proving illegal acts by the President. Our first attempt to "assemble" the evidence against Richard Nixon served as a sobering reminder of how flimsy a basis existed for any formal investigation.

More frustrating than the lack of hard evidence was the absence of any obvious *line* of investigation by which additional facts could be uncovered. Only a few people could tell us anything about Nixon's role in the cover-up. Haldeman, Ehrlichman and Mitchell could be written off. Dean would not agree to further interrogation without a grant of immunity. And our attempt to obtain White House documents that might shed light on the Nixon role had been stymied by White House obstructionism and delay. Executive privilege and "national-security" claims would also block our path to any additional information. Where were we to go? An active investigation of the President would mean tramping around in a lot of unknown territory. Each step of such a march ought to be supported by strong factual justification, justification that had not yet materialized.

Except in cases of blatant wrongdoing the responsible federal prosecutor is usually reluctant to launch an investigation of an elected public official—not only because of the politician's power but also because of his role in the political system. The very existence of an investigation may substantially damage the politician's career; indictment may terminate it, regardless of the outcome of any trial. The prosecutor, too, rarely emerges from such a contest unscathed: even if he obtains a conviction he will inevitably be accused of political bias, of fronting for the politician's political opponents, and of usurping the role of the electorate in policing the morality of its public officials. If the jury acquits, these accusations will be confirmed and the prosecutor will suffer the consequences.*

In the case of the President—head of the political system and symbol of our democracy—the stakes were multiplied manyfold. We were fearful of the tremendous power Nixon wielded and his undoubted willingness to use it. There was no question in our minds that the continued viability of all our investigations could be jeopardized by a foolish confrontation with the President that gave him an excuse to act against the whole office.

Jim Neal, a tireless purveyor of (sometimes fractured) Tennessee aphorisms, had one for this situation that he often cited at us: "If you shoot at a king, you better aim for the heart." † Our aim might be true, but the ammunition was lacking.

In truth, Neal himself entertained few thoughts during the summer of 1973 that the President might have been criminally involved in Watergate. Yet, despite the fact that overt mention of Nixon's personal culpability was a virtual taboo within the office, Neal had a number of private chats with Cox about the delicacy of directly investigating the President. Cox was pessimistic, he told Neal, that such an investigation could ever really be mounted.

Besides, assembling good cases against the President's closest aides seemed to be the most responsible long-range approach to ascertaining the President's true role. To this end we were already working seven-day weeks. Without John Dean as a government witness the prospects of convicting Haldeman and Ehrlichman were far from certain. We were too worried about their cases, where solid evidence of criminality was already manifest, to be overly concerned about more speculative investigation of President Nixon.

---

* One of Watergate's legacies may be to change this equation, at least for the short run: the prosecutor who lacks self-confidence may jump into an unwise prosecution for fear he cannot weather the public criticism inherent in *declining* to bring charges against a public figure whom the media have implicated in questionable conduct.

† Or, as Justice Oliver Wendell Holmes was accustomed to recollect it, "When you strike at a king, you must kill him."

The same cautious and deferential posture characterized our quest for White House documents and other physical evidence. Documentary evidence can make or break a case like Watergate. Defendants inevitably seek to discredit insider witnesses by painting them as liars, or attempt to explain incriminating conversations in which they participated by interpreting the conversations in an innocent light. Documents like action memoranda, however, are difficult to "reinterpret." And, of course, it isn't too easy for a defendant to take the stand at trial and claim that a written instruction bearing his signature never happened. Diaries, meeting logs and other records showing the physical movements and meetings of a potential defendant serve as leads from which a good investigator can expand his inquiries. They also limit the options available to the subject of the investigation: the prosecutor knows that the defendant will have to fashion explanations for his actions within the framework of the documentary proof. In short, there is nothing a criminal investigator likes to find more than a good "trail of paper."

However, the Special Prosecutor, not the Watergate Task Force, was making decisions about our efforts to obtain documentary evidence from the White House. Cox's patience, his desire to lean over backward to be fair, his deference to the White House, and his willingness to assume good faith on their part until facts conclusively proved otherwise combined to produce a drawn-out, frustrating series of skirmishes over documentary evidence that by late summer had netted us little of consequence.

In the first weeks after the birth of the Special Prosecution Force, a naïve confidence prevailed that any White House documents needed for the investigation would be forthcoming. During the first week of June, when the Special Prosecutor was still working out of a three-room suite at the Justice Department, Frampton suggested that we should pursue formal arrangements with the White House to impound and protect certain important, selected categories of documents. Cox told him that this was no problem, because everything necessary to the office's work would be provided. He had "firm assurances" of this from Attorney General Richardson, Cox said, and was prepared to rely on them.

Cox's early optimism soon paled in the face of White House obstruction and delay. Within weeks it became apparent to most of us that we would get nothing voluntarily. Our plight was compounded by an early tactical mistake. The very first request made by our office was not for a few, identifiable items, but for a complete inventory of White House files. Given the size of the task and the small legal staff the President had assembled, this blunderbuss request was one no reasonable observer could expect the White House to complete in a short time. Thus we could hardly fault them for their indefinite delay. Worse, the information was really of little use to us. The request was made at a time when only a few experienced prosecutors were on board. Cox was still preoccupied with office organization, making sure that a basis would be laid for investigation of all matters that theoretically fell within the broad scope of the Special Prosecutor's charter.

We quickly remedied our error with a request that turned up more useful information. We demanded a list of the dates and times of the President's meetings and phone conversations with a select group of his aides who had evidently been involved in the cover-up. This was a tough one for the White House to deny. The original prosecutors already had obtained similar information from Haldeman, Ehrlichman, Mitchell and others. Our new request was brief and specific. Since we weren't seeking information about the substance of the conversations, executive privilege was not applicable. Before long we began to receive long lists of the dates and times of conversations between Nixon and such people as Dean, Haldeman, Ehrlichman, Mitchell, Colson and others. The information was priceless to us in pursuing new leads, conducting grand-jury interrogation, and eventually for pinpointing important Nixon tapes.

Almost all our other requests to the White House for documentary evidence were met with carefully couched excuses, delay, and sometimes a lack of any response at all. When Cox politely reiterated our requests, the White House just as politely persisted in putting him off. Subpoenas for evidence were not seriously considered. Cox determined to press for the voluntary cooperation he believed he had been promised, even when it seemed obvious to most of us that it simply wasn't going to be forthcoming.

If the handful of young prosecutors working under Neal's supervision on the Watergate Task Force had had their druthers, a more aggressive approach would have been adopted in trying to get hold of White House documents. Ranging in age from the midthirties downward, our investigative group shared the attitudes of a generation raised and educated during a period that saw urban riots, the Vietnam War and other national unrest. Undeniably, as a group we had come to have less regard than our parents for the probity and integrity of public officials simply by reason of the fact that they had attained high office. By nature, we were more suspicious, more skeptical.

Then, too, our role in the office brought us into more intimate contact with the evidentiary aspects of Watergate than our boss, the Special Prosecutor. For us, unlike Cox, Watergate was a prosecutive rather than an institutional problem. Our job was to investigate and prosecute as vigorously as we knew how. In the early stages, the need for factual reconstruction was paramount. We were expected to put the jigsaw puzzle together. If someone had a piece of the puzzle, we wanted it, no matter who he was.

Our day-to-day immersion in the facts gave us a perspective somewhat different from that of the Special Prosecutor, too. We knew perhaps better than anyone else in the country how circumstantial was the evidence against the President, but we also knew how damning those circumstances were. Having lived for several months with the details of Richard Nixon's desperate attempt to conceal his role in the collapse of the cover-up, we were quite a bit less cautious than our superiors about pursuing the evidence to build a stronger case against him.

In any event, by August Archibald Cox's reluctance to ferret out a trail of paper in the White House was largely mooted by disclosure of the President's taping system. A "celluloid trail" was more than we had ever dreamed of finding. When the existence of the tapes was made known, Cox did not hesitate to move with alacrity.*

* See Chapter 5.

CHAPTER **4** **The Linchpin—John W. Dean III**

JOHN DEAN was thirty-one years old in July 1970 when he became counsel to the President of the United States. He was a comer. In a Republican Administration that boasted few attractive young lawyers, Dean—bright, congenial, good-looking, and very ambitious—was one of those obviously headed for bigger things.

In spite of his youth and his relative inexperience in government, Dean had managed to add a number of pearls to his string of credentials. First there was a marriage to the stepdaughter of a Midwestern Democratic United States senator, a millionaire in her own right, that proved the source of many congressional contacts. The marriage would turn out to be unsuccessful. Then a brief sojourn as an associate in a politically connected Washington law firm, which ended, however, in a falling-out between Dean and a senior partner over an investment that Dean was contemplating with some of his wife's money. The partner believed Dean was putting his own interests above those of the firm and even accused him at one point of an unethical conflict of interest. The charge was later retracted.

After a brief stint as a minority counsel for the House Judiciary Committee, Dean served for two years, from 1967 to 1969, on the staff of the National Commission on Reform of the Criminal Laws. Ironically, it was in this capacity that he became one of the architects of the new federal immunity statute enacted by Congress in 1970, part of an omnibus anticrime measure strongly advocated by Nixon and Mitchell. The statute was instrumental in piercing the Watergate cover-up and opened the way for Dean to implicate Richard Nixon in Watergate before a national television audience.

After his Reform Commission service, where he caught the eye of John Mitchell, Dean was brought by Mitchell to Justice as an "associate Deputy Attorney General"—an impressive-sounding title traditionally reserved for one or two bright young men on the Attorney General's staff. It was from there that he was called to the White House as counsel to the President, a position vacated when its previous occupant, John Ehrlichman, was promoted to coordinate the Administration's domestic programs. Dean's promotion was a result of his being "noticed" by the White House and later tapped by H. R. Haldeman after a personal interview at San Clemente. Mitchell was set against Dean's departure from Justice. "John," the Attorney General confided, "they'll eat you alive up there." But the lure of the big time proved too great.

The position Dean inherited at the White House did not have quite the scope of the one Ehrlichman left behind. Of course, there was an office in the White House, a most impressive title for such a young man, and an equally impressive salary ($42,500) to match. Beyond that, the work was not exactly heady. Ehrlichman had been an "assistant to the President"; Dean was not. Under Dean, the office of counsel was charged almost exclusively with routine legal business and liaison with law enforcement agencies. But Dean had time to keep his eyes and ears open, to cultivate his new White House contacts, and to make a good impression on the likes of Haldeman and Ehrlichman by zealously pursuing their pet projects.

The one substantive responsibility Dean inherited from John Ehrlichman was coordinating and disseminating domestic-intelligence reports that came to the White House from other law enforcement agencies. Dean soon learned of the voracious White House appetite for domestic intelligence. The President was titillated by it; Haldeman and Colson demanded more and more. The first year and a half of the Nixon Administration had seen continued Vietnam War protests, a series of criminal-conspiracy trials of political dissidents, the Cambodia invasion setting off a new wave of student protests throughout the nation, and finally the tragedy at Kent State. In the siege mentality that prevailed at the White House the President was perceived, in apocalyptic terms, to be involved in a many-faceted struggle against a single, undifferentiated "enemy." The struggle constituted no less than a total crisis of Presidential authority and credibility. The White House staff was especially eager for any intelligence that could be used as ammunition against this "enemy" (whether it be newsmen, students, politicians, or left-wing rabble rousers).

Dean took intelligence seriously, since it was an area where his work would be noticed. Yet, as White House counsel, his role in domestic-intelligence-gathering was never going to be a central one. All in all, intelligence was not the sort of major project Dean had in mind when he pondered how he could make his mark at the White House.

In mid-1971, when the White House began to plan in earnest for Richard Nixon's reelection campaign—another and even more critical battle in the President's struggle with his amorphous foe—Dean was asked to shoulder a greater intelligence load. But this task was soon turned over in large part to CRP. It had been decided that CRP should have its own "counsel" to handle the joint responsibilities of campaign funding law and "campaign intelligence." Dean himself helped locate the man for the job: G. Gordon Liddy.

When Liddy presented his proposal for a million-dollar CRP intelligence program to John Mitchell in January and February of 1972, Dean was invited to attend the meetings in his capacity as White House intelligence coordinator. He did not like what he saw. What with chase planes, kidnapping and hired prostitutes, the plan was something the White House should have nothing to do with. Dean reported as much to Haldeman. Haldeman agreed. It was all a little too flaky, a little too dangerous for the White House.

With the apprehension of Liddy's wiretap crew at the DNC offices in Watergate on June 17, however, Dean finally got the chance he had been waiting for to prove his mettle to the President's inner circle. Now the White House was presented a *fait accompli*. Like it or not, Liddy's program had gone forward and been bungled. With the election less than five months away, protection of the President's reelection became paramount. The political damage could be narrowly limited if the connection between the burglars and the CRP hierarchy could be concealed. The existence of the Liddy program that had been discussed at CRP and the White House would have to be kept secret.

No command decision was made to put a vast cover-up into motion. It was just instinct, political instinct, sharpened in the crucible of three years of White House paranoia, three years of White House struggle with the forces that were out to demolish "Presidential authority." The cover-up was another skirmish in this war. The Hunt-Liddy connection with the Plumbers and Hunt's previous work for Colson upped the ante. The Administration's abuses of power, what

John Mitchell called "the White House horrors," had created a reservoir of secrets in the White House that had to be protected. Some could harm the President's reelection prospects even more than the truth about Watergate; thus the high priority of containing the investigation into the bugging. As John Dean told us in describing how and why the cover-up first began, "There wasn't any articulated plan or motive. It was just assumed that this had to be done. It just happened."

Dean was uniquely situated to take day-to-day charge of the cover-up. He had proved himself trustworthy to Haldeman and Ehrlichman. As a former protégé of Mitchell's, Dean was the ideal White House liaison to CRP. He could keep the palace guard fully informed of what Mitchell's men at CRP were doing to head off the criminal investigation. Dean also had personal relationships with other CRP officials: Magruder (a former Haldeman aide) and Mardian (who had been an Assistant Attorney General while Dean was at Justice). And, of course, it was Dean's counterpart at CRP, Gordon Liddy, who had masterminded this disaster.

At the same time Dean could serve the conspirators as a conduit to the criminal investigation itself. As counsel and White House liaison to Justice, he would normally be assigned to keep close touch on that agency's investigatory progress. At Justice, Dean had personal relationships with Attorney General Kleindienst (Dean's former boss) and with FBI Acting Director Gray (who had also been an Assistant Attorney General under Mitchell). Dean used these contacts to extract detailed information about the progress of the FBI and grand-jury investigations on the grounds that as the direct, personal agent of President Nixon he needed to keep the President informed. In reality, Dean passed along the information to CRP and White House aides to help them stay one jump ahead of the investigators.

Finally, Dean was an excellent choice for Haldeman and Ehrlichman to insulate themselves from any direct contact with the cover-up. They could count on their ambitious, self-starting young subordinate to protect them judiciously while acting aggressively to do what he realized they wanted done. (The President, of course, was kept even further above it all: Dean had no access to him and rarely saw him except on ceremonial occasions.)

So John Dean's big chance was at hand. Success was critical to the reputation of John Mitchell, Dean's sponsor and one of the President's closest friends. It was of utmost importance to the President's reelection. This would be Dean's major test in the eyes of Haldeman and Ehrlichman: a test of loyalty, ability, discretion.

The word went out: Dean was "handling" Watergate for the White House. And handle it he did. It was no exaggeration to say, as Dean told the President in a taped conversation in March of 1973, that he was "all over the thing like a blanket."

When federal indictments of seven men, no one higher than Liddy, were finally returned on September 15 and Dean met personally with Haldeman and the President to receive the President's praise for his work, Dean felt that he had met the challenge. Nixon told Dean that, like the young hero in the Dutch legend, he had successfully "kept his fingers in the dike."

When the cover-up collapsed, the White House would claim that Dean had masterminded it. The charge was too severe. Dean's role could more accurately be likened to that of White House platoon sergeant: directing the daily battle order, keeping in touch with the flank unit at CRP, and keeping his commissioned officers informed. Like any good noncom Dead did not have to consult the White House brass at every step; he knew what was required. But the major decisions and strategic planning were theirs. In the final analysis they gave the orders; Dean carried them out.

By February of 1973 the storm clouds were on the horizon. Some of the seven men recently convicted in the Watergate trial were sure to be immunized by the federal prosecutors, the newly formed Ervin Committee, or both and forced to tell what they knew about higher-ups. They, in turn, were complaining vociferously that the financial commitments made to them had not been kept.

Dean had become the object of a tug-of-war between the Senate Judiciary Committee and the White House over his testimony at the confirmation hearings of FBI Acting Director L. Patrick Gray. The committee wanted to make the hearings a full-scale inquiry into the FBI's handling of the Watergate investigation, and they wanted to hear from Dean. In August of 1972 the President, in a mood of exuberance, had stated in a press conference that Dean had conducted a full investigation of Watergate and given the President a "report" establishing that "no one in the White House staff" was involved. The statement was a blatant falsehood. (Even Dean's deputy Fred Fielding, who had little contact with Watergate matters, knew full well Dean had not authored such a report; when Fielding first spoke to

Dean after the President's surprise announcement, Fielding said, "Well, John, I guess you better get busy and write a report.") The committee naturally wanted to know about the report. The White House was claiming that it—and any testimony by Dean about his "investigation" for the President—was covered by executive privilege.

In February and March Dean began to meet with the President alone. They talked about the Gray hearings, the law of executive privilege, and Watergate. The President gave Dean the impression that he did not truly appreciate the dangers that lay in store for his Administration if the existence of the cover-up were revealed. A message Dean received from Howard Hunt in mid-March demanding an additional $120,000 shook even the cool young lawyer. If the money wasn't forthcoming, Hunt threatened, he would tell about the "seamy" things he had done for the White House, and that meant more than just Watergate.

Realizing that a critical moment was at hand, Dean decided to brief the President extensively on the details of the cover-up and the new Hunt threat. On the morning of March 21, Dean warned his President that Watergate was a "cancer on the Presidency" growing and compounding itself with every passing day. The young lawyer advised Nixon to seize the initiative and "cut his losses"—even if it meant sacrificing some White House aides, including Dean—before the President was too deeply involved personally to extricate himself. Dean warned the President that it was only a matter of time before the cover-up came unstuck.

Dean's "cancer on the Presidency" speech and the meetings that followed it on March 21 and 22 made little impact on Richard Nixon. The President did not comprehend the gravity of the situation. The cover-up would continue. The President himself was actively involved. The only decision to emerge was that Dean should write a "report" about Watergate purporting to set forth all the facts. What the President, Haldeman and Ehrlichman had in mind was a report that, in essence, implicated Magruder and others at CRP in the bugging, probably condemned Mitchell, played down and falsified the existence of any cover-up, and exonerated the White House entirely. If the true story later came out, the President could claim he relied on Dean's report.

Dean could not carry out his new assignment. If he wrote anything close to the truth, he would damn them all, the President included.

If he wrote what was expected of him, the document would heavily incriminate Dean while protecting his superiors at the White House whose orders he had carried out.

On March 23 Dean's prediction about the cover-up was fulfilled when James McCord wrote a startling letter to Judge Sirica claiming that higher-ups were involved in Watergate and that perjury had been committed at the Watergate burglars' trial. McCord's information, Dean knew, was only hearsay, but it reached Magruder and Mitchell, and probably Dean. Mitchell, Dean knew, would not crack. But Magruder, who had testified at the trial and had indeed committed perjury, was something else. An "anonymous-source" news story reported on March 26 that Magruder and Dean had been implicated in the Watergate bugging. Dean sensed in telephone conversations with Magruder that Magruder was panicking—it wouldn't be long before he would break.

At the same time Dean was beginning to receive some disturbing signals from Haldeman and Ehrlichman, suggesting that the President and his two closest aides had decided to take Dean's advice and "cut their losses" by cutting loose John Dean. Dean would be made the sole White House scapegoat for deceiving the President and the President's aides. Haldeman and Ehrlichman would slip the noose.

Dean was at the crossroads of his life. The young lawyer considered the alternatives open to him and evaluated them in terms of probable long-range outcome. He decided he would be better off in the long run if he went to the prosecutors and told them what he knew about the bugging and a good part of what he knew of the cover-up—at least, the involvement of Haldeman, Ehrlichman, Colson, himself and the CRP officials. He was a dead duck anyway. If he were the first major figure to cooperate, he could expect to receive consideration for coming forward. He would insure that the full story came out, that he alone did not get blamed as the head honcho in the cover-up. Speed was now of the essence, for if Magruder and others beat him to the courthouse door, Dean might lose the advantages that could accrue to an early, "voluntary" cooperator.

For his attorney Dean chose a brilliant, aggressive criminal lawyer named Charles N. Shaffer. Shaffer was a liberal Democrat and former Kennedy Justice Department prosecutor who had previously worked with Jim Neal on a prosecution of James Hoffa. Ben-Veniste had also dealt with Shaffer in connection with Shaffer's representation of an important witness in the Voloshen-Sweig case. When Shaffer debriefed Dean, he was stunned to learn the extent of the information Dean stood to provide the prosecutors. In early April Shaffer approached Earl Silbert. Citing the wealth of valuable information his client was prepared to divulge, Shaffer requested immunity for Dean. Silbert and his team were reluctant. Before making that decision they wanted to hear from Dean himself.

Accordingly, Dean began meeting secretly with the original prosecutors during the second week of April on an "off-the-record" basis. Dean agreed to relate what he knew so that the prosecutors could evaluate his usefulness as a witness and decide if immunity was warranted. They, in turn, agreed not to use Dean's disclosures against him but to consider them only in making their immunity decision. The meetings continued into early May before being discontinued.

Dean told the prosecutors a great deal about Watergate, including most of the facts about the involvement of himself, Haldeman and Ehrlichman. But he did not tell them much about his meetings with President Nixon, and he didn't implicate the President in the cover-up. What he told the prosecutors indicated that the President had remained ignorant of what his aides were doing. Perhaps Dean held back from more complete disclosure because of uncertainty about his status at that time. He may have felt constrained, even at that late date, by the President's assertion of executive privilege over all his personal conversations with aides. More likely Dean was motivated by a combination of continued loyalty to and fear of the President. Implicating the President directly would be a momentous step, different in quality from simply telling the prosecutors about Haldeman and Ehrlichman. And it would be dangerous. The confrontation of Dean and the President would be one man's word against the others; Dean could get way out on a limb.

What Dean did disclose made it obvious that he would be a valuable witness. At the same time, the prosecutors realized how deeply Dean had been involved in the cover-up. He had fingered his superiors, but Dean was no small catch either. The counsel to the President of the United States might not count for much in the White House inner sanctum, but to the prosecutors and the country he was a very high-ranking national official. The decision to grant him testimonial immunity would make it extremely difficult to prosecute him for his role in the cover-up. That they could not risk. Besides, other witnesses were by this time coming forward in droves. Some of them, particularly Magruder and LaRue, implicated Dean. A good case could now be mounted against Dean on the basis of others' testimony.

In early April the prosecutors told Shaffer that they would not grant Dean immunity. Instead they offered to accept a guilty plea to one count of conspiracy to obstruct justice in satisfaction of all potential criminal liability Dean had incurred. Shaffer and Dean hemmed and hawed. The prosecutors subpoenaed Dean to appear before the grand jury, but he asserted his Fifth Amendment privilege. Without immunity, there would be no testimony.

In the meantime the Ervin Committee was courting Dean zealously. They had no compunction about offering him testimonial immunity, and they had the power to do it under the new 1970 statute. They didn't have to worry about prosecuting him, now or at any time. They needed a star witness for their hearings. Dean began to make preparations to testify before the committee.

We feared that Dean's upcoming Ervin Committee appearance would be a tactical loss for the prosecution. He would be telling his entire story for the first time under oath without the thorough preparation and cross-examination that often goes on in the prosecutor's office before a major witness's testimony is committed to a written record. With such a vast amount of material it was natural that Dean's recollections would not always be perfectly accurate. This loss was substantially ameliorated in Dean's case, though, by Dean's remarkable memory, the acuity and drive of Charlie Shaffer, and the material made available to Dean by the Ervin Committee staff to help him refresh his recollection. To prepare for his appearance, Dean retraced his White House career in large part by reviewing daily news stories and recalling what he had been doing in relation to the events reported in the papers. Indeed, this was a crucial feature in understanding the cover-up: the conspirators were constantly reacting to daily crises, not looking and planning ahead.

As we later discovered, Dean had startling powers of recall. Strangely enough, he sometimes remembered things in visual terms and by details, rather than by the momentous aspects of the events. He could tell you where he had been sitting at a certain meeting, what color shirt Haldeman was wearing, what Ehrlichman was eating, what the demeanor of other participants was even when he could recall little of the substance of the conversation.

Shaffer played a crucial role in assisting Dean's preparation of a written opening statement for the Ervin Committee. Shaffer debriefed Dean, drove him, harangued him, subjected him to hours of mock cross-examination. Shaffer did not need to point out to Dean that in testifying under immunity it is to the witness's advantage to disclose every bit of wrongdoing in which he was engaged. But knowing that intellectually is not the same as acting on it. Shaffer reached into the corners of Dean's recollection and pulled chunks out. Shaffer also impressed on Dean the fact that his credibility depended in large part on his coming completely clean. The result, a 245-page typewritten statement, was a testimonial to the touch of a fine trial lawyer.

The Ervin Committee could have helped itself and the prosecutors by being a little less hasty in putting Dean before its national television audience. Bringing Dean on early in the hearings was a public-relations success but an investigative mistake. Once Dean had testified publicly, Haldeman, Ehrlichman and others could shape their testimony to Dean's, meeting his points where they could, sliding around them when they could not. The more astute course would have been to hold Dean's appearance until after the testimony of others had been placed on the public record.

A few days before Dean's scheduled appearance, we filed a bulky package with Judge Sirica to be sealed and put away in court files. The package summarized all the evidence against Dean assembled by the prosecution and included excerpts from some of the pertinent testimony relating to his role in the cover-up. If we had to prosecute Dean, it would be incumbent on us to prove that we had not used his immunized Ervin Committee testimony to gather evidence against him. The package might aid our proof by showing what evidence we had already accumulated by the time Dean testified. The procedure was a novel one. It had recently been suggested by a federal court as one way to deal with problems posed by the 1970 immunity statute. Frampton dug up the case and showed it to Neal. We had no idea whether it would eventually prove useful in a prosecution of Dean or not: the law surrounding the new immunity statute was in a state of uncertainty. But it seemed worthwhile to try; it couldn't hurt.

On June 25 Dean began his Ervin Committee testimony by reading his prepared written statement. It took the entire day. Whatever had been the cause of Dean's caution during his earlier interviews with the federal prosecutors, his newly conferred formal immunity and the unrelenting attacks on him that emanated from the White House in May and June had changed his mind. The best weapons he had to defend himself from the White House onslaught were the information he possessed and his extraordinarily keen memory. Before the nation on live television he had chosen to use them both. Dean was finally going the "hang-out route."

The prosecutors paid close attention to Dean's television debut. His testimony unquestionably was detailed, thorough and well documented. Potentially he would make an excellent trial witness, though his pedestrian interrogation by the President's supporters on the committee provided no clue as to how he would stand up to searing cross-examination.

But we were put off by his demeanor. He seemed a little too cold, a little too calculating. Though he appeared to be telling the truth, there was sometimes an annoying self-serving turn to his account. Was the cornucopia of factual detail he had poured out before the committee merely a clever device to gain credibility in shading his testimony against his superiors, throwing off the major blame onto them? We were truly astonished that Nixon could have selected such a person as counsel to the President. Dean's parting words to Nixon in which he expressed the hope that the President would not be impeached seemed a bit hard to take on the basis of the relatively meager evidence Dean had to support such a cataclysmic result. We were left with a decidedly unfavorable impression of Dean.

Notwithstanding our personal reservations about Dean, we soon discovered in our investigation that time after time Dean's Ervin Committee statement was corroborated by other testimony or evidence, even when it appeared initially that he had been wrong. His uncanny accuracy became something of an office joke. With respect to those portions of Dean's account about which we were able to garner any kind of independent information, Dean was right on the button to an astonishing degree. That we were able to corroborate his story so fully made believers out of those on the task force who had originally been skeptics.

We could not properly evaluate Dean's truthfulness or his effectiveness as a witness, however, until we had an opportunity to interview him personally. After Dean's Ervin Committee appearance Neal reiterated to Shaffer the prosecution's offer to accept a plea of guilty to one count of conspiracy to obstruct justice in connection with

Watergate. Neal told Shaffer that we were not inclined to grant Dean immunity. Shaffer said they would think it over.

The Watergate Task Force regarded the securing of Dean as a government witness to be the key to our entire case. Haldeman and Ehrlichman had acted almost exclusively through him. Without Dean, there were few direct witnesses against either Haldeman or Ehrlichman. There was no one else who could testify of his own personal knowledge to the full spectrum of their activities in the cover-up. Without Dean, for instance, only Herbert Kalmbach tied Ehrlichman to the hush money, and he could testify to only one incriminating conversation. Without Dean, only Haldeman's assistant Gordon Strachan could testify to Haldeman's transfer of the $350,000 cash fund to CRP. Strachan claimed to be a mere courier who had no knowledge of the purpose or background of the transfer and knew nothing of payments to any burglars. Magruder and the CIA chiefs could give testimony about personal conversations with Haldeman, but Magruder's testimony was suspect and Haldeman defended his part in the meeting with the CIA officials on national-security grounds.

If Dean could not testify for the prosecution, this about summed up the case linking Haldeman and Ehrlichman personally to corrupt activities. Of course, both Haldeman and Ehrlichman had acknowledged participating in some of the activities attributed to them by Dean in their grand-jury and Ervin Committee testimony. These "admissions" would be admissible evidence that could be read to the jury by the prosecutors in the government's case at trial. However, their versions of these actions were relatively exculpatory, and in any event our case would appear flimsy indeed if most of it consisted of proof out of the defendants' own mouths.

Compare this to the case against John Mitchell. Both Jeb Magruder and Fred LaRue had agreed to plead guilty. Both, of their own personal knowledge, would implicate Mitchell in a wide variety of incriminating pre– and post–June 17 activities. Dean's testimony against Mitchell would be primarily corroborative of others'. In contrast, Dean was virtually a prerequisite to a respectable case at trial against Haldeman, Ehrlichman, Colson and possibly others at the White House.

At the same time, we remained steady in our resolve that, based on the extent of his involvement in the cover-up, Dean must be prosecuted if he didn't accept our offer to plead guilty to one count of conspiracy. Dean was too deeply involved, too culpable, too big a fish, to get a "free ride"—total immunity from prosecution—even in exchange for valuable testimony against his superiors.

Archie Cox was particularly firm in his personal determination that Dean be prosecuted no matter what. Dean became an *idée fixe* for Cox. True, as a witness Dean would cement otherwise weak cases against Haldeman and Ehrlichman. But Cox preferred, if forced to choose, to take the relatively sure shot at Dean rather than the long shot against Dean's superiors. When the Saturday Night Massacre loomed close, it might have been propitious for Cox to make a deal with Dean and secure Dean's testimony against President Nixon as another weapon to hold the President off. Even then Cox's determination did not waver. With all the uncertainties of Watergate that swirled around him—the weakness of the evidence against Nixon's top aides without Dean's testimony, the possibility of Presidential culpability, the problems of obtaining White House evidence and of dealing with "national security"—Cox saw Dean's guilt as the one enduring constant. During a particularly difficult period Archie remarked to us, "If everything else goes down the drain the one thing I can cling to is Dean's venality."

Moral balancing aside, the realpolitik of the situation was that Dean would not be an effective witness at trial if he got a free ride. His credibility would be substantially diminished by his making a deal with the prosecutors to implicate others only if the prosecutors completely forgave his own deep involvement. The evident effect of Dean's prison sentence, later, on the jurors at the Watergate cover-up trial confirmed our tactical judgment. As a man who was already serving a long jail term for doing what he testified he had been instructed to do by Haldeman and Ehrlichman, Dean made a measurably greater impression than if he had never been charged or punished for his acts.

Our decision to prosecute Dean if he did not plead guilty, coupled with the necessity to use him as a prosecution witness against his White House chiefs, left us only two strategic alternatives. We could indict Dean first, try to convict him, and then use him as a witness against the others; or we could indict Dean simultaneously with (but separately from) the other participants in the cover-up, postpone

Dean's trial, grant him testimonial immunity, compel his immunized testimony against the others at *their* trial, and then try Dean by himself at a later time.

Neither of these alternatives was attractive, but trying Dean first was the worse. It would mean a long delay before trial of the "Big Three"—Haldeman, Ehrlichman and Mitchell. Moreover, if we failed to convict Dean he would come on as a witness against his superiors having beaten the rap he was trying to pin on them. That would hurt his credibility and ours: if Dean escaped, why shouldn't they?

On either course a Dean prosecution was far from being a sure thing. Dean's interviews with the original prosecutors back in April and his immunized Ervin Committee testimony in June posed some thorny legal problems.

The original prosecutors had agreed that Dean's disclosures to them would be "off the record"—that is, they promised that if Dean were eventually prosecuted he would not be confronted in court with having admitted certain things during these conversations. As they understood it, their arrangement did not forbid them to use what he told them to develop evidence against him. However, the terms of the arrangement had never been recorded in writing. If Dean's lawyer now claimed that the understanding they had entered into was broader—that it precluded any use of Dean's revelations directly or indirectly to develop leads against Dean—we would have to prove in court that not a shred of our trial evidence derived in any way from these conversations. That would be almost impossible.

Dean's Ervin Committee testimony had been given under a formal, statutory grant of "testimonial" immunity. Since, in legal terms, he had been compelled to testify despite his Fifth Amendment right to remain silent, we were constitutionally foreclosed from using that testimony against him even though we ourselves had not been the ones to extend the immunity. The formal grant of immunity unquestionably barred us from using his compelled testimony against him either directly *or indirectly* as leads to additional evidence. The package of evidence filed with Judge Sirica under seal before Dean's Ervin Committee appearance would show we had already developed a comprehensive case against Dean without his testimony. But the law of testimonial immunity was comparatively new and its outlines were still unclear. For instance, we might be required to prove that our access to Dean's immune testimony had not even influenced the tactical decisions about how to present at trial evidence which we had obtained prior to Dean's appearance but which was confirmed by Dean's own compelled testimony. This was a burden we probably would not be able to meet.

The legal uncertainties posed by Dean's disclosure to the prosecutors and the Ervin Committee could be avoided, Ben-Veniste suggested, if we could bring charges against him in an area, however narrow, not covered in his immunized testimony. Did such an area exist? To answer this question Peter Rient, Judy Denny and Jerry Goldman of the task force mounted a mini-investigation into the course of our own investigation of Dean. They interviewed the original prosecutors in depth. They interviewed the rest of the task force. They interviewed each other. They reconstructed the way we had acquired information relating to Dean. As a result, they came up with one approach that might work.

There was an area Dean had not discussed with the original prosecutors at all. It was a relatively minor aspect of his total involvement in the cover-up: the veiled offer of executive clemency extended by the White House to James McCord in early 1973 through McCord's friend Jack Caulfield, the investigator Dean inherited from John Ehrlichman. The offer was intended to induce McCord to plead guilty at the original Watergate trial rather than "tough it out" and drag out the trial. We had learned about Dean's role not from Dean but from Caulfield, McCord and others. And we had learned about it well *before* Dean confessed to it in his Ervin Committee testimony. Thus we could prove that nothing the prosecution learned from Dean contributed to development of this information.

A draft indictment was prepared charging Dean with conspiracy to obstruct justice based on this one distinct segment of the cover-up. We were not eager to proceed against Dean on this indictment. Its purpose was to confront Dean and his attorney with a concrete and immediate choice: either plead or face imminent indictment. We hoped Dean would choose to plead. Jim Neal contacted Charlie Shaffer and told him time was running short. If Dean was still unwilling to accept our offer to plead guilty to a broad charge of conspiracy, we would indict him in this one smaller area where no attractive immunity defense appeared to be available. Shaffer consulted with his client. The carrot and the stick we were wielding were an unusual combination. We were threatening to indict and try Dean on a charge factually more limited than the one we were asking him to plead to. Either way, Dean's maximum liability would be the same: a five-year prison sentence. On the face of it, not much of a deal.

Dean's position was an unusual one, too. Locked in a high-stakes credibility duel with President Nixon, confronting the full force of White House political and media power, Dean was now compelled, for the sake of his self-respect and his public credibility, to demonstrate— as he was claiming—that he had come clean in the national interest. The prosecution was offering Dean an opportunity to make such a public demonstration: to admit his guilt formally, "switch sides," join the prosecution and become a cooperating witness. The alternative open to Dean was to be indicted and then fight conviction with all his legal resources. Since Dean had already admitted his moral guilt on public television, the latter choice would not be a happy one for him.

Would Dean come around, or would he hold out and make us prosecute him? Our ability to proceed quickly and effectively against the entire Nixon coterie rested in the balance of his decision.

CHAPTER **5** **The Bugging of Richard Nixon**

ON JULY 16 Alexander P. Butterfield, a former White House aide uninvolved in Watergate, startled a national television audience by revealing that Richard Nixon had been tape-recording his own conversations since 1971. While the controversy still raged over whether Nixon had had advance knowledge of the Watergate bugging, we were now told that the President had bugged his own White House. In the midst of the bitter debate about the truthfulness of Dean's allegations, here was the *deus ex machina* that could resolve the dispute. The most imaginative novelist would never have dared invent it.

Butterfield, the author of this bombshell, had for several years managed the President's daily schedule in the Oval Office. In succeeding months we came to know the former Air Force colonel as an enigmatic figure with a military bearing, a plainly visible pride in his integrity and an eager-to-please manner that sometimes cloaked his intelligence. Butterfield's most distinguishing characteristic was a well-developed view of life in terms of personal duty. It was this code of duty, he said on television, that made him decide to reveal the full story of the President's tapes when called in for a routine interview by Ervin Committee investigators. The same unusual sense of duty, peculiarly enough, kept Butterfield loyal to the President much later, even when he was helping *us* with technical problems relating to the tapes.

However, our first reaction to Butterfield's revelation was that we were being set up. How could such a closely held secret be divulged unless the President directed it? Who was Butterfield, anyway? What were his motives? Was this the prelude to some canny strategy in which the President would now release a few "transcripts" allegedly made from actual tape recordings and blow John Dean out of the water? Was it a feint, a diversionary tactic of some kind?

Jim Neal was more suspicious than anyone else. He warned Cox,

111

"It's bound to be a ruse. The President's sent Butterfield up there to tell about these tapes, but they're all going to be exculpatory. They're trying to lead us into a cul-de-sac. Nixon will say, 'Well, executive privilege and national security, but I'm going to give them to you anyway,' and then they won't show a damn thing. Public opinion will have turned against us and we'll all be thrown out of this job."

Trick or not, one thing was obvious. We had no choice but to subpoena some of those tapes right away. If they really existed (and if they could be obtained) the tapes seemed certain to make or break John Dean's testimony. Probably they would determine the outcome of our case against Haldeman and Ehrlichman. In the bargain, the tapes, if legitimate, would undoubtedly tell us a good deal about the extent of the President's own involvement.

The sooner we acted, the better. Once under subpoena the tapes could be tampered with only at the risk of criminal liability for contempt of court and obstruction of justice, a risk we hoped would be sufficient to deter their destruction.

From the moment we decided to seek a subpoena our eyes were on the Supreme Court. If the President asserted executive privilege on the tapes, he would undoubtedly appeal any adverse decisions in the lower courts all the way up. That meant we had to construct a successful pilot case or test case that would put the facts in the best possible light once the case reached the highest court. Under legal precedents, when a claim of privilege is asserted in opposition to a grand-jury subpoena the dispute often boils down to whether the prosecutors can show that the jury has a "particularized need" for the material subpoenaed. In other words, we had to show that the tapes were important to the resolution of factual issues actually being considered by the jury in its investigation. Since the importance of the tapes to the investigation was the main thing that the courts would weigh against the President's privilege, a good test case required that we select only those tapes that were unquestionably central to the cover-up. If even a single subponeaed tape appeared to be peripheral— if it looked as though we were going on a fishing expedition for new evidence—the whole case could be jeopardized. We also wanted to limit our subpoena to a small number of tapes in order to head off any claim by the White House that compliance with the subpoena would be "burdensome" or time-consuming.

Working round the clock, the legal staff plunged into research on executive privilege and on the technical problem of "serving" a subpoena on the President of the United States. Meanwhile, the task force pinpointed nine tapes as the critical ones. All but three of these were tapes of conversations about which John Dean had testified before the Ervin Committee. These tapes would present our best chance in the courts. There was a live witness who had testified to their relevance to the grand jury's investigation, and that same witness—John Dean—was also a target of our investigation. However, Dean had had no significant contact with the President in the first months after the Watergate arrests. We did not want to stake our entire case on Dean or to ignore the early period of the Watergate cover-up. So we also decided to subpoena tapes of three conversations on June 20 and June 30, 1972, within a few weeks of the break-in.

On June 20, 1972, John Mitchell had talked by telephone with President Nixon in the early evening. It was the first time the two had spoken, as far as we knew, since the Watergate burglars had been arrested in the early-morning hours of June 17. Then, on June 30, the day Mitchell resigned as chairman of CRP, he had met with the President and Haldeman at the White House. It was the last meeting they had that summer. We knew of these conversations from the White House lists of meetings between the President and Mitchell. Tapes of both were added to our list.

We had also become intensely interested in another conversation on June 20, 1972, ever since preparation of a comprehensive "chronology" of the events that followed the Watergate arrests. In a textbook prosecutorial technique, the task force had used all of the testimony and evidence available to us (including desk diaries and meeting logs kept by secretaries to Haldeman, Ehrlichman and others) to reenact the movement of all the principal actors connected with Watergate. A highly suspicious sequence of events had occurred on June 20, the first day the President and Haldeman were back in Washington after a trip to the Key Biscayne White House over "Watergate weekend." On the morning of the twentieth Attorney General Richard Kleindienst (formerly Mitchell's deputy at Justice) came to the White House to meet with John Ehrlichman. As the morning wore on, Haldeman, then Dean, and finally Mitchell joined the meeting. When the meeting broke up, Ehrlichman and then Haldeman went in to talk to President

Nixon. From their diaries we could not be sure whether they had seen the President separately or together.

Here were all the major figures in the cover-up (according to John Dean, at least) meeting with the head of the investigation, Kleindienst, on the first day the President was back in town, following which the President's two closest advisers met with the President personally. Dean had testified in the Ervin Committee that Watergate was the subject of conversation during the meeting he attended. But his testimony was inconclusive and he had not been cross-examined about it by the committee. Surely, we thought, the President's conversations with Haldeman and Ehrlichman were key. The President's aides must have reported what they knew of Watergate, and suggested what should be done. If any of these people were in on the cover-up, there had to be some discussion of it then. So the final conversation on our subpoena list was the President's June 20 conversation with Haldeman and Ehrlichman.

The task force also insisted that the Special Prosecutor now make a formal demand for some White House documents in addition to tapes. From a former White House secretary we had recently learned that Haldeman's political aide, Gordon Strachan, kept his boss regularly informed during the 1972 Presidential campaign about CRP's activities through biweekly "political matters memoranda." Strachan admitted destroying one of these memoranda after the Watergate break-in during his attempt to "cleanse" his boss's files. In our subpoena, we would ask for the rest—and hope that a copy of the one Strachan had destroyed might still be lying around.*

Because we thought our court case would be strengthened by a showing that we had first sought voluntary disclosure in good faith, the first step was not a subpoena but a formal request for cooperation. On July 18, two days after Butterfield's televised testimony, Special Prosecutor Cox wrote a letter to the White House requesting the nine tapes on our list and arguing that executive privilege could not legitimately be asserted to deny us access to them. Two days later President Nixon left Bethesda Naval Hospital, which he had entered for treat-

---

* The political-matters memos turned out to be a good choice for our subpoena. When, months later, they were finally produced they turned up a detailed record of the Nixon reelection effort, including a passel of embarrassing, improper and probably illegal activities. Not only did the memos provide the Watergate Task Force with useful information, they opened up many of the most significant investigations carried out by the Campaign Financing Task Force.

ment of "viral pneumonia" reported to have been brought on by exhaustion, but there was no announcement from the White House about the President's position on the tapes.

The Watergate Task Force, meanwhile, was becoming increasingly worried that no steps had been taken to deter tampering with the tapes. So on July 20 the Special Prosecutor addressed another letter to the White House, urging that action be taken to keep the evidence intact and to limit access to it until the legal issues were decided. Five days later the President's counsel Fred Buzhardt replied with assurances that the tapes were under the President's "sole personal control," in "secure conditions," and that access to them was being "carefully documented." Only much later would we discover how empty those assurances were.

On July 26, six days after our formal request for the tapes, President Nixon announced he would not surrender any of them to the grand jury or the Ervin Committee. We had to move with a subpoena that day.

If the President had received more astute legal advice on July 23, he might have plotted a course designed to delay substantially a judicial ruling on executive privilege. The legal research conducted by Phillip Lacovara's research staff found little precedent for subpoenaing a sitting President of the United States. Such a thing had not even been attempted for over a century. What if the President took the position that he could not even be "served" with a subpoena, that he was totally exempt from ordinary legal processes? Such a defense could become an important "threshold" issue to the more central issues surrounding the tapes. Ordinarily, a subpoena is "served" by handing it to the person being subpoenaed. Usually this is done by a prosecutor (if he has personal contact with the witness) or by a federal marshal. But how could we personally serve Mr. Nixon? Obviously, neither Cox nor a marshal could expect to march through the White House gate, proceed into the Oval Office, and lay a subpoena on Nixon's desk. We might even be refused access to Nixon's lawyers. Further legal complications would ensue if service were made only on a guard at the White House gate and not on the President personally. This position might give Nixon an opportunity to litigate and appeal the preliminary threshold issue of service all the way to the Supreme Court, using up many months. Even if we ultimately won, issues like executive privilege would then have to be litigated again, beginning in the trial court and moving up to the Supreme Court a second time. The technical details of service had plagued us for days, and of course we had no idea what the President's strategy might be.

Our worries were soon put to rest. A telephone call was made to the President's lawyers: would they "accept service" on behalf of the President? No problem, they said, bring it over. Before they could have second thoughts, Lacovara and Peter Kreindler quickly covered the seven blocks from our office to the White House.

Within days the President's lawyers told the court they would not comply with the subpoena. Judge Sirica, at our request, issued an order formally joining the legal issue. Thus began three weeks of concentrated effort by the Special Prosecutor, Lacovara and his research staff, and the task force, shaping and honing our legal papers for the argument before Judge Sirica.

It was a measure of our institutional uncertainty that in the opening rounds of the tapes legal battle we could not even make up our minds whether the legal pleadings should say "the United States moves for such-and-such action" or "the Government moves . . ." or "the Special Prosecutor moves . . ."

Cox himself, from this point on, devoted a substantial majority of his time to the legal battle over the tapes. This was his turf. Where constitutional law was concerned, he was one of the country's best, and he loved it. In fact, Lacovara and the other scholars who worked on the brief were often put out to find that areas Archie delegated to them usually came back from Cox's "editorial" pencil completely revised to fit Cox's own thought and style.

Our desire to avoid public reports that we were investigating the President directly, together with Cox's overwhelming desire to proceed cautiously with the White House and prevent any charges of unfairness, prompted the omission from our litigation papers of the most pressing reason for getting the tapes, in the minds of most people —to find out if the President himself had been involved in Watergate. To the public and to the Ervin Committee the tapes were important to the *President's* case. They might show "what the President knew and when he knew it." But no mention of any curiosity about the President's involvement graced our lengthy factual justification for the subpoena (our showing of "particularized need" for the tapes). Rather, our brief stressed the need for the tapes to determine the culpability of the President's *aides* and, particularly, to determine whether Dean had told the truth in his Senate testimony. Our argument sometimes sounded as though the President were nothing but an accidental participant in these conversations: he and his hidden microphones just happened to be there at the right time.

The arguments we advanced were perfectly legitimate ones, but of course they were partially disingenuous. We too were intensely interested in the President's role, and we could hardly wait to see what the tapes would reveal about it. We would not have been doing our duty had we not gone after the tapes for that very reason. Cox's charter specifically instructed him to investigate "allegations . . . against the President." However, for both legal and practical reasons that motive remained unspoken. The grand jury had not been investigating the President directly. The mere existence of tape recordings didn't alter that fact. For the moment, therefore, the tapes were not directly relevant to any issue about the President's culpability that the jury had before it. To announce in our legal papers that an investigation of the President had now been opened would have done more than cause a public uproar, it would have immeasurably weakened our case. The President could then claim (and rightfully so) that we were on a true fishing expedition, looking for evidence to start a new investigation where none existed to justify such a move. Based on what we knew, we could not even have replied that we expected to find hard evidence of the President's criminality in the tapes. Had we taken this route, weakening the factual basis of our case, our entire legal position as well as the quick ruling we hoped for would have been jeopardized.

Cox's preoccupation with the constitutional questions at stake in the tapes dispute contributed to the failure by our office to seek a court order protecting the tapes from tampering. A protective court order might have required the White House to segregate the subpoenaed tapes at the White House under special guard or deliver them to the federal court for safekeeping. We had already made that demand in a letter, of course, and had received Buzhardt's assurances in reply. However, both Ben-Veniste and Frampton expressed their concern—sometimes vociferously—that more should be done about the potential for destruction and tampering.

Seeking a court order was seen by those working primarily on the constitutional issues as petty and punitive. Both Cox and Lacovara insisted that we had no choice but to assume good faith on the part of the White House. There was a desire on their part to keep the case clean and elegant, to focus on the ultimate issues, not to clutter the constitutional confrontation with messy details about custody and protection. Anyway, there was considerable doubt that Judge Sirica would grant such an order. If we pressed for a specific anti-tampering order and lost, we would have weakened our overall position. And any such request would be taken by the White House as an exacerbation of the already deteriorating relationship between the President and Cox. So suggestions for additional protective measures were turned aside.

On July 30, testifying before the Ervin Committee, H. R. Haldeman disclosed that way back in April at the President's request he had listened to two of the tapes the grand jury had now subpoenaed. One of these was the tape of the March 21 "cancer on the Presidency" meeting between Dean and Nixon. Having listened to the tape, Haldeman now contradicted Dean's account on the meeting on a few crucial points.

While the President must have regarded Haldeman's testimony as critical to support him in his dispute with Dean, it certainly did nothing to help him in his dispute with us over the tapes. That the President had directed Haldeman to listen to the two tapes and that Haldeman had now testified about them undercut completely any good-faith claim by Nixon that executive privilege still applied to the two recordings. The purpose of the privilege, it was said, was to protect the "confidentiality" of the President's conversations with aides, in order to insure that free and uninhibited discussion on matters of government policy would not be deterred by fear that such discussions might later become public. But there could be no reason for keeping confidential a tape of a conversation about which *two* witnesses had now testified under oath, and which the President himself had described in public statements. We could now argue that the purpose for which the privilege existed (if it existed at all) had disappeared in the case of this March 21 tape.

On August 22, the tapes subpoena case was argued before Judge Sirica. The basis of the arguments had already been set out in a fifty-page brief filed by Charles Alan Wright, the conservative constitutional lawyer from Texas drafted by the White House, and a sixty-eight-page written argument submitted by Cox. Wright's principal argument was that the President simply was not subject to the ordinary processes of the law. One man, above the law, he was "beyond the process of any court," as Wright put it. In his secondary argument Wright advanced the claim of executive privilege.

Cox cited the grand jury's need for the tapes in order to complete its criminal investigation. The closest he came to an accusation against the President was his remark that there was "strong reason to believe that the integrity of the executive office has been corrupted." Peering at the judge over the half spectacles that customarily perched low down on the bridge of his nose, Cox cited the medieval legal scholar Bracton to support our contention that *no* man, however powerful, is above the law.

Wright, in his oral argument, raised another issue which came straight out of the blue. He claimed that disclosure of some of the subpoenaed tapes might be injurious to the national interest because of sensitive "national-security" information contained in them. Why, Wright said, the President had told him personally that one of these tapes (he didn't say which one) contained a matter so sensitive that the President couldn't even hint to Wright what it was—and Wright (as he proudly told the court) had a top-secret security clearance.

This was an outrageous argument, one that had never been made in any of the legal papers filed by the White House. The proper way to present any "privilege" based on national security is to claim it formally in writing and, if required, submit a description of the matter in secret to a judge for his determination. Besides, a generalized allegation like Wright's simply wouldn't support refusal to turn over an entire tape just because an alleged secret was supposed to have been discussed on a portion of it, much less all the tapes. Wright's allusion appeared to be one more example of the ingrained habit of the Nixon Administration to cry "national security" when investigators got too warm.

When the President was ultimately ordered by the courts to turn over all relevant portions of the tapes, not a single claim of national security was advanced with respect to any of them, proving that either Nixon had misled Wright or Wright was overdramatizing. The only genuine national-security problem that *ever* arose in connection with any Presidential tape recordings occurred much later, in 1974, when the President was forced to turn over additional tapes to the prosecution for the Watergate cover-up trial. One of those tapes did contain a very highly sensitive matter pertaining to national security. Unnoticed, the White House turned it over to us anyway. An FBI clerk assigned to help us transcribe tapes brought the matter to our attention. How could the White House release such a piece of information? She was right. We immediately impounded the tape and copies of all transcripts, notifying the court and the White House. The secret remained intact.

A week after the oral argument Judge Sirica rejected the President's contention that he was not subject to the legal process: "In all candor the court fails to perceive any reason for suspending the power of the courts to get evidence . . . simply because it is the President of the United States who holds the evidence." The judge ordered the President to turn the tapes over to him for his determination of whether or not they were covered by executive privilege. This was a victory for us and, we thought, for the principle of law. However, the judge did not go as far as we had wanted him to. In effect, he had ruled only on the first of two issues in the case, whether the President was subject to the legal process like other citizens, and not on the second issue of whether executive privilege applied. We had sought a definitive ruling that the privilege was inapplicable and that the grand jury should get the tapes forthwith.

The White House response was at first somewhat threatening. The President, his spokesman said, "would not comply." He was considering appeal or "how otherwise to sustain the President's position." The next day the President met with his lawyers, and they appealed to the U.S. Court of Appeals.

We were in a quandary. Procedurally the President could appeal the one issue on which Judge Sirica had ruled all the way to the Supreme Court. If he lost, he could then begin again in the district court, before Judge Sirica, to litigate the effect of executive privilege—and appeal again if he lost on that second issue. Giving Nixon two bites at the apple meant it would be many months before the grand jury would ever see any tapes.

Yet we were reluctant to appeal ourselves and risk what we had already won. Judge Sirica had credibility with both the public and the appeals court; to challenge his decision might be to cast ourselves in the role of victors demanding an extra measure of the spoils. Finally we decided that legal requirements had to take precedence over these considerations. So we too appealed, asking the Court of Appeals to affirm Judge Sirica and in addition to rule in our favor on the issue of executive privilege.

Less than a week later, after another hasty exchange of written legal briefs, the case was argued before the Court of Appeals, in the barn-like ceremonial courtroom of the U.S. Courthouse. The argument lasted a little over three hours. In addition to arguing that the President was above the criminal process, Wright claimed, as set out in his legal briefs, that it was "more important that the privacy of the Presidency be preserved than that every possible bit of evidence that might assist in criminal prosecutions be produced." Pressed in cross-examination by one of the judges, Wright also said, "It is clear beyond peradventure that if the President had engaged in a conspiracy, he would be wholly beyond the jurisdiction of the grand jury or this court. That no President can be indicted before he is impeached is as clear as anything can be."

In the context of the tapes case, Wright's no-indictment argument was a classic non sequitur: whether the President could be indicted had nothing to do with whether he could be subjected to subpoena by the grand jury. The issue Wright addressed, however, was soon to become paramount inside our office.*

Reluctant to tangle with the constitutional question unless it absolutely had to, the Court of Appeals first tried to promote compromise. On September 13, the court made public an interim order suggesting that the parties see if they could work out a settlement. Accordingly, Cox entered into discussions with White House counsel about such a compromise. They were willing to concede nothing that would give us meaningful access to the tapes for use as evidence. A few days later, both sides told the court that compromise was hopeless.

Having allowed only a few days to prepare written and oral arguments, saying that the case must be decided quickly in order to get Supreme Court review, the Court of Appeals now proceeded to devote a full month to deciding the questions presented by the appeal. Frustrated, we waited week after week for a decision.

Meanwhile, a few blocks away at the White House, the President set in motion a plan for listening to each of the subpoenaed tapes, and transcribing them. The events that flowed from this order and the role of the President's secretary Rose Mary Woods and others in handling the tapes would become the subject of hearings in Judge Sirica's courtroom later that autumn, hearings that gave us our first crack at the

* See Chapter 10.

Nixon White House.* The importance of the President's timing has never been appreciated. As early as September, he was obviously anticipating another beating in the courts. He was beginning to think ahead toward the possibility of countering that defeat, not by continuing appeals through the courts but instead by "enforcing" a solution in which his own *edited transcripts* rather than *tapes* would be produced, and the Special Prosecutor would be cut off from further access to any White House material.

Just a few weeks later he began to put that strategy into operation.

* See Chapter 7.

CHAPTER 6 Saturday Night Massacre or Saturday Night Suicide?

ON FRIDAY, OCTOBER 12, over a month after it had heard oral arguments in the tapes case, the U.S. Court of Appeals ruled in an extensive opinion that the President must comply with the grand jury's subpoena. The court meticulously spelled out procedures under which the tapes would be turned over to Judge Sirica and reviewed by him to resolve any further disputes. Watergate-related portions of the taped conversations would then be given to our office for presentation to the grand jury. The Court of Appeals embraced our legal position in almost every respect. This time our victory was total.

The court gave the President until the following Friday, October 19, to decide whether to file legal papers seeking review in the Supreme Court. The President, however, had already made up his mind. Going to the Supreme Court was not in the cards. On Monday, October 15, the curtain would go up on the drama President Nixon intended to play out during that week with Archibald Cox and Attorney General Elliot Richardson. The prologue, however, had begun back in July, long before the Court of Appeals decision.

ON JULY 3, when Elliot Richardson conveyed to Cox the President's protest at reports that we were investigating the financing of San Clemente, Richardson told Cox that Nixon thought it was none of Cox's business how he had financed his San Clemente home. Cox agreed to issue a statement saying we were conducting no investigation. But he objected strongly to Richardson's telling him this was something he *could* not investigate if serious allegations of criminality should arise. The Special Prosecutor's charter, now embodied in fed-

123

eral regulations, forbade the Attorney General to exercise that kind of authority. Cox's rebuff of Richardson left the matter unsettled. But, in retrospect, the first seed had been sown.

On July 12, Cox met with Richardson to go over administrative problems. Some of the things that had come up during the past few weeks, Richardson said, necessitated a "reexamination" of the way in which matters reached the attention of the Special Prosecutor. Factual allegations should be screened by the Justice Department, which would then forward to us only those deemed to be "substantial." Cox immediately objected. Richardson's plan would be at least a technical invasion of our jurisdiction, he pointed out, and perhaps worse. Richardson withdrew the proposal. The matter didn't seem very significant. However, a pattern was already beginning to suggest itself.

July 23 was the day we served White House counsel with the historic grand-jury subpoena for nine Presidential tapes. The same day, Alexander Haig called Richardson to complain: the President wanted a "tight line" drawn on Cox without any "further mistakes." Haig warned that if Cox wouldn't agree to that, they would get rid of Cox.

That afternoon, Cox and two aides met with Richardson at the Justice Department. The Attorney General complained that it was "improper" for our office to want to interview Thomas C. Huston, author of a comprehensive domestic spy plan developed by the White House in 1969 that was supposedly torpedoed by J. Edgar Hoover. The President, Richardson said, was afraid Cox wanted to investigate *all* government intelligence activities (a fear that can be well understood in light of subsequent disclosures about the intelligence community). Cox said we had no such intention. But Huston would have to be interviewed pursuant to our investigations of the Plumbers unit and the Ellsberg psychiatrist break-in. Cox reminded the Attorney General that these matters unquestionably fell within our jurisdiction.

After the full meeting broke up, Cox and Richardson met alone. Richardson wanted to take up the question of the so-called "national-security wiretaps." These were a series of wiretaps ordered by the President to be placed on certain of his own staff—primarily aides of Henry A. Kissinger—and on newsmen in 1969 and 1970. The program had proceeded with the utmost secrecy. In some cases the taps had continued long after it was clear that no national-security information would be obtained—if indeed that had been the original intent. The taps were of questionable legality in any event. Richardson told Cox he believed that the taps were perfectly legal and was inclined, in effect, to "rule" that way, thus foreclosing any investigation by Cox. Cox responded sharply to Richardson's suggestion, lecturing his former pupil in professorial but firm tones. Not only did Cox rebut Richardson's legal arguments, he also warned the Attorney General that he had better reread his own congressional testimony about the Special Prosecutor's authority before he started telling Cox what was and what was not within Cox's jurisdiction.

Rebuffed, the White House apparently decided that the best way to deal with the wiretap problem was to take the matter away from Cox altogether. On August 15, Richardson proposed that the Special Prosecutor's mandate be "redefined"—in other words, narrowed. Specifically, this narrowing would serve to exclude any investigation by Cox of the national-security wiretaps.

On August 24, Richardson presented Cox a draft of "guidelines" that would accomplish this feat. Nothing was said in this document about Cox's authority to look into offenses by "Presidential appointees" or "allegations against the President." This part of his jurisdiction, evidently, was just going to be written off. But the kicker was left till last: the new guidelines, said Richardson, would not have to be made public! In other words, the scope of the Special Prosecutor's authority would be narrowed secretly, without anyone knowing about it.

This was too much. Cox told Richardson that not only did he find the changes objectionable, but any proposed revision of his authority would have to be made known to the public. Richardson then unveiled another proposal. He suggested that Cox accept a "special consultant" on national-security matters who could serve as an "intermediary" between the Special Prosecutor and the Administration. For this job Richardson proposed a longtime, high-ranking CIA official who was about to retire from The Company.

Cox strongly resisted any narrowing of his jurisdiction. This would be a violation of the commitments he (and Richardson) had made to the Senate when first appointed. His resistance eventually forced Richardson to stop pressing his proposals. Had the President's concern been genuine, he could of course have had Richardson take the matter to the Senate, openly. Obviously the President was not willing to take the heat that a congressional fight over Cox's mandate would have entailed. Besides, he had quicker and neater solutions in mind. Throughout September Nixon was occupied with the criminal problems of his Vice President, Spiro T. Agnew. But in early October, well before the Court of Appeals had ruled on our tapes subpoena, the President told Richardson that now that the Agnew matter had been resolved "we can go ahead and fire Cox."

In retrospect, the then secret Cox-Richardson conversations reveal an unmistakable course of intention on the part of President Nixon to contain the criminal investigation into the White House. As the summer of 1973 wore on, the President more clearly perceived the genuine threat that the Special Prosecutor's investigation posed to him personally. The existence of our office alone did not in itself inevitably present him a problem; the office was nothing without a leader who possessed the temperament to take the investigation wherever it might lead. Rather early the President must have realized that Archibald Cox was such a man, that Cox would not be Elliot Richardson's factotum. When he learned that Cox could not be controlled there was only one solution: Cox had to go. What was lacking prior to the Court of Appeals decision on October 12 was not the will but an acceptable scenario for carrying it out. The court decision presented the opportunity for mounting such a putsch. That the President might engineer a successful plan to avoid disclosing his tapes must have seemed to him an equally attractive benefit of this opportunity; he could eliminate two of the chief threats to his continuation in office —the militant Special Prosecutor and possible public exposure of his own tapes—with a single stroke.

ON MONDAY, OCTOBER 15, three days after the Court of Appeals decision, Cox was urgently summoned to the Justice Department by Attorney General Richardson. Richardson warned that "serious consequences" might ensue if Cox did not agree to a compromise proposal on the tapes that was going to be made to him. And his agreement had to come before Friday of that week, October 19, the date by which the President had to either seek Supreme Court review or agree to turn over the tapes to the grand jury under the Court of Appeals order. Richardson's proposal involved the use of Senator John C. Stennis of Mississippi, a devoutly conservative, pro-Nixon Democrat who had recently advised Mr. Nixon publicly to "tough it out" in his Watergate fight. Stennis would receive from the White House transcripts, prepared by the President's legal staff, of portions of the subpoenaed tapes related to Watergate. These transcripts would not be verbatim transcripts; they would omit or characterize certain portions of the tapes. The decision as to what was "related to Watergate" was in the hands of the White House alone. Stennis would then listen to the portions of tapes from which the transcripts had been made and "verify" that the transcripts were substantially accurate. We would then receive Stennis-verified transcripts in place of the tapes.

The Stennis proposal originated earlier that day in discussions among Richardson, Alexander Haig and Fred Buzhardt. The President's advisers told Richardson that the President had decided to impose on Cox a final solution to the tapes problem. Nixon would prepare a summary of the tapes. He would then instruct Cox to accept this summary in lieu of the tapes themselves, and to withdraw the grand jury's subpoena. If Cox refused, the President would get rid of him. Maybe he would get rid of him in any event. When Richardson objected to this plan Haig consulted with the President and proposed a new idea to Richardson: the use of Senator Stennis as a verifier of the summaries was injected into the plan. It was a clever addition. If Cox objected to the President's ultimatum he would appear to be questioning Stennis' integrity and would risk alienating a powerful bloc of senators.

From the beginning the President was intent not only on denying Cox the tapes already subpoenaed by the grand jury but also on compelling him to agree not to seek any additional White House tapes or documents. Cox would get a few transcripts this one time, but no more. In the future, Cox would be prohibited from seeking the help of the judiciary in our quest for evidence from the White House. What has never been adequately explained is why Elliot Richardson did not spell out this White House understanding to Cox in their first meeting on Monday, October 15, or in any of their subsequent meetings.

In their first meeting on Monday, Cox pointed out to Richardson that there was no need for any rush in considering the proposed accommodation. The President could go ahead and seek Supreme Court review while talks progressed. Reasonable men didn't negotiate under a deadline when they didn't have to. But Richardson was adamant. The deal must be cut by Friday. Richardson's anxiety and haste tipped his hand. The President did not have genuine negotiations in mind. In the guise of a compromise Cox was being presented an ultimatum.

On late Wednesday afternoon Cox received Richardson's written formulation of the President's plan. It said nothing at all about Archie agreeing not to subpoena any *further* tapes. There was a reason for the omission. In drafting the plan Richardson had wanted to stipulate that the "Stennis Compromise" would apply only to the tapes Nixon had already been ordered to give the grand jury. Cox's future access to White House evidence could be settled later. But Haig and Buzhardt said no: Richardson couldn't include that kind of limitation. So the written plan given to Cox was silent on the question of his future authority. There was no doubt at the White House that Cox would have to pledge not to subpoena more tapes, but the written proposal, by its silence, cleverly kept Cox in doubt. As for Richardson, he either misunderstood what was going on or, understanding it perfectly, helped perpetuate confusion between Cox and the White House in hopes that other elements of a bargain could be struck first and the confusion cleared up afterward.

Richardson's proposal was unacceptable to Cox for at least two reasons. First, the tapes would be important evidence at the trials of major potential defendants: Haldeman, Ehrlichman, Mitchell. The transcripts might be sufficient for the grand jury, where few limitations exist on what kind of evidence can be considered. But at trial the prosecution would be obliged to produce the genuine article, the original tape recording itself. Summaries or transcripts purporting to say what was on the tapes according to the President or a third party would not be admissible evidence at trial. Thus our objection to getting transcripts was fundamental, unless the President could guarantee that the tapes themselves would be produced for trial if needed.

Second, there were substantial difficulties with the use of Senator Stennis as a "verifier," indeed with having the job done by any single person. The seventy-two-year-old Stennis was still physically ailing from near-critical gunshot injuries to his head suffered as a victim of a recent robbery attempt. His hearing, in any event, was none too good. Scrupulous review of the tapes would require excellent hearing as well as physical stamina. Making accurate transcripts even from the best of recordings is an arduous and sophisticated task: Stennis had never tried it to our knowledge. Ordinarily, the job is best performed by someone who has intimate knowledge of the case, since nuances in transcription can have an enormous impact. Above all, Stennis was already committed to President Nixon's innocence in the whole Watergate matter. He would have no incentive that we could perceive to push his physical capabilities to the limit in order to catch the President in discrepancies. Naturally, Cox could not articulate *that* objection in answering the President's proposal, lest he fall into the trap set for him. Thus only objections that did not go to Stennis personally were incorporated in Cox's responses.

Cox drafted a reply to Richardson's written proposal and had it delivered to Richardson on Thursday afternoon. He counterproposed that a panel of "special masters" answerable to Judge Sirica be appointed by the judge to do the verifying of transcripts. Cox also wrote that while transcripts might be sufficient for the grand jury, the President would have to produce actual tapes in the event of a trial. In addition Cox noted that the proposal did not deal with the problems of access to additional tapes and documents, including papers we had requested from the White House long ago but never received. But he left the door open to further discussions, saying, "I am glad to sit down with anyone in order to work out a solution if we can."

The detached, analytic tone of the Special Prosecutor's reply to Richardson contrasted sharply with the pace of onrushing events. Cox was attempting to proceed in a rational way, assuming to the bitter end the possibility of good faith on the other side. The White House was interested only in whether Cox would capitulate; probably the President hoped that he would not, since the alternative of sacking him was what the President had been building himself up to all these months. Cox's negative reply meant to the White House that Cox would not agree to lie down and play dead. Thus the need for further pretense was at an end.

That same Thursday evening the President's lawyer Charles Wright called Cox at Cox's brother's home, where he was about to have dinner. Cox, sitting on the floor and surrounded by nieces and nephews, listened to Wright deliver in arch tones what was unquestionably an ultimatum. There was no attempt now to hide the President's demand that Cox give up hope of getting additional White House evidence. Wright told Cox he must not only agree to accept the transcripts as verified by Stennis but also agree not to seek additional tapes and documents in the courts. If Cox was not willing to accede, there was nothing more to be said. Cox was stunned. Wright's second demand added a new and totally unacceptable dimension. To acquiesce in giving up the right to seek evidence would be to negate an essential part of his charter authority—and kill the hope of seeing the Watergate investigation through to an honorable conclusion. Wearily, Cox asked Wright to put the terms of the ultimatum in writing and send it to the office as early as possible the following morning (Friday).

IN THE MEANTIME a second and separate drama was being played out that week that would also have a crucial impact on the future of our investigation. After the Watergate Task Force warned Charlie Shaffer that we were prepared to prosecute John Dean on the narrow grounds of Dean's offer of clemency to McCord if he did not plead guilty, Shaffer had consulted with his client. Dean told Shaffer that he had already decided to plead. At the end of the previous week, Shaffer had communicated this decision to the task force.

This marked the successful culmination of a decisive and honorable strategy by Cox. The signals from the White House earlier that summer that dire consequences would follow if the Special Prosecutor "fished" in waters relating to the President might have led another man to make an early deal with Dean in order to get Dean's evidence. As a potential government witness, Dean would have been a significant piece of ammunition in Cox's arsenal for any confrontation with the President. But Cox had remained firm: there would be no free ride for Dean regardless of what could be gained by the prosecutors vis-à-vis the White House. Cox's persistence had paid off.

Jim Neal responded with a strong and somewhat peculiar request to Shaffer: he now wanted to conclude the plea bargain and seal it by having Dean enter his plea in open court as soon as possible—no later than Friday, October 19, and earlier that week if possible. Shaffer and Dean agreed.

On Wednesday, October 17, Dean and Shaffer had slipped up surreptitiously to the ninth floor of 1425 K Street by a back entrance, after most of the other employees had left the building for the day. Late into the night and early morning hours, around a large conference table, negotiations continued between the task force and Dean over the precise language of the conspiracy charge to which Dean would plead guilty and the terms of the letter of agreement sealing the arrangement. Not until 1 A.M. did we reach agreement on the "information"—the prosecutor's formal accusation—to which Dean would enter his plea. Then we turned our attention to drafting a letter from Cox to Shaffer setting forth the scope of the bargain.

White House charges that Dean had lied when he implicated the

President before the Ervin Committee now presented us a significant problem. We did not believe those charges. In fact, our willingness to accept a plea from Dean was tacitly based on his counsel's assurances that Dean had been candid in his congressional testimony. But what if the Nixon tapes proved us—and Dean—wrong? Then we wanted to preserve our prosecutive options. From our point of view, we believed that Dean's one-count plea should relieve him of potential criminal liability for all past Watergate misdeeds *except* perjury, should we find evidence upon which to charge him of that crime.

Fortunately, Dean and Shaffer readily agreed that this exception should be made explicit in the letter setting forth the plea bargain. They realized that without it Dean's motive in pleading guilty might be misunderstood as an attempt to insulate himself from a perjury charge just before the prosecutors got the tapes that would resolve the credibility battle between him and President Nixon. The perjury exception would signal to the world that Dean was standing firm by his account of the cover-up, at the peril of criminal sanctions.

At about 3 A.M. Thursday, after every paragraph of the letter had been revised and re-revised, a consensus was finally reached and the deal was concluded. Dean would enter his plea Friday morning, pursuant to Neal's request for a quick consummation of the bargain. Only then, moments before he stood up in court, would Dean discover the reason for Neal's urgency.

On Friday morning at 10 A.M. Cox accompanied the Watergate Task Force to Judge Sirica's courtroom. The press had been alerted that there would be some kind of "court proceeding" that morning, but there had been no notice that we had finally succeeded in winning a guilty plea from John Dean, thus clearing the way toward making him a government witness. When Archie Cox turned up in the courtroom with our whole task force, there was a murmur of surprise. Then Dean and his lawyer Charles Shaffer entered, and the reporters guessed what was up, rushing for the hall telephones even before the judge entered the courtroom.

A few minutes before Dean was scheduled to enter his plea of guilty, Jim Neal took Charlie Shaffer aside and told him the reason for Neal's mysterious haste in consummating the deal. Neal said he didn't think Archie was going to be around after the weekend. Shaffer hurriedly consulted Dean, who decided to go through with the plea anyway.

The formal acceptance of Dean's guilty plea before Judge Sirica that morning was Jim Neal's last act as chief of the Watergate Task Force. Neal had perceived from the outset that concluding a plea arrangement with John Dean was far and away the most important step in the entire investigation and a prerequisite to building strong cases against its major targets: Haldeman, Ehrlichman and Mitchell. He had given this task his highest priority. When the agreement was reached the previous Wednesday night for Dean's plea, Neal announced to the task force that he would resign on the day the plea was entered. He could no longer neglect his two-man trial-law practice in Nashville and was therefore forced to end his association with the force.

We were sorry to see Jim leave, especially on the eve of this showdown with the White House, but there was hope that he might later return for the major Watergate cover-up trial. When he departed Ben-Veniste became the chief of the task force. With Neal's departure, the average age of the seven attorneys now working actively on the Watergate investigation had dropped to twenty-nine and a half.

When we returned from the courthouse to our offices, flushed with accomplishment, Wright's letter was waiting. For the first time, the entire Watergate Task Force learned what Cox had suspected as early as Monday and known for sure the previous evening—that the ongoing "negotiations," the polite point-counterpoint, had never been designed to achieve any compromise. They had been intended to maneuver Cox into a position where he would either have to surrender or be shot. There was no mistaking the tone of Wright's letter or the threat contained in it. The President's proposal, Wright stated, was reasonable, was in the national interest, was designed to "put to rest any possible thought that the President might himself have been involved in the Watergate break-in or cover-up." (Had the President's ultimatum been rammed through, it probably *would* have put the issue of his involvement "to rest" by burying it too deeply for disinterment.) Cox's objections to the proposal were "unacceptable." If Cox would not reconsider, "we shall have to follow the course of action that we think in the best interest of the country." What this last phrase portended was unclear. The language was characteristic of autocracy, not democracy. One thing seemed perfectly clear: none of us was likely to have a job come Monday. Beyond that, we could hardly imagine what the President might do: Declare the investigation at an end? Supplant the judicial process? Go after us personally?

Cox immediately responded by messenger that what was proposed now was totally at odds with the independence accorded Cox in his appointment.

Wright fired back a written reply of his own: "[F]urther discussions between us . . . would be futile." This time, Wright noted that the President's lawyers would "be forced to take the actions that the President deems appropriate in the circumstances." Whether these actions would be consistent with the law Wright did not say.

As Friday wore on a heavy pall hung over the office. Cox waited in his office. Rumors came and went: the President would have a press conference at 3 P.M., then at 4 P.M. When four o'clock passed we reckoned that the deadline for the President to file for review by the Supreme Court had passed; then it turned out the rule permitted filing at any time up until midnight, and on this Friday a Court employee would stay late at the Supreme Court clerk's office to receive any papers from the White House. Television crews were staked out at the Court. The public knew nothing of what had been going on that week behind the scenes. There was no public expectation that the President would do anything but take his appeal. As the hours crept by, though, it became more and more apparent to us that the President was not going to file.

The young lawyers sharing Cox's ordeal felt the helplessness of being swept along with him toward a tragic climax. The President had used every legal weapon to contain our investigation and had failed. His imminent decision to abandon the resort to lawful process and turn to the vast arsenal of lawless executive power left us completely vulnerable. Against the might of the President's mailed fist, the strong bonds of trust and respect formed among the prosecutors these past months—and the solid progress we had made—seemed insignificant. All of a sudden our work seemed little more than an intellectual exercise.

As strong as our own fears were, the young prosecutors' emotions were subordinate to what Cox himself was going through. The last two days had shattered him. The string had run out—there seemed nowhere to turn. In fact, Cox had telephoned a friend to supply the names of some "elder statesmen" whose advice Cox could seek about his predicament. "Gee, Archie," his friend told him, "*you're* one of the elder statesmen." At this point, Cox told us, he realized how alone he really was and how difficult were the choices he was going to have to make.

What was happening was against the grain of everything Cox was prepared to believe about the President and his staff, for he had willed himself to the conclusion that they would act honorably and obey the law. All the premises on which he had based his conduct toward the White House had been cut from underneath him. And he could no longer transmit his faith that the law would command the allegiance of every man, no matter how powerful, to younger and more cynical staff members who hadn't been so sure how Richard Nixon and his henchmen would react if cornered. None of the cynics said, "I told you so." The depth of our affection and respect for Cox was too great.

About 6 P.M., as the news came and went, Cox announced he was leaving for the day—he wasn't going to sit around waiting to be psyched out by the President. Earlier that afternoon the President had addressed a letter to Elliot Richardson instructing him to tell Cox to "make no further attempts by judicial process to obtain tapes, notes, or memoranda of Presidential conversations." Around 6:30 P.M. Richardson telephoned Cox and read him the President's letter "for your information." Richardson's phrasing was significant: he was not conveying the President's order to Cox, as the President had asked him to do; he was just letting Cox know where everyone stood.

Shortly before 9 P.M., the White House released a statement announcing that the President would not appeal the Court of Appeals decision. The language of that release provided a fascinating psychological portrait of Richard Nixon. Citing the "strain" imposed on the "American people" by Watergate and "apprehension" over a possible "constitutional confrontation," the President concluded that "our government, like our Nation, must remain strong and effective. What matters most, in this critical hour, is our ability to act—and to act in a way that enables us to control events, not to be paralyzed and overwhelmed by them." What leaped out from the statement was not just the absence of any reference to the rule of law but also the ambiguity of the first-person plural ("*our* ability to act," *we* must not "be paralyzed"). Was Nixon referring to his country, to his government, to his tiny coterie of advisers, or subconsciously to himself?

The White House statement revealed that the President had proposed to Cox that in lieu of the subpoenaed tapes we accept a "summary" of them verified by "a very distinguished man, highly respected by all elements in American life for his integrity, his fairness, and his patriotism." In return, Cox would subpoena no more tapes or Presidential documents. Then, in a major surprise, the statement went on to say not only that Senator Stennis had agreed to fill the role of verifier but that Senators Ervin and Baker had accepted the proposal, too, as a satisfactory resolution of the Ervin Committee's demand for tapes. Cox, the President continued, had rejected it. Nonetheless, in the name of "overriding national interest" Nixon had decided not to seek Supreme Court review and not to comply with the Court of Appeals order—instead, Cox could take the Stennis Compromise or nothing.

The concurrence of Ervin and Baker was an unexpected and nasty surprise. Nixon's use of Stennis already made rational objection to his plan on its merits risky lest it be twisted into personal criticism of Stennis. The added endorsement of Ervin and Baker could make it impossible to impress on the public the complete illegitimacy of Nixon's position. Cox had been stabbed in the back by the leaders of the Senate Watergate probe at the same time he had been stabbed in the chest by the President.

Our anger was fueled by the fact that Judge Sirica had just two days previously, on Wednesday, October 17, rejected the Ervin Committee's civil lawsuit to get the Nixon tapes it had subpoenaed back in July. We had won our tapes case in the trial court and the Court of Appeals. The Ervin Committee's suit appeared to be dead, for the basis of Judge Sirica's ruling made a successful appeal highly unlikely. Whatever crumbs of evidence the committee could scrounge off the President's table were more than it was going to get through the courts. With the Senate's Watergate investigation trailing off, we felt that Ervin and Baker had decided to squeeze a little more life out of their own probe, no matter what the effect would be on the Special Prosecutor's office. Within a day or two both of them, realizing they had been used, jumped off the Stennis Compromise bandwagon. They had not been told by the President, they said, that the plan would be used to foreclose *Cox* from getting the evidence *he* needed through use of the courts. Much later, Stennis himself claimed that he too had been misled by the White House regarding the role he was to play.

Saturday morning, October 20, most of the staff were on hand at the National Press Club on Fourteenth Street, where a large banquet room had been made available for a press conference to be held by Cox. As soon as it was announced, the major television networks decided to cover it live. Just before the press conference began, we knew, Cox had taken a telephone call from Richardson. What we did not know was that Richardson had read to Cox a copy of a letter to Nixon refusing to pass along the President's orders to the Special Prosecutor. Cox entered to the sound of sustained applause. He had forsaken his customary and symbolic bow tie; it just wasn't formal enough for the occasion.

In the understated, slightly professorial manner so familiar to us, Archie began by virtually apologizing for the crisis that the President's ultimatum—and Archie's response—had thrust upon the country. Sometimes he feared that he was "getting too big for his britches." He had not sought this confrontation. "I'm certainly not out to get the President," he declared in a tone that conveyed genuine disbelief that anyone could think the contrary for a moment. But summaries of the type the President proposed to substitute for tapes just wouldn't suffice for the prosecution. Summaries would not be accepted as evidence in court. Besides, the President's order effected a "basic change in the institutional arrangement." If Cox abided by it, the Special Prosecution Force simply would not be able to conduct its investigations thoroughly. Thus capitulation would be inconsistent with the pledge of independence made at the time of his appointment "through the Senate to the American people."

No one was more astonished than we at Archie's superb ability to communicate in down-to-earth terms the gravity of the situation, the enormity of what was at stake not just for the investigations but for the whole country. His low-key, down-Maine demeanor was consummate television—not the television of the professional actor but that of the man who had argued many complex cases before another difficult tribunal, the Supreme Court. Archie made it so simple. Of course he could not surrender to the President's will, for the only *responsible* course was to go on, and he was a responsible man. It was a matter of principle. The main issue as he saw it was "what seems to me to be noncompliance with the court's order." So, he said, he would go to court and bring that to the court's attention. What the President did was up to the President.

As the press conference continued, there emerged a vivid picture of Cox's own personality: his integrity, his passion for fairness and for the rule of law, and a warmth and sense of humor too. Why did he get into this in the first place? he was asked. Well, he thought it was important. If he could complete the job, it would be a service to the country; if not, "What the hell? It was worth a try."

Would he resign? He would not. (He had told a UPI reporter who asked him the same question the night before, "Resign? No—hell, no.") Moreover, he put it squarely on Elliot Richardson. His "respect and affection" for Richardson were undiminished. Cox emphasized that some elementary legal research showed that only the Attorney General—who had hired him—could now fire him. Cox reminded the press of another President, Andrew Jackson, who had trouble with his Secretary of the Treasury and had to appoint several men to the post before getting one who would carry out his will.

By roping Richardson into this standoff, Cox had raised the price to the President of firing him. Cox knew that his defiance had probably cost him his job; but if the President realized that Cox would take Richardson down with him, Nixon might have second thoughts. Watching from the side of the press club banquet room we felt a good deal of anxiety about Archie's approach. After all, what if Richardson didn't stand by him?

Earlier that week, Cox had had some of the same doubts himself. Commiserating with Neal about the awful dynamic the White House had set in motion and the impossibility of an executive officer truly investigating the President himself, Cox had confided that his greatest fear was that when push came to shove Richardson would not back him up. To suggestions that Richardson was a political animal, that he would make whatever compromises he had to make, Cox had maintained a brave front. "I know Elliot," he said. "He'll do what he says. He'll abide by his pledge to me." But Cox acknowledged that if Richardson failed him, it would be one of the most devastating things that had ever happened to him personally.

Now, from the telephone conversation that preceded his press conference, Cox knew that he had Richardson's moral proxy in his pocket.

When the press conference broke up, the task force repaired to a local restaurant for hamburgers and beer. After a glum hour spent keeping an eye on a large color television set for the anticipated news bulletin announcing that Cox had been dumped, we trudged back to our offices, and to an afternoon of restless waiting. There was nothing to do; nothing happened. Archie left in midafternoon, but the rest of us waited. The President, we reasoned, couldn't delay too long if he was going to fire Cox. Archie's stubborn resistance had been so forthright. By nightfall there seemed to be nothing to do but leave. It didn't appear likely that after waiting all day the President would throw his thunderbolt on a Saturday night.

Unknown to us, the President had been trying to unsheath that thunderbolt all afternoon without notable success. Within the hour of Archie's press conference Alexander Haig, on behalf of Nixon, phoned Elliot Richardson and instructed him to fire Cox. Richardson already had his letter of resignation in hand. Well, he told Haig, he couldn't do that, so he better come to the White House and tender his resignation. When the Attorney General arrived at the White House the gatemen to the Oval Office, Haig and Buzhardt, once again hammered him with the crisis of the war in the Middle East, just as they had all week. Richardson's defection could have international implications, they exclaimed. Couldn't he at least fire Cox and *then* resign? No. Richardson had a short audience with the President and returned to the Justice Department Building to clean out his office.

As Richardson arrived at his office to chat with aides and with his deputy (now acting Attorney General) William Ruckelshaus, Haig phoned again, this time for Ruckelshaus. Now he wanted Ruckelshaus to do the deed. Ruckelshaus demurred. Haig almost audibly pulled himself to attention on the other end of the line: "Your Commander in Chief has given you an order. You have no alternative." Yes he did, Ruckelshaus replied. He could resign. And he did. (The President announced that Ruckelshaus was "fired" before Ruckelshaus had a chance to submit his formal letter of resignation; seconds-in-command do not get Oval Office audiences to announce their defiance of the President.)

That left Robert Bork, the conservative former Yale Law School professor and Nixon-appointed Solicitor General. Some hurried research had disclosed that he was the third in line at Justice, and thus had become acting Attorney General. Now Haig phoned the Justice Department a third time, for Bork. Bork agreed to fire Cox. (As Ruckelshaus had told Haig, "Bork's your man.") Within a short time, by now well into the evening, Bork sent a short note notifying Cox of his ouster to Archie's home by Justice Department chauffeur. At 8:25 P.M., a tight-lipped Ron Ziegler entered the White House press room to read a statement: Cox had been fired, he announced, Richardson and Ruckelshaus removed, and the Special Prosecutor's office "abolished." At 9:05 P.M., FBI agents acting on orders from Haig marched into 1425 K Street and seized control of our offices.

Some of the staff had already arrived when the agents burst in. Others heard the news on the radio or from friends and rushed to the office in shock and confusion shortly thereafter. Behind "Checkpoint Charlie," prosecutors and other staff members were welcomed by Hank Ruth's bitter comment, "Welcome to Moscow."

Our office library, on the tenth floor, was not within the "security perimeter" and was unoccupied by the FBI. Shortly after Frampton and Ben-Veniste arrived, Ruth (now acting Special Prosecutor) went up there—as much to escape the visual shock of what was happening downstairs as for any other reason. Newsmen who had been crowding around the door to the office followed him. At an impromptu press conference, Ruth tried to choke back tears of frustration as he read a short written statement: "I must say I suppose that human emotions take over because one thinks in a democracy this would not happen."

The small library soon became a staging area for the curious and outraged "outsiders" who rushed to 1425 K Street on the heels of the first news bulletin. Consumer advocate Ralph Nader materialized before the TV cameras in the library to denounce Nixon's action. An investigator from journalist Jack Anderson's office foraged about the library shelves, seeking cannon fodder for Anderson's column, and came up with a checkout list for lawbooks which showed that Cox had personally done his legal homework.

We were not the only ones whose roles had suddenly been turned topsy-turvy. Some of the FBI agents summoned by Haig's order and propelled to 1425 K Street for the occupation had been working with us on the cover-up investigation. In fact, a few had been with the case since June 1972. They shared our attitudes about Watergate. Like us, they had a professional commitment to a thorough investigation. They had an emotional stake in it, too, for the FBI itself had been obstructed by the White House during the original Watergate investigation. Suddenly the agents were told by the same White House they had been investigating that we were no longer their co-workers but should be regarded as their adversaries. From whom were they supposed to protect the fruits of our joint investigation? Some of the agents were trying to look calm and authoritative, but it wasn't fooling anybody. They were obviously upset, and more than one seemed a little frightened.

When the agents arrived they had usurped the control of the FPS officers who had jurisdiction over all the office security arrangements. During the many late evenings and weekends the task force had spent working on the investigation we had been befriended by the FPS officers, a hand-picked crew operating under the security chief of the Justice Department, Win Joy (a man who took his job so seriously that he once staged a personal raid on the office to test his own security precautions, leaving little red cards on our desks to be found the next morning). To break up the mutual long hours we often chatted with them or inquired about what they were reading. A few studying criminology and related subjects used the late nights to catch up on course assignments. On Sundays we would share a football game on TV. We especially admired their gourmet "camp cooking," which became more and more sophisticated though carried out on little more than a couple of hot plates. They never failed to offer to share it with us.

The personal relationships and the FPS officers' intimate knowledge of how hard we were working and how much we cared about what we were doing contributed to the sense of loyalty they had naturally developed toward the office. And, of course, since they were responsible for the physical integrity of the premises, their sense of territoriality about the place was at least as strong as ours. So it was no surprise when some of the heavily armed FPS personnel confided in us that when the band of G-men from the FBI showed up to take over the office there were some mighty tense moments. By the time most of the staff arrived, the FPS, which was also under the authority of the Attorney General (if anybody could figure out who that was at the moment), had uneasily ceded their control to the agents. They continued to man the entrance to the office, however, and some of them were looking at us as if to say, "Just say the word and we'll throw these bums out of here." That most of the FPS crew were black and the FBI agents all were white didn't contribute anything to the lessening of tensions.

Behind the "checkpoint" there was utter confusion. Despite the "seizure" it appeared that the office was not about to just disappear. The agents were there, they told us, not to keep us from getting in but to prevent us from taking anything out. In other words, they were there to protect the files from their creators. It was pure Alice in Wonderland. The person with the greatest motive for doing away with the files was the man in whose name the agents had been ordered to seize them.

Actually, copies of all potentially explosive documents had *already* been removed for safekeeping several days before. On the previous Thursday evening, members of the Watergate Task Force had made copies of key prosecution summaries and memoranda and spirited them away. Though we had not been kept fully informed about every step in Cox's "negotiations" with Richardson we had had a strong enough sense of impending danger to act. The bulk of useful files went to a locked cabinet in the musty basement of Frampton's grandmother in Arlington, Virginia (unbeknownst to her). Others went to back closets. On Friday, Cox himself had gathered up status memoranda and a few other important documents from each task force for storage in two safe-deposit boxes near the office.

Alexander Haig later tried to justify his order to seize our offices by claiming he had received reports in the wake of Archie's press conference that afternoon that "members of the staff were leaving rapidly with huge bundles under their arms." This was a demonstrably bogus explanation, for by that time there was nothing important that had not been already spirited away. Besides, Haig's claim didn't explain the FBI seizures of the offices of Richardson and Ruckelshaus. (In the following weeks we continued to be uncertain about the ultimate outcome of the Massacre. Reluctant to bring all the files back to the office, where they might again be seized, we sometimes had to share copies of these key materials at the office while additional copies remained stashed away outside.)

Phil Lacovara had talked to Acting Attorney General Bork on the telephone. Bork told Ruth and Lacovara that as far as he could figure out we had not been fired and that our investigations now were under the jurisdiction of the Justice Department; Bork said he would place Criminal Division chief Henry Petersen in charge. In a series of meetings in Ruth's office, accompanied by a great deal of milling about, Ruth told us about his phone conversations. The "office" might have been abolished, but we remained Justice Department attorneys attached to the investigation, Ruth said. Or at least we might as well act that way until the situation was clarified.

Jill Volner had left Washington early that evening for the wedding of a close friend in New York, hoping that nothing would occur overnight. Frampton called her hotel from the Special Prosecutor's office to reassure her that the office apparently still existed. When she arrived in the hotel lobby at about 2 A.M. a uniformed desk clerk came rushing across the lobby, calling, "Mrs. Volner, Mrs. Volner, you have messages." Volner was perplexed, since the hotel staff had no reason to know who she was. The message from Frampton, slightly garbled, read: "FBI has seized your office; everything OK."

In fact, there continued to be confusion for days about our precise status. It remains unclear whether Nixon's failure to fire us all and issue a formal regulation abolishing the entire office was intentional, or whether it was an oversight or just a muffed job. There have been reports that the President really thought he was getting rid of everybody, or that he imagined that by chopping off the head the body would die. Reports have surfaced that he instructed Bork to fire Ruth, Lacovara and Ben-Veniste as well as Cox but that Bork refused on the ground that that would be an outright obstruction of justice, an attempt to emasculate the entire investigation. Bork has said it didn't come to that, but has admitted that Alexander Haig regaled him with the alleged "bias" of the Cox staff.

The President's failure once again to do his dirty work artfully would come back to haunt him. It was the same pattern we had seen over and over again in the White House containment of Watergate— equal measures of corrupt intent on the one hand and incompetence on the other.

The reaction in the nation which began to erupt within minutes of the first news broadcasts was as astonishing to us as it must have been to the beleaguered White House. Thousands and thousands of unsolicited telegrams and telephone calls began to pour into Washington —to the White House, to our office, anyplace people could think of to direct them. Many had seen Carl Stern of NBC and Nelson Benton of CBS first reporting the news of the Massacre as they stood breathless and shaken on the White House lawn. Both networks prepared for ninety-minute specials later in the evening. Reporters and network cameramen rushed to the Ruckelshaus and Richardson residences, badgering them for some statement or explanation. Democratic senators immediately issued vehement and outraged counterattacks, calling the President's action "reckless" and saying that it "smacked of dictatorship." Republican senators, including Senator Edward W. Brooke of Massachusetts, mentioned impeachment for the first time. (Vice President Gerald R. Ford said that "the President had no choice" but to fire Cox.)

From his home Cox issued a simple one-sentence moral call to arms: "Whether ours shall continue to be a government of laws and not of men is now for Congress and ultimately for the American people."

The network specials galvanized millions of Americans. Perhaps it was the replays of Archie's press conference juxtaposed against the film of FBI agents waving network cameramen away from the door of our offices. Or perhaps the air of crisis. Every Washington newsroom was in an uproar. It was as though war had broken out on Seventeenth Street.

The President was made to bear witness to the nation's immediate outrage and alarm. Thousands of demonstrators appeared out of nowhere to besiege the White House gates. Dozens of them sported picket signs urging passing motorists to join them: "Honk if you think Nixon should be impeached." During the live TV coverage the raucous sound of honking could be heard in the background late into the night. It continued for days, reportedly interrupting the President's sleep.

Two of the picketers that first night were neighbors of Jim Doyle, our press officer. Soon after they had taken up their positions a Metropolitan Police cruiser drove by and its two occupants gave them the once-over. A few minutes later the cruiser came slowly around the block again and the officers looked them over a second time. Jim's neighbors began to be uneasy. When the cruiser pulled slowly abreast of them for a third time they thought something dire was about to happen. The cops slowed almost to a halt; they were eyeball to eyeball. Then the cruiser honked twice, and drove off.

What was Nixon thinking? What aberration prompted this monumental miscalculation, as Carl Stern put it that night, "to jump out of the frying pan and into the fire"? The elder statesman of the White House PR team, Richard Moore (a man who had had some prickly entanglement of his own in the Watergate cover-up), told one newsman triumphantly that this was Richard Nixon's greatest coup—an apt phrase. The President, he said, had finally taken bold action to put the nation back on course. This was a classic Nixon approach. The confusion between national and individual persons. And the deep-seated inability to see his problems in anything but public-relations terms. The White House evidently perceived the problem to be too much public exposure to Watergate. If the public didn't hear anything more about it, then the problem would be solved!

Another White House aide told a reporter that Cox was "uncontrollable." That was true, but it was not the heart of the problem. It was the criminal-justice process (as John Dean had once warned the President) that was uncontrollable, once set in motion. It was this the President failed to perceive.

Sunday there was hardly anyone at 1425 K Street. Most of the Watergate Task Force, together with some of the other younger prosecutors, gathered at a palatial Georgetown town house where Chuck Breyer, a member of the Plumbers Task Force, was house-sitting. We wanted to know what was happening and to stick together, but we also wanted to stay away from the office and even from our own homes—just in case someone came looking for us. Slumped in lawn chairs, drinking beer or wine, we made periodic telephone calls to see how our absent brothers were doing. Our mood was bizarre, a combination of bitterness, nostalgia, desultory plotting and talk of resignation, occasional hilarity tinged with hysteria.

The events of Saturday night had left a residue of genuine paranoia. Might our homes be searched? What if someone found the materials we had removed from the office? To what lengths might Nixon go?

Our fears, as it turned out, were not so farfetched. A manifestation of what the President could do occurred just a few days later when early-morning news shows on Thursday reported that Nixon had declared a worldwide alert of all United States military forces. (The White House hadn't announced it; the media found out for themselves through logistical activities that couldn't be hidden by the military.) All over the globe America's nuclear forces were poised to respond to a Soviet threat. But what threat? The Middle East war was tapering off. Nobody knew of any threat. "The details are as yet incomplete and sketchy," said the news broadcasts.

At midday Henry Kissinger held a press conference. The alert, he claimed, was in response to "information" that the Russians *might* be mobilizing some troops within the Soviet Union for transport to the Middle East *if* the cease-fire declared there failed to hold up. What information? Why this drastic response? Kissinger: "We have tried to give you as much information as we decently and safely and properly can." Sometime in the future "we will be able to judge whether the decisions were taken hastily or improperly."

The Administration compared the crisis with the Cuban missile crisis, but the only similarity was in the fright both caused to the American public. Spasms of military might tend to create crises even where they didn't exist before: what would the Russians do now?

The questions posed to Kissinger at his nationally televised press conference echoed our sentiments. Could Kissinger comment on the "speculation" that the alert was prompted as much by "domestic requirements as by the real requirements of diplomacy"? More to the point, was the President's order a "totally rational decision"?

What made us so uneasy about the alert was not the suspicion reflected in the first of those questions. Use of the time-honored technique of engineering some foreign intrigue or crisis to divert attention from problems at home was no less than we would have expected of the President. The tactic was a Nixon trademark and had been used by Presidents of both parties. Kissinger himself admitted the linkage, the need to demonstrate firmness abroad (however irrationally) when faced with a weakened home front: "One cannot have crises of authority in a society for a period of months without paying a price somewhere along the line."

We did not genuinely fear some kind of military coup, although Haig's earlier remark to Ruckelshaus about his "Commander in Chief," when coupled with the alert, recalled a facetious remark made during the summer by Ben-Veniste that we would know we were in real trouble when General Haig began to wear his uniform to work.

What we feared was the suggestion contained in the second question put to Kissinger: whether the President these days was "totally rational." On that Thursday morning a new element crept into our calculations about the effect our actions might have on the President, a factor that was to remain present throughout that winter and spring. (No satisfactory explanation of the alert or any additional information about it was ever made public, Kissinger's promise notwithstanding.) What might the President do if he felt the investigation was pushing him too far? If indeed, as it seemed to some of us, there was a streak of instability there, then it meant we would have to be extra careful to keep from pushing Mr. Nixon over some invisible line into disaster—maybe disaster for all of us.

The President's press conference on October 26 confirmed fears felt by many of us. It was terrifying to see the controlled fury in the President's face, the familiar inappropriate smile and the awkward laugh breaking out at just the wrong time. Still smarting from the effect of the Saturday Night Massacre network specials, the President lit into TV and radio, calling the reporting "frantic, hysterical, . . . outrageous, vicious, distorted." Perspiring heavily, he asserted, "The tougher it gets, the cooler I get." When the ordeal was finished, the President appeared disoriented in time and space. The cameras focused on him as he walked up to the technician in charge of TV lighting and started chatting with him awkwardly. Watching this performance at our K Street office, some of the task force members remained silent for a very long time. Had Richard Nixon finally gone around the bend?

Notwithstanding the hint of paranoia still present on Sunday following the Massacre, we were not as deep in despair as we had been the night before. The avalanche of public support, the outraged comments from every sector of public and national leadership reported in the newspapers and throughout the day on radio and TV, the calls for impeachment, all lent some hope to our situation. Surely, we thought, the public will not let the country become a virtual police state. Yet we had no plan; there was no obvious action we could take. We seemed dependent on events. Sunday afternoon at 1425 K Street Jim Doyle held his own press conference. He told his many friends in the media defiantly, "The mood of the staff is that we're going to continue." It was a strong, forthright thing to say—much stronger than the true confusion many felt.

Monday, a holiday, saw most of the Special Prosecution Force's staff at our K Street office bright and early. When we arrived we found that the FBI agents had been replaced by U.S. marshals, charged with the same duty of preventing files from leaving the office. The first order of business was a meeting of task force chiefs and most of the Watergate Task Force with Hank Ruth and his aides. As we gathered in Ruth's office someone raised a startling question: Hadn't the occupation of our offices for two nights made this an entirely new ball game? What about the possibility of electronic surveillance having been installed? It was farfetched, but it couldn't be ruled out. We decided to go elsewhere. Joe Connolly, chief of the ITT investigation, quickly arranged for the use of a conference room in a law office a few blocks away.

Once installed in the conference room of the nearly empty law office, we began to consider what alternatives we had to respond to the President's refusal to obey the Court of Appeals. Should we make a direct request to Judge Sirica (to whom, according to the court orders, the tapes were required to be produced) that he hold the President in contempt of court for failing to obey? Ordinarily a district judge has broad powers to use contempt as a means to compel compliance with a subpoena: he can impose a jail sentence pending compliance, or levy a heavy fine on a daily basis until the subject gives in. But if the *President* were held in contempt, how could the judge make his ruling effective? There was no question of incarceration. Was it conceivable that a fine would be levied? Could a President's salary be docked?

Another alternative suggested was for our office to recommend to judicial authorities in New York and California that President Nixon be disbarred. But this solution hardly seemed pertinent to the problem of compliance with the subpoena.

Back and forth we went, growing more dejected as the meeting continued. There was little consensus even about the propriety of our seeking a contempt citation—that step seemed too bold to contemplate in our shattered condition. The fact was, we really had very few "alternatives" indeed. We were lucky just to be around. Someone brought in coffee and tea from the next room on a plastic tray. With the coming and going of those making coffee, a few of the lawyers in the law firm who had come in for a quiet holiday at the office stared curiously in on our "board meeting." To us, it had more of the flavor of the Mad Hatter's tea party. By a freak of chance, at one point who should stick his head in but Frank Mankiewicz, renowned Nixon-baiter and top aide and press secretary to Nixon's unsuccessful challenger in the 1972 Presidential election. Apparently Mankiewicz had some business with a lawyer in the firm that day. Whatever he thought about our cabal, he was discreet enough to say nothing and withdraw.

At midday on Monday, a small delegation from our office consisting of Ben-Veniste, Tom McBride (chief of the Campaign Financing Task Force) and Bill Merrill (chief of the Plumbers Task Force) went off to a secret rendezvous with John Dean in a rented room at the Statler

Hilton Hotel. The purpose of this meeting was to find out whether Dean had any major "bombshells" about Nixon that he hadn't already set off in his public testimony. The fact that the meeting had to be held shows how little confidence we had that in a day or two we were still going to be part of this investigation—or that there was going to be any investigation. Dean suggested a few leads, but nothing of major import.

That evening there was a staff meeting in a large conference room on the eighth floor of 1425 K Street belonging to the National Endowment for the Arts. The room was the only one around that was large enough to hold all the staff, and we doubted that anybody would have bothered to bug it. Hank Ruth began the meeting by announcing that as he understood it we were all still employed by the Justice Department, that the office apparently would remain together, but that it would be under the jurisdiction of the Criminal Division of Justice. Henry Petersen was apparently in charge of all our operations, at least temporarily. Hank said he and Phil Lacovara were to meet with Petersen and Bork that afternoon to find out more about the situation.

There was an air of tension overriding the exhaustion in the room. Widely differing opinions about what we should do were expressed. A few suggested mass resignation. Phil Bakes, one of the two assistant prosecutors on the Plumbers Task Force, pointed out that as long as we were not going to get White House evidence his investigation would be a fraud. Whether we actually resigned or not didn't make much difference, he said. The point was, who wanted to continue after what had happened? Bakes urged selective resignations. After Harvard Law School, Bakes recounted, he had traveled extensively in South America on a fellowship in a reconverted 1955 Wayne school bus. "It looks like time to get back into the bus and just take off," he said. A somewhat similar view was propounded by Phil's colleague on the Plumbers Task Force, Chuck Breyer, a former assistant DA from San Francisco.

These views appealed to everyone emotionally. Our fighting instinct had been blunted first by shock, then by fatigue, and finally by the seeming hopelessness of our position. The President had shown us where the power lay in the country when the chips were down, and it did not—it seemed—lie in the law. As emotionally and physically drained as we were, most of us were quite ready, even eager, to accept the idea that it should be all over. More than anything it would have been a blissful relief just to go home and try to forget that all of this had ever happened.

But mass resignation didn't gain too much currency. How could it help us? There must be something we could do that would advance our cause beyond that.

Hank Ruth made a strong pitch to the entire staff to stay on out of professional responsibility. These were our cases, he said. The cases were the most important thing. We had an ethical and professional duty, as well as a duty to the country, to see these investigations through to an honorable conclusion if possible. We couldn't just get up and walk away from them because we were dissatisfied. Important work remained to be done, he pointed out, whether we could get access to White House evidence or not.

Frampton spoke up against this theme. He argued that a decision to stay on the investigation indefinitely under circumstances in which we would not be permitted true independence was intolerable and would be perceived as acquiescence in the President's action. In the long run if we stayed on while the President's position remained static we would be helping Nixon weather the firestorm by appearing to accept the conditions laid down. What we should do, Frampton suggested, was seek an unambiguous issue on which to assert our independence regardless of the President's orders. If we were not permitted to take that stand, like Cox, then we should resign. The first such opportunity was the following day, when the President would have to answer the court order. Frampton urged that we recommend to the judge that he hold the President in contempt of court for refusing to obey the Court of Appeals. If Ruth were not amenable to that, then we should reevaluate each day whether the conditions under which we were operating truly hindered our investigation. Once that occurred, we should protest and, if necessary, resign.

Lacovara and Ruth both rebutted this view. There was no need to take an apocalyptic approach, they said. Going forward as best we could was the better course. If conditions became intolerable, of course anyone was free to resign. But for the moment they stressed the importance of maintaining a united front. They opposed seeking a contempt citation.

Ben-Veniste also urged everyone to stay, pointing out the practical ramifications of the various alternatives. "It's surprising we're still here," he remarked, "but since we are, why waste our resignations when the whole country already assumes we've been fired and has counted us out of the fight anyway? If we're going to resign, let's do it when it can make an impact. Our best approach is to stick to it, show the President we won't give up, that we can't be intimidated. Over at the White House they must be convinced that we'll all resign in protest like the good little liberals they've got us pegged for. Let's give the other side as much hell as we can and no more Mr. Nice Guy."

Everyone decided to stay. Some had grave reservations. Frampton was one; he felt that every hour that went by made him more of a collaborator. What none of us could know was that the very next day, the President would take action resolving our dilemma.

By Monday night the full force of the firestorm was being felt. The AFL-CIO called on the President to resign. Chesterfield Smith, president of the American Bar Association, issued a surprisingly strong statement for that ponderous body, accusing the President of trying to "abort the established processes of law." Senate Republicans told the President's aides they would not fight off an impeachment inquiry. Republican Senator Robert Packwood of Oregon observed, "The office of President does not carry with it a license to destroy justice in America."

By Monday evening 150,000 telegrams on the Massacre had come into the District of Columbia—"the heaviest concentrated volume on record," according to Western Union. Ten thousand of these went to the White House, and most of the rest to the Special Prosecutor's office and to the Hill (which usually receives less than six thousand a *week* on all subjects combined). The verdict was almost unanimous. Many of the telegrams to Congress bore only two words: "Impeach Nixon." "Nobody in the company," a Western Union official said, "could ever remember anything like it." By Wednesday evening the number had grown to 220,000; in ten days, 450,000 telegrams flooded into Washington.

Beginning Tuesday morning, forty-four bills related to Watergate would be introduced in the House; twenty-two called for Richard Nixon's impeachment.

TUESDAY, OCTOBER 23, was an extraordinary day for us. It marked a transition from the old, with Archie Cox's leave-taking; the reaffirmation of a constant and reliable factor in the Watergate equation—

the authority of Judge Sirica; and the effective beginning of the end for the Nixon Presidency.

Early that morning Cox visited the Watergate offices for the first time since the Saturday Night Massacre, to bid the staff farewell and to offer his encouragement for the honorable completion of the task we had sworn to undertake. As we crowded around him, some standing, some sitting on secretaries' desks in the small anteroom outside his former office, Archie spoke in familiar professorial tones and syntax, but his message was far more emotional than his vocabulary or style was used to conveying. Leaning against a pillar, his familiar bow tie once again firmly in place, Archie began by observing, "Perhaps, as in most important things, there is nothing to say." Nevertheless he continued, expressing his hope that the viability of our organization, which he described as the most dedicated and professionally skilled that he had ever worked with, would be preserved. "I cling to the faith that [the merit of our work] will appear to the American people and those who make decisions for them. And that you will be able to continue to do what you came here to do. I do think, at least, that that chance should be preserved, that one should bet on it just as we all bet on that chance when we came to begin with. Because life isn't a sure thing in these areas." He then thanked us for the support we had provided him over the past week and the sense of camaraderie that he had found enormously important. As he described his plans for spending the winter on the coast of Maine and thereafter returning to Harvard, the reality of Archie's departure struck home—coming from his own lips it was now certain. Susan Kaslow, who had typed the legal briefs in the tapes case, and some of the other staff members began to cry. No one left the anteroom without a lump in his throat.

The Watergate Task Force left immediately for court, where Judge Sirica had asked us to assemble both of the grand juries that had been conducting investigations under our direction. Fearful that the grand juries might feel isolated and be tempted to "go public," we had already advised the foreman of the Watergate grand jury that the Special Prosecutor's office was still intact and intended to pursue the investigation vigorously. There was no ambiguity in Judge Sirica's position: come hell or high water the grand juries would not be deterred from completing their investigations. Judge Sirica, in an even, measured voice told them, "The court and the country are grateful to you," and said that he wanted to "alleviate some of the anxiety" that they might be experiencing regarding their "role as grand jurors and the role of the grand juries themselves." He asked the jurors to be patient while the various problems surrounding their investigations were resolved and assured them, "In due course the questions which now plague us will be answered, and you may rely on the court to safeguard your rights and to preserve the integrity of your proceedings." After exhorting them to "steadily and deliberately pursue" their investigations, and reminding them of their oath in which they were sworn to maintain the secrecy of their proceedings, the judge emphasized to them that they were not dismissed and would not be dismissed "except as provided by law upon the completion of your work or the conclusion of your term."

We were just a bit miffed that the judge made no reference whatever to us, sitting there in front of the jurors at counsel table. Perhaps he, like us, was still in a quandary about our precise status and authority.

To underline the fact that, whatever was going on elsewhere, Judge Sirica was very much alive and well, he brushed aside a suggestion made by law professor John F. Banzhof III that the court appoint an attorney to succeed Cox as legal adviser to the grand jury. "If the court feels it is necessary it needs no help," the judge snapped.

We barely had enough time to grab a bite to eat before we were due back in court to hear President Nixon's formal response to the Court of Appeals decision ordering him to produce the tapes. The President had been unequivocal that it was either the Stennis Compromise or nothing. It would be interesting to see what would happen when the "nothing" was formally articulated in court, for, Cox or no Cox, the subpoena was still outstanding and the Appeals Court ruling was still binding on the President.

The courtroom that afternoon must have been a curious sight. Packed together around the table reserved for "the government" (Which "government"? we asked ourselves) were Hank Ruth, Phil Lacovara, the Watergate Task Force, the other task force leaders (Connolly, Merrill, and McBride) and Ruth's aides Kreindler and Feldbaum. If the head had been lopped off, the body lived. In fact, we were uncertain of whether we were supposed to be there at all. But in our thinking we were still "attorneys for the grand jury," and it was in that capacity that we had come. Somebody had to be present to represent the interests of the enforcement of the law.

At opposing counsel table sat Charles Alan Wright, the Texas law professor who, justifiably or not, represented to us what power could do when advocacy failed. The courtroom was packed with newsmen and lawyers.

We had no idea what would happen that afternoon. Would the judge ask whether "the government" had decided to withdraw its subpoena in accordance with the President's instructions? We had no intention of making such a statement. If the judge turned first to Wright and he refused to comply, would the judge then turn to us for a recommendation? Ordinarily the court would not move toward contempt without seeking the views of prosecutors. But we had made no decision. We didn't have a position, except to make no recommendation of contempt. Would the judge take it upon himself to hint at contempt?

There was no need for any decision on our part. At eight minutes past two, Judge Sirica strode into his courtroom, his face set with determination. Without delay he began in stern, almost harsh tones to read some of the more compelling passages from the Court of Appeals order. The tension mounted. He was making no bones about what the Court of Appeals had required the President to do. Simply by reading the court's opinion he seemed to be putting it to Wright.

Revealing the tension felt by all in the hushed courtroom, Judge Sirica looked at his notes and announced, "The court will now read the order—" then, catching himself, murmured, "I've already read the order." There was no room for procrastination—the slowly grinding wheels of justice had meshed. As Judge Sirica called for the President's professor to approach the lectern "to file with the court the response of the President," the courtroom air was as charged as with a jury returning its verdict. Wright, wearing a lime-green shirt with his brown suit, walked briskly to the podium. Much of the arrogance of posture exhibited in his earlier appearances was gone. He stunned everyone in the courtroom by announcing, "Mr. Chief Judge, may it please the court, I am not prepared at this time to file a response. I am however, authorized to say that the President of the United States will comply in all respects with the order of August twenty-ninth as modified by the order of the Court of Appeals."

Judge Sirica, as if unable to believe his own ears, asked Wright, "As I understand your statement, that will be delivered to this court?"

Wright: "To the court *in camera.*"

A smile began to form on the weary judge's face. "You will follow the decisions or statements delineated by me."

Wright: ". . . will comply in all respects with what Your Honor has just read."

It was as though a giant force had exhaled the tension of the courtroom, spewing reporters through the double doors toward their telephones.

Professor Wright went on: "As the court is aware, the President yesterday filed with the clerk of the court a response along different lines, along the lines indicated in the statement to the country on Friday. That statement, if it was ever officially filed with the court, is now withdrawn." The President was actually backing down! When it came to a choice of defying the court in the charged atmosphere following the Saturday Night Massacre or giving up the tapes, he had chosen to give in.

The President's lawyer, relishing the stunned silence his announcement had created, made a last attempt to justify the Stennis Compromise but admitted that the "events of the weekend" had demonstrated that the White House gambit was not going to defuse a constitutional crisis. Wright finished with a ringing declaration: "This President does not defy the law, and he has authorized me to say he will comply in full with the orders of the court." Of course what everyone in the courtroom knew was that the President wasn't going to defy the law *on this occasion* because he believed that the American public wouldn't let him get away with it.

Relieved of the terrible burden of deciding what to do if the President refused to comply with the court's order, Judge Sirica was thinking more pragmatically. After expressing his happiness with the President's decision to comply, he discussed with Wright the timetable for production of the index and analysis which would precede the actual transmittal of tapes. Receiving a satisfactory answer from Professor Wright, Judge Sirica asked, somewhat rhetorically, whether we had any further business and promptly adjourned the court.

It is no exaggeration to say that we were dumbfounded. As we tried to come to grips with our surprise we were struck with a new and horrible possibility. Perhaps the genius of the President's grand strategy had only now been revealed, showing what a potent and resourceful adversary he truly could be. Having risked the firestorm to withhold the tapes, would the President now surrender them and compound his dilemma if they actually contained anything harmful to him? No. It must be that he had decided to use the tapes confrontation as basis for getting rid of Cox, knowing all along he could give in and produce the tapes because there was nothing on them to damage him. Worse, the President could now argue that his whole dispute with Cox was one of "principle" rather than a desperate attempt to bury incriminating evidence. By first withholding the tapes and then giving them up the President would regain lost credibility, survive the firing of Cox, and maybe now be in a good position to terminate our investigations. It was a little far out, but diabolical. Back at 1425 K Street, as we kicked around the possible reasons for the President's reversal, there seemed only two theories: either he had euchered us, the Congress and the American public in a daring gamble or he was merely buying time to escape the extraordinary public outcry his continued defiance of law would bring.

Later on Tuesday, after Wright's startling courtroom announcement, Acting Attorney General Bork officially abolished the "Watergate Special Prosecution Force" and created the "Watergate Special Prosecution Office" within the Department of Justice. Henry Petersen was designated to take charge of the office, which would continue with its personnel intact in the same location at 1425 K Street. Ruth had agreed that each task force would brief Petersen about the status of its investigation.

On Tuesday afternoon Petersen and Bork addressed the task force leaders. Petersen began the meeting by announcing that nobody would be fired. Those who felt they could not continue, he said, were "quitters." The task force leaders bombarded Petersen and Bork with hostile questions. Bork defended his decision to fire Cox by saying, "I had ten minutes to make up my mind and if I didn't do it, somebody else would have." He insisted that Richardson and Ruckelshaus had both urged him not to resign. That obscured the fact that, resign or not, he had carried out the order to fire Cox even though his two superiors had refused to do so. Had Bork refused to fire Cox it is likely that the President would have been temporarily stymied, since beyond Bork no clear line of "succession" to the post of Attorney General existed in the Justice Department. Had Henry Petersen, as the senior

Assistant Attorney General, taken over after a Bork resignation he too probably would have refused to fire Archie. In short, Bork had been instrumental in doing the President's bidding. Whether he liked it or not, he was going to be identified in history for following orders rather than for acting to preserve the integrity of the criminal-justice process.

Would Bork support appointment of another independent special prosecutor? Again he waffled. The "Department" would undoubtedly oppose that, he said, whether he was acting Attorney General or not. After Archie's firing, a series of small posters bearing Bork puns had gone up around our offices to raise morale: "Nixon's Bork is worse than his bite," "Bork if you think Nixon's guilty," "End Nixon's aBorktion," and so on. The jokes seemed even more appropriate after his performance on Tuesday.

Wednesday the task force leaders met with Petersen to discuss with him what his procedures would be in respect to getting evidence from the White House. Petersen was in a bit of a reflective mood. He explained that both he and Bork had been prepared to resign on Tuesday afternoon had the President refused to comply with the Court of Appeals order. What they had in mind was to demand the evidence and resign if it was not forthcoming. But the President's reversal made that unnecessary. Petersen agreed to continue requesting information from the White House.

Later Petersen met with Ben-Veniste, Volner and Ruth concerning the cover-up investigation. Ben-Veniste put to Petersen the concern of the entire task force that as a potential witness in upcoming Watergate trials Petersen had a very strong conflict of interest in being responsible for our investigation. Phil Bakes, on the Plumbers Task Force, had already objected to Petersen's intimate participation in its investigations on the same grounds. Petersen said he would consider the problem. Petersen admitted that he'd been pretty relieved to have the Watergate investigation taken off his back when Special Prosecutor Cox had been appointed in May. It was a responsibility he hadn't relished. Now he wasn't too happy to have it again, but he wanted to see it through.

We surely were a lot better off with Petersen than with almost anyone else imaginable as an ultimate "supervisor" from the Justice Department; he had already been around the Horn with Nixon once on this, back in April when the cover-up was collapsing and Petersen was urging the President to fire Haldeman and Ehrlichman. But it was a blow to morale to see the new security badge with Petersen's picture go up on the board at the entrance to our office.

On Thursday we petitioned Judge Sirica for a "protective order" making us custodians for the grand jury of all the prosecutorial files connected with the jury's investigation and forbidding anyone besides ourselves and Henry Petersen from having access to them. The court's supervision of the grand jury and its activities laid the proper legal basis for this request. The next day the judge signed the order.

Still feeling very much in limbo, we had begun during the week to make some attempts to get our grand-jury and witness-interview schedule back in shape. It wasn't easy. Some witnesses' attorneys were uneasy about our status, as were we. There had been a movement in Congress for legislation authorizing the court to appoint its own special prosecutor to undertake our investigation, but the fate of these efforts was unclear. Our morale could not be helped by the fact that the President was now officially in direct control of the investigation, through the Justice Department.

The one thing that more than any other kept our spirits up was the unprecedented outpouring of public support. Telegrams and letters were arriving at our office faster than they could be handled. To save the effort of delivery, Western Union set up teletype machines in our office which proceeded to spew out telegrams from all parts of the country almost twenty-four hours a day. Bags of mail arrived hourly. The letters and wires had to be stacked, bagged, wrapped, and stored in nooks and crannies throughout our offices just to get them out of the way so that more could come in. We felt the country communicating with us directly, urging us to stick in there, praising Cox, condemning the President, emphasizing the importance of the job we were doing.

Carl Feldbaum memorialized some of these messages on Halloween. The weekend after the Massacre he got hold of dozens of small pumpkins. When we arrived on Tuesday morning, October 30, each staff member found a pumpkin on his desk and attached to it a telegram cheering us on.

The folks who kept those cards and letters coming (and they did keep them coming, for weeks and even months) could scarcely have realized how much they meant to our morale in a very trying time.

CHAPTER **7** **The Tapes Hearings: no more Mr. nice Guy**

EXACTLY ONE WEEK after Professor Wright announced that the President would comply fully with the tapes subpoena, J. Fred Buzhardt, the mild-mannered, bespectacled Mississippian who replaced John Dean as counsel to the President, made a startling announcement in the privacy of Judge Sirica's chambers. Ben-Veniste listened in controlled anger to Buzhardt's almost whispered revelation that tapes of two of the conversations about which the nation had been plunged into controversy since July did not exist.

Buzhardt explained that his inquiry into the matter led him to the conclusion that the June 20, 1972, telephone conversation between Nixon and John Mitchell—the first communication between the two after the Watergate arrests—had never been recorded because Nixon spoke from the upstairs residence of the White House on a telephone which was not bugged. According to Buzhardt, the second missing conversation, a face-to-face meeting between Nixon and John Dean on the evening of April 15, 1973, the day the President learned that Dean was cooperating with the prosecutors, was not recorded because the timer in the EOB taping system had malfunctioned on that day (a Sunday) and no Secret Service technician was on hand to change the reels of tape.

The significance of both conversations to the Watergate investigation was enormous.

The immediate question was whether to accept the White House explanation for the missing tapes or to conduct an open court proceeding in order to test Buzhardt's claims under cross-examination. We demanded a hearing. At Ben-Veniste's request, Buzhardt agreed to make the Secret Service technician most familiar with the White House taping system available for interview as soon as possible. Perhaps after listening to an informal exposition on the details of the system, the President's lawyer suggested, the special prosecutors would change their minds as to the need for a court hearing.

Raymond C. Zumwalt, a portly former military communications expert and designer of President Nixon's surreptitious electronic eavesdropping system, was the White House choice as the man who could pour oil on the troubled waters raised by the two missing Nixon tapes. On October 31, Zumwalt showed up at Ben-Veniste's office in the tow of a young White House staff lawyer who insisted on sitting in during the interview. To us the parallel between this search for truth and the earlier investigation, when it was John Dean and CRP lawyers who sat in on investigators' interviews, was too close. We could not tolerate the presence of White House lawyers during our interview. The White House knew it was the wrong time to do battle with us on this issue and backed down.

Zumwalt's demeanor led us to believe he had been regaled with tales of horror about the wild beasts at the Special Prosecutor's office. The time would have been better spent going over the facts with him. Despite Buzhardt's explanation that the system had malfunctioned on April 15, 1973, Zumwalt, the expert, told us he had never heard about any malfunctions. Ben-Veniste concluded that there would be no time like the present to get started on a public hearing and phoned Buzhardt to suggest that Zumwalt testify that afternoon. The White House counsel was obviously not pleased but went along with the suggestion that perhaps this could all be cleared up quickly.

The hearing that afternoon was in many ways typical of a pattern of unfortunate and frequently avoidable mistakes which was to dog the Nixon White House virtually until the President's resignation. No tactician could have arranged the sequence of events in a more disadvantageous order: first the bombshell announcement, next the simplistic explanation (sometimes coupled with a salvo against an identifiable Nixon enemy), eventually the proof that the explanation was erroneous. Yet it was the Nixon team which largely had control over that sequence.

The tapes hearing began in Judge Sirica's crowded courtroom at 3:30 P.M. on Halloween Day. Fred Buzhardt, dressed in his best blue suit, made a brief, low-key statement in which he explained that the

April 15 Nixon-Dean conversation "was not recorded due to a malfunction of the system." He then called brother Zumwalt "to throw some additional light on the problem." Zumwalt, looking a bit more confident but no happier than he had looked that morning, testified that he assumed a seven-day timer hooked into the taping system of the President's office in the Executive Office Buildings had "failed to switch the machines that night."

On cross-examination Ben-Veniste focused in on why the witness had suddenly "remembered" a malfunction after his interview in our office that morning. The answer: Buzhardt had told him of it! Thus the expert who was to enlighten the court was in fact himself in the dark except for the answers spoon-fed to him by Nixon's lawyer.

On leaving the courthouse, a reporter asked Buzhardt, "Do you think the public will believe this?"

"I don't know," replied Buzhardt, heading for his limousine.

The Watergate team returned to K Street in high spirits. In the brief skirmish that day we had done pretty well. This was the first time anyone had crossed swords with Nixon's legal department in a courtroom confrontation. Here there was no hiding behind the verbal mush of a Ziegler-controlled news conference, enjoying the flanking movement of a reliable senator or employing the artful leak to a hungry newsman.

The press corps was out in force the next morning as we arrived at the entrance to the courthouse. The morning papers screamed headlines announcing the nonexistence of two key tapes the White House had "pledged to let Sirica hear." All of a sudden, the press had discovered that Cox's staff was alive and well and was determined to make up for lost time. A ritual began that was to continue for the rest of our tenure. Cameramen with the agility of pro football defensive backs skipped backward to keep us in range as we walked toward the courthouse from the street; sound technicians thrust obscenely phallic shotgun mikes at us, fine-tuned to overhear any conversation or banter; correspondents, always waiting for a quote for the day's story or a statement predicting events, or summarizing, jogged alongside. We consistently adhered to the canons of professional ethics and the sage advice attributed to President Coolidge: "You don't have to explain what you ain't said."

In court, Fred Buzhardt revised his explanation of the day before. Instead of a faulty switching device being responsible for the failure to record the April 15 Nixon-Dean conversation, Buzhardt now blamed Nixon's loquaciousness—the tapes, which would hold only six hours of conversation, had been all filled up by the time John Dean ambled in.

Zumwalt was only too pleased to testify to this new explanation. But the hapless technician soon got further mired down when cross-examined about the records kept to document withdrawals from the White House tape bank. It appeared that the vault in which the tapes were kept, electronically secured by a computer, was impregnable. The only trouble was that whenever a member of the President's staff with sufficient clout to requisition some tapes from the Secret Service guardians did so, there was no system designed to keep track of where they went or whether or not they were returned. While normal custodial procedure of tape recordings would require careful documentation and a rational system to identify the materials logged in and out, the best that poor Zumwalt had done was to jot down the information on pieces of brown paper that looked to be torn fragments of grocery bags. A sharp counterpoint to the legendary Prussian discipline and regimentation of the Nixon White House!

Typical of the tapes hearing, as soon as one fire was doused, two others spontaneously ignited to take its place. The moment the White House got its story together on the faulty-timer-versus-garrulous-Chief-Executive issue, it next appeared that the Scotch Brand tape box containing the filled-up reel of April 15 Presidential conversations had the pencil marking "Part I." If there was a Part I, where was Part II? Nobody knew. To make things worse, it turned out that the April 15 tape was among a baker's dozen loaned to Bob Haldeman in July 1973, months after Haldeman, by then a major target of the investigation, had left the White House. In certain instances there were no records reflecting return of large numbers of tapes.

The White House lawyers attempted to recoup some lost ground by presenting professionally printed charts of the tape system's wiring, and transparencies of the President's daily log for April 15, 1973; the log was displayed on a large movie screen in a darkened courtroom. The sophisticated audience of journalists who packed the courtroom gallery and even, with Judge Sirica's dispensation, the jury box, thought little of this dog-and-pony show. Their *sotto voce* wisecracks were audible even to us. One wondered if the easel upon which the White House charts rested was the same one G. Gordon Liddy had used to display *his* very polished charts outlining the million-dollar Gemstone plan for Attorney General Mitchell. Another was heard hawking peanuts and popcorn. A third announced that the White House had originally intended a screening of *Patton* but had inexplicably lost the second reel.

In agonizing detail we took the Secret Service technicians through the procedures by which they had planted bugs behind the wall sconces in the Oval Office and the Cabinet Room, how they had drilled holes in the historic mahogany of the President's own desk to install tiny voice-activated microphones. Only the equipment in the Cabinet Room could be turned on and off manually, by buttons disingenuously marked "Haldeman" and "Butterfield" at the President's chair. The voice-activated machinery dispensed with the drudgery of human decision—any sound made in the President's vicinity was automatically recorded. However, the Cabinet Room equipment with its manual buttons was a constant nuisance to the technicians. Tourists taken through the Cabinet Room on White House tours had the infernal habit of pressing the buttons, which resulted in hours of tour-guide spiel being recorded for posterity.

Even Nixon supporters must have been rankled by the thought of sharp steel drills biting out hunks of historic American furniture— particularly since the incumbent during the 1972 campaign had made such a big deal about having made this or that historic decision while sitting at President Wilson's desk in the Oval Office. Imagine desecrating the desk of a man the likes of Woodrow Wilson! It was not until long after Nixon's resignation that we learned that all through the 1972 campaign Bob Haldeman had been receiving persistent notes from the curator of the Senate Museum, pointing out that while Mr. Nixon did have *a* Wilson desk, the original owner had not been Woodrow but rather the somewhat more obscure Henry Wilson, Vice President under Ulysses S. Grant.

Throughout the hearings we were learning a great deal about the inner workings of the White House—and getting important documents we had previously asked for in private letters. White House counsel were now reluctant to refuse our public requests before Judge Sirica. Thus, we became aware of detailed logs accounting for every moment of the President's day—valuable evidence of his meetings and telephone conversations which we later put to good use in framing our second tapes subpoena. These logs, a composite of information supplied by a network of sources close to the President, were synthesized into a final summary and maintained for historical purposes by an affable and scholarly-looking archivist named James Nesbitt, detailed to the White House from the National Archives.

Called to the stand to demonstrate from the Presidential logs that Nixon had more than six hours of conversations on April 15 before Dean arrived, thereby corroborating the "tape ran out" theory, Nesbitt promptly admitted that the April 15 log had been ordered *revised* on July 26, 1973—three days after our subpoena was served on the White House. Very nasty coincidence. We continued to demand and receive bits and chunks of Nesbitt's Presidential logs (filling in important gaps in our knowledge of Nixon's meetings during the period the cover-up was collapsing) for weeks thereafter until one day Nesbitt received a memo stating that the practice of maintaining the logs had been discontinued. When we asked him if he could explain the policy change, Nesbitt could only surmise, "I guess the President got tired of being hit with his own bat."

The White House took the position that its witnesses had already cleared up the entire controversy. But we demanded that additional witnesses be called, and Judge Sirica agreed.

The next day's first witness was Presidential assistant Stephen Bull, a slender man in his early thirties who had taken over many of Butterfield's responsibilities after Butterfield left to become head of the Federal Aviation Agency. A clean-cut former Marine, wearing the obligatory White House hardware of American-flag lapel pin and Nixon tie clasp, he obviously had been given the mission of rescuing the White House from its current dilemma. He was, after all, the first *real* member of the White House team to take the stand in this hearing; clearly the Secret Service boys hadn't cut the mustard, but this would be different.

It *was* different—worse; and the media now had the opportunity of hearing the young man who had the office "contiguous to the President," as he put it, testify under oath. The problem was that in his effort to impress everyone with his erudition and command of the situation, the former junior executive at Canada Dry could rarely utter a simple declarative sentence. Thus, what should have been "Butterfield told me the tape-recording system in the Cabinet Room was of

poor quality" became "Mr. Butterfield had indicated that the repro-
ductive capability in the Cabinet Room was something less than satisfactory." The gallery tittered.

Bull revealed that he had conducted a fruitless hunt for the elusive
April 15 tape at Camp David, the Presidential retreat, at the request
of the President (who, Bull told us, was reviewing all the subpoenaed
tapes) on September 29, 1973—a full month before the news of nonexistent recordings was relayed to Judge Sirica. Yet Buzhardt had
proclaimed at the start of the hearings that the two conversations had
not been found to be missing until October 27 or 28—more than a
week after Cox had been fired.

We also learned from Bull that Nixon had spent twelve full hours
back on June 4, 1973, reviewing various recordings in his EOB office.
Bull couldn't remember whether or not the April 15 Nixon-Dean conversation was one of them, though the Secret Service records showed
the April 15 reel among those requisitioned by Bull for the President's
use. Since the tape-recording equipment in the President's EOB office
was not disconnected until July 18, Ben-Veniste pointed out, the automatic voice-activated taping system must have made a tape of
Nixon listening on June 4 to his own past tapes. If the April 15 Dean
tape once existed, we might find a recording of Nixon listening to it on
June 4.

Judge Sirica, in his folksy way, looked over to Buzhardt. "Well, it
wouldn't hurt to find it and find out what it was and what was on it."

Buzhardt reacted to the suggestion that the White House produce
the "tape of the tapes" like a vampire to a crucifix. "Your honor, I don't
have authority from the President to disclose any more tapes."

It would be several months before we got the June 4 tape—and discovered that nothing related to the "missing" April 15 tape was discussed on it. But Nixon's unwillingness to produce it at the hearing
added more fuel to the growing fires of speculation.

The revelations brought to light since October 23 made the motive
of the President in putting forth the Stennis Compromise even more
suspect. We now knew that Nixon had reviewed his tapes on September 29—after Judge Sirica had upheld the grand jury's subpoena but
before the Court of Appeals had ruled—a month earlier than his
lawyer had reported. Given Stennis' age, physical condition, poor
hearing and previously announced support for the President, together
with his well-known deference to executive claims of national security,

how would the question of the two missing tapes have been handled? Would the White House have found any need to tell the public about gaps in other tapes? How accurate would the "summaries" of the remaining conversations have been? We suspected that none of the matters embarrassing to the White House that were being disclosed in public hearings would ever have seen the light of day if Archibald Cox had acquiesced in the Stennis Compromise.

Unknown to us at the time, Stennis had acquired the nickname of "the undertaker" among the Nixon coterie because matters referred to the Senate Armed Services Committee (of which he was chairman) that the White House did not want made public stayed very professionally buried. In connection with his former position as counsel to the Defense Department Fred Buzhardt had come to work closely with Senator Stennis on matters such as the infamous My Lai Massacre and the Pentagon Papers. The White House had intended that in implementing the Stennis Compromise none other than Buzhardt himself would work with the Senator in verifying the accuracy of White House "summaries."

THE POLITICAL REPERCUSSIONS of the missing tapes, the confusing explanations for their disappearance and the inept White House security for the recordings that remained added substantially to the pounding the President had taken over the Saturday Night Massacre. The *New York Times,* in a lengthy Sunday editorial, said, "The one last great service that Mr. Nixon can now perform is to resign." The *Detroit News* and the *Denver Post,* both of which had supported Nixon in Presidential campaigns, called for resignation. Most dramatically, *Time* magazine, in its first editorial in fifty years of publication, declared, "The most important decision of Richard Nixon's remarkable career is before him: whether he will give up the Presidency rather than do further damage to the country." Although the magazine had editorially supported Nixon in 1960, 1968 and 1972, *Time* now concluded that he had "irredeemably lost his moral authority, the confidence of most of the country, and therefore his ability to govern effectively." Indeed, on the anniversary of Nixon's landslide reelection, the Gallup pollsters found the President's support down to a mere twenty-seven percent of the electorate—a stark drop from the sixty-eight percent he had enjoyed in January.

More ominously for the President, many leaders of his own party began to ask embarrassing questions in public. Senator Barry Goldwater was quoted as saying that Nixon's credibility had reached "an all-time low from which he may not be able to recover." Senator Brooke became the first Senate Republican to publicly call for Nixon's resignation. In fact, Presidential denials that resignation was being considered had become virtually a daily occurrence.

The second week of tapes hearings opened with some new discoveries. On Monday, the White House acceded to our demand that it produce logs showing the whereabouts of various tapes between July 18, 1973, the day when the tape system was turned off, and the present. From these logs we learned that the President's secretary, Rose Mary Woods, had kept a batch of subpoenaed tapes in her office for two weeks while transcribing them in late September, and that she had carried the tapes to the Florida White House at Key Biscayne on the weekend of October 3. From further cross-examination of Steve Bull, it emerged that Bull had personally told the President on September 29 that the April 15 Dean tape could not be located. And according to the new custodian of the tapes, John C. Bennett (an aide to Haig who was himself a retired major general), Rose Mary Woods still had eight tapes in her possession. Not copies, but originals. All this was a far cry from Buzhardt's earlier assurances that the tapes were in a safe place under the President's personal custody, and, more pointedly, from Buzhardt's statement in open court only a week before that all the tapes were now intact in the White House vault.

Bennett presented the image of the ramrod-straight, well-organized military man—clearly the most competent of the White House witnesses to take the stand so far. He disclosed that just the day before Rose Mary Woods had mentioned she was having trouble with a tape she was playing. It had a "gap" in it. But Bennett confessed he had not wanted to get involved with Woods's problem. He had told her to do her best and then jackrabbited out of her office without finding out more. Of course, we were alarmed that at this late date original tapes rather than copies were being used for transcription. To alert Judge Sirica to the dangers involved, Ben-Veniste, while cross-examining the head of the Secret Service's Technical Services Division, Alfred Wong, held up a piece of tape similar to that used by the White House taping system and pulled gently at both ends. The tape became a strand of spaghetti. The demonstration made clear what would happen if original White House tape recordings were stretched or mangled in the machinery of a tape-recording machine while being transcribed.

November 8 was the first round in one of the most interesting confrontations of Watergate, Jill Volner against Rose Mary Woods. Miss Woods, brought on to tell what she knew about the "gap" mentioned by General Bennett the day before, was first questioned by White House counsel Samuel J. Powers, a private Florida attorney freshly recruited to bolster the reeling Nixon legal team. She took the stand in a bright-orange dress and a string of pearls. Her heavy makeup was contrasted with Volner's peaches-and-cream complexion.

Powers, wisely taking the initiative, had Woods immediately defuse the explosive revelation of a "gap" in the tapes. According to Woods, her discussion with Bennett related to her inability to find a conversation between Nixon and John Dean on the sixteenth of April *not* called for by the subpoena. She had since found the elusive tape and was "perfectly satisfied" that "there was no gap." (How this testimony could conceivably square with the subsequent revelation that Woods knew there was a gap in a different tape is another matter.)

Under Volner's cross-examination Woods described how she had struggled for twenty-nine hours trying to transcribe the first taped conversation given her. We were later to learn that this was the famous Nixon-Haldeman tape with the eighteen-and-a-half-minute gap.

When Volner began to question her about the procedures used to insure that no harm would come to the original tapes that were being used to make typed transcripts, Woods became suddenly snappish, her face coloring with indignation.

> VOLNER: Were any precautions taken to assure you would not accidentally hit the erase button?
>
> WOODS: Everybody said be terribly careful. I mean, I don't think, I don't want this to sound like I am bragging but I don't believe I am so stupid that they had to go over it and over it. I was told if you push that button it will erase and I do know even on a small machine you can dictate over something and that removes it and I think I used every possible precaution to not do that.
>
> VOLNER: What precautions specifically did you take to avoid . . . recording over it, thereby getting rid of what was already there?
>
> WOODS: What precautions? I used my head. It is the only one I had to use.

H. R. Haldeman followed Woods to the stand, admitting his participation in ordering the installation of the taping system at the request
of the President in order to provide "a complete, accurate record of
conversations held by the President . . . for his reference and for historical purposes." Haldeman could provide no convincing explanation
as to why he had received twenty-two tapes on April 26 but had
listened, he said, to only one conversation. Nor could he explain the
discrepancy between his recollection that he had returned the tapes
the same day and the Secret Service logs which indicated that they
had not been returned to the vault until nearly a week later.

At the end of the day, obviously in reaction to Ben-Veniste's "suggestion" in court that the tapes be copied and the originals immediately turned over to Judge Sirica for safekeeping, Powers announced
that copies were in fact being made "to make sure that all recordings
of subpoenaed Presidential conversations were preserved," i.e., that
copies would be made of originals. We felt that we had won a minor
victory—and indeed the institution of this procedure became an important factor in our eventual success in getting the "smoking pistol"
tape of June 23, 1972—but as far as the eighteen-and-a-half-minute-
gap tape was concerned it was locking the barn door after the horse
had bolted.

FOLLOWING THE CONCLUSION of the hearing that afternoon, while
Powers was "clarifying" the day's inconsistencies for the press, a group
of prosecutors departed for Fred Buzhardt's office to meet with him
about selecting a panel of experts to analyze the tapes and determine
whether there had been any tampering. The points we had been
scoring against the White House legal team had put the prosecutors
in a lighthearted mood. Buzhardt's chambers in the Old Executive
Office Building right across from the White House were large and
well-appointed. Ben-Veniste, Hank Ruth and Carl Feldbaum were
ushered in and made themselves comfortable on an overstuffed couch
just a short jog from Buzhardt's desk. The President's lawyer then
briefly excused himself. Before long it became apparent that the
prosecutors' wool suits, selected for brisk November weather, were
especially inappropriate for the near-tropical temperature in the room.
The sudden heat wave was particularly puzzling because only the
night before President Nixon had solemnly promised the nation on

TV that he was going to do *his* part to fight the energy crisis by lowering his thermostat to sixty-eight degrees and keeping it there throughout the winter—a patriotic gesture somewhat reminiscent of Lyndon Johnson's widely publicized program to cut down on expenses by seeing that all unnecessary lights in the White House were turned off.

Ben-Veniste sauntered over to the handsome thermostat-clock-barometer gizmo prominent on Buzhardt's wall and noticed that the temperature indicated seventy-nine degrees. Returning to his briefcase, he removed a five-by-seven index card and printed in block letters:

WARNING!
YOU ARE IN VIOLATION OF THE
PRESIDENT'S 68° EDICT.
TURN DOWN YOUR THERMOSTAT!
THIS IS YOUR FIRST WARNING.

Ben-Veniste placed the card on top of the thermostat and took his seat.

Shortly afterward, Buzhardt bustled in with a National Security Agency expert, Howard Rosenblum, in tow. Ben-Veniste directed Buzhardt's attention to the thermostat: "Fred, a man in a military uniform came through here and left something on your thermostat."

Buzhardt read the card, his head slowly shaking to and fro in resignation.

"What's wrong, Fred, what does it say?"

Buzhardt read the note aloud.

"Fred, what happens if you get another warning?"

The harried Presidential counselor thereupon launched into a detailed exposition of the picayune trivia with which unseen functionaries at the White House were intent upon squandering his time. They were always "gigging" him about something, he complained. "Shoot, the damn thermostat doesn't even work. Want to see how to achieve sixty-eight degrees around here?" With that Buzhardt turned on the air conditioner full blast. So much for the White House's response to the energy crisis. At least when you drove past LBJ's White House you could tell if the lights were out.

The purpose of the White House meeting was to discuss joint selection by the prosecutors and the White House of a panel of

scientific experts who would, under Judge Sirica's auspices and supervision, study the subpoenaed tapes to determine whether they
had been edited or otherwise altered.

The discussion about detecting tape alterations was eye-opening.
Carl Feldbaum quizzed Rosenblum on the means for detecting a
splice through a telltale "click" on the tape, and how a "click" would
sound if the tape were played backward. The expert explained that
this was such a new field that scientists, engineers and technicians
would be creating a new technology in serving as experts in this
matter. It was important to know, he said, what our time frame
would be, as the possibilities for testing and experimentation were
limitless.

"Sometime before the next three years are out," replied Ben-
Veniste.

The background for the next major tapes flap had been laid by
Ben-Veniste's earlier request that we be given the President's Dictabelt recording of his own recollections of the meeting on April 15
between himself and Dean. Back in April 1973, the President had
committed an unfortunate faux pas in describing his April 15 conversation with Dean to Henry Petersen. "I have it on tape," the
President had maintained, insisting that the prosecutors were trying
to attack the White House by offering Dean immunity from prosecution (a charge Petersen had denied). On June 11, Archibald Cox,
who had learned about the President's remark, had written to Buzhardt asking for the tape that Nixon had offered to let Petersen hear.
But Buzhardt wrote back that "the tape to which the President referred in his discussion with Mr. Petersen was a tape on which the
President dictated his own recollection of that conversation [the April
15 meeting with Dean] after it was finished. It would, of course, not
be appropriate to produce that tape."

At the time of Buzhardt's reply, we had been suspicious that the
White House was simply trying to throw us off the track; after all,
why would Nixon offer to let Petersen listen to Nixon's own recollections of the Dean meeting? Butterfield's revelations about the
taping system bolstered our suspicion that perhaps there never was
any Dictabelt and that Nixon (and Buzhardt) well knew it. However, the White House had affirmatively represented that there was
such a recording, and in the absence of an actual April 15 tape the
Dictabelt recording of the President's recollection was the next best

thing. It was covered by our subpoena, too. So we asked for it. Would the White House now be trapped into admitting that it had been deceitful in the first place in responding to Cox's initial request? Would the President try to manufacture a Dictabelt?

Buzhardt was the next witness called by us in the public hearings. A good bit of time was spent probing his response to Cox's letter of June 11 asking for the Nixon-Dean tape of April 15. Ben-Veniste especially attempted to ascertain whether the President had instructed Buzhardt intentionally to mislead the Special Prosecutor by stating that what Nixon had been referring to in the Petersen conversation was a Dictabelt, not a tape.

Not only did Buzhardt begrudgingly admit that there was no April 15 Dictabelt, but he also now revealed that he, Nixon and Haig knew that no such Dictabelt existed as of November 5—the same day deputy White House press secretary Gerald Warren was telling newsmen in Florida that the Dictabelt did exist and that it would be made available to the court. What was the reason for a week's delay in advising the court? Had Nixon planned to *manufacture* an April 15 Dictabelt in order to continue the lie which was started back in June as the result of Cox's request? After all, his voice would be the only one on the Dictabelt; perhaps he could just crank out a fresh "recollection" of the April 15 meeting with Dean. Had Nixon abandoned this plan only after being advised of the ingenious methods available for detecting forgeries made on magnetic tape?

Buzhardt's demeanor on the stand was that of a soldier emerging from a foxhole. He spoke in a voice just above a whisper and was admonished by the judge more than once to speak up. Questioned repeatedly by Ben-Veniste about his conversations with the President concerning the nonexistent Dictabelt, Buzhardt instead lapsed into vague evasive answers and the stock White House approach when all else failed: "I can't recall."

The cross-examination then moved to the promises made by the White House regarding the safekeeping of the tapes, as compared with the true facts that had come out so far in the hearing. How could Buzhardt have stipulated at the beginning of the tapes hearing that all the tapes were locked in the special vault, when in fact Rose Mary Woods had at least seven of them since September 28? Buzhardt answered that nobody had told him. How could Buzhardt justify his July 25 letter assuring Cox that "the President has sole personal control of those tapes and they are being adequately protected under secure conditions [and] all access . . . is carefully documented" in light of the tapes being transported to Key Biscayne and Camp David by Rose Mary Woods, and in view of Zumwalt's brown-paper-bag "records"? Why, Ben-Veniste asked, were the tapes even now being kept outside the vault, in Miss Woods's office, even though she was finished transcribing them?

Buzhardt replied, "I am not sure I know the specific reason. I don't know of a specific reason except the fact we . . . or they were probably not delivered. I am sure that the President is aware we have to have access to those tapes and probably for the court procedures and they are perfectly safe there."

How wrong he was.

FOR THE REMAINDER of the tapes hearings we would be consulting closely with the independent panel of tapes experts chosen jointly by us and by the White House to test the tapes for alterations.

On a Sunday evening, we met with White House counsel and with the scientists in a large conference room in the Executive Office Building. Our dealings with the experts themselves proved to be one of our most rewarding Watergate experiences. The clarity of their thought and expression provided a welcome gust of fresh air for those of us jaded and dulled by rhetoric and evasiveness. The men who assembled in the EOB conference room that evening immediately launched into enthusiastic discussion of how to meet the challenge of determining whether the tapes they would be examining were genuine or bogus, pristine or edited. The credentials of these men were more than impressive: Richard H. Bolt, chairman of the board of Bolt, Beranek and Newman, Inc.; Franklin Cooper, president and engineering director of Haskins Laboratories; James L. Flanagan, head of the acoustics research department of Bell Laboratories; John G. McKnight, an audio and magnetic recording consultant; Thomas G. Stockham, Jr., a professor in the computer science department of the University of Utah; Mark R. Weiss, vice-president for acoustics research of the Federal Scientific Corporation.

As the evening wore on and the discussion became more and more arcane—analysis of flutter and wow, spectrographic examination, the capacity for analyzing high- and low-frequency hum—the scientists became increasingly animated and, absorbed in their own intellectual world, discontinued the simultaneous translation they had been providing for the lawyers. At one point during the discussion of "hum analysis" the tensions of the preceding weeks seemed to strike White House lawyer Leonard Garment and Ben-Veniste simultaneously. Both left the room quickly and under cover of a nearby stairwell broke into uncontrollable gales of laughter in contemplation of spending the foreseeable future trying to learn the ins and outs of flutter and wow. The membership in this stairwell asylum was quickly doubled as Carl Feldbaum from our office and Douglas Parker from the White House staff defected from the meeting. With tears of laughter streaming down his face Len Garment suggested that as reasonable lawyers we make an attempt at compromise in lieu of having to learn all this mumbo jumbo: suppose he could deliver a guilty plea from Ron Ziegler and a nolo contendere from Kissinger. Nothing doing—we wouldn't settle for less than a future draft pick for a Vice President. About five minutes later, fully composed but drained near exhaustion by laughter, the four attorneys reentered the conference room. The scientists, still debating, were oblivious to the lawyers' reentry into the world of sanity.

That week, the media had not let up on the President, headlining the disclosure of the missing Dictabelt and reviewing in their editorials the holes in the White House explanations served up during the two weeks of hearings. The Nixon credibility gap was growing geometrically. The response of Richard Nixon to his faltering position was as unsuccessful as it was predictable. He took to the South—his remaining enclave of popular support—to launch a new offensive. In one of the most unfortunate public utterances in the history of the Presidency, Richard Nixon assured the nation in a televised press conference that he was "not a crook." He was obliged to explain why he had paid less in taxes than the great "silent majority," why he had authorized a tap on his own brother's telephone and why he had been unable to produce three of the subpoenaed tapes. In answering a question about his April 1973 endorsement of Haldeman and Ehrlichman as two of the finest public servants he had ever known, the President misspoke, "I hold that both men, and others who have been charged, are guilty until I have evidence that they are not guilty." After leaving the press conference (held, appropriately, near the gates of Fantasyland at Walt Disney World), it was learned, Nixon approached a portly, balding man and a boy who were standing at a fence. "Are you the boy's mother or his grandmother?" the President asked the man. After an incredulous pause, the citizen replied that he was neither. "Of course you're not," chirped the leader of the free world, who then slapped the man's face soundly and walked off.

Less bizarre only by degree was the title given the new Nixon offensive—"Operation Candor." Under its rubric the President assured a conference of Republican governors in Memphis that there were no new "bombshell" revelations in Watergate, and that all the remaining tapes were audible. The unwary governors trumpeted their party leader's assurances, unaware that the very next day just such a bombshell would explode and that the "Nixon offensive" would be shown to be offensive only to the truth.

OF ALL THE MAJOR revelations of Watergate, the eighteen-and-a-half-minute gap must rank among the most surprising. Adding to the nation's shock that a most important portion of a conversation between Nixon and Haldeman had been rendered unintelligible were the facts which emerged about how the White House had waffled in finally disgorging the unpleasant news.

Early on the morning of Wednesday, November 21, J. Fred Buzhardt telephoned the new Special Prosecutor, Leon Jaworski, to ask if he could come up to our offices to discuss a matter of some importance. It was Buzhardt's first visit to 1425 K Street. He had a problem, a very big problem, and he wanted the Special Prosecutor's cooperation. Something had happened to a June 20, 1972, tape of a conversation between Haldeman and the President—one of the seven to be produced. For some eighteen minutes, instead of conversation there was only a buzzing noise—first low and then louder. Apparently Rose Mary Woods had caused this obliteration while the tapes were in her possession. Buzhardt had tried unsuccessfully to duplicate the sound of the buzz, experimenting with non-Presidential tapes. He could offer no innocent explanation for the obliteration.

What was worse, Haldeman's contemporaneous notes of the conversation indicated that Watergate had been discussed during the meeting; Buzhardt admitted that this conversation must have taken place on the obliterated portion of the tape. A mathematician was later to estimate that the random chance of this happening on this portion of the tapes was several million to one.

Buzhardt's audience was aghast. With all of our warnings about safeguarding the tapes, how could this have happened? At the very least, this revelation represented gross malfeasance by the President.

"How long," Leon Jaworski asked Buzhardt, measuring his words, "had you known about this before today?"

Buzhardt allowed as how he had known since he had listened to the tape for the first time on the previous Thursday (the day after the nonexistence of the Dictabelt was disclosed).

"What do you intend to do about this?" asked the Texan, sinking back into his chair.

Buzhardt said he needed time. Would Jaworski consent to a few days' delay before the news was made public, to give the White House a little more time to get its explanation straightened out?

Jaworski's eyes narrowed as he faced the President's lawyer. His response was unequivocally to the point. Either Buzhardt would go with us to inform Judge Sirica this very moment or we would go ourselves. Jaworski was not about to become the White House's partner in a cover-up of this information—not for a few days, not for an hour.

Shortly afterward, the White House lawyers, Jaworski, Ruth, Ben-Veniste and Volner met with Judge Sirica around the conference table in the windowless jury room adjacent to his courtroom. Buzhardt repeated his sorry tale, with a court reporter making a verbatim transcript. The judge, who had by this point in Watergate attained a very high threshold of surprise, shook his head sadly.

THE COURT: Then there is a lapse?
BUZHARDT: Yes. Then the circumstances are even a little worse than that, your honor.
THE COURT: I don't know how it could get much worse.
GARMENT: Just wait.

Buzhardt then explained that the gap apparently came during a discussion of Watergate.

Judge Sirica announced that in view of "what has transpired" he was asking the President to turn all the tapes over to the court on Monday—days ahead of schedule. "This is just another instance that convinces the court that it has to take some steps, not because the court doesn't trust the White House or the President, but because the court is interested in seeing that nothing else happens." Moreover, public hearings would resume on Monday to explore what had caused the eighteen-and-a-half-minute gap, rather than awaiting the experiments of the tape experts as previously planned.

On Monday, November 26, the rest of the world learned that Rose Mary Woods was the chief suspect in the eighteen-and-a-half-minute-gap caper. The President's secretary was far more subdued than in her first appearance, but now she was represented by prominent Washington attorney Charles Rhyne—an old friend and former law-school classmate of Richard Nixon's—who more than compensated for her loss of volubility. It was Rhyne's contention that Rose Mary was being served up as a sacrificial lamb—a very ambitious argument in view of the fact that Rhyne was in no way blaming Nixon for Rose Mary's plight. Instead, Rhyne attempted to cast none other than Buzhardt and Garment in the role of bad guys taking undue advantage of the "unsophisticated secretary."

Jill Volner's questioning of Rose Mary Woods took on a much more serious tone, beginning with Volner's advising the witness of her constitutional right against self-incrimination. Woods claimed that through some "terrible mistake" she had obliterated a portion of the June 20 tape while listening to it on October 1, 1973, in her office at the White House. According to Woods, her phone rang, and as she turned around to her credenza to answer it, she pushed the "record" button on the tape recorder instead of "stop." But the safety features of the tape recorder she was using were such that depressing the "record" button alone would not be enough to erase the tape— the "forward" or "rewind" button would also have to be pushed simultaneously. This, of course, could not have squared with an accidental erasure. But if the foot-pedal control, which is used by secretaries to free their hands for typing while transcribing tapes, were depressed, the tape could be erased. So, Woods testified, she must have kept her foot on the foot pedal while pushing the "record" button and while turning to answer the phone. On further probing by Volner, Woods stated that she spoke on the phone from four and a half to five minutes—she didn't think the conversation lasted eighteen and a half minutes. Coincidentally, the first portion of the hum which obliterated the conversation, a softer hum, lasted for four and a half minutes, thus setting the stage for an argument that "someone" must have come along later and erased the balance.

Volner shifted her questioning from the manner in which the gap was caused to the inconsistencies now revealed in Woods's prior testimony. How was it that if the "accident" occurred on October 1, Woods did not mention it when she first testified under oath in Judge Sirica's courtroom on November 8? On that occasion, Volner had asked her what precautions she had taken to avoid erasing the tape. Woods had snapped, "I used my head. It is the only one I had to use." In fact, the skeptical Judge Sirica specifically asked that this portion of the prior testimony be read back. Woods's explanation strained credulity as much as her stretch for the telephone with one foot on the pedal would have strained the human torso.

Woods claimed that after she hung up the phone she realized what she had done and rushed over to Nixon's office, telling her boss she was "terribly embarrassed" by her "accident." The President was most understanding, according to Woods. "He said, 'Don't worry about it, that is not one of the subpoenaed tapes. It is too bad, but don't worry about it.'" Indeed, it turned out that she had been quite forgiven: we learned to our horror that despite the June 20 tape erasure Woods had had *original* tapes in her possession as late as that very morning, November 26. How brazen could the White House get?

The explanation that she believed the tape she had erased was not one of the subpoenaed tapes provided Rose Mary's excuse for not mentioning the embarrassing mishap in her prior testimony. It was "my very first time in a courtroom and I was petrified, and I understood that we were talking about only the subpoenaed tapes. All I can say is that I'm dreadfully sorry."

The strategy for the next day centered on recreating the exact manner in which Woods claimed her mistake had been made. Volner demanded that Woods demonstrate the "Rose Mary stretch" with a Uher-500 tape machine plugged in before her on the witness stand. Woods's resulting contortion involved taking off her earphones, reaching with her left hand to depress the lighted button on the telephone, lifting the phone receiver from its distant position on her desk, mistakenly pushing the "record" instead of the "stop" button on the tape recorder with her right hand, and all the while depressing a small foot pedal with her left foot. No other combination would have caused the machine to erase the tape. Not surprisingly, in reaching for the make-believe telephone to her left Woods lifted her foot off the foot pedal, causing the tape reel to stop turning. The error in recreating error did not go unnoticed by Volner, who in true Perry Mason fashion declared, "You just picked your foot up off the pedal." All similarity to the Perry Mason script terminated abruptly, however, as Woods snapped, "That is now because I don't happen to be doing anything." Undaunted by her failure to duplicate her stretch, not to mention the deficiencies in the logic of her explanation, Rose Mary continued to contend that on October 1 she must have kept her foot on the pedal.

Our work was cut out for us after court on November 27. As implausible as Woods's testimony may have been on its face, there was more to do. We requested photographs of the scene of the erasure. Then Volner went off to the White House with the White House lawyers, Charles Rhyne and the official White House photographer. Color eight-by-ten glossies of Rose Mary doing her now famous stretch were produced for posterity. Volner made sure that nothing had been rearranged recently in Woods's office, so that the distance of the stretch was accurately portrayed in the photos. Dust marks on a telephone table provided the basis for a heated argument between Volner and Rhyne as to whether the phone had been moved. For some inexplicable reason Rhyne insisted that photographs be taken of *all* telephones in the President's office as well as in Woods's. This produced quite a surprise the next day when among the batch of photos presented to us was a color eight-by-ten glossy of the Presidential commode with its handily mounted wall phone nearby.

Back in court the next morning, Rose Mary Woods continued to insist she had not spoken on the phone more than five minutes and therefore could not have caused an eighteen-and-a-half-minute gap. The photographs of Miss Woods carried on the front page of most newspapers the next day trying to duplicate the rubberized stretch she had described in testimony over the prior two days gave great currency to the saying that a picture is worth a thousand words. The obvious anomaly of Rose Mary smiling cheerily in the photos as her sinews seemed about to snap undoubtedly made her all the more testy in response to Volner's barrage of questions. At one point, in a humanitarian effort to mitigate the acrimonious turn the dialogue had taken, Judge Sirica got himself into hot water with the Women's Liberation movement, cautioning interrogator and witness, "All right, now—we have enough problems without two ladies getting into an argument." The remark broke the tension of the moment, but later earned the judge not a little criticism.

Next to take the witness stand was Fred Buzhardt—up at bat for the second time during the hearings. The judge immediately instructed his clerk to increase the volume on the microphone in the witness box. Buzhardt had more than a little explaining to do. How could he have given Nixon the opinion that the "gap tape" had not really been subpoenaed? Even Judge Sirica, who had thus far kept his personal feelings hidden, reacted with incredulity at Buzhardt's strained explanation, which hinged on a supertechnical reading of the subpoena.

"You mean to say it took a careful reading of that paragraph to conclude that the subpoena called for the conversation of Mr. Haldeman and Mr. Ehrlichman?" asked the judge. Buzhardt's then partner Samuel Powers, it developed, had only to glance at the subpoena to determine that the Nixon-Haldeman conversation was among those to be produced.

Buzhardt was unable to provide answers to Ben-Veniste's questions as to how it was that Rose Mary Woods had been given still more original tapes to transcribe (related to another request by the Special Prosecutor) *after* Buzhardt had told General Haig that he knew of no innocent explanation for the gap, or how Nixon could have honestly stated there were no new "bombshells" since he knew of the eighteen and a half minutes of obliteration of a subpoenaed tape well before he addressed the governors' conference in Memphis. How was it that Buzhardt had not mentioned the existence of the gap during the Sunday-night convocation of the experts at the White House, but had learned through his staff what technology was available to detect tampering with the tapes? "I don't think it occurred to me at that point to advise the experts," was the best he could do.

Buzhardt left the stand pale and weary. His unhappy plight was not mitigated by the fact that even while he was testifying that day, White House spokesman Ron Ziegler was publicly expressing dissatisfaction with the White House legal team and predicting a shakeup. Confronted by the press with Ziegler's rebuke at the courthouse door, Buzhardt quietly answered, "I never pretended I was perfect."

That evening we learned that Ron Ziegler had not confined his criticism to his own team. One of the handful of former confidants still in residence at Fort Nixon, Ziegler admitted failure to find any takers for the derogatory stories he had tried to float out about the

Watergate prosecutors, and took on the task himself. Summoning moral outrage from who knows what source, Ziegler bitterly complained that while Jaworski was a "very respected and fair man," the staff which he had inherited from Professor Cox had displayed "an ingrained suspicion and visceral dislike for the President and this Administration."

Imagine the compliment we felt—the best that the President's Disneyland-trained press secretary could do was excoriate us for being *suspicious?*

The next weekend the experts began their tests on the tapes. An elaborate security system had been designed to protect the tapes received by Judge Sirica from the President. They were stored in a large safe in the judge's chambers which was constantly under surveillance by federal marshals through a remote television hookup. Only the judge and his law clerk, Todd Christofferson, had the combination to the safe, and deposits and withdrawals of tapes were meticulously documented. Whenever tapes had to be transmitted for testing at one or more of the experts' laboratories, U.S. marshals carried them in special antimagnetic containers and stayed on guard at the labs until the tapes were returned. Additionally, representatives of the Special Prosecutor's office as well as the White House were present as observers when any testing was to be done. Our representative was usually Jim Boczar, a tall, thin computer specialist who was in charge of the computerized information retrieval system we had inherited in part from the Ervin Committee. Boczar had been obliged to work at night, since access to computer time was available to us very economically in the late-night and early-morning hours. Hence Boczar's nickname "Dracula." The tape experts were also obliged to do much of their work very late at night —also because of the limited availability of special computer machinery which was needed for large segments of time. Consequently, while the White House "observer"—usually an attorney—was fast asleep in his chair dreaming of better times, Boczar was picking up very useful advance information about the results of the testing.

THE TAPES hearings resumed on December 4 with the testimony of Lawrence Higby, former aide to H. R. Haldeman. Higby, a blond, clean-cut graduate of Haldeman and Ehrlichman's alma mater, UCLA, had earned the dislike of many White House staffers to whom he had brusquely barked Haldeman's commands. There was something about this inexperienced young advertising executive, still well short of thirty years old, exhorting men quite senior to him to get on the stick, that rubbed many the wrong way. Haldeman's use of Higby as his factotum as well as go-for contributed to the rich idiom of the Nixon White House. Soon after the 1969 inauguration, when the lines of responsibility and power were sorted out, it became *de rigueur* for those with any standing at all to have their own "Higby." Thus, coffee-break gossip would often focus on whether so-and-so would be granted a Higby of his own. Higby's own assistant, naturally, was known as "Higby's Higby."

General Haig, the next witness up, proved to be the toughest customer we had to deal with in the tapes hearing. His answers were crisp and well thought out. Although he was new to the courtroom procedure, Haig's analytically trained mind kept him out in front of most of the questioning—anticipating the points to be made and tailoring his responses accordingly. Indeed, on one occasion Haig responded by saying, "I don't understand the *purpose* of your question." Ben-Veniste suggested that understanding the question was all that was normally required to answer truthfully.

The main focus of our interrogation of the highest member of the Nixon Administration aside from the President himself was to get an explanation for the relationship between the missing and altered tapes and the earlier Stennis Compromise. Through the use of logs and transcripts of other witnesses' testimony, Haig was obliged to admit that both he and the President knew that two of the subpoenaed tapes were missing and that Rose Mary Woods had obliterated a portion of another tape all before the Stennis Compromise was proposed by Nixon as a substitute for delivering the actual tapes to the grand jury. Ben-Veniste's attempt to draw Haig into an explanation of this "coincidence" was strenuously objected to by White House counsel. Judge Sirica was not inclined to have that can of worms opened; he sustained the White House objection pending a determination of whether it was "relevant and material to the issues . . . being discussed in this proceeding." As Haig was the last witness, except for the experts, the inquiry was foreclosed.

Before Haig was finally excused, however, he made a slip that haunted him for some time afterward. Ben-Veniste inquired as to whether the White House had an explanation for the discrepancy between Woods's testimony that she spoke on the telephone for only four and a half to five minutes and the fact that the tape gap lasted for eighteen. Haig responded that a "devil theory" had been formulated whereby "there had been one tone [of hum] applied by Miss Woods in accordance with her description to the President of four and a half to five minutes' gap, and then perhaps some 'sinister force' had come in and applied the other energy source and taken care of the information on that tape." With this, Judge Sirica chimed in, "Has anyone ever suggested who that sinister force might be?" Haig helpfully provided the information that only Woods and Stephen Bull had access to the tape. The headline of the always proper *New York Times* read: "Haig Says White House Suspected 'Sinister Force' Ruined Tape But Now Feels Miss Woods Is To Blame." Haig offhandedly told reporters outside the courthouse that Woods probably miscalculated the length of her telephone conversation—"I've known women that think they've talked for five minutes and have talked an hour." Judge Sirica had been replaced as target for the Watergate Women's Liberation ire.

The final phase of the tapes hearing, the report of the expert panel, brought responsibility for the eighteen-and-a-half-minute gap to Nixon's doorstep. The experts had worked long and hard, some refusing compensation, to reach their conclusions. In a large sense they had created a new technology, synthesized from their varied specialties, in the course of their development of tests and procedures to detect the possibility of tampering with magnetic tape recordings. The expert panel had functioned as an orderly team, delegating different tests among themselves and convening in various parts of the country for the purpose of conducting tests as a group and discussing the meaning of their findings.

Some of the equipment employed by the experts was so sophisticated it boggled the minds of the lawyers. For example, a machine invented by one of the experts, Mark Weiss, called the "coherent spectrum shaper," happened to be the best available device for removing distortion from the tapes in order to enhance the intelligibility of the conversations. Unfortunately, only one coherent spectrum shaper existed in the world, and it was nestled in the bosom of the CIA, for whom it was designed. With remarkable alacrity, the CIA responded to a request by Judge Sirica to borrow the device for use by its inventor. Such was the power of the federal judge that the CIA delivered it to the courthouse with no more fanfare than if it had been a borrowed cup of sugar.

The reunion of Weiss and his brilliant assistant, Ernest Aschkenasy, with their brainchild, the coherent spectrum shaper, was something to behold. They cooed over its circuits and tubes, setting it up in the jury room next to the judge's courtroom. Judge Sirica came in for a look at Weiss's darling, approaching the gizmo with considerable deference. The tapes would be run through the machine (which needed twelve hours just to warm up) and copied around the clock until the task was completed.

Boczar and White House lawyer Richard Hauser were to keep Ernie Aschkenasy company during the all-night vigils in the deserted courthouse. Aschkenasy, a squat, bearded ball of energy, donning the ever present skullcap worn by the most observant branch of the Jewish faith, occupied one of his midnight breaks mimicking witnesses from the tapes hearing, scrabbling about the courtroom to make arcane points on the blackboard, while Hauser examined from the lectern and Boczar solemnly presided from the judge's chair. Early the next morning, Judge Sirica, a very early riser, greeted the trio. Aschkenasy asked the judge if there were a quiet place where he could chant his morning prayers. Judge Sirica immediately invited the scientist to use his private chambers. As the judge looked on with curiosity, Aschkenasy removed his prayer shawl and phylacteries from a small leather pouch and, winding the latter around his left arm and his forehead in the ancient manner, began his morning devotions. Each of the succeeding mornings during the tape enhancement process, Judge Sirica would greet Aschkenasy warmly and invite him in for the morning prayer session.

The release of the experts' report on January 15, 1974, produced a shock wave which swept across the nation, further eroding the remaining enclaves of support for the President. The report demolished the explanation provided by Rose Mary Woods as to how all or part of the eighteen-and-a-half-minute gap had been caused. The conclusion dictated by the experts' findings was simple: either Woods was lying or someone, without her knowledge, had come along after her "accident" and deliberately erased the tape.

The amount of information the experts were able to glean from the June 20 tape was nothing short of astonishing. First of all, through the use of specialized digital computers and by a process of "developing" magnetic tapes (invented in the course of the investigation by the panel members), they were able to determine that magnetic "signatures" which appeared on the tape were caused by the *hand operation* of the recorder's keyboard—not by the foot pedal, which produced different signatures—and that the eighteen-and-a-half-minute obliteration was caused by *at least five* distinct segments of erasure. This finding was totally at odds with the suggestion that the gap was caused by the scatterbrained actions of a confused secretary who kept her foot on the *pedal* continuously for eighteen and a half minutes while gabbing on the telephone. Further, the cautious panel could say "almost surely" that the same Uher-500 tape recorder used by Woods at the White House was the one on which the gap was caused. Lest there be any doubt about it, the panel was able to conclude that the obliterated portion originally contained human speech, and that it was impossible to "recover" the speech which had once been on that segment of the tape.

The latest "bombshell" was detonated just at the moment President Nixon's new special counsel, James D. St. Clair, arrived on the scene. Hopes that the highly respected St. Clair would be able to shake the experts (who were, after all, the product of joint selection by the Special Prosecutor and the White House) from their conclusions went unrealized.

While the experts would not go so far as to state that the erasure was a deliberate act, they did agree with Ben-Veniste's analysis that their findings were "consistent" with the concept of someone trying to erase a certain portion of a tape by repeatedly listening for a while, rewinding, erasing and rewinding again. Put another way, if the eighteen-and-a-half-minute gap had been caused *accidentally*, the same "accident" would have had to be repeated five times. St. Clair quickly learned during cross-examination that he was in deep water trying to challenge the experts. Not only were they among the most brilliant in their respective disciplines, but the experts, many of whom were teachers, proved to be extremely articulate and well able to fend for themselves on the witness stand. For example, St. Clair questioned whether fragments of admittedly unintelligible human speech could be detected through three separate "windows" in the obliterating hum in the eighteen-and-a-half-minute segment. Each of the "windows" (which were all less than three quarters of a second in length) occurred at a spot on the tape missed by the "erase head" of the recorder when it began erasing one of the five segments; the experts claimed they could determine the existence of human speech in the windows by use of spectrographic analysis and the human ear. Thomas Stockham, the digital-computer expert and professor at the University of Utah, answered St. Clair's question with a loud and staccato "You bet." He then pointed out to St. Clair that it had taken him less than *half* a second to utter these words. Stockham, dressed in a blue blazer and modishly flared plaid bell-bottom trousers, was clearly in control. St. Clair, having in mind Woods's testimony about the foot pedal, challenged Stockham on whether it was not possible for the erasure to have been caused by something other than a finger pushing a button. "Perhaps with a stick," was the response. St. Clair soon had had enough.

The impact of the experts' findings was so overwhelming that it obscured new developments in the tapes mystery: gaps in two other Presidential Dictabelts. In the case of each of the Dictabelts, including a recording of Mr. Nixon's contemporaneous recollection of his March 21, 1973, meeting with John Dean, the voice trailed off in mid-sentence. J. Fred Buzhardt attributed these gaps to the President's lack of skill in operating his Dictaphone.

Reaction to the panel's report was particularly damaging to the President among the leaders of his own party. Typical was the articulate response of Representative John B. Anderson of Illinois, leader of the House Republican Conference, who saw the latest development "as approaching the final denouement in this drama." Anderson said, "This is the most serious single bit of evidence to date. The theory that there has been a conscious effort to conceal evidence is no longer a theory." He described the report of the tape panel as the "penultimate link in the chain of evidence that has steadily been forged to show that there has been a conscious deliberate effort . . . to obstruct justice." The ultimate link, he said, would be to show that this obstruction was directly ordered by the White House. "Not only was the tape doctored deliberately, but it probably occurred on the machine that Miss Woods used." Certainly a very limited number of people in the White House would have had access to that machine.

Republican Senator William E. Brock III of Tennessee likened the release of the report to waiting for another shoe to drop, and added, "I don't know how many shoes there are to fall. I feel like I've been dealing with a centipede this last year." Conservative columnist George

F. Will, in an article entitled "End of the Nixon Administration," wrote that the scientists' conclusions had moved the Watergate affair from the "White Queen stage," in which the White Queen had bragged to Alice that she could believe six impossible things before breakfast, into the "impeachment stage"—because now "we *know* that there is corruption in the precincts of the Oval Office."

The Nixon loyalists were tepid, at best, in their defense. Vice President Gerald R. Ford said through a spokesman, "This is a technical and confusing matter about which I have no personal knowledge. Therefore I have no comment on it."

We had indeed come a great distance in the period of two and a half months since Fred Buzhardt assured us that any questions about the tapes would be answered by one witness, Ray Zumwalt, the Secret Service technician.

On January 18, 1974, Judge Sirica made the decision to refer the matter to the grand jury for further investigation. The grand jury, which turned up little significant information beyond what had been developed in the court hearings, did not return an indictment connected with the eighteen-and-a-half-minute gap, nor did we recommend that it do so. Similarly, the House Judiciary Committee, which months later conducted its own investigation, was unable to lay the blame for the gap on any one individual.

The cast of plausible suspects for deliberate erasure of the tape had been narrowed to a few—much like the murder mystery where the lights go out in a locked room, someone is murdered, and each of the persons remaining has a motive to kill the victim but swears later that he didn't do it and doesn't know who did. A less conservative prosecutor's office might have recommended indictment on the basis of abundant circumstantial evidence. Ours did not.

CHAPTER **8** **Archie's Orphans Meet the Silver Fox: Jaworski Arrives**

To SAY THAT WE HAD very little confidence in our new boss, Leon Jaworski, on the day he was sworn in would be putting it mildly. To us, Jaworski represented no less than the man President Nixon had procured to perpetrate the biggest fix of all time. Sure, the President had acquiesced in getting himself another Special Prosecutor—when public opinion and the Congress threatened to force one on him by legislation. Our office was still alive not because of any Nixon commitment to a continued investigation but only because of Nixon's apparent blunder in not firing us all—and because of the firestorm that followed the Saturday Night Massacre. For good reason, we put no stock in the Administration's assurances that our investigation would be accorded continued "independence."

On October 26, only three days after he changed his mind about the tapes, the President announced that Acting Attorney General Bork would appoint a new Special Prosecutor. The new man, the President said, hopefully would "bring Watergate to an expeditious conclusion." In the same breath the President also allowed as how the new appointee would *not* receive any Presidential tapes or documents. That would not be "necessary," he said, because if the problem arose he was sure he could work out a compromise with his new Special Prosecutor. The President then had the gall to cite the by then thoroughly discredited Stennis Compromise as a "reasonable" example.

By this time, the Senate was already considering a bill that would authorize the federal courts to appoint their own special prosecutor to conduct the Watergate investigation. The bill acquired the sponsorship of fifty-five senators. For the President, getting a puppet to replace Cox was obviously preferable to having someone appointed by, say, Judge Sirica and endowed with total independence by congressional fiat. In mid-December congressional efforts to pass a special-prosecutor bill eventually bogged down: senators could not agree on a single approach that would survive a Presidential veto. Some judges opposed a court-appointed prosecutor, too, and Leon Jaworski, who was by then on the scene, pledged his independence to the legislators. But the Senate threat had done its job.

We knew that if the President found some hack willing to take the Special Prosecutor's job on the President's own terms, i.e., on terms Cox had rejected, that would be the end of any vigorous investigation. The new "Nixon man" would put each of us on a spot because sooner or later we would have to resign rather than continue to be part of a throttled prosecution. What we were hoping was that no responsible person could be found who would be willing to undertake the task given the guidelines the President had apparently laid down.

Our fears were strengthened when Alexander Haig promised a few days after Nixon's press conference that the new Special Prosecutor would not be required to "pledge" to refrain from seeking Nixon's tapes. The public welcomed this as a relaxation of the President's position. We saw it as camouflage: The President had realized that if his puppet looked like a puppet, the public would not be satisfied. Of course Nixon's new Special Prosecutor wouldn't have to "pledge" not to subpoena tapes. The President would find an appointee who had no *desire* to go after Presidential evidence in the first place.

Besides, something more than another warm body to fill the office of Special Prosecutor was needed to restore momentum to our investigation. Only a new appointee willing to demonstrate his independence to the public actively and aggressively was going to be able to do that. Even before the Massacre, the problem of getting leverage on potential witnesses had been complicated by the possibility that when the chips were down the President would quash prosecution of his closest associates. The Massacre proved that the President was willing to incur dire risks to himself before letting the prosecutors get too near pay dirt. If he had done it once, he could do it again—to protect others as well as himself.

Prosecutors are ordinarily said to represent "the government," but we appeared to have the power of the Executive, the Nixon government, arrayed against us. Nixon's former aides could now even more confidently discount the long-range chances of successful prosecutions ever being mounted against them. As long as we seemed to be on the losing side of the political battle, there was no incentive for anyone to cooperate with us. So we needed a new Special Prosecutor who would make plain right off the bat his zeal, his independence, his intention to see Cox's effort through to the end. It seemed unlikely, to say the least, that the President would seek out and appoint such a person.

On November 1, the President announced that Leon Jaworski had been selected as the new Special Prosecutor. The same day, Bork told the press that the President had given Jaworski "personal assurances" of independence. Bork said that Jaworski would have the same mandate as Cox and that if Jaworski decided to seek Presidential documents there would be "no restrictions placed on his freedom." Coming from the man who had fired Cox when his two superiors thought such an act violative of basic personal and jurisprudential principles, Bork's statement did little to reassure us.

That Jaworski was a Democrat and had an impressive list of credentials made things worse. We reasoned that the President would hardly have appointed Jaworski unless Leon had agreed to play by Nixon's rules. It was a bad omen that the President was able to snag such a prestigious person to play the role of fixer.

Chesterfield Smith, then president of the American Bar Association and a close friend of Jaworski, echoed our thoughts when he announced on November 2 that he still favored a court-appointed prosecutor. In spite of his friendship and respect for Jaworski, Smith said, the "appearance of justice" required a more independent prosecutor.

There were personal, psychological ingredients in our skepticism about Jaworski, too, that arose out of the divergence in age and background between us and the new Special Prosecutor. Though the Cox staff represented a much more diverse set of attitudes than was generally realized, the universe that encompassed our backgrounds was quite different from that of Leon Jaworski. Most of us had gone to school and worked in the East, New York and Washington, often in government rather than in the private sector. Most had what the press would call "liberal" attitudes toward law enforcement and the criminal-justice system. Jaworski's impressive legal credentials—the same credentials that made him a popular public choice—gave us pause.

They were centered in a different personal and professional universe. Some said Jaworski was a wheeler-dealer. It was clear, in any event, that he was a skillful politician. He had made his way to the top in the councils of the private bar: a highly structured, unforgiving atmosphere where you had to be able to see behind you without turning your head. Jaworski had conservative views about politics and the law. He was the leading light in one of the two most prominent Texas law firms. (The other was John B. Connally's firm.) His culture, his experience, his instincts were substantially different from ours.

In fact Jaworski's background augured more than we gave him credit for. A minister's son from Waco, Texas, he had been an early achiever, winning a law degree from Baylor University at the age of nineteen and a graduate law degree from George Washington University in Washington, D.C. (As it turned out, Jaworski had lived with several fellow students during that year in Washington in a house just across the street from our offices at 1425 K Street, and he later recounted to us his many fond memories of the time he spent there.) Jaworski made his reputation as a trial lawyer in Texas and eventually rose to become president of the American Bar Association. In between, however, he had put in a stint as a legal officer at the Nuremberg war crimes trials, an experience that made a significant impression upon him. In 1960, Jaworski represented Senator Lyndon Baines Johnson in a lawsuit against Johnson to prevent him from simultaneously running for Vice President and for reelection as senator from Texas. Characteristically, Jaworski won. He went on to become a close adviser and confidant of LBJ during the 1960s. Jaworski served on both the President's Commission on Violence and the important Commission on Law Enforcement and the Administration of Criminal Justice. On both panels, he displayed outspoken conservative, minority views. In 1962, however, at LBJ's urging, Jaworski had agreed to serve as a special federal attorney to prosecute Governor Ross Barnett of Mississippi on charges of defying a federal court order integrating the state university. Jaworksi had performed admirably an assignment that he must have known would win him few friends among his natural constituency.

One thing we had heard about Leon Jaworski gave us hope. He was said to be a man of considerable personal pride and ego, with a tangible patriotic belief in service to his country. Jaworski seemed to be a man who had already achieved all the success one could desire within his profession and evidently had no future political ambitions. Once he was involved in the professional challenge of the Watergate investigation, perhaps his pride and patriotism would compel him to see the job through in a fashion in which both he and the country could be proud.

When Jaworski's appointment as Special Prosecutor was confirmed by the Senate on November 5, he came immediately to our offices at 1425 K Street and addressed the entire staff, secretaries and clerks as well as lawyers, in the central file room, the only place big enough for an "office meeting." His debut was not auspicious.

A hush fell over the room as Jaworski entered, bulky in a dark suit and white shirt. His white hair reaffirmed his establishment credentials, the florid complexion and bulbous nose were something of a surprise. The atmosphere was sullen as he made his pitch. We figured the burden was on him to convince us that he intended to be his own man rather than the President's puppet. And the burden was a damn heavy one. We were feeling like martyrs: forlorn and alone. We were Archie's orphans.

Instead of wooing us, however, Jaworski issued what amounted to a challenge. He began by telling us, as he had the Congress, that he had been guaranteed complete independence. There would be "no restraints" on him. He noted that he had originally been approached for the job in May of 1973 but refused it at that time because he did not feel that enough independence was assured. Now he had won a pledge that he could not be fired without the concurrence of a substantial majority of a group of eight bipartisan congressional leaders. He intended, he said, to obtain whatever evidence was needed for the investigation. (Left unsaid was whether he would be willing to subpoena more tapes if the President refused to supply them. One staffer asked him that question point-blank. Jaworski answered affirmatively, but the fact that he had not brought the matter up himself worried us.) To stress his personal independence of the President, Jaworski mentioned that Nixon had asked to meet with him but he had refused, preferring to deal instead with Alexander Haig.

Jaworski went on to say that he had been told by White House people that some of the assistant prosecutors were out to get the President and were not acting professionally—that they should be fired. But, Jaworski said, he had replied that he alone would make that determination. For the time being, he was asking everyone to stay. He wanted to meet and get to know each of us. He had talked with Cox and had been told of our abilities and dedication. He had the highest respect for Cox. Jaworski wanted to make it clear that he expected the highest professionalism from each of us.

A good number of the staff went away from the meeting muttering. Jaworski had put the burden on *us* to prove we were proceeding in a professional manner. "I'm thinking of keeping you fellows around," he had said, in effect, "don't screw up." We had just spent five months proving our professionalism, only to have the President do us in with a political coup. We didn't feel obliged to justify *our* abilities to this interloper from the Texas establishment.

Instead of saying anything, Jaworski should have cited the much abused Nixon maxim "Watch what I do, not what I say." Within just a few weeks, Jaworski made believers out of us. After discussions with each of the task force leaders about the status of the various investigations ongoing in the office, Jaworski made it plain that each task force would continue to make everyday decisions. The second day on the job, Jaworski made his first formal request to the White House for documents in a letter requesting certain files dealing with the ITT investigation. The following day he addressed another letter to the White House requesting Plumbers documents. And a week later, on November 25, he signed a request proposed by the Watergate Task Force asking for tapes of certain conversations between the President and Charles Colson that had taken place in January of 1973. The testimony of John Dean, corroborated by considerable circumstantial evidence from meeting logs and diaries, suggested that in these meetings Colson had approached the President about making assurances of executive clemency to Howard Hunt at a time when those involved in the cover-up wanted Hunt to plead guilty in the Watergate bugging trial.

When very little was forthcoming from the White House in response to his initial requests, Jaworski scheduled a meeting with Alexander Haig and Fred Buzhardt at the White House on November 13. At the meeting, he stressed that prompt action was important to keep the grand juries on schedule. On November 19, Jaworski sent a letter reiterating requests for all the documents and tapes already requested by our office under Cox. The tone of his letter went beyond anything Cox had written to the White House. Jaworski said that the White

House foot-dragging was "delaying and in some cases *impeding* our investigations." Jaworski demanded a prompt timetable for decisions by the White House on whether to comply. The message was clear both to the staff and to the White House: Jaworski meant business. He wasn't going to be horsed around. The language itself was the kind lawyers use when they want to make a record for the future. The President at that time was calling for a quick conclusion to Watergate investigations. Jaworski was saying: If there's delay, let it be on *your* head.

The firmness of Jaworski's letter produced a quick response from Buzhardt, saying that some of the material would indeed be produced, but pleading the pressure of time. Jaworski was unrelenting. He fired back a letter saying that "unequivocal response" to our remaining requests "should be forthcoming in another week or ten days."

In the next week, more requests were made. No tapes were forthcoming from the White House, despite their previous willingness to provide a few that we had asked for. On December 6, Jaworski took another bold step. He wrote that certain materials, including tapes and documents relating to the Plumbers and to the milk price support scandal, were needed immediately and that if they were not forthcoming within a few days we would subpoena them. In effect, Jaworski was committing himself to go the full mile, to do what Cox had been fired for doing.

Two days later, the White House produced eight tapes relating to ITT, milk prices and the Plumbers. Other material was also forthcoming. Not only had Jaworski gone to the wall for the integrity of our investigations, he had won. The President, obviously, was not in a position to claim that Jaworski was "out to get him" only a month after he had appointed him. That would have been suicidal. On December 13, Jaworski could write Senator James O. Eastland, chairman of the Senate Judiciary Committee, that the White House had manifested "significant cooperation" with him.

The Special Prosecutor's aggressive stand on Presidential tapes and documents heartened us. So did his support of the task force in pressing the White House during the tapes hearings in Judge Sirica's courtroom. By that time the nonexistence of two subpoenaed tapes had come to light, and the eighteen-and-a-half-minute gap. Jaworski supported Ben-Veniste's conduct of the hearings down the line, despite the obvious embarrassment they were causing the White House. Sometimes Leon even seemed to enjoy them a bit. As a trial lawyer, he could appreciate a good scrap.

The new Special Prosecutor also surprised us by according the task force almost total autonomy in the management of our continuing grand-jury investigation. In fact, he exercised quite a bit less supervision than had Cox. He wanted an overall picture of what we were doing, and he wanted to be consulted on major decisions. Otherwise, it was our investigation. Jaworski viewed his own role as that of policy-maker and representative of the investigation to the White House, the Congress and other institutions. The fact that Jaworski seemed to manifest confidence in *our* judgment was certainly encouraging.

There was another thing that surprised and impressed us. Contrary to everyone's expectations, Jaworski brought no one with him from Texas or elsewhere as a personal aide or adviser, nor did he hire any new prosecutors. He did not even bring his own secretary. He just moved into Cox's austere office and picked up the entire administrative superstructure already in place. Given our age, our backgrounds, and what must have been some suspicion of our bona fides on Jaworski's part, this seemed to us a particularly courageous approach, one that demonstrated his good faith toward us in deed as well as in word. Even Cox, when first appointed, had turned first to close friends and associates from Harvard Law School for help. Probably Jaworski's decision to go it alone with the entire Cox staff was a result of his own considerable self-confidence. As Special Prosecutor he, of course, controlled all the important decisions. Yet it was a symbol that meant a great deal to us.

Of course, the town-meeting days of the Cox period were gone. Archie had encouraged open, even rambunctious argument about every issue; no one's opinions were excluded. Any staff member not satisfied with the opportunities presented by numerous staff meetings could walk into Cox's office and take up a problem or an issue. The feeling of inclusiveness had been a major factor in making the office under Cox an enjoyable place to work in, giving the younger staffers team spirit and a sky-high feeling of morale.

Jaworski's style was cooler, more formal, and more private. He was most comfortable in one-to-one conversations. Yet he was available to the task force. Jaworski and Ben-Veniste had a cordial, if wary, relationship despite differences in style and personality. Moreover, Jaworski had given our task force so much independence that we were making almost all of our own decisions anyway.

If it was hard at first for us to get comfortable with the idea of Leon Jaworski as new Special Prosecutor, it must have been at least as difficult for him to adapt to the Cox staff. Our allegiance really belonged to his predecessor. Certainly, in style and demeanor we were different from anything he had ever encountered. In the rigid atmosphere of big Houston law firms, we were told, a patriarch like Jaworski need have personal contact only with a few senior partners on the one hand and God on the other. Certainly Jaworski was unaccustomed to having junior attorneys display anything but the greatest deference. We heard that on Saturdays associates and junior partners in Jaworski's Texas firm were granted the dispensation of wearing bright-colored sport coats and ties to the office rather than business suits, in order to be prepared for an afternoon at the golf club or at cocktail parties. At the Watergate Special Prosecution Force, nearly all the line attorneys were in their late twenties and early thirties. On Saturdays, we had often gathered in Cox's office in blue jeans, T-shirts and tennis shoes to have an informal go-round. In these interchanges, practical experience and good sense counted far more than age and seniority. Jaworski was undoubtedly more comfortable dealing individually with the older and more senior people in the office than with a gaggle of irreverent young prosecutors. If Jaworski was taken aback by our informality, he never displayed the slightest visible reaction.

As tolerant as he was with his inherited staff, the staid Texan drew the line with the ever-experimenting personnel czar, Dan Mann. In response to Jaworski's need for a personal driver, Mann suggested that it was well past time for the federal government to accord homosexuals equal employment opportunities. He had just the fellow in mind to be Jaworski's chauffeur. One can merely speculate what ran through Leon Jaworski's mind at this point, but he was seen still shaking his head days later.

As it turned out, Leon was a delightful and skilled raconteur who enjoyed entertaining the younger prosecutors with stories about his own experiences that only occasionally seemed designed to make a salient point about our investigatory problems. He rather appeared to relish his new audience, particularly in the late afternoons when he could begin to relax from a long day.

The one significant policy disagreement between Jaworski and the Watergate Task Force during these first months illustrates the positive working relationship that had developed. The White House refused to supply us with the requested Colson-Nixon tapes from January 1973, claiming they had no relevance to Watergate. The task force pressed Jaworski on this matter, taking the firm position that such assurances were not enough. The Colson-Nixon conversations went to the heart of the President's involvement in Watergate. Any discussion of clemency during those meetings would tie the President directly to the cover-up. We simply could not take the White House's word for his innocence.

Jaworski accepted our position and went back to the White House. The President, however, was adamant: these tapes involved highly sensitive national-security material and would not be produced. The President would, however, permit Jaworski to come to the White House and listen to these tapes—*alone*. Neither his deputy, Henry Ruth, nor the head of the Watergate investigation, Ben-Veniste, would be permitted to hear them.

Right away, we smelled a rat. We argued to the Special Prosecutor that this was not a rational response and would set a very bad precedent. We should not accept. At least three people should listen. Jaworski was willing to hear us out, and in meetings with several task force attorneys the point was vigorously argued. At these meetings, everyone was permitted to speak his piece and to challenge Jaworski's approach. In the end, he did not agree with us. The White House had made a fair offer, he said, and we should accept and see what was on the tapes. If anything seemed fishy, we could consider what to do next.

Jaworski did listen to the tapes alone and reported back to us that the President was correct in his claims that Watergate was not discussed on them. The tapes contained no real "national-security" material, however, but only a disgusting display of uncontrolled backbiting by the President and Colson regarding other White House aides of the highest rank. The tone of the tapes had obviously pained Jaworski greatly. He was tremendously disillusioned with both Nixon and Colson. Some of us were still unsatisfied and even suspicious about these tapes. But the Special Prosecutor had won access for himself and had considered our views before deciding to accept the White House offer. We had no right to expect anything more.

When it became apparent that Jaworski's independence was going to be a thorn in the President's side, White House aides stepped up their attacks on the investigation by criticizing the staff to Jaworski. The Special Prosecutor relayed a few of these complaints, which came primarily from Alexander Haig, to us. The Watergate Task Force and Ben-Veniste in particular came in for some harsh words from Haig, who told Jaworski that his staff was biased and should be disciplined or fired. Jaworski repeated to us on a number of occasions that he had rebuffed this criticism and supported us.

In retrospect, the President's decision to fire Cox may have been one of the worst in a series of bad decisions made by Richard Nixon in Watergate. Until the Saturday Night Massacre, Cox's cautious approach to investigating the President, his deference to the office of the Presidency and his determination to lean over backward to be fair to Nixon had combined to give the President a much better shake than he deserved.

In Leon Jaworski, the President thought he had found a more sympathetic and politically compatible Special Prosecutor. Jaworski did bring to the job many of the same attitudes of restraint and institutional deference Cox had displayed. With a Texas background, Jaworski was just as conscious as Cox of the public's deep-seated respect for the office of the Presidency and was perhaps more determined than Cox not to be too far out ahead of public opinion. But Jaworski was also a courtroom lawyer, a skilled politician in his own right and an eminently practical man who savored the smells and sounds of the arena. Jaworski did not like to be threatened or intimidated. In his experience, the best way to deal with those who attack you was to counterattack. True, Jaworski was consistently reluctant to move against the President. But when he had pondered his course in the privacy of his own mind and made a decision, he was ready for bold action—he wanted to move in the most effective way, and he wanted to move quickly. The weighing and reweighing of the ultimate fairness of what he was about to do was not his style. For the greatest gut fight of his career, President Nixon made the mistake of choosing as an opponent a first-class gut-fighter. It was a decision that he came to regret deeply.

All in all, as we neared the end of 1973, our spirits had once again been raised. The grand-jury investigation was proceeding apace.

Jaworski was giving us our head in the investigation and tapes hearings, and support in the quest for White House evidence. And we had some dynamite evidence in the tapes.* The same things that had made us wary of Jaworski—his prominence in the private bar, his Texas-establishment background and so on—gave him a great deal of credibility with the public. He had proven he had the clout to win evidentiary battles with the White House. Once we got the tapes subpoenaed by the grand jury, it became obvious that another battle with the White House—this one for higher stakes—was going to be inevitable.

* See Chapter 9.

CHAPTER **9** **Cancer on the Presidency**

FOR SEVEN WEEKS after Charles Alan Wright's startling courtroom announcement that the President would turn over the tapes subpoenaed by the grand jury we waited patiently for the President's decision to bear fruit. In early November the White House submitted to Judge Sirica original recordings of seven of the nine subpoenaed conversations. (The other two, allegedly never recorded, had become the object of the tapes hearings in the judge's courtroom.) Copies of the originals were made and the tapes were then deposited in a safe in Judge Sirica's private office under an elaborate closed-circuit-television security system.

Pursuant to the procedures laid down by the Court of Appeals in its tapes decision, White House counsel submitted to Judge Sirica written claims that certain portions of the tapes were unrelated to Watergate and therefore should not be turned over to us. Using copies rather than originals, the judge and his law clerk reviewed all of the tapes and ruled one by one on the President's claims, sustaining some and rejecting others. Copies of the tapes with irrelevant portions excised would then be given to the prosecutors for presentation to the grand jury.

Finally, on December 12, the first tapes were delivered to our offices. By virtue of his work with the tapes experts selected to test the eighteen-and-a-half-minute gap, Carl Feldbaum, Hank Ruth's assistant, was designated the "tapes impresario" of the Special Prosecutor's office. He was given charge of a file safe in the Special Prosecutor's office where our copies of the tapes were kept at all times. When one of the Watergate Task Force prosecutors wanted to use a tape he would find Carl and check out the tape from the front office, signing his name and the time. Later the tape would be returned to Carl and signed back into its secure resting place in the safe.

On that first afternoon Feldbaum brought several ordinary-looking reels of Scotch open-reel recording tape direct from the courthouse to Ben-Veniste's office. A battered and ancient Tandberg tape recorder was placed on top of a pile of papers on the desk. The door was firmly shut, and six of us squeezed into the modest-sized office to hear what President Nixon's taping system had wrought.

One of the tapes released to us by Judge Sirica was that of the March 21, 1973, meeting between Dean and the President, the "cancer on the Presidency" meeting. That was the one we wanted to hear first. There was some fumbling with the tape machine. Although the "record" button had been disabled to eliminate any possibility of accidental erasure—a procedure we fervently wished had been followed elsewhere—we were still nervous about handling the thing. With the exception of the judge and his law clerk nobody outside the White House had ever heard anything like what we were about to hear.

Some of us donned headsets that were plugged into the recorder, Feldbaum pushed the "play" button, and we were off to the Oval Office. After some banging of doors and scraping of chairs we heard the instantly recognizable voice of John Dean. Just as he had recounted it six months earlier to the Ervin Committee, Dean launched into his "cancer on the Presidency" speech.

The recording was of unfortunately poor quality in many places. Only later would we obtain better copies approximating the audio quality of the originals, and still later a "second generation" of tapes processed by computers to eliminate background noise. Nevertheless, a good deal of the conversation could be made out clearly. Dean's voice was almost always sharp, with a well-modulated nasal timbre. Listening to him on tape was exactly like debriefing him in person, as Frampton had been doing in our offices for the past two weeks. As we listened to more tapes we would discover that due to the placement of the microphones in the President's Oval Office desk the voices of those talking to the President were always more distinct than the President's voice. The President's speech was more difficult to distinguish. The pitch of his voice was lower and he sometimes mumbled and ran his words together.

What were we listening for? Dean had testified that on March 21 he laid out the cover-up for the President in great detail, making no bones about the illegality of what had been done and the White

House involvement in it. In subsequent public statements, President Nixon had disputed Dean's version. The President had told the public that when Dean briefed him on March 21 it was the first time he had had any inkling of the cover-up. He was "surprised and shocked," he had claimed. Would the tape bear him out?

Dean had also testified that he told the President about the distribution of hundreds of thousands of dollars in cash for hush money and warned him—citing a recent demand by Howard Hunt for $120,000 —that continuing the cover-up would require much more of the same. In one of his March conversations with the President, Dean had testified, Nixon wanted to know how much the continued payment of hush money would cost over the next few years. Dean estimated it might cost a million dollars. The President responded, according to Dean, that that was "not a problem." Dean's testimony on this point had over recent months become the subject of a raging controversy central to President Nixon's repeated claims of innocence in Watergate. Haldeman had told the Ervin Committee in July that on the basis of his review of the March 21 tape the substance of this exchange was quite different from the way it was portrayed by Dean. What actually happened, Haldeman had testified, was that when Dean mentioned a million dollars the President responded, "There is no problem in raising a million dollars, we can do that, *but it would be wrong.*" Our ears were tuned to catch this tiny segment of the conversation: would the tape vindicate Dean, or would it support the President's and Haldeman's version?

As we listened, we heard John Dean lay out for the President of the United States coldly and articulately chapter and verse of the greatest governmental scandal in American history. Seemingly discomfited at first, Dean gained confidence as he went along, picking up one thread after another. Little of importance was left out. With a few minor changes it was like hearing a fifteen-minute summary of our case. The crimes came spilling out, one on top of another.

And the President: at first he seemed to be taking it all in. There wasn't much of a reaction from him at all. But as Dean began to pick up speed, pointing out the vulnerable points in the cover-up and the potential criminal liabilities, Nixon began calmly to interject comments of his own. Hunt could possibly implicate Colson, Dean remarked. The President, unaware of a 1970 change in the federal perjury statute which abolished the "two-witness rule," said, "Hunt isn't enough; takes two, doesn't it?" Dean noted that before the election he had worked on a theory of "containment" of the federal criminal investigation. The President: "Sure." Dean described the hush-money operation. The President: "They put that under cover of the Cuban Committee . . . I would certainly keep that cover, for whatever it's worth, don't you agree?" But Dean expressed concern about the money payments. The President: "I think you should handle that one pretty well." Dean said that Krogh had perjured himself. Nixon: "Perjury's an awful hard rap to prove." Dean concluded that he himself had been involved in a criminal obstruction of justice. The President: "It could be cut off at the pass," and later, "I think we can handle that." The problem of defendants' demands for more hush money. Nixon: "Let me put it frankly, I wonder if that doesn't have to be continued." And finally, if Haldeman and others were indicted? The President: "We just better then try to tough it through."

It almost seemed as if the President were trying to soothe Dean, make this jumpy young fellow realize that there was no need to get upset. The President was calm, calculating, bloodless.

We were stunned. Even now it is impossible to describe the depth of our reactions that afternoon. We held no brief for Richard Nixon. President or not, he had set out to destroy our investigation and he was our adversary in the struggle to vindicate it. Yet emotionally we were not unmoved by the prestige of the Presidency, its mythic power. We may have been part of the cynical generation of the sixties, but we began our education in the fifties. We learned that when the President of the United States met in the White House Oval Office with his closest advisers this was the most important policy-making forum in the world. And on that December afternoon in 1973 when we donned headsets to eavesdrop on that forum we did so with a sense of awe.

What we were hearing was a violation of all those deeply embedded emotions. It wasn't so much the substance of the conversation that was shocking as its flavor. There wasn't any moral framework lurking here; there weren't even any moral overtones. This was the amoral intercourse of political technicians. Dean, the more farsighted technician, saw the inevitable denouement. Gently, he was urging the President to cut his losses while he could. Nixon, the canny old politician, was the obtuse technician; he could not relate to Dean's message. Dean had told us that in the days after June 17, 1972, the cover-up was never planned, it was just "assumed." On the March

21 tape the conversation never touched the question of whether the cover-up *should* go on. It was just assumed that a cover-up had been inevitable up until that time. Despite difficulties ahead, it must in one way or another be continued.

Early in the tape Dean mentioned the million dollars. The President responded, "We could get that. . . . On the money, you need the money . . . My point is, you can get a million dollars and you can get it in cash. I know where it could be got. I mean, it's not easy, but it could be done. But the question is, who the hell would *handle* it? Any ideas on that?"

So Dean had been right. The President echoed the sentiment about the million dollars time and time again. In fact, he kept breaking away from other topics of conversation to return to it: "We could get the money. There is no problem in that. We can't provide the clemency. The money can be provided. Mitchell could provide the way to deliver it. That could be done. See what I mean?"

When Haldeman entered the meeting, about halfway through the tape, the three continued to discuss the problems that would be involved in continuing to make hush-money payments. Nobody suggested it would be "wrong" to do it. Dean, however, cautioned the President that continued payments might not work. The burglars wouldn't care how much money they were getting if they were rotting away in jail. They expected executive clemency to get them out. In order to be successful, continued payment of hush money had to be joined with grants of executive clemency. Politically, clemency was out of the question. It was too hot.

The problem with the option of continued payoffs, then, was not moral or legal, it was practical: could the White House keep the deliveries a secret, Mafia style; and if so, would they succeed in keeping the burglars silent?

By the time we had heard all this on the tape, our curiosity had long passed the nuance of the President's reaction to getting a million dollars in cash sometime in the hypothetical future. The recorded conversation had taken a new and more concrete turn, one that we had not anticipated. Dean was telling the President about Howard Hunt's latest demand for money, a demand that had apparently *not yet been satisfied*. And the President was telling him—and Haldeman —what to do about it. This revelation was the most astonishing of all, for we were completely unprepared for it.

Before listening to the tape, we had assumed that Hunt's demand to the White House for $120,000 and the resulting delivery of $75,000 by Fred LaRue to Hunt's lawyer, Bill Bittman, had all taken place *before* March 21. True, nobody could pinpoint the date, but the consensus seemed to be that it was March 19 or 20. No one had hinted that the President himself was involved in this payoff in any way whatever.

The tape itself placed all the facts in a completely new perspective. Hunt's demand for money, it appeared, had not yet been satisfied on the morning of March 21. It was the overhanging threat behind Hunt's demand that served as the catalyst for Dean's briefing of the President. Dean was bringing the problem directly to the Oval Office. He was using it as a lever to prod the President into action that would put an end to the obstruction of justice.

The President understood the danger Hunt posed, but his reaction was different from what Dean had anticipated: "Don't you, just looking at the immediate problem, don't you have to handle Hunt's financial situation damn soon? . . . It seems to me we have to keep the cap on the bottle that much. . . . Otherwise we won't have any options. . . . Either that or it all blows right now." In the President's thinking, keeping Hunt from "blowing" was necessary for the moment in order to have time to consider what new strategy was best. "We better take the Hunt thing, that's worth it at the moment. . . . Worth buying time on." And later, to Haldeman: "First you've got the Hunt problem, that ought to be handled right now." And again: "You've got no choice with Hunt. . . . You better damn well get that done."

The tape was difficult to make out, and we had no transcript. For hours we took the recording back and forth on the machine over the most important segments—partly to contstruct a rough transcript, partly to convince ourselves we were not imagining what we were hearing.

The possibilities of this new evidence were startling. If in fact the $75,000 in cash had been delivered to Bittman for Hunt not on March 20 but *after* the Nixon-Dean-Haldeman meeting of March 21, then the impetus for the delivery may well have come right out of the Oval Office—from the President's own lips. If the proof established a direct link between the tape and the payment of cash to Hunt, then the President would unquestionably be guilty of obstruction of justice, conspiracy, bribery and probably other crimes. Even without such a link the tape was far more damaging to him than we had ever dreamed it would be.

The tape not only corroborated Dean's principal allegations, it went far beyond his Senate testimony on matters other than the hush money. The tape showed that Nixon not only had condoned the cover-up but had reassured Dean they could continue to conceal what had been done. Dean had testified that there was a discussion of various options and that his recommendation to "go the hang-out route" was rejected. There was a discussion of options on the tape all right, but none of them included any voluntary disclosure to legitimate law enforcement agencies. The options were all different strategies for continuing the cover-up. They all had one thing in common: as the President put it, "I don't want any criminal liability . . . for members of the White House staff, and, I trust, for members of the Committee [to Re-Elect the President]." In a classic passage, the President educated Haldeman in the points of giving evasive testimony under oath about possibly incriminating matters: "If you're asked, you just say, 'I don't remember, I can't recall, I can't give an answer to that that I can recall.'"

When we finally switched off the Tandberg late that afternoon, we sat motionless—silent, exhausted. We knew that we had turned the corner of Watergate. We knew now how important it was that we had kept the investigation alive to get this evidence, and why Nixon had fought so bitterly over it. We could have more confidence in that continuing struggle now because we held a trump card. Each of us, too, felt a measure of dismay. The ordinary-looking tape reel sitting on the desk in front of us was one of the most sordid, disillusioning pieces of historical evidence in the saga of American government. No one who listened to it could ever again feel quite the same way about the American Presidency.

In a stage-managed press conference with newspaper editors a month before, the President had been asked about his personal finances. He had reacted angrily. "People have got to know whether or not their President is a crook," he said. "Well, I am not a crook." Even to us, at the time, it had seemed an overreaction. The nakedness of the word was a little shocking. The idea of the President of the United States being a "crook" was almost unthinkable. On December 12 we realized why the President so curiously lashed out to deny that appellation. He *was* a crook, and we had the evidence to prove it.

Why, after two missing tapes, a missing Dictabelt and an eighteen-minute gap, had we gotten *this* damaging tape intact? Obviously, the President's eagerness to use the tape in his dispute with John Dean over the March 21 conversation had tied his hands. Once H. R. Haldeman reviewed the tape and testified about it in detail before the Ervin Committee, telling the committee that he had found no gaps on it, the President was locked into turning it over unharmed.

In the days following December 12, we received the rest of the subpoenaed tapes from Judge Sirica and reviewed them eagerly. None was as dramatic, standing alone, as the tape of the March 21 morning conversation. Together, however, the tapes formed an incriminating pattern more definitive than any one tape taken by itself. The tapes showed that even before March 21 the President knew that a cover-up was going on and knew that CRP and White House officials were involved. The tapes also showed that the President had become actively involved in furthering the cover-up after March 21 as the situation collapsed in on the White House, and that he had consistently lied to the public about his conversations with Dean, Haldeman and Ehrlichman and about his own motives.

For example, on the afternoon of March 21, the President first suggested that a grand jury might be convened to investigate the White House and announce that all White House personnel were innocent. As he put it, if they went that route it would be necessary to "keep criminal liability off of" Haldeman, Ehrlichman, Dean, Strachan, Mitchell and if possible Magruder. Other possibilities included a deceptive public statement or a Dean report to the Cabinet along the same lines: "Haldeman is not involved, Ehrlichman is not involved."

By March 22 a strategy had been evolved. Dean would write a "report" to the President purportedly setting forth everything he knew about Watergate. In fact the report would disclose only those facts it could be anticipated would be disclosed by others. It would trace the origins of the bugging at CRP, but would say little about any cover-up. It would exonerate the White House. It would be a "modified, limited hang-out." The beauty of this strategy was that the report would be something the President could later say he "relied on." As Ehrlichman argued, "Assuming some corner of this thing comes unstuck, you are then in a position to say, 'Look, that document I published is the document I relied on, that is, the report I relied on . . . And now this new development is a surprise to me. . . .' You have to bottom your defense, your position on the report. The report says nobody was involved and you have to stay consistent with that." The President told Dean on March 22 that containment had been the right approach through the 1972 election and afterward, but now their strategy had to change.

After the March 21 morning meeting, there was little discussion on the tapes about Hunt's demand. The President apparently assumed that, according to his wishes, that had been "taken care of." Dean told him on the afternoon of March 21 that Mitchell and LaRue were "aware of" the problem.

Between March 22 and April 15, 1973, the President continued to hide the facts from law enforcement authorities. It was only after Dean and Magruder had spilled the beans to the prosecutors—and after Assistant Attorney General Petersen had gone to the President on April 15 and demanded that he fire Haldeman and Ehrlichman— that the President even admitted he had learned the intimate details of the cover-up almost a month before, on March 21.

To MITIGATE the outcry over the two missing tapes, the White House unexpectedly had turned over to Judge Sirica two tapes not specifically called for by our subpoena. Remarkably, both provided additional evidence of criminality. The first was a Dictabelt recording of the President's reflections on the events of March 21, 1973, as dictated in his own voice late that same evening. In the Dictabelt, the President recounted that the day had been fairly "routine" except for his conversation with Dean. He went on to detail some of Dean's account, observing that Magruder was obviously a "weak" link, that Krogh had perjured himself, and that Strachan had been a "real courageous fellow." The President noted that he "felt for" all involved because they had gotten into this with the "very best of motives." Hunt, he said, seemed to be a "real problem," but the past payments of hush money didn't pose as much of a threat as Dean seemed to think they did. The President reflected that if Mitchell put his mind to it they might work out "some sort of a course of action we can follow. It seems to me just to hunker down without making any kind of statement is really too dangerous as far—" At this point, the Dictabelt broke off and was followed by fifty-nine seconds of silence.

The Dictabelt recording, of course, laid to rest the President's contention that he had any desire to get the facts out to the public after his March 21 meeting with John Dean. The recording reflected no such desire, no contemplation on the President's part of any moral or legal duty to act, no instinct except that for self-protection.

The other unsolicited tape surrendered by the White House was a recording of a conversation between the President and Dean on April 16, 1973. We had subpoenaed a Dean-Nixon conversation on April 15; it was one of the conversations the White House claimed had not been recorded. Instead, the President's lawyers produced the tape of the meeting of the sixteenth, saying it covered much the same ground. By April 15 and 16, President Nixon knew that Dean was cooperating with the prosecutors. In the tape of the sixteenth, the President for the first time seemed conscious of the tape machines revolving silently in the White House basement. In subtle ways, Nixon seemed to be "reminding" Dean of certain things that, as Dean told him, "didn't exactly happen that way." He encouraged Dean to testify that the President really knew nothing before March 21, and impressed upon Dean his desire that Dean reveal nothing about Dean's direct conversations with him. It would be hard to call this subornation of perjury, but intimations of it were there.

The process of transcribing the President's tapes proved a more difficult, time-consuming and tiring chore than we had imagined it would be. Most of the tapes had portions that were inaudible. The microphones in the President's desk in the Oval Office picked up the slightest physical vibrations in the desk itself and recorded these as sound waves on the tape. Whenever the President's cottage-cheese-and-catsup lunch was placed on his desk or he slammed a drawer shut the tape contained a painful explosion of sound. Many difficult portions of the tapes *could* be made out but only after repeated listening. Often dozens and dozens of passes were required just to catch one word. Different ears were good for different tapes, and we soon found that some of us were far more skilled at recognizing patterns of speech than others.

It was essential to have accurate transcripts. With transcripts, the recordings would be far more intelligible to the grand jurors. Yet we were afraid that if the transcripts we presented to the jurors later proved to have even the smallest errors, our objectivity would be attacked. So a great deal of work went into honing the transcripts. Most of the work was done by the task force attorneys. We were the ones most familiar with the case, and we wanted to retain complete control over the quality of the work. If there were any mistakes they would be ours alone.

The White House had produced transcripts of several subpoenaed tapes. These transcripts were turned over to us, unsolicited, in late December. Invariably, we found that the White House transcripts were incomplete and inaccurate. Sometimes they omitted clearly relevant and highly damaging portions of a conversation.

As the task force reviewed the tapes and began constructing transcripts, we kept Special Prosecutor Jaworski apprised of the factual pattern that was developing. Within a few days of our listening to the March 21 tape on December 12, Jaworski also listened to the recording in his office. Later he reviewed three of the other tapes, and the President's Dictabelt of his recollections of March 21. Jaworski quickly absorbed the implications of this new evidence. He said very little about it to us, but it was obvious to look at him that he was carrying a new burden. Jaworski now knew that he would be confronted with far more difficult decisions than he ever anticipated when he accepted the job as Nixon's second Watergate Special Prosecutor.

The President, in fact, seemed to be pushing the Special Prosecutor toward those decisions. Not only was Nixon ignoring the evidence he had turned over to us, he was out in the country proclaiming his innocence in the PR blitz of Operation Candor—in terms so sweeping and categorical that he almost seemed to be challenging us to bring this evidence to light. Was this a strategy of irrationality and desperation, a bluff the President hoped would never be called? Or did the White House have some elaborate plan in mind?

Among those who were going out on a limb for Nixon was his newly appointed Vice President, Gerald R. Ford. It was clear that Ford had not been shown the transcript of the March 21 tape—only a fool would have so staunchly proclaimed Nixon's total innocence otherwise. One evening Ben-Veniste and Volner found themselves attending the same banquet as Ford at the Shoreham Hotel in Washington. It was difficult for the two prosecutors to resist the impulse to advise Ford, quietly, that he should lower his Watergate profile or demand to hear the March 21 tape. The nation would not be well served, they felt, by having its next President unnecessarily enmeshed in Watergate. Nevertheless, Ben-Veniste and Volner knew that it would be most improper to meddle in such extraordinarily sensitive political matters—indeed, the potential for disaster should Ford or his advisers choose to misinterpret the bona fides of the message was enormous. Instead, they chatted pleasantly with the new Vice President about his confirmation hearings.

Meanwhile, Jaworski expressed his concern to us that the President didn't seem to be considering imminent resignation. In the two months following the Saturday Night Massacre the President had suffered the missing tapes, the eighteen-and-a-half-minute gap, the humiliating tapes hearings, new revelations in the ITT affair, income tax problems, Krogh's repudiation of "national security," and new disclosures about the milk price support scandal. He must know that the evidence he had turned over to us would wound him fatally. Surely a rational man would contemplate resignation "in the national interest" while he could still convince some that he was innocent—especially if resignation could be exchanged for a termination of the investigation and avoidance of further public ignominy.

In a number of meetings with Alexander Haig, Jaworski tried to impress on Haig that the tapes presented both the White House and the prosecutors "a completely new situation." But Haig was not receptive to Jaworski's none-too-subtle warning. Haig maintained that the President had committed no crime, that in the March 21 tape and other tapes the President was simply exploring "hypothetical courses of action." Moreover, Haig and other White House lawyers insisted privately to Jaworski that Nixon had never done an illegal *act*, that the last payment of $75,000 in hush money to Howard Hunt had been made on March 20, *the night before* the President speculated on March 21 about paying Hunt.

Jaworski did not directly contradict the White House legal theories. Instead he told Haig that the President ought damn well better get himself a good criminal lawyer, someone who knew the law, and ask *him* about such matters. What Jaworski did not say was that he knew his Watergate Task Force was developing the hard evidence to refute the President's position on the timing of the final payoff to Hunt; evidence that would make inevitable in the next few months perhaps the most difficult decision Jaworski would ever have to make—a decision about what action he and the grand jury should take to deal with President Nixon's criminality.

CHAPTER **10** **Le Grand Fromage**

THE QUESTION OF HOW to proceed with the evidence against President Nixon preoccupied us from December 1973 until March of 1974, when indictments in the cover-up case were finally returned.

During December and January very little was said about it openly, even among the few prosecutors in the office who were aware of how incriminating the tapes really were.

But Jaworski did ask Phillip Lacovara to have his research team begin work on a comprehensive legal memorandum setting forth the law relating to possible indictment of a sitting President. Lacovara assigned one of his staff members, Richard Weinberg, to prepare the memorandum, in close consultation with him. The work on this project went forward in total secrecy; not even the Watergate Task Force was informed that Jaworski had commissioned it.

The Weinberg memorandum, forwarded to the Special Prosecutor in early January, concluded that nothing in the text of the Constitution or in legal precedents explicitly barred the grand jury from indicting President Nixon. But the memorandum expressed grave doubts about the institutional "propriety" of indicting a sitting President. Weinberg's conclusion echoed research done by the original Watergate prosecutors, and by the Department of Justice during the Agnew case. The lengthy Justice Department review had concluded that while ordinary civil officers subject to impeachment (such as judges and Cabinet officers) can be indicted before being impeached (and that included Agnew) the President was a special case. On account of the symbolic damage to the Presidency and the concrete damage to the functioning of the government that might be caused by a criminal proceeding against a sitting President, the Justice Department had concluded in its study, the criminal process should not go beyond the point where the President's performance of his official duties would be impaired.

In transmitting Weinberg's study to Jaworski, Lacovara included his own memorandum that expanded on the practical and institutional drawbacks to the indictment of a sitting President but nonetheless concluded that there was no explicit *or implicit* constitutional bar to indictment.

Lacovara's memo sounded two additional themes. One was the suggestion that the propriety of an ordinary criminal indictment of President Nixon might depend in part on the probability that "alternative mechanisms" would play their role in bringing the President to account for his criminal role in the cover-up, i.e., impeachment. By January it seemed certain that the House Judiciary Committee would follow through with a full-scale impeachment inquiry. The second theme was that some "disposition or settlement in the public interest" might be arranged. This was a long-winded way of saying that the President might be persuaded to resign in exchange for a pledge that he would not be prosecuted.

Lacovara's two suggestions illustrate the dilemma we faced from the beginning of our deliberations about how the criminal-justice system should deal with President Nixon. On the one hand, we wanted to proceed strictly according to the Constitution—to put aside political considerations and to approach the problem strictly from a professional, legal point of view. It was not our place to decide whether the public interest would be served by the President's remaining in office. On the other hand, in assessing the constitutional principles involved in the matter, it would be necessary to decide whether and to what extent deference to other branches of government—especially Congress—was required. Inevitably, the legal question of whether a sitting President could be indicted would depend to some degree on a comparison of the public interest in avoiding interference by the criminal law in the functioning of the Executive, versus the public interest in vindication of the criminal-justice system itself. In the large sense, these were "political" considerations; but they were considerations that we could not avoid taking into account in deciding the right "legal" answers to our questions.

While the legal researchers were plunging into the constitutional issue, the Watergate Task Force had other chores awaiting it. Our first investigative priority was to pinpoint the exact date and time of the final payment of $75,000 of hush money that had been made to Howard Hunt—to determine whether the payment had flowed from the President's instructions that could be heard on the March 21 tape to "buy time" by meeting Hunt's demand. So far in our investigation we had found no one who could firmly establish the date of the payment; all thought it had been made on "about" March 20.

LaRue remembered that on the evening the money was delivered he had entertained friends at his apartment. After dinner, LaRue gave one of the guests, Manyon Millican, a sealed envelope and asked him if he would deliver it to the home of Howard Hunt's attorney, William Bittman, in Potomac, Maryland. Millican, having no idea what the envelope contained, followed LaRue's instruction to place it in Bittman's mailbox. LaRue could not fix the exact date of this delivery but thought it "probably" had been made on March 20. Millican, who had been interviewed by the FBI, was unable to fix the time more precisely than "late March." Dean could not help. Bittman admitted receiving the envelope, and he and Hunt agreed that Bittman had in turn given it to Hunt "a day or two" before March 23. That was where the matter stood.

In late December Ben-Veniste and Frampton (who had compiled the evidence relating to the hush-money scheme) met with LaRue and Millican in our offices. Together and separately, the two witnesses were quizzed about *anything* they could recall, any records they possessed, that might help pinpoint that date. (We had, for instance, obtained telephone company charge records of John Mitchell's long-distance toll calls in the hope that through them we could identify the date Mitchell gave LaRue the go-ahead to pay Hunt. The records were inconclusive.) Neither LaRue nor Millican had appointment books or other records fixing the date of the party. Well, what about the dinner party? we asked. Was there anything they could recall about it that was in any way unusual, anything they had done that same day (such as going to a restaurant for lunch and using a credit card) that could help us establish the date? Millican mentioned that there were several other people at dinner that night, including a gentleman "from Ohio" whose name he couldn't recall.

Millican also remembered that the dinner had taken place in LaRue's new apartment. It had been a cool night, and LaRue had started a roaring fire. Unfortunately, an exhaust fan malfunctioned and smoke filled the apartment. We went back to LaRue. Did he recall the problem with his fireplace? Yes, now he remembered that that had happened the same night in late March he asked Millican to deliver the envelope to Bittman. Millican, we told LaRue, said there was someone from Ohio at the dinner party. Who would that have been? After a typical LaRue pause, the Mississippian came up with a name: Sherman Unger, a prominent attorney from Cincinnati and a Republican who had served briefly as general counsel to the Housing and Urban Development Administration under President Nixon. Finally we had a lead.

Ben-Veniste phoned Unger. "You won't understand why this is important," he said, "but we want to know if you can help us fix the exact date last March when you had dinner at Fred LaRue's apartment." Did Unger recall a dinner party when the fireplace backed up? "Sure," he said. He wouldn't soon forget that. Ben-Veniste: "Do you have any records that could help us pinpoint that date?" He did. Unger had been on a business trip to New York and Washington. He had stayed only one night at each place. Unger kept a desk diary, and he had hotel bills and airline ticket charge slips from the trip. He didn't know what this was all about, but he'd be happy to help.

Unger quickly phoned back. That night was March 21, he said. No doubt about it. His records established it. Bingo! Ben-Veniste asked Unger to send us photocopies immediately and make arrangements to come to Washington with the originals. We wanted him to appear before the grand jury, we told him; this had nothing to do with him or his friend LaRue (we didn't want to "spook" Unger, who promised to be a friendly, cooperative witness), but it was *very* important to us.

Now that we knew the money had been delivered to Hunt on the evening of March 21, the question was whether the payment stemmed from the President's instructions during his meeting with Dean and Haldeman that morning. If we could prove that Haldeman phoned Mitchell right after the Nixon-Haldeman-Dean meeting on the morning of March 21, then we would be able to show that Haldeman had had the opportunity to pass the President's instructions on to Mitchell before Mitchell told LaRue to pay Hunt. Dean told us he thought Haldeman had made such a call. Could we document it?

Quickly we pulled out the detailed logs of Haldeman's telephone calls kept by his secretary, subpoenaed by the original prosecutors back in May 1973. Excitedly we turned to March 21, 1973. The log for the morning and early afternoon of March 21 was missing! Only "page 2" of the log for March 21 had been supplied to the grand jury. This was the only day in the entire three-year period covered by Haldeman's phone logs for which a page was missing. We must really be onto something now! Haldeman's attorneys claimed they didn't have the missing page, either. They had the same photocopy we did; it had been supplied by the White House. The original phone logs were still at the White House, they told us.

Eventually, when we obtained "page 1," it showed as we expected that Haldeman talked to Mitchell on the telephone directly following his March 21 morning meeting with the President and Dean. The story of how we got the missing evidence tells a great deal about the kind of cooperation we were getting from the White House by early 1974.

After the tapes hearings, the FBI had been brought in to investigate missing and altered Presidential tapes and documents. When we asked the White House for "page 1" of Haldeman's March 21 phone log, their first response was that they couldn't find it. So we quickly added that item to the FBI's investigatory list. As a result of FBI pressure, Haldeman's former deputy Larry Higby was asked by the White House counsel's office to search Haldeman's files for the document.

Higby wanted to perform this search by himself. However, much to his annoyance, an assistant to James St. Clair (the President's counsel) insisted on going along. The assistant, Cecil Emerson, an experienced prosecutor from Texas who soon quit the White House, didn't think it was right for Higby to be handling important evidence without a formal representative of the White House legal staff. So, protesting all the while, Higby gained access to the room where ex-aides' files were locked up and began looking for Haldeman's phone logs.

After a short time, Higby announced to Emerson that the log didn't seem to be there. Emerson, who had been looking over Higby's shoulder the entire time, pointed out to him that he was looking in the wrong place. "Try over there," he said, pointing to a different file cabinet. Sure enough, there was "page 1." Emerson demanded a photocopy on the spot and then turned the copy over to FBI agents.

Mitchell and Haldeman, of course, denied that they discussed any Presidential order to pay Hunt in their telephone conversation on March 21. The documentary evidence we received from Sherman Unger and from Haldeman's phone log did, however, together with other testimony, establish a direct chain of events beginning with the

President's expressed desire on tape that Hunt be paid "damn soon," and ending with the payment of $75,000 to Hunt's attorney that same night.

BY MID-JANUARY we had finished transcribing most of the Nixon tapes. The next step was to play them for the grand jury. This task required some logistics to find the most sophisticated tape player and to rig up a set of earphones for each grand juror so that all could listen simultaneously through an optimum sound reproduction system. (Use of earphones results in substantially better audibility than use of open loudspeakers.) None of the task force prosecutors had said anything to the grand jury about what was on the tapes up until then. We wanted to do absolutely nothing that might prejudice the jurors in any way—we wanted the record to be clear that we had presented the tapes to the grand jury cold, without any prior interpretation or characterization. We were eager to see their reactions: whether twenty ordinary people well versed in the facts of the case but lacking a lawyer's perspective would find the tapes as startling and as damaging to the President as we had found them.

Special Prosecutor Jaworski decided that it would be appropriate for him to address the grand jury in advance. He would tell them we would now be presenting a "new line" of evidence "more sensitive than any they had heard before." We would ask the grand jury to keep a completely open mind until all of the tapes were played for them and not to give the prosecutors any reactions until then. That could take a number of days. On January 16, we began playing the Nixon tapes for the jury.

In early January, President Nixon had appointed noted trial lawyer James D. St. Clair of Boston as his chief counsel for "Watergate-related" matters. St. Clair was not a criminal-law specialist, but he was reported to be tough, savvy, and at home in the courtroom. In fact St. Clair proved to be the man President Nixon had been looking for. His arrival signaled an abrupt end to the White House cooperation with the Special Prosecutor that had seemed so promising in November and early December.

On January 9, Jaworski signed a letter drafted by the Watergate Task Force requesting tapes of twenty-five additional Presidential conversations that we believed contained more evidence concerning the cover-up. When no answer was forthcoming, Jaworski reiterated the request at a meeting with St. Clair on January 22. Even though we produced detailed documentation backing up our evidentiary demand, St. Clair airily claimed that the new tapes we wanted would merely be "cumulative" of what we had already obtained. But he didn't give us a definite no. He said instead that a decision would be forthcoming shortly. It was obvious that we were now in for the same tactics Special Prosecutor Cox had faced in the summer of 1973 from the White House: endless foot-dragging without any concrete refusal to provide evidence.

Obviously, the White House was worried most about impeachment. Nixon didn't want to give us any more evidence out of fear we would simply serve as a conduit, handing the material over to the House Judiciary Committee. But he didn't want to say no to our requests, either. A flat turndown would give Jaworski grounds for reporting to Congress that the White House had stopped cooperating. Since Jaworski had recently reported to Congress that the White House *was* cooperating, a contrary report now would be very bad for the President's impeachment defense. Accordingly, St. Clair would occasionally send over some scrap of evidence already promised us by his predecessors (with a cover letter saying the item was "solely for your use in presenting evidence to the grand jury") while he postponed indefinitely answering all our new requests for additional evidence.

Jaworski had already tried to calm White House fears that we were going to ship our Presidential documents and tapes to the Congress wholesale. In early January the Special Prosecutor gave an interview in which he stated that Presidential material gathered in the Watergate investigation would *not* be turned over by the prosecutors' staff to the House Judiciary Committee. This would violate legal rules of grand-jury secrecy, Jaworski was quoted as saying, and would be contrary to the Court of Appeals tapes decision by which we obtained the tapes explicitly for grand-jury use.

Some of the Watergate Task Force prosecutors were none too happy at Jaworski's position, because we thought the legal issue was far from clear. The right of Congress to obtain evidence for impeachment of a President derives from a high constitutional duty that conceivably could take precedence over traditional rules of grand-jury secrecy. We recalled that in April 1973 Assistant Attorney General Henry Petersen told President Nixon that if any evidence incriminating the President turned up, Petersen would "waltz it right over" to the House of Representatives. Besides, the rules for criminal practice in federal courts guaranteeing grand-jury secrecy provided that a federal judge *could* order disclosure of grand-jury information "in connection with a judicial proceeding." This clause would make it quite plausible for us to apply to the court for permission to turn our evidence over to Congress on the ground that impeachment constituted just such a "judicial proceeding."

The Special Prosecutor's assurance that we had no intention of serving as a conduit for the House Judiciary Committee—that we wanted evidence solely in order to fulfill our own responsibilities—undoubtedly put us in a stronger tactical position to obtain needed Presidential materials. But not strong enough. The President had made up his mind that cooperation was at an end. On January 30, Jaworski asked the White House for a decision on all our outstanding requests for Presidential evidence. That evening, President Nixon delivered his State of the Union address. Nixon told a joint session of Congress, "One year of Watergate is enough." The President called for a speedy end to Watergate probes and vowed he had no intention of resigning. He said that he had provided the Special Prosecutor with "all the material he needs to conclude his investigations and to proceed to prosecute the guilty and to clear the innocent."

The next morning, St. Clair intimated in a courthouse TV interview that no more tapes or documents would be handed over. But privately, to Jaworski, he continued to hold out some hope. More "review" was necessary, he said. Now it was obvious that St. Clair was just jerking us around. On February 8, St. Clair suggested that some tapes might be forthcoming if we would agree not to request any more for the grand jury's investigation. Jaworski indicated tentative approval of such a possibility. But on February 13, St. Clair reported that the President refused to reconsider his position. Only then did Jaworski write to the Senate Judiciary Committee that the White House had now cut us off.

Of course, we could have subpoenaed the additional tapes. But the legal battle over the subpoena would have consumed months. We had enough evidence to indict those who were target defendants in the cover-up. And we had enough evidence to conclude that President Nixon himself was implicated. The nation had already waited eight months for indictments and could not be asked to wait much longer.

At the same time we were seeking more of the President's tapes we were also seeking his live testimony for the grand jury. On January 22 the Special Prosecutor first raised the question with St. Clair in a meeting at the White House. Jaworski suggested that it would not be necessary for the President to "appear" at the U.S. Courthouse in downtown Washington. The grand jury would come to him. It would take his testimony in secret, at the White House. St. Clair acted horrified. The idea was totally unacceptable. He countered that perhaps we should consider submitting written questions ("interrogatories") to the President which the President would then answer in writing.

The task force pointed out to Jaworski that evening that St. Clair's suggestion had a familiar ring to it. John Dean had told us that in February or March of 1973, when the Senate Judiciary Committee was after him to testify about Watergate at the confirmation hearings of L. Patrick Gray, the President had suggested to Dean that Dean might offer to answer written interrogatories instead. That way, the President had pointed out, Dean could always dodge the hard questions. The President had repeated the old lawyer's maxim about submitting written answers in lieu of appearing in the flesh: "You can't cross-examine a piece of paper."

Jaworski agreed with our protestations, but he pointed out that the chances of Nixon's agreeing to appear before the grand jury even if subpoenaed were nil. And there was legal precedent he could use to support a refusal to appear. On our present schedule we did not have the time to force the issue by litigating a subpoena. We did not believe that the President's personal testimony was important enough to delay indictments for months. Jaworski suggested that written answers, under oath, might be better than nothing. Some of the staff disagreed, arguing that the President could then tell the public that he had "cooperated fully with the grand jury" when in reality he would have given us nothing useful.

The upshot was a letter from Jaworski to St. Clair saying that written interrogatories were in general unsatisfactory but asking more specifically what the President had in mind. Would he answer under oath? How long would this take? Would staff members from the task force then be permitted to interview Mr. Nixon, using the written answers as a basis for the interview? Would the President provide additional tapes as a basis for his answers? In truth we were more interested in getting tapes than in getting live Presidential denials; if agreeing to submit written questions to the President would get us additional tapes, the trade might be worthwhile. On January 25, St. Clair responded that the President would swear to his answers but that no further tapes would be produced. St. Clair said that Jaworski could personally interview the President after the written questioning was finished, but nobody from our staff could accompany him. This arrangement was simply unacceptable.

Consequently, in late January we decided to ask the grand jury whether it wanted to make a formal request to the President that he appear. It did. A letter from the grand-jury foreman, Vladimir Pregelj, to the President was prepared, setting out the jury's request. In the utmost secrecy, on January 30, the letter was hand delivered to the President's counsel.

Only two copies of the foreman's letter were made, one for our office and the other for the foreman to keep for the grand jury itself. The evening the original letter was delivered to the White House, several of us dropped Mr. Pregelj off at his house on Capitol Hill late in the day. As he got out of the car, he discovered to his horror that he could not find his copy of the letter. Apparently it had dropped out of his coat pocket somewhere in the courthouse or possibly on a sidewalk in downtown Washington. We never did find it. But no account of the grand jury's formal request to the President surfaced in the press. The President himself was the first to disclose the invitation publicly, a month or two later.

Somewhere in Washington there may be a citizen with a unique historical memento hanging on his wall.

President Nixon quickly let us know that he had absolutely no intention of testifying before the grand jury. His response informed the grand jury that in light of the "constitutional separation of powers" it would be "inappropriate" for him to subject himself to questioning by the jurors. This was another bit of meaningless legal gobbledegook, but no matter. We had already decided not to challenge it.

As JANUARY wore on, the task force began to draft an indictment charging conspiracy and obstruction of justice in the Watergate cover-up. Although we were then in the process of presenting to the grand jury direct evidence implicating President Nixon in these crimes, there was little consensus within the task force about where the President should fit into our plans. Not that we didn't discuss it—we began now to talk about it constantly. But this was a decision Special Prosecutor Jaworski would ultimately have to make. He had initiated no discussions with the task force about how to proceed against the President or whether evidence against him should be transmitted to the Congress for use in the impeachment inquiry. Without knowing Jaworski's mind, our own discussions pretty much went in circles.

The Special Prosecutor's silence, in fact, began to worry us. We wondered what courses of action he was considering, whether he had weighed the various choices open to him. Nothwithstanding the legal research done by Lacovara's staff, it was doubtful that the Special Prosecutor would find indictment of Mr. Nixon very palatable. What were the alternatives?

Traditionally, federal grand juries have had the power to do more than simply vote to indict or not to indict. They have sometimes returned "presentments" instead of indictments. A presentment is similar to an indictment in that it exposes wrongdoing, except that it does not initiate a criminal prosecution against the accused. On occasion grand juries have chosen on their own initiative to present rather than to indict. At other times presentments have occurred because a grand jury was frustrated by prosecutors in its desire to indict. A federal statute requires that every indictment must be "signed" by the "attorney for the Government," i.e., the prosecutor; thus the prosecutor must concur before the grand jury can return a valid indictment. Where prosecutors have refused to sign indictments voted by grand juries, "runaway grand juries" have sometimes caused the unsigned indictments to be made public in open court, resulting in what amounts to a presentment.

In addition to presentments, federal grand juries can issue "reports" of one kind and another. These reports have ranged from formal legal charges (like the presentment) to accounts of evidence heard by the grand jury (often dealing with governmental corruption) to recommendations about law enforcement directed to police and prosecutors. A few grand juries have summarized evidence about local political corruption or organized crime in public reports and blasted authorities for not being more zealous in attacking it.

The presentment was a device by which the Watergate grand jury could express a formal conclusion of "probable cause" to believe President Nixon was criminally involved in the cover-up, without actually indicting him. A grand-jury report might be a vehicle for transmitting our evidence to the House Judiciary Committee. Finding some way to get the evidence against the President over to Congress seemed highly desirable to the Watergate Task Force. Indeed, at this time the House Judiciary Committee was so frustrated at lack of access to important evidence that some members were talking about subpoenaing *the grand jury* for Nixon tapes if the committee could not get them direct from the White House. With the grand jury, the judge, the prosecutors, the House committee and the President all involved as parties, some legal donnybrook *that* would have been!

We did not know whether Jaworski was actively considering these alternatives to indictment. But we did know he shared our view of the evidence. Perhaps more than the younger prosecutors on the staff, he had been appalled by the Nixon tapes. Long before the task force finished transcribing all the tapes, Jaworski had heard enough to make up his mind. Whether the taped evidence was enough to establish *criminality* by Mr. Nixon beyond a reasonable doubt was beside the point so far as the Special Prosecutor was concerned. Morally, Nixon was guilty. In Jaworski's judgment the public and the national leadership regardless of party were never going to tolerate the moral implications of the tapes. Had the evidence been of a different kind, Jaworski might have been slow to trust its interpretation by the young prosecutors he had inherited for a staff. No interpretation of the tapes was necessary. This was evidence the Special Prosecutor could hear with his own ears. Like others who played important investigative roles in the Watergate scandal, Leon Jaworski had been "radicalized by the evidence."

From what little the Special Prosecutor said to us in December and early January about President Nixon it appeared to the task force that his central concern was to see President Nixon removed from office. In the first place, Jaworski had obviously concluded that on the basis of the evidence such a person should not in the national interest continue to lead the country. Moreover, Jaworski calculated that the President probably would not be able to cling to his office for long after the tapes were made public. In Jaworski's mind, seeing Richard Nixon out of the White House was the most important achievement he could render the country as Special Prosecutor.

Of course, this was a path strewn with pitfalls. The evidence might eventually drive the President from office, but that evidence was now unknown to the public—and the desired result was at that time unimaginable to a majority of citizens. Jaworski could simply make the evidence public on the ground that it was relevant to impeachment. However, that course might be counterproductive as well as unethical. The President could then attack the prosecutor for lack of impartiality and create a diversionary issue. When the tapes finally surfaced, Jaworski wanted to make sure that the evidence, not the prosecutors, would be the focus of public attention.

In order to accomplish this feat, in Jaworski's calculations, we had to maintain our credibility and our reputation for fairness to the President; we had to avoid any missteps that could open us up to attack; and we had to beware of getting too far out ahead of either prevailing public sentiment or public knowledge of the evidence against the President.

Jaworski often shook his head and wondered aloud, "I don't understand why he doesn't do his duty and resign, you know? He must know he's finished—it's just a matter of time. Why can't he do what's best for the country and get out now?" Jaworski held the trump card that could bring about this result, but it had to be skillfully played to avoid national trauma and upheaval.

Late January was the beginning of a very unsettling period in the Special Prosecutor's office. The task force and a few of the other young prosecutors learned that Jaworski had been having discussions with his deputy Hank Ruth and with Phillip Lacovara for almost an entire month about how to proceed against the President, but the task force had not even been told about these discussions, much less consulted.

For instance (we learned quite later on), Lacovara had secretly forwarded additional legal memos and recommendations to Jaworski following the comprehensive study of the President's indictability. Peter Kreindler had been asked to research the constitutionality of the grand jury's returning a "presentment" charging that the President had been involved in a criminal conspiracy. Not only did Kreindler conclude that the grand jury could return such a presentment, he came up with a precedent. In 1811 a county grand jury in the Mississippi Territory had returned a presentment to the House of Representatives charging impeachable offenses against a federal judge named Harry Toulmin. Lacovara had recommended in writing to the Special Prosecutor that he should advise the grand jury about its power to return a presentment which "states its conclusions [about the President] based on the evidence it has heard" either publicly or in secret, and submit this presentment as well to the House Judiciary Committee. Lacovara had written that he favored the Special Prosecutor's advising the grand jury that we thought the President could be indicted but that because of the "considerable doubt" about it and the "severe dislocations that would immediately flow from naming a sitting President as a criminal defendant, it would be preferable to leave formal proceedings to the House of Representatives."

Our disquiet upon learning of these developments can be explained only against the backdrop of our service under Archibald Cox before the Saturday Night Massacre. Cox had fostered an internal dynamic that led each of us to believe and expect we would have a full hearing on the important decisions affecting *our* case. The open-ended and freewheeling atmosphere encouraged by Cox was, of course, gone; Jaworski didn't favor town meetings, but preferred smaller private chats with senior prosecutors. Nonetheless December and January had been a honeymoon period in our relationship with the new Special Prosecutor. The task force had made almost all of the decisions relating to the cover-up and tapes investigations and had been fully consulted when decisions were made by the Special Prosecutor. Now we were facing our biggest decision of all, and suddenly the closed style of Leon Jaworski's decision-making had manifested itself.

More was at stake than just eagerness to make our opinions known. The decision that confronted us had many facets. There was the question of whether the grand jury should formally accuse the President of criminal conduct, by indictment or in some other fashion, or leave this to the House Judiciary Committee. There was the question of whether evidence should be transmitted to the House Judiciary Committee by the grand jury and, if so, whether the jury should analyze or comment on the evidence as well. There was the question of what role President Nixon would play at the trial of his aides if he were not indicted with them. An informed decision on these issues couldn't be made unless all the alternatives, all the ramifications of various choices were thoroughly and exhaustively explored. We were afraid that no comprehensive consideration of all the choices open to us and of our responsibilities in the matter was going to be encouraged within the office.

The public too had a right to expect that any action by the Special Prosecutor and the grand jury having a critical impact on the President

Le Grand Fromage   225

would be taken only after an exhaustive review of all the competing factors involved. We were not unmindful of the historical implications of the decision-making process. In our view, on this issue the Special Prosecutor unquestionably had an obligation to the public to make a "record" for history showing that the whole spectrum of views was assessed and that advocates of different positions had an opportunity to set forth their arguments. Only this kind of process could insure that the wisest decision would ultimately be made.

In addition, we were afraid that Jaworski might not have considered as thoroughly as he should have the consequences that his decision about Nixon would have on the chances of convicting Nixon's subordinates.

Even if Nixon were not indicted, our strongest case at trial against his aides would be one that presented to the jury the whole story of the cover-up—including the President's role. An indictment must fairly define the contours of the prosecution's case in order to inform the defendants of the charges they will be required to meet at the trial. The indictment would therefore have to make clear our belief that the President participated in the cover-up. Ordinarily, the proper way to do this would be for the grand jury to charge the President as an "unindicted co-conspirator," listing his name in the indictment as a person who participated in the charged conspiracy but was not being formally indicted for it and brought to trial. Unindicted co-conspirators are usually those who have received immunity from prosecution or who have already pleaded guilty to the charges.

If the President were not numbered among the conspirators in the indictment, wouldn't that limit the scope of the case we could put on at trial against Nixon's associates? Moreover, we wanted to be able to admit the tapes into evidence at trial. But tape recordings that are shown to be authentic are admissible evidence at trial only if they satisfy other rules of evidence. For example, a defendant's prior "admissions" about the events with which he is charged are admissible against him, so the taped statements of Haldeman and Ehrlichman could be used at trial against them. However, the taped statements of the President would constitute "hearsay" at a trial of his aides: they would be allegations by a third party, not a defendant or a witness in the courtroom. Hearsay is ordinarily not admissible evidence. In a conspiracy case, however, hearsay statements may still be admissible evidence if they are made by *conspirators* and *in furtherance of the conspiracy*. In legal parlance, this is called the "co-conspirator exception to the hearsay rule."

If the taped conversations between the President, Haldeman, Ehrlichman and Dean were conspiratorial conversations, then, we would be able to play the entire conversations for the jury. If they were not conspiratorial conversations, then we would probably be forced to fragment the tapes and play for the jury dozens of isolated taped statements by Haldeman and Ehrlichman. Obviously, the effect of this on our case could be devastating. The latter process might make the prosecution's case unintelligible for even the most intelligent jury.

Had the Special Prosecutor taken all this into account in his thinking about how to proceed? We didn't know, but we were afraid he hadn't.

Although the problem of how to proceed with our evidence against the President was constantly on our minds, we had to exercise a great deal of circumspection in talking about the subject. Conversations begun inside our office were sometimes continued in the car on the way to the courthouse, on the street, or in local cafeterias and coffee shops where we went for lunch. At this time the media and the country were still asking themselves whether on March 21 the President had said "it would be wrong" to raise a million dollars. We were asking ourselves what to do about a President who had committed crimes.

In deference to the need for caution in discussing this matter, Ben-Veniste began to refer to the President as Le Grand Fromage (the Big Cheese). Soon the code name became automatic; after a while, the President was hardly ever referred to as such by the young prosecutors even in mundane contexts, but only as "G.F." Inside the office too the term was used, out of courtesy to those whose pulse rate quickened precariously when they overheard staff members discussing the eventual fate of the President of the United States.

Before the task force prosecutors tried to open a dialogue with Jaworski about the alternatives available in proceeding against the President, we wanted to have a concise factual account of our case against the President in hand. In late January, Frampton hurried to complete a project begun several weeks earlier: a 128-page prosecutive memorandum summarizing and analyzing all the evidence against President Nixon. We knew it would show the evidence of Nixon's criminal conduct to be indeed overwhelming—that failure to take action could not be justified for want of a strong enough case.

Delivered to the Special Prosecutor in early February, the Nixon prosecutive memorandum stressed the President's role in the cover-up in March and April of 1973. It dwelt primarily on the events surrounding the final payment of hush money to Howard Hunt, the meetings on March 21 and 22, and the President's joint effort with his aides to foment a new strategy as the cover-up came tumbling down around them. However, the memorandum went on to show that the techniques used by the President and his aides in this late period were conceptually the same ones that had been employed by others throughout the cover-up. There was the resort to hush money (in order to "buy time"), the revelation that the President knew of an offer of clemency, the President's attempt to obtain information from the Justice Department about the case under false pretenses, the encouragement to his aides to give evasive testimony, and the preparation of written (the Dean "report") and oral "scenarios," i.e., cover stories, to cloak the President's own actions.

The memorandum concluded that on March 21, 1973, President Nixon joined an ongoing conspiracy to obstruct justice on the part of his closest White House aides and high officials of his reelection committee by (1) urging that a cash payment be made to Howard Hunt, and (2) approving a new strategy to continue the cover-up that contemplated limited disclosure of some information together with continued concealment of the most damaging evidence. The memorandum also stated that the President's "persistent refusal" to cooperate with the prosecution's investigation, the intentional destruction of evidence under the President's custody and control (the eighteen-minute gap), and the considerable evidence of the President's role in the cover-up prior to March of 1973 might also constitute evidence against him.

Based on his own actions, the memorandum said, the President might be prosecuted for obstruction of justice, for bribery, for obstruction of a criminal investigation, and for conspiracy to commit all these offenses. In addition, he could conceivably be charged for having "aided, abetted, and counseled" the payment of a bribe, for having failed to report what he knew about the cover-up as an "accessory after the fact," and for misprision of a felony.*

---

* An updated version of this same memorandum authored by Frampton in June of 1974 has been published, except for several sections of detailed analysis, as "The Case Against Richard Nixon," Chapter Eleven of Leon Jaworski's recent book, *The Right and the Power* (Reader's Digest Press, 1975).

Jaworski had been waiting nervously for the memorandum and waded into it as soon as it was finally completed. While it made an obvious impact on him, it did not serve to begin any dialogue.

In the first few days of February four of the younger prosecutors—Frampton, Rient and Goldman on the Watergate Task Force and Ruth's assistant, Feldbaum—became actively alarmed about the course of decision-making. There had still been no discussion whatsoever of the Nixon problem between Jaworski and the Watergate Task Force. There were intimations that the Special Prosecutor was reluctant to take any action relative to the President at all. The four prosecutors decided to articulate in writing and submit to Jaworski a statement of their personal views about the Nixon decision, in an attempt to open up the decision-making process.

While the four prosecutors were drafting their statement, the task force learned indirectly that the Special Prosecutor had in fact already made up his mind about how to proceed against the President. He had decided against any recommendation to the grand jury that they indict President Nixon, or that they make a "presentment" naming him, or that they issue a report. He had also ruled out naming the President as an unindicted co-conspirator. However, we were told, his mind was still open about the possibility of suggesting to the jury that they transmit the tapes to the House of Representatives for use in the impeachment inquiry.

Realizing that a memorandum stating their views would probably have very little impact at this late date, the four authors submitted it to the Special Prosecutor anyway on February 12. They fully realized there were risks in injecting themselves into the decision-making process like this, especially in committing themselves to paper. They sensed that the intrusion would not be welcome, because of the anxiety and sensitiveness with which Jaworski was approaching the issue of the President. The Special Prosecutor placed a high premium on loyalty. He tended to treat the expression of views contrary to his as a manifestation of disloyalty. But the authors preferred the risk of losing their credibility with Jaworski to remaining mute and seeing the decision made without a full canvass of all the competing factors and possibilities.

The memorandum contended that the grand jury had a duty to reach some conclusion about the President's role in the Watergate cover-up and express that conclusion through appropriate action, be it indictment or, if indictment was constitutionally inappropriate, either a presentment or a report. The arguments for and against indicting a sitting President for serious crimes were set forth, but no conclusions were drawn about that course. The important thing was for the grand jury to manifest its findings in some form or another. A presentment would avoid most of the problems of indicting a sitting President and still make it clear that the jury had found "probable cause" to believe that the President had acted unlawfully—that, but for the fact that he was President, Richard Nixon *would* have been indicted.

In arguing their conclusion, the authors pointed out that the Special Prosecutor's "duties and responsibilities" under his charter included "full authority for investigating *and prosecuting* . . . allegations involving the President." By the appointment of a Special Prosecutor the Congress and the public had committed the decision of the President's involvement in Watergate to the traditional processes of law enforcement, they said. If the grand jury was not permitted to play its customary role in this process the vitality of the criminal-justice system—and the principle that "no man is above the law"—would be called into question.

The authors argued further that impeachment was essentially a political process designed to determine not whether unlawful acts had been committed but rather whether the President was fit to continue in office. The criminal process and the impeachment process were not identical. For the grand jury to stand aside and throw up its hands would set a dangerous precedent confirming the very fears the Special Prosecutor was appointed to allay: that responsibility for criminal conduct by the most powerful people in the country could not be assessed by the criminal-justice system but only through the political process.

Besides, the memorandum argued, leaving to Congress the issue of the President's commission of illegal acts meant that the question might never be determined authoritatively by anybody. We would be remiss indeed if we did not transmit to Congress the evidence we had gathered that was critical to the impeachment question.

The four prosecutors' substantive arguments had very little impact on the Special Prosecutor. However, the memorandum itself had a dramatic personal effect on him that quickly led to a deterioration of communications within the office and, for a short period of time, to bitter personal differences.

The four had vastly underestimated the suspicion and anxiety their expression of opinion would cause in Leon Jaworski's mind. If the Watergate Task Force had remained somewhat wary of Jaworski's ultimate intentions, he must have remained at least as wary of the aggressive young prosecutors he had inherited from Cox. While he always supported his troops, Jaworski was sensitive to protestations from the White House that the task force was composed of politically biased zealots out to humiliate Richard Nixon. Many of the White House complaints had been aimed at Ben-Veniste, who believed that his prior record of prosecuting crooked public figures of both parties, including the administrative assistant to Democratic former Speaker of the House John W. McCormack, served as a precious amulet to ward off the more virulent of these attacks. However, the public exposure gained by Ben-Veniste and Jill Volner during the tapes hearings remained a source of concern to Jaworski and others in the office, principally Ruth and press officer Jim Doyle. Jaworski had endorsed Ben-Veniste's strategy decisions during those hearings, but the Special Prosecutor and others in the office were bothered by feelings that the task force was too eager to take on the White House at every opportunity. They were also troubled by the fact that Ben-Veniste and Volner had thereby reaped such a huge amount of personal media coverage. Ben-Veniste's direct and irreverent personality was unlikely to assuage the Special Prosecutor's concern, particularly given the not inconsiderable ego possessed by Leon himself. Jaworski did not doubt our abilities; he just didn't fully trust the maturity of our judgment.

When the four prosecutors submitted their memorandum to him, he must have perceived a mutiny on his hands. Certainly the views expressed in it ran largely counter to his own at that time. Moreover, the fact that the authors had set their position down on paper must have troubled the Special Prosecutor. Why would they make a paper record except for the purpose of undercutting him?

Jaworski's touchiness about the Nixon decision was also exacerbated by his constant fear of leaks. For months our office had kept from the press the slightest intimation of the dynamite that was in the Nixon tapes. Nevertheless, the fear of some dramatic piece of evidence being disclosed prematurely continued to be on the Special Prosecutor's mind. Perhaps the Special Prosecutor feared that the authors were planning to leak their position—and the existence of a dispute between him and his staff—to the press.

On February 13, Jaworski made clear in a meeting with Ruth, Ben-Veniste and Volner that he *had* reached tentative conclusions about the President. Jaworski told Ben-Veniste in no uncertain terms that he did not favor indictment, presentment or naming of the President as an unindicted co-conspirator. The third alternative would be unwarranted and unfair, he said. Jaworski showed Ben-Veniste what he had in mind instead: a draft statement by the grand jury, couched in the most neutral terms, stating that the jury was transmitting certain tapes to the House Judiciary Committee "in case" they were relevant to its inquiries. When Ben-Veniste cautiously began to explore other alternatives, Jaworski's temper flared. The Special Prosecutor heatedly accused Ben-Veniste of disloyalty, claiming that he had put the four young prosecutors who drafted the Nixon memorandum up to it as "front men" for himself. The task force was trying to foment disunity in the office, Jaworski said, in order to limit his freedom of action.

Ben-Veniste volubly informed the Special Prosecutor that his charge was unfair. In fact, Ben-Veniste had declined to be part of the memorandum written by the four prosecutors. While he agreed with some of their views, Ben-Veniste disagreed with the proposition that the grand jury could discharge its duty only by rendering an accusatory presentment about the President's criminality. Ben-Veniste thought that a grand-jury report that transmitted evidence to the House Judiciary Committee and, in addition, provided some coherent analysis of the evidence would amply fulfill the jury's function. Such a report would also have the desired effect of making it clear to Congress that the grand jury believed the President was criminally involved in Watergate.

When the flare-up subsided at the February 13 meeting, Ben-Veniste explained his personal opinions about the Nixon decision to Jaworski. He said he did not believe that an accusatory presentment was required. But he did urge the Special Prosecutor to consider something more than a mere shipping of the tapes to Congress; perhaps a summary of the evidence could be included with the tapes. Jaworski did not react favorably. He was not entirely placated either. After the meeting, Ben-Veniste took a long walk to cool off. Jill Volner, looking shell-shocked, informed the rest of the task force what had happened.

Jaworski's reaction demoralized the task force—it seemed that the Special Prosecutor now saw all of us as virtual renegades. This made any effective advocacy by us now impossible. Ben-Veniste had declined to be part of the four prosecutors' "petition" in part because he wanted to maintain his own freedom of action to take a more compromising approach with the Special Prosecutor. But that possibility seemed to be gone. Volner was the only one who had not alienated herself from Leon Jaworski. During the February 13 meeting she had hardly said a word, shrinking from the battle of personalities and hoping to wait out the storm.

In retrospect, the four authors of the Nixon memorandum failed to pay sufficient heed to two factors uppermost in the Special Prosecutor's mind. The first was his strong desire not to get out ahead of public opinion, not to appear to be "challenging" the President on the basis of evidence not yet in the public domain. In Jaworski's mind, such a course could in the long run be fatal to all our efforts because it would make the propriety of our actions, rather than the evidence, the central public issue. He wanted to be extremely cautious that whatever action we took was *perceived* to be eminently fair to the President by a public not yet inclined—as were the young prosecutors in our office— to view their President as a criminal.

Second, Jaworski had set two priorities for himself: successful resolution of the Nixon problem and successful prosecution of the President's highest aides. Taking an aggressive stance on the first problem, he feared, could well prejudice success in the second. If we indicted President Nixon along with his aides, the President would surely take the constitutional question of his indictability to the Supreme Court. While the law appeared to be on our side, Jaworski was not so sure the Court would ultimately see it that way. More important, a great deal of time would be lost before we could prosecute Nixon's subordinates. During that time, with the President under indictment, the country would be severely disrupted. During that time, also, the public would focus on the issue of whether the President could be indicted. This was a fight Jaworski saw no need to get into in light of the other important tasks ahead of us. It would be a diversionary fight. It was the wrong issue on which to take on the President.

THE FEBRUARY 13 wrangle between Jaworski and Ben-Veniste occurred hard on the heels of another debate within the office, over the disposition of charges against Herbert Kalmbach. Kalmbach had been a central figure in the distribution of hush money to the Watergate burglars from June until September 1972. However, he had voluntarily disclosed most of the facts concerning his participation in this scheme to the original prosecutors. For that reason, and because his primary involvement in alleged improprieties during the Nixon Administration had to do with his political fund raising, the Watergate Task Force was inclined to use Kalmbach as a witness at the cover-up trial rather than to seek his indictment.

On one important point, however, we were skeptical of Kalmbach's testimony: his professed naïveté about the purposes for which the hush money had been raised. (Later, at the cover-up trial, Judge Sirica echoed our doubts, repeatedly questioning Kalmbach on the point himself.) Told in the first week of February that Ruth and Jaworski had decided to permit Kalmbach to plead to two technical violations in the campaign-financing area, the Watergate Task Force unanimously expressed strong objections. In fact, almost no one on the staff agreed with the plea bargain except Tom McBride, chief of the Campaign Financing Task Force. But our arguments were to no avail. Jaworski was determined to go through with the deal, and Kalmbach agreed to plead guilty to the relatively minor charges.

The Special Prosecutor saw the disposition of the Kalmbach case in broader terms than the task force prosecutors. To him there was great significance in the fact that the President's personal attorney was pleading guilty to crimes. We took a more traditional prosecutorial view, evaluating the fairness of the disposition and the tactical ramifications of it within the context of our own investigation and that of the campaign contributions task force.

McBride's vigorous advocacy of the Kalmbach disposition had caused a minor revolt among his own staff. Just a few days before February 13, McBride's staff prosecutors and some others from the legal research staff had met en masse with Jaworski to protest his decision about Kalmbach. So, Jaworski's squabble with Ben-Veniste on the thirteenth must have appeared to the Special Prosecutor as confirmation that the whole office was rising up against him.

Kalmbach's was not the first case in which the staff had been at odds with the Special Prosecutor over plea bargaining. In early January, the Watergate Task Force warned John J. Wilson and Frank Strickler,

the lawyers who had been representing both Haldeman and Ehrlichman, that their position could involve a serious conflict of interest. As
a result, Ehrlichman retained a well-known California lawyer, who
immediately entered into one-on-one discussions with Leon Jaworski
about Ehrlichman pleading guilty to a single charge in the Ellsberg
psychiatrist break-in case, thus avoiding being charged with covering
up Watergate.

When the Watergate Task Force got wind of these negotiations we
took strong exception to any bargain that would allow Ehrlichman
to finesse culpability in the Watergate cover-up. We also insisted that
Ehrlichman must demonstrate prior to acceptance of any plea that he
was really going to come clean. Jaworski's discussions, however, had
gone too far for us to prevail in our first argument. Apparently he had
already agreed "in principle" to permit Ehrlichman to plead to the
Ellsberg case and escape our task force. As a fall-back position, we
attempted desperately to draft a single information that encompassed
both the Fielding break-in and the Watergate cover-up. As it turned
out, Ehrlichman saved Jaworski from what might have been a poor
bargain by cutting off negotiations. We speculated that the prospect
of telling us what he really knew, including information about the
President, had been the sticking point for Ehrlichman.

It was at about this same time that the Watergate Task Force attorney primarily responsible for drafting our legal memoranda, Peter
Rient, took it upon himself to try his hand at drafting a presentment
naming President Nixon. We were by then well along in formulating
the text of an indictment charging between five and ten persons with
conspiracy and obstruction of justice in the cover-up. Rient simply
adapted some of this language to produce a draft of a document entitled "presentment" and naming the President alone. Finding himself
temporarily without secretarial help, Rient asked Henry Ruth's secretary to type up the three-page draft for him, pledging her to secrecy
and telling her that this was simply an attempt by the task force to
see how such a presentment might look.

While the draft was lying face up on the secretary's desk, Ruth
walked by on the way into his office and happened to notice it. "The
United States of America versus Richard M. Nixon," it read. "Criminal
No. _____; Violation of 18 U.S.C. 201 (d) [the bribery statute], 371 etc.
The Grand Jury charges . . ." and so on. Ruth was apoplectic. A mild-
mannered man with a wry and nonassertive personality, Ruth had

spent much of his career as a criminal-justice administrator. He had survived in a number of difficult bureaucratic situations where he had been able to promote professionalism and values he cared deeply about under trying political circumstances only by exercising the utmost caution and discretion. Ruth had already realized that if the relationship between the Watergate Task Force and the Special Prosecutor deteriorated further, he might be the only one who could communicate successfully with both sides and keep the situation from breaking down altogether. The last thing he needed now was for Special Prosecutor Jaworski to come upon a document like this. Ruth rushed off to Rient, feeling relieved that he had "rescued" the draft in time, and, rolling his eyes, warned Rient that this was not a very productive thing to be doing just at that moment.

On February 14, Valentine's Day, the entire Watergate Task Force met with Henry Ruth to explore where Jaworski stood on the question of the President. Jim Vorenberg was also present, as were Phil Lacovara, Peter Kreindler and Carl Feldbaum. Ruth announced that Jaworski had already made up his mind what to recommend to the grand jury about Nixon—but nobody, Ruth said, knew what he had decided! Moreover, the task force was told, we had no right whatsoever to meet with Jaworski to discuss it with him. He had made his determination after discussions in January with Ruth and Lacovara. "All the considerations" had been canvassed. Ruth agreed that he would meet with Jaworski as our emissary and ascertain what the Special Prosecutor had decided to do. He promised he would report back to us.

Needless to say, by this time we were profoundly upset. The task force had very little confidence that among the three of them Jaworski, Ruth and Lacovara had thoroughly explored "all" of the alternatives or that they had calculated the practical effect of various choices on the cover-up prosecution of the President's former aides. The following day Ruth and Feldbaum went from task force to task force to explain to all the attorneys in the office that there was substantial evidence against the President and that Jaworski was considering how to proceed. This series of meetings was promptly dubbed "the traveling road show." The primary result of it was to stimulate a flood of memoranda from other staff members not directly concerned with the Watergate cover-up investigation, urging the Special Prosecutor to consider more fully a variety of possible actions. Lacovara drafted a list of the "questions still open" as he understood them. Frampton drafted a "counter-list" of "questions for consideration." Frampton's list implicitly urged consideration of something more than a transmission by the grand jury of raw evidence. It pointed out also that important issues such as how to approach the grand jury and how extensively to brief them on the legal and constitutional issues involved still remained to be resolved.

The grand jury had, up to this time, pretty much been left out of our thinking—an arrogant oversight in view of the fact that it was they who would be called upon to make the final decisions. The Watergate Task Force assumed that the grand jurors would be influenced considerably by the thoroughness with which various alternatives were sketched out for them and by what the prosecutors recommended. Of course, the grand jury could not indict the President, even if it wanted to, without the Special Prosecutor's concurrence. Nonetheless, if the grand jury were told it had the power to return an accusatory presentment naming the President, it might decide to do that even though the Special Prosecutor strongly opposed such action. While we thought the grand jurors probably would concur in a suggestion to transmit their evidence to Congress, it was certainly possible that they would also demand to characterize, summarize or comment upon that evidence even if they were told the prosecutors did not think that was a good idea.

Some of the staff attorneys by this time were holding out private hopes that if the Special Prosecutor told the grand jury it should do nothing at all the jury would rebel. We knew from our close relationship with them that they were in a militant mood and would certainly not blindly follow a recommendation simply because it came from the Special Prosecutor's office. They were a pretty independent bunch and they believed, rightly so, that they had at least as much at stake in the success of this investigation as we did.

The same possibility must have occurred to the Special Prosecutor. Theretofore, he had addressed the grand jury only twice, and very briefly. The task force had worked with the jury almost daily for nearly eight months and had built up a considerable rapport with them. Jaworski may have feared that the Watergate Task Force might take our dispute with him directly to the jurors, urging them to disregard his recommendations. We did not entertain such thoughts. We intended to press our views within the office. If the Special Prosecutor ultimately recommended to the grand jury a course of action some of us felt to be completely wrong, a few entertained the thought of quiet resignation. But there were no circumstances that could prompt us to go behind the Special Prosecutor's back to the grand jury.

Nonetheless, Jaworski did broach the possibility that Ben-Veniste should confine himself to the investigation into the eighteen-minute gap, becoming the head of a "special task force" to be set up for this purpose. Phil Lacovara, Jaworski suggested, could take over the grand-jury proceedings, relating to indictment and to the President, with the assistance of Volner and the rest of our task force. Both Ben-Veniste and Volner argued vigorously that this plan did not make practical sense. The real basis for the suggestion was left unspoken—by either side—and it was soon dropped. The Special Prosecutor's suggestion did not, however, do anything to improve the deteriorating atmosphere in the office.

On February 15, the Watergate Task Force and a few other young prosecutors in the office sat down to parse out the practical problems posed for our case by the Special Prosecutor's apparent decision concerning the President. Our main problem was how to put together a vigorous prosecution of Nixon's aides if the grand-jury indictment failed to identify the President himself as one of the principal actors in the cover-up.

Four former Assistant U.S. Attorneys from the Southern District of New York—Ben-Veniste, Richard Davis, Frank Tuerkheimer and Peter Rient—reflected on the uniqueness of their situation. For the first time in their professional careers they were being forced to calculate not just the merits of the case at hand but also the internal politics within the office which affected it. At the same time they had to consider the psychological process of recommending to their boss decisions on issues in the case.

Our discussions quickly led us to the conclusion that notwithstanding the moral question of excising Nixon's role from the indictment, prosecution of Nixon's aides for conspiracy in the cover-up would be seriously threatened if the President were not included in our allegations and our proof at trial as a member of that conspiracy. Tuerkheimer had already come to this conclusion independently, and he had discussed it with Jaworski privately for several hours.

What would happen if the grand jury returned an indictment that did not "fit the evidence"—that failed to name the President as an unindicted co-conspirator and ignored the President's participation in the cover-up? We might then be barred at trial from presenting evidence about Nixon's plotting with Haldeman and Ehrlichman in March and April of 1973. That was some of our best evidence. The trial jury would certainly be suspicious if we put on a transparently truncated case.

Worse, our discussion made it crystal clear to us that if we did not explicitly conduct the prosecution on the theory that Nixon was a conspirator we probably could not get the tapes admitted into evidence in their entirety. The taped conversations would be admissible as units only if all the participants in them were alleged conspirators.

There was no question but that naming Richard Nixon as a conspirator was essential to mounting a strong prosecution against his former aides.

Yet Special Prosecutor Jaworski had apparently ruled out that course. And it wasn't going to be easy to change his mind. It was true that naming the President as an unindicted co-conspirator had some of the advantages of a "presentment"—it would answer our trial-connected needs without taking the radical step of bringing the President into the criminal dock. But we knew that there was great resistance on Jaworski's part to taking this step. Shortly before the Saturday Night Massacre the White House had heard a rumor (completely unfounded) that Archibald Cox was planning to "name" the President in an indictment in the milk fund case. Cox had gotten a lot of flak from the White House about it, and within the office he had expressed his view that such a course would be consummately unfair—as he put it, "stabbing the President in the back." The root of Cox's objection was that an accusation by the grand jury short of indictment offered no way for the President to respond to the charge in a court of law (although, of course, he had the forums of public opinion and now of the impeachment inquiry in which to defend himself). Jaworski knew of Cox's comment and had once quoted it back to us.

Tuerkheimer was the first to point out a way around Jaworski's opposition to naming the President publicly in the cover-up indictment as a conspirator. He suggested that the indictment could remain silent on the identities of unindicted co-conspirators. He observed that conspiracy indictments usually charge that the named defendants conspired with other named persons and "with persons unknown to the grand jury." In our indictment we could just say that the named defendants conspired with "others *known and unknown to the grand jury*" without saying who those "others" were. This wouldn't relieve us of the eventual obligation to name co-conspirators: the defendants had a right to be informed before trial of the details of the charges they would have to meet at trial, including the nature and membership of the alleged conspiracy. But disclosure of those alleged to be unindicted co-conspirators could be delayed. Technically, after the return of the indictment but at least a month before trial, the defendants would be entitled to a "bill of particulars" in which we would be required to name all alleged conspirators.

Tuerkheimer pointed out that by that time the impeachment inquiry might have progressed to a point at which the public had fully accepted the possibility that the President had been criminally involved in Watergate—especially if the tapes we had were transmitted to the House Judiciary Committee, and the committee made them public. If the public atmosphere and the amount of evidence in the public domain made the act of naming the President seem less of a political affront, the Special Prosecutor might be more amenable to our naming the President in a bill of particulars four or five months down the road than he was to our doing it in the indictment. At the least, since Jaworski seemed unalterably opposed to naming the President at the present time, we would lose nothing by postponing the decision.

Ben-Veniste observed that Tuerkheimer's suggestion had one major flaw. If the impeachment inquiry did not make progress but bogged down in the next few months, Jaworski might be even more reluctant to name the President in a bill of particulars than he was to name him in the indictment. By naming him in the indictment, the prosecutors would share any public criticism of the act with the grand jury. Since the jurors were the ones who voted the indictment, any perceived confrontation with the President would be a confrontation between the jury and the President, not Jaworski and the President. But if the indictment remained silent and *then* the prosecutors alleged later in the bill of particulars that the President was a member of the conspiracy, Jaworski would be vulnerable to charges that he had "overreached" his own grand jury. The Nixon propaganda machine would have a field day. "The grand jury refused to name the President," Nixon loyalists would say, "because the evidence was insufficient. Now the prosecutors are unhappy, so they're superseding the grand jury. They're substituting their own judgment for the jurors.' They're out to destroy the President." Faced with taking sole responsibility for naming the President as a co-conspirator, Jaworski might find the decision even more unpalatable politically in six months than he did now.

Ben-Veniste proposed a solution to this problem, unprecedented as far as we knew in practice. Suppose the grand jury were to vote *now* to authorize us to name the President *later* in the bill of particulars, even though the indictment itself would remain silent on the identity of co-conspirators. We could then record this vote in the formal (secret) minutes of the grand jury. This approach would give us the option to name the President as a co-conspirator well after the return of the indictment, protect our trial strategy, maintain a posture of fairness toward the President and still enable us to invoke grand-jury support for the action later on.

The approach was a natural. It satisfied all our trial-related needs and also the Special Prosecutor's strong desire to avoid public confrontation with the President. When it became necessary to name the President, Jaworski could defend that action by arguing that it was a prerequisite to effective prosecution of Nixon's aides, and that we had taken every step possible to avoid prejudicing his impeachment defense. If the President resigned or were impeached in the interim, neither we nor the grand jury could be accused of contributing improperly to the political process. And the approach might defuse a potential confrontation between the Special Prosecutor and the jury, which might rightfully resist a recommendation to tell less than the full story in its indictment.

Finally, we could argue to Jaworski that obtaining grand-jury *authorization* didn't obligate him to drop the other shoe in public; it just preserved his options. If Nixon's aides decided to plead guilty, for example, there would be no trial and no legal requirement that the grand jury's action ever be revealed. This final argument was, of course, slightly disingenuous. Our hope was that getting the grand jury on record would create not-so-subtle pressures on the Special Prosecutor to permit us to follow through when the time came.

The task force discussions also focused on the question of transmitting our evidence against Nixon to Congress for use in the impeachment inquiry. The Special Prosecutor apparently had decided to recommend to the grand jury that it send the most damaging Nixon tapes to the House Judiciary Committee. In Jaworski's thinking, the grand jury had the authority to do this, while the prosecutors did not. If the Special Prosecutor could get the grand jury to send to the House committee a "report" containing the tapes, he could leapfrog the legal barriers to our sending the tapes directly to the committee ourselves.

Beyond that, we thought that more than new tapes would be needed to get the House committee up to speed on the available evidence. The atmosphere surrounding the impeachment inquiry at that time was still avowedly partisan and political. There were quarrels about staffing, about procedures and about scheduling. The committee had even been engaged in a running battle among its members and with the White House over what constituted an "impeachable offense."

John Doar, the House Judiciary Committee's chief counsel, had launched an exhaustive staff effort to gather and cross-index every fact, however insignificant, that related to the committee's inquiry. In an ideal world and with infinite time this endeavor could have proved useful. Under the circumstances, however, it precluded immediate action to what was most urgently needed: an attempt to summarize the most *important* evidence against the President in a meaningful way, so that it could be readily understood and assessed by Congress and the public. In the meantime the President, seeing the Judiciary Committee's slow start and realizing he could win easily if the issue were brought to a head soon, was calling for a quick vote on impeachment. If the President succeeded in forcing a vote before Doar's "information-gathering" machine shifted gears and began summarizing the case, or if the committee split hopelessly over preliminary procedural issues, the momentum for impeachment might be shattered no matter how strong the evidence.

The Judiciary Committee's plight convinced some of us that members of Congress from both sides of the aisle were going to have to have the significance of the evidence spelled out for them in neon letters before they would act. The Watergate Task Force believed that the grand jury should be told it could make a report to the Judiciary Committee that not only transmitted evidence but summarized and commented on it. The summary, we thought, could articulate the "theory of the case" against the President. It could show how the tapes and other evidence fit together and demonstrate that the President had been trying to hold the cover-up together in March and April of 1973. The report could also juxtapose the President's public statements denying knowledge of the cover-up with evidence from the tapes showing he really knew far more.

But the Special Prosecutor already had ruled out any analysis or summarization of evidence by the grand jury. Raw evidence, Jaworski argued to us, spoke for itself. Summarization meant the grand jury was "interpreting" the evidence. That was just as dangerous as drawing conclusions from evidence, Jaworski said. The grand jury, he claimed, could be drawn into a position vulnerable to criticism.

Something else worried Jaworski. He professed to uncertainty about Judge Sirica's reaction to an attempt by the grand jury to make a report. Sirica, then Chief Judge of the United States District Court, "presided over" all grand juries in the District, including the Watergate grand jury. All indictments were "returned" in his courtroom. Technically the Watergate grand jury would make any report on President Nixon directly to Judge Sirica. The grand jury would have to request the judge to pass the report along to the House Judiciary Committee. There were plenty of legal precedents for a grand-jury report. But a report about the President of the United States would present a unique legal question, especially if it accused the President of a crime. Jaworski seemed convinced Sirica wouldn't accept a report that was accusatory of the President.

We didn't agree with the Special Prosecutor's argument that summarizing the evidence was tantamount to accusing the President, nor did we share his concern that Judge Sirica might not honor a grand-jury request to transmit such a summary to Congress. But Jaworski would not be swayed. The task force then suggested there was a middle course. Without analyzing the evidence, the grand jury could nevertheless arrange it in a format that made its significance as clear as possible. Even better, the jury could supply the House Judiciary Committee with an "index" to the evidence showing how various pieces fitted together. The phrase we coined for this index was "the road map." We argued to the Special Prosecutor that transmission not only of raw evidence but of a road map to the evidence could avoid the drawing of formal conclusions by the jury. In truth, though, we hoped that a road map could serve as a do-it-yourself kit for the

Judiciary Committee, helping it reassemble the individual pieces of grand-jury testimony and other evidence into a coherent theory of a criminal case as we and the jury saw it.

On February 18, the four young prosecutors who had earlier urged in writing that the grand jury return a presentment met with Jaworski and Ruth, at Jaworski's invitation. They suggested transmission to Congress of a road map to accompany tapes and other evidence. The Special Prosecutor was noncommittal, but he did not rule out the idea.

Two days later, Ben-Veniste met with Jaworski to urge on him our idea of seeking grand-jury authorization now to name the President as an unindicted co-conspirator at some later time. Ben-Veniste downplayed the moral and constitutional aspects of the Nixon problem. Instead he appealed to Leon Jaworski the trial lawyer—to Jaworski's strong desire to mount an airtight prosecution against Haldeman, Ehrlichman and Mitchell—and to Jaworski the political professional, who could appreciate the insulation that grand-jury authorization would give him if he later decided to name the President in the bill of particulars. Jaworski seemed receptive to the idea of grand-jury authorization. He asked Ben-Veniste to prepare a written memorandum outlining the procedure.

Later that same afternoon the task force met with Jaworski to review the cases against several potential defendants. Jaworski brought up the subject of grand-jury authorization. He intimated that it made good sense, and said he was mulling it over. But time was getting short. We wanted to return our indictment no later than the end of February, a week and a half away, and we still had no firm decisions on Nixon.

At about noon the next day the Special Prosecutor called Ben-Veniste to his office. He had made up his mind, he said, to suggest to the grand jury that it transmit evidence about the President to the House Judiciary Committee. However, he said he had ruled out summarizing the evidence, making any accusations or drawing any conclusions. He said nothing at the meeting about naming the President as an unindicted co-conspirator.

The task force now concentrated its efforts on the concept of a "road map." Jaworski did not seem to have ruled out that possibility by his decision that the grand jury could "report" evidence to the House Judiciary Committee but must not analyze or summarize the evidence. Frampton began to assemble all the pertinent evidence before the grand jury that we wanted to send to the House. Together with others, he began to draft a road map to go with the evidence. We wanted to be prepared with a draft if the Special Prosecutor gave us the go-ahead. Perhaps if Jaworski saw in black and white what we were contemplating he would give his consent.

The task force was scheduled to meet with Jaworski Saturday morning for final consideration of the perjury charges that we would ask the grand jury to include in the comprehensive cover-up indictment. When discussion of the perjury counts concluded we turned to the road map. Well, said the Special Prosecutor, he could go along with such a thing, but it must be scrupulously neutral—no inferences, no characterization of evidence. Frampton explained what we had in mind: a series of short statements setting forth indisputable facts, each of which would be followed by a list of tapes or other evidence supporting the statement. In using tapes, we would cite to page numbers of tape transcripts wherever possible. "Try your hand at it and let me see what you come up with," Jaworski replied. That was all the go-ahead we needed.

As the meeting broke up, Jaworski gave Ben-Veniste a typed draft of what he proposed to say to the grand jury about President Nixon. The Special Prosecutor had informed us the day before that he intended to accompany us to the courthouse and address the jurors personally first thing Monday morning. The draft advised the jurors that it would "not be responsible conduct" to indict the President, because of the uncertainty of the law, the "trauma the nation would suffer" while the legal issue was resolved, and the appropriateness of Congress rather than the grand jury dealing with the evidence against Mr. Nixon. However, Jaworski proposed to tell the jurors, they could transmit evidence to the House Judiciary Committee by way of a "report," and the prosecutors would assist in this task in any way desired by the jurors. Again, nothing was said about authorization to later name Nixon as an unindicted co-conspirator. Was this because he intended to leave this matter for later discussion with the grand jury or because he had changed his mind?

We decided that the grand jury ought to get in one sitting our total decision on how to deal with Nixon. For nearly two hours we drafted and redrafted an addition for Jaworski's proposed statement to the grand jury which included a request to the jurors to authorize us to name President Nixon as an unindicted co-conspirator at a later date. The insertion amounted to three sentences. The question now was how to submit it to the Special Prosecutor as gently as possible.

Almost two months earlier, well before relations between the task force and Leon Jaworski had soured, we had decided to give a dinner party for the Special Prosecutor and his wife. At the time, we wanted to show our hospitality to Jaworski. A nice, relaxed social evening would be just the thing, we reasoned, to convince Jaworski that he need not feel isolated or uncomfortable with us on account of differences in age and style. Long ago, the dinner party was set for the home of Jill and Ian Volner on this very Saturday night, February 23.

While our rapport with Jaworski was now on the mend, there was still wariness and reserve on both sides. And all of us, the task force and the Special Prosecutor, were exhausted by the workload and the tension of the decisions we faced. Jaworski more so than anyone, because of the prodigious pace he maintained for a man of sixty-eight and the strain of having the Nixon problem constantly staring him in the face. Moreover, Jaworski was always his most chipper and at his best for business first thing in the morning. By late afternoon—especially at the end of a long week—he was often too tired or wound up to concentrate on new problems. He preferred to relax, reminisce, spin a few yarns. Given the events of the past month within our office, a Saturday-evening dinner party attended by the entire task force and the Special Prosecutor seemed the worst possible setting in which to approach Jaworski for the final time with the most important bit of business our office ever had to deal with. But we had little choice. In order to accommodate the schedule we would have to present our redraft to Jaworski at the party.

That night, the Special Prosecutor's Justice Department driver got hopelessly lost, delivering the Jaworskis to the party well past the appointed hour. Jaworski was his courtly and charming self, as usual, but the tension and fatigue that were affecting all of us showed on his face. During pre-dinner cocktails, the atmosphere was cordial but guarded. Jaworski appeared to assume the air—if not the physical posture—of one intent on keeping his back to the wall at all times. As casually as possible, Ben-Veniste took him aside and mentioned that we had tried our hand at redrafting a few lines in his proposed statement for the grand jury for Monday morning. Ben-Veniste pulled the papers out of his pocket and handed them to Jaworski. Glancing at them, Jaworski told Ben-Veniste he'd think the matter over. The Jaworskis departed immediately as dinner finished, and the rest of us struggled home shortly afterwards to try for a little sleep.

Bright and early Monday morning, the Special Prosecutor came down the hall to the task force offices. His secretary had not yet arrived and he wanted one of our secretaries to type something for him. Only Frampton was in. He was surprised to see the Special Prosecutor, for Jaworski hardly ever came down to the task force offices. Frampton promised to get the material typed as soon as someone came in to do it. "It's what I'm going to tell the jury," Jaworski said, and he departed for his own office. Frampton whipped through it. The Special Prosecutor had bought our approach! The statement said that co-conspirators would be named "at a later date" and that a list of persons "including the President" would be discussed with the grand jury and their "authorization" sought to name them in the "bill of particulars."

At ten o'clock that morning, February 25, Leon Jaworski addressed the grand jurors on the subject of President Richard Nixon. The jurors besieged him with questions. Most were tough and intelligent ones. Some jurors expressed views much like those we on the task force—and the four young prosecutors who had started the whole dispute—had voiced within our office. Sitting with Jaworski in the grand-jury room, some of us could hardly suppress wry smiles. The give-and-take between the jurors and the Special Prosecutor seemed a brief but thorough reprise of the discussions within the Special Prosecutor's office that had raged over the past month. Jaworski ably defended his recommendation. It was obvious to us that the logic of his position was winning the jurors' approval.

When the Special Prosecutor had fielded the grand jury's questions, he departed. The task force remained to show the grand jurors a draft of our proposed indictment and the list of conspirators we proposed to name, arranged in alphabetical order. Then we left the jurors to digest and discuss our recommendations among themselves.

After due deliberation, grand-jury foreman Vladimir Pregelj informed us that the jury had voted 19–0 to authorize us to name each of the recommended co-conspirators. The vote was not unanimous. Twenty of the twenty-three jurors were present that day (all who remained active on the jury), but one abstained. Whether the one juror was recording a protest against our refusal to seek the President's indictment or whether, on the contrary, he wanted no part of accusing Mr. Nixon we were not entitled to know. One of the two regular stenographers who had taken down testimony for the grand jury throughout the investigation was summoned. Ben-Veniste "read into the record" the grand jury's authorization vote and the list of co-conspirators. When he reached "Richard M. Nixon" in the alphabetical procession, the stenographer's eyes bulged. When she finished she said to Frampton, "I guess you want this typed up right away, huh?"

Frampton and other members of the task force were now working feverishly to finish the road map and collection of evidence to be transmitted so that we could show a draft to the jury. The form already chosen for the report was a series of "statements of fact," most of which were one or a few sentences long. Each "statement of fact" was numbered. Each was followed by a list of evidence that supported the numbered statement: a tape, a few pages of recorded grand-jury testimony, a document. (Later, we were flattered by the fact that the House Judiciary Committee staff copied our format precisely for presenting all its impeachment evidence to the committee members and the public.) We wanted to be sure that everything we had gathered that contributed to the case against President Nixon was sent over to the Judiciary Committee. More important, we wanted the road map to make "perfectly clear" how each piece of evidence fit together in the overall scheme.

Jaworski himself had drafted the preamble to the report, requesting Judge Sirica to transmit the enclosed evidence to the House Judiciary Committee. As drafted, the preamble stated that the grand jury had "heard evidence relating to" the impeachment inquiry but had concluded it should "defer to" the House and let the House decide what action was warranted, if any, by this evidence. When the preamble and the road map itself were presented to the grand jurors for their consideration, they were generally pleased. There was only one major change upon which the jury insisted. The preamble, as approved by the jurors, was changed to say that they would "presently" defer to the Judiciary Committee and allow the committee to decide what should be done "at this time." This language was a none-too-subtle hint to the Congress that the jury would still be around to move against the President if the politicians faltered. Strangely, when the preamble eventually was made public, none of the media commentators remarked on these highly pregnant phrases.

From a constitutional standpoint they were perhaps the most important words in the report!

Throughout the last week of February the task force was preoccupied with presenting the indictment and report to the grand jury and with summarizing the evidence against the defendants. (The cases against the Big Three had been reviewed with the jury the previous week. Only the more difficult decisions were left for presentation the final week prior to indictment.) By Thursday afternoon we were ready to return the indictment and report. That night, Frampton and Volner packaged together the road map and the evidence—tape boxes, retyped tape transcripts and other material, all neatly numbered to coincide with the references in the road map. We had intended to put all of the evidence into two briefcases to give to the judge, but we decided to see if it would all fit in one big government-issue case. It did, barely. The last tape box had to be pounded to fit it in. For good reason, the press would call this the "bulging briefcase."

Some weeks before, Frampton had received from a friend a screaming orange anti-Nixon automobile bumper sticker that proclaimed in bold letters, "SAY GOODBY, DICK," a play on the traditional ending of the *Laugh In* television series. On Friday morning, as we were departing our offices for court and the return of our indictment, we affixed the sticker to the outside of the briefcase containing the report. Nervous but exhilarated by the imminent conclusion of our long investigation, we thought the sticker would make a good practical joke on the Special Prosecutor. With a fine irony it bespoke the months of professional restraint we believed we had exercised under siege from the Nixon forces—people who were seldom restrained by legal or ethical niceties in the way they exercised *their* power. And the sticker was perfect counterpoint to the scrupulous objectivity we had labored to bring to the grand jury's report itself. Frampton flashed the bumper sticker at Hank Ruth. Ruth laughed briefly—like a man with a bone stuck in his throat—and then started to make menacing noises. We decided it would be better not to try the prank out on Leon. The sticker came off the bulging briefcase and went into Frampton's suit pocket instead.

The grand jury had already reviewed the indictment and report in final form by Friday morning. That day, the task force and the

Special Prosecutor met with the jurors for a brief formal session in the jury room. We then proceeded together to Judge Sirica's courtroom, via the back elevator. Our office had announced there would be a "proceeding" in court that morning, following the usual practice of giving the press some short warning of official court action. Since Jaworski had earlier announced that we hoped to recommend action to the grand jury by the end of February (this was March 1) and since there had been press speculation that action would come this week, there was a huge crowd of TV newsmen and reporters on hand at the courthouse.

When Judge Sirica entered, Leon Jaworski rose to inform the judge that the grand jury had "material to be delivered" to the court. The jury foreman, Vladimir Pregelj, then came forward from the front row of spectator benches, where the entire grand jury was seated, and handed the judge two envelopes. One contained our indictment charging seven men—Mitchell, Haldeman, Ehrlichman, Colson, Mardian, Strachan and Parkinson—with conspiracy in the Watergate cover-up; the other contained what Pregelj told the judge was "a sealed report." In fact the second envelope contained the preamble to the report and road map, asking the judge to forward the evidence in the separate, bulging briefcase on to the House Judiciary Committee.

In dead silence, the rasp of his letter-opener cutting clearly through the hushed room, Judge Sirica slit open the two envelopes. He glanced at the indictment, then briefly read the preamble to himself.

As he appeared to finish it, Ben-Veniste arose and brought forward from under our counsel table the chocolate-brown bulging briefcase containing the tapes and other evidence and our road map. He asked to "hand it up" to the court. "If it please Your Honor," he said, "this is the material made reference to in the document you just read." Ben-Veniste explained that the briefcase was locked and that the key to it was contained in a sealed letter-sized envelope given to the judge along with the preamble to the report.

So far, spectators and press had learned nothing, since the judge had not read out loud either the "caption" of the indictment (revealing the names of those indicted) or the preamble to the report. The judge thanked the grand jurors, reminding them that they had further business and that they should not discuss the case with anyone, and dismissed them. There was then a brief exchange between the judge and Ben-Veniste about setting the date for arraignment (the time when indicted defendants are required to surrender to the court and enter their formal pleas of guilty or not guilty). Ben-Veniste suggested that the following Saturday morning should be convenient to defendant Mitchell, since Mitchell was then permanently occupied five days a week in New York being prosecuted in the so-called Vesco case.* There was a murmur in the courtroom at Mitchell's name. It was no surprise, of course, but his was the first one mentioned. The formalities completed, we left the courthouse by the basement parking-garage exit as the press ran for the court clerk's office on the second floor of the courthouse to get their copies of the indictment.

WOULD THE WATERGATE grand jurors have indicted President Nixon if it had been left up to them? The events of March 1 suggest they would have.

On the afternoon our indictment was returned, the task force gathered with Hank Ruth and a few of the other younger prosecutors in Leon Jaworski's office. Jaworski had already left for a weekend in Texas, as much to escape reporters as anything; we too were looking forward to a few days of sleep. Totally drained by the tensions of ten months of seven-day work weeks, by the Saturday Night Massacre and by everything in its wake, we felt for the first time that something concrete had been achieved. There had been many times when it seemed that this day would never come. But the prosecution was still on track, and evidence against the President seemingly was on its way to the House Judiciary Committee. No matter what happened now, in Congress with impeachment or in the political arena, we could be proud of what we had done and how we had done it.

Our investigation had been conducted with fairness and integrity. The President had attacked us and had made what we knew to be false statements about the tapes. But we had kept the secret of the

---

* In that case, Mitchell and Maurice Stans, former Nixon campaign finance chairman, had been indicted for conspiracy and perjury in connection with an alleged attempt to improperly influence an SEC investigation into the affairs of international financier (and Nixon contributor) Robert Vesco. Both defendants were eventually acquitted on all charges.

tapes for three months. We had answered the President in the only responsible manner: by according him every consideration to protect his rights, and by playing it straight down the middle.

Then, in the space of forty-five minutes, our feeling of well-being was shattered by two telephone calls from the media. A *Newsweek* editor phoned to say that the magazine had a great deal of "leaked information" that would be published in its Monday issue about the indictment and the grand jury's report. Almost immediately there was a second call, from the *Washington Post*. It had a story that the grand jury had taken a "straw vote" on indicting President Nixon and had voted 19–0 in favor of it. The *Post* wanted a comment from the Special Prosecutor or from public-affairs officer Jim Doyle—who had, like Jaworski, left on a vacation a few hours before.

The *Post* story was especially alarming, because it seemed so far off base. If the story was a misinterpretation of the grand jury's authorization to name the President as a conspirator its publication would not only destroy the secrecy of that action and thus defeat our objective of not appearing to prejudice the President's impeachment defense, but would also make the jury's action seem worse than it really was. Or else the story was a complete red herring that *we* would be accused falsely of leaking. The alleged source for the story could not be anyone in the Special Prosecutor's office because, as far as we knew, nothing of the sort had happened.

The *Post* story placed us in quandary. If it ran, it would obviously be harmful to us, to the grand jury, and to our case. We were wary of initiating any request to *Post* officials not to run the story, lest we be accused of trying to manage the news. At the same time, the story seemed to us to be wrong. John Barker, assistant press aide, made several attempts to reach Jaworski at the airport in Texas where he was due to arrive from Washington. Interspersed with these calls were conversations with Ben Bradlee, the managing editor of the *Post*, and attempts to reach Katherine Graham, *Post* publisher, at an airport in Connecticut.

Barker tried to find out in more detail what the *Post* was going to print. It appeared that in fact the *Post* was wavering a bit. Maybe it had only one source for its story; under informal guidelines for its Watergate investigative reporting, the *Post* ordinarily did not run an "anonymous-source" story without confirmation from at least two such sources. Barker, then Jaworski, told the *Post* that while we could not comment formally on its story, the grand jury had never taken a straw vote on indicting the President under our auspices, nor did we have any knowledge of such a vote. They told the *Post* editors that the story would be very harmful to everybody if it weren't true, and urged them to double- and triple-source the story before printing it.

While these phone conversations were going on, we recalled two comments made by grand jurors the previous week that had made no sense at the time. On Tuesday the grand jury had had one of a number of private sessions (without any prosecutors present) to discuss matters relating to the report and indictment. Afterward the grand-jury foreman, Vladimir Pregelj, mentioned to us that the grand jury had "voted on the President, twenty-six to nothing." When the entire task force reentered the jury room, another juror mentioned some kind of "vote," and said jocularly, "Well, it was thirty-eight to nothing." Since there were only nineteen grand jurors present that day, the implication seemed to be that the jurors were so enthusiastic that when a hand vote was called some or all raised two hands rather than just one. But at the time we were at a loss to explain the jurors' reference to a "vote," since we had not asked them to take any vote during that particular session. At the time, we passed off the remarks as references to the vote the jury had taken the day before, Monday, to authorize us to name the President as an unindicted co-conspirator. Now, in light of the *Post's* claim, the remarks took on new meaning.

Nevertheless, remonstrations with *Post* officials continued. Our suspicions notwithstanding, we believed it was fair to represent to the *Post* that the prosecutors had nothing to do with any vote to indict President Nixon and had no knowledge of such a vote. We also wanted to be sure that the *Post* story, if ultimately published, made it plain that the "anonymous source" was not in our office. This was the closest we ever came (so far as we know) to an attempt to get a story killed by going to media management. In this case, however, there was no direct plea not to run the story but rather a disclaimer that we had anything to do with the alleged event, coupled with exhortations about checking additional sources in light of the sensitive and potentially harmful subject matter. But our efforts did amount to something more aggressive than the "negative guidance" sometimes afforded by press officer Jim Doyle as a service to inquiring reporters checking out apparently spurious "tips."

Evidently the *Post* never found a second source for its account or was wary of it for some other reason. The news story that was eventually published, based on "courthouse sources," stated only that the grand jurors would have willingly indicted the President if permitted to do so. Similar stories about the grand jury's attitude appeared in other news media at about the same time. On March 5, Daniel Schorr reported on *CBS News* that the grand jury had actually taken a straw vote on the issue and had voted unanimously in favor of indictment; by that time, Schorr's report was little noticed.

By the second week of March our office was besieged with press queries about our widely reported decision to steer the grand jury away from possible indictment of the President. A short formal statement was drafted by Leon Jaworski to answer these inquiries. In a situation of "legal doubt," his statement said, it would not be "responsible" to entertain an indictment of Mr. Nixon (even if the evidence justified one) only to have the Supreme Court rule much later that such a course had been unconstitutional. The statement also mentioned that "another sound reason" for avoiding indictment was that the House Judiciary Committee was a more "appropriate" body for handling evidence relating to the President "in the first instance." The final words were added to echo the grand jury's changes in the preamble to their report, reserving for themselves the right to come back and consider indictment at some later time if Congress did not act.

Although the grand jury did not, in the end, make any formal public accusation of the President, the course chosen by Special Prosecutor Jaworski and endorsed by the grand jury had virtually the same impact. The indictment itself caused a major public reassessment of the nature of the evidence and the way that that evidence surrounded the President on all sides. The media succeeded in convincing the public—rightly or wrongly—that the grand jury *would* have indicted Richard Nixon outright but for the fact that he was President. The road map transmitted to the House Judiciary Committee spurred that body on. And the grand jury's transmission of tapes defeated the President's strategy of keeping them from Congress, thus forcing him within a short time to publish his own tape manuscripts.

All these, together, resulted in a massive erosion of public confidence in the President and his protestations of innocence. By the time the public learned, several months later, that the grand jury had authorized naming the President as an unindicted co-conspirator in the cover-up trial, the disclosure of this fact was almost anticlimactic in its effect on public opinion. In short, our strategy succeeded.

THE INDICTMENT HANDED up to Judge Sirica on March 1 charged seven former Nixon aides and associates in the Watergate cover-up with a massive criminal conspiracy to obstruct justice, commit perjury, and "by deceit, craft, trickery and dishonest means" defraud the United States by manipulating the CIA, the FBI and the Justice Department. Four of the defendants—John Mitchell, H. R. Haldeman, John Ehrlichman and Charles Colson—had been perhaps the most powerful people in the government aside from the President himself during the first Nixon administration. Robert Mardian, former Assistant Attorney General under John Mitchell, had been an assistant to Mitchell at CRP. Kenneth Parkinson, a Washington attorney, had been retained by CRP after the Watergate break-in to defend a civil suit by the Democratic National Committee. The seventh defendant, Gordon Strachan, was the young lawyer who served as Haldeman's chief political assistant and his liaison with CRP during the 1972 election campaign. Never had so many powerful and close associates of an American President been charged with crime, much less in a single indictment. In the caption at the top of the first page of the indictment, Mitchell's name was (intentionally) listed first. Thus the case would be known officially as *United States v. Mitchell et al.*

The indictment alleged that the conspiracy in which all seven defendants eventually participated began within hours of the arrest of the Watergate burglars on June 17, 1972, and continued up to the present. Its purpose was to "conceal and cause to be concealed the identities of the persons who were responsible for, participated in,

255

and had knowledge of (a) the activities which were the subject of the initial Watergate investigation and trial, and (b) other illegal and improper activities." Part (b) reflected our theory that the cover-up had been designed to keep secret not only Watergate but also the Fielding break-in and the other "White House horrors" investigators might stumble over in looking into Watergate. The indictment made clear that the overriding aim of the conspirators had been to protect President Nixon—first his reelection and after November 1972 his political future. When the cover-up got rolling, of course, the conspirators also had to conceal the existence of the cover-up itself.

In addition to the conspiracy charge, all the defendants but Mardian were charged with actually obstructing justice. The Big Three—Haldeman, Ehrlichman and Mitchell—were charged with a number of counts each of lying to the grand jury and the Ervin Committee. Ehrlichman and Mitchell were each charged with making false statements to the FBI, also a felony.

The indictment was more than a cryptic legal formality. We knew the document would be widely read and publicized. We wanted it to "tell the story" of the cover-up in narrative form and in language that ordinary citizens—and, when we got to trial, the jurors themselves—could easily understand.

Count One, the conspiracy charge, first set forth the different phases of the conspiracy conceptually, charging that a number of "means" were used to further the conspirators' illegal ends. Incriminating documents were "removed, concealed, altered and destroyed." The cover story involved "planning, soliciting, assisting," and actually giving "false, misleading, evasive and deceptive statements and testimony." The indictment charged that the conspirators would "covertly raise, acquire, transmit, distribute and pay cash funds to and for the benefit of" the burglars to induce their silence. Finally, it alleged that offers of "leniency, executive clemency and other benefits" were extended to the burglars and later to higher-ups.

The indictment then told the story over again, chronologically. The law of conspiracy requires not only that there be an illegal "agreement" but that at least one "overt act" have been committed to carry out the agreement. We were legally required to allege only a single overt act; but since we wanted to list as many of the important events in the cover-up as possible, we included forty-two. The majority dealt with the payment of hush money. In our minds, this was our most impressive evidence. The motives of Haldeman, Ehrlichman and Mitchell for approving the payments were simply not subject to innocent interpretation. The defendants could say anything they wanted about that money, but no rational jury was going to conclude that the most powerful men in the United States had secretly caused that kind of cash to be ponied up to a bunch of third-rate burglars out of the goodness of their hearts.

The indictment was as notable for what was *not* included as for what was.

President Nixon's name nowhere appeared, and intentionally so. Nonetheless, the document was just as much an indictment of the President, in a popular sense, as of his aides. The overt acts focused attention on the final payment of hush money to Howard Hunt on March 21, 1973, and the circumstances leading up to it—including the President's meeting that same morning with Dean and Haldeman. Then, in Count Eight of the indictment, Haldeman was charged with perjuring himself when he told the Ervin Committee that Nixon had declared at the March 21 meeting that *"it would be wrong"* to get more hush money. Since the President had publicly endorsed Haldeman's account, now alleged to be a lie, the indictment constituted a direct challenge to his position as well as Haldeman's.

Curiously enough, the fact that so many of President Nixon's former aides were included in the indictment seemed in following weeks to deal a more severe blow to him in the public eye than any imputations about his own actions. Indictments of many of his chief advisers had been predicted by the media and expected for months; the grand jury's action certainly came as no surprise. Yet the impact of the indictment on the public appeared to be greater than some of the unanticipated disclosures of the past few months—the missing tapes, the eighteen-minute gap, the cloud on the President's taxes. Obviously, indictment of so many of the President's intimate associates was the kind of thing public opinion did not "discount" in advance.

Perhaps the stamp of legal formality placed on these charges—even charges that had been circulating in the public arena for months—had greater currency with the American people than anyone expected. If so, it is an interesting commentary on the public's ability to distinguish between the flood of allegations emanating from congressional hearings and the news media, on the one hand, and charges generated through the criminal-justice system. Or, it may be that the indictment simply provided an index of the erosion in public confidence in Nixon that had begun with the Saturday Night Massacre and continued throughout the winter of 1973–74.

THE USE OF President Nixon's name was not the only thing we consciously avoided in the indictment. Nobody was actually charged with ordering the Watergate bugging, to take one example. And there was no explicit description of the White House attempt to use top CIA officials to narrow the FBI's Watergate investigation, an attempt about which the CIA chiefs had testified publicly. These omissions bore witness to the "defensive" approach we had adopted in preparing the charges.

That process started in early January. The Watergate Task Force took to spending most of each Saturday discussing the shape of our case and how it should be presented at trial, and reviewing weekly revisions of a draft indictment prepared by Peter Rient. Hours were devoted to thinking through the different charges. What tactics would defense lawyers employ? How would we respond? The object of these sessions was to eliminate anything that might make the prosecution vulnerable at trial. Some of our best evidence—the tapes, the money— left room for no effective trial defense. Why pile on additional evidence that opened up lines for effective rebuttal by the defense or tactics that might divert the jury? Every proposed addition to the tight core of our case was evaluated by its downside risk: What was the *worst* we could expect from the defense at trial if we included the additional matter in our indictment?

We quickly decided to concentrate on the cover-up alone. The testimony documenting the cover-up was far stronger than the proof of who knew about the bugging in advance. There was some evidence to suggest that three or four of the defendants named in our indictment knew about the bugging attempt prior to June 17. But intimation is not proof. We had live testimony against only one: John Mitchell. That testimony was conflicting. Jeb Magruder told us that Mitchell had approved the $250,000 Gemstone plan. But Mitchell's former confidant Fred LaRue held to his original recollection that Mitchell deferred action on the program.

Technical legal problems also deterred us from charging some but not all of the defendants with planning the break-in and bugging. If the planning and the cover-up were held to be "separate conspiracies," then evidence admissible at trial against some of the defendants might be inadmissible against others.

As prosecutors, we felt no moral or professional obligation to "assess responsibility" for the Watergate bugging. In our view the cover-up had been more pernicious than the bugging. The bugging was a CRP operation. The cover-up became a White House project, an attempt by the highest government officials charged with enforcing the criminal law to subvert it.

Finally, we wanted to be as certain as we could of winning convictions. Faced with a potential defendant who has engaged in a variety of criminal activities, the prosecutor usually "takes his best shot." The strongest evidence we had was evidence of the cover-up; that was our best shot.

Our most difficult decision in drafting the indictment was whether to include the intervention of top CIA officials shortly after the Watergate break-in to restrain the FBI's rapidly developing investigation. Our problem was not that the evidence against Haldeman and Ehrlichman was equivocal. Rather, we feared that if the defendants were given the slightest opening they would throw up national security as a smokescreen at trial. If they could convince the jury that legitimate national-security considerations motivated even one minor aspect of their early participation in the cover-up, the jury might wonder if national security justified the rest of their misdeeds too. The possibilities for generating smoke were endless. The defendants might claim that only the President knew about certain secret Mexican operations, and try to call him as a witness; the President could then refuse to testify and the defendants could move to dismiss all the charges against them on the ground that a vital part of their defense was being denied to them. Or Haldeman might take the position that he knew what was involved but it was too secret to divulge to the judge and jury.

If allowed to bring up national security, Haldeman and Ehrlichman might try to mount an entire trial defense without ever addressing themselves to the questions we knew they could *not* answer satisfactorily: Why was money paid to the burglars? Why did White House aides fail to inform investigators that the bugging was part of a program approved by the highest officials at CRP, even when they knew perjury was being committed?

Reluctantly, we concluded that while evidence of CIA intervention would be helpful in the prosecution's case at trial, the downside risk was far greater than the possible benefit. Consequently, the indictment did not commit us to prove the incident at trial, but left the option open.

Another early decision was to charge the major participants in the cover-up under the federal conspiracy statute. There was sardonic irony in this choice. Abuse of this same conspiracy law to prosecute political opponents of the Vietnam War had become a trademark of the first Nixon administration, and particularly of John Mitchell's Justice Department. The chief architect of a series of conspiracy prosecutions against antiwar figures had been Robert Mardian, the ultra-conservative lawyer from Phoenix, Arizona, brought into the Justice Department by Mitchell to head its revived Internal Security Division.

To be fair, criticism of the law of criminal conspiracy did not begin with the Nixon Administration's excesses. Lawyers and laymen have long deplored a number of distinct hazards to individual rights posed by conspiracy prosecutions. Chief among these is the possibility that the prosecutor may charge conspiracy (i.e., an agreement to commit illegal acts) when he cannot marshal sufficient proof of the actual illegal acts the conspirators are alleged to have plotted. (Some European "civil law" countries permit conspiracy prosecutions only upon a showing of concerted action by all conspirators to commit the most serious crimes.) Another is the rule that the conspirators need not have physically come together and made a formal pact to break the law— or even met each other. The prosecution must prove only that by their actions the alleged conspirators were "aware of" and "acted in furtherance of" a common scheme. Criticism has also been directed at the wide procedural latitude permitted the prosecution at conspiracy trials.

The Nixon Administration conspiracy prosecutions embodied most of these dangers. Usually, the purported "agreement" either was little more than a hypothetical political discussion never followed by meaningful action to achieve illegal ends (as in the prosecution of Philip Berrigan and others for conspiring to kidnap Henry Kissinger) or involved a number of people conducting similar activities with little or no evidence of any common plan (as in the "Chicago Seven" trial of antiwar activists for conspiracy to incite a riot at the 1968 Democratic national convention). Often the basis for the alleged conspiracy

consisted not only in a series of acts legal in themselves, but in constitutionally protected free speech (a characteristic of the prosecution
of Dr. Benjamin Spock and his associates for conspiracy to counsel
draft evasion, first brought by the Johnson Administration, as well as
of the Chicago Seven trial).

Had our case been like these, we would indeed have been troubled
by choice of the federal conspiracy statute. But the need to reform
and limit modern conspiracy law does not mean it should be thrown
out altogether. There are two areas in which use of the conspiracy
concept remains legitimate, where it is an essential law enforcement
tool, and where potential abuses and dangers can be strictly controlled: political corruption and so-called organized crime. The typical
characteristic of organized crime is the existence of a hierarchical
structure in which the bosses get the organization's foot soldiers to do
the bidding, thus insulating themselves from apparent responsibility.
In a typical case there is no question that illegal acts have been carried
out; the question is, who is responsible? How far up the chain of command did the orders originate?

In this respect the Watergate cover-up resembled an ordinary
organized-crime case. Serious offenses *had* been committed: obstruction of justice, tampering with witnesses, payoffs, misuse of investigative information, perjury. All of the defendants had some knowledge
of what was going on. They met and discussed the problems that the
federal criminal investigation posed for them. Each of the defendants,
in our view, personally acted to help further the cover-up. We intended to ask the trial jury to assess each defendant's guilt or innocence of conspiracy by judging *his* acts, not those of his associates.
The fact that each defendant played an active role in the cover-up
blunted the possibility of unfairness that arises in some conspiracy
prosecutions where the acts of the most aggressive conspirators are
attributed to their passive associates. The issue presented by the
cover-up case was not whether crimes had been committed but who
was to be held responsible for conceded offenses by lower-level officials. Were their superiors responsible? Or, as the superiors claimed,
should their subordinates shoulder all the blame?

The conspiracy charge would also give us an important trial advantage in playing Presidential tapes which contained discussions of how
to further the cover-up. Under the "co-conspirator exception to the
hearsay rule," the complete taped conversations of the President,

Dean, Haldeman and Ehrlichman would be admissible evidence at trial if the conversations were "during and in furtherance of" the conspiracy.

Each of the defendants but Mardian was charged with actually obstructing justice as well as with conspiring to obstruct justice. Under present federal law a conspirator can be held responsible for the substantive crimes committed by his co-conspirators even though he personally committed no such crimes himself. This rule is usually known as the "Pinkerton doctrine," after a 1946 Supreme Court case, and is one of the most criticized features of conspiracy law. Theoretically, any one of our defendants found guilty of *conspiracy* to obstruct justice could *automatically* be held liable for obstruction of justice itself. We decided not to rely on the Pinkerton rule. Not only did it seem to us unfair, we were afraid it would seem unfair to the trial jury—too automatic, too gimmicky. We didn't need to reach out for obscure theories of criminality when there was evidence of each charged defendant's personal involvement. As in the conspiracy count, we decided to premise our case of obstruction of justice on the evidence about each defendant's *own* actions, not the actions of his associates.

ONLY WHEN the conspiracy and obstruction-of-justice charges were well formulated did we turn to possible perjury charges. The final version of the indictment charged the three major defendants with a total of eleven counts of perjury and making false statements to the FBI.

For example, during the initial Watergate investigation John Mitchell had sworn to the grand jury that he knew nothing about Liddy's intelligence-gathering program—a denial that had been essential to implement the conspirators' cover story that Hunt and Liddy were on a lark of their own. Mitchell's testimony was an obvious candidate for a perjury charge.

Haldeman and Ehrlichman too had testified before the grand jury under oath on a number of successive occasions, but it appeared that they had adopted a deliberate strategy to avoid being caught in outright lies by claiming they "could not recall" most of the salient events about which they were interrogated. The March 21 tape strongly supported our suspicion. In the conversation, President Nixon had lectured Haldeman and Dean that one of the advantages of secret grand-jury sessions was that they could avoid the tough questions by claiming they didn't remember, couldn't recall, couldn't give an answer that they could recall.

Legal requirements make perjury much more difficult to prove than most people realize. The burden is on the prosecution to rebut beyond a reasonable doubt the possibility that the defendant was honestly mistaken or beset by a faulty memory. It is not uncommon for persons charged with perjury to win acquittal by convincing the jury they might have been "upset" by having to testify, that they had inadequate time and documents to prepare for their testimony, that they were busy people who paid little attention to the matters in which the jury was interested, or that they wanted to be especially careful in their testimony by not testifying to something unless they were one hundred percent sure of it. Proof of what is in a man's mind—his "intent"—is never easy. Obviously it must usually be demonstrated by circumstantial evidence.

Sometimes, however, the prosecution has concrete evidence to help prove intent. In charging Haldeman with lying about the March 21 meeting, for example, ("it would be wrong") we had Haldeman's notes of the tape of that meeting and an admission from him that he had reviewed those notes shortly before giving sworn testimony contradictory of them. Moreover, we felt certain that Nixon's "I can't recall" lecture would make an important point with the jury when it came time to decide on Haldeman's truthfulness.

The indictment handed up by the grand-jury foreman on March 1 was the product of more than nine months of intensive investigation and more than two months of drafting and redrafting. It marked the transition from one phase of our work to a new and more important one—preparing for the trial itself. Based on the program set out in the indictment, we were confident that when the time came, the trial jury would agree with our analysis of the evidence and convict those of the Nixon palace guard who had played key roles in the cover-up.

CHAPTER **12**   **The Unindicted Co-conspirator**

WHEN WE HANDED the grand jury's report to Judge Sirica on March 1 we hoped he would zip it over to the House Judiciary Committee that same day. If he did not, the President's lawyers might intervene; then there would be a hearing, appeals to higher courts, and months of delay before the House committee saw any evidence.

Judge Sirica hesitated, but to our surprise the President did not object to transmission of the report. Instead, his former chief of staff H. R. Haldeman appeared as the President's stalking horse, claiming that his own rights would be infringed if the report were sent over to Congress. The President—to all appearances—stood above the fray. His counsel James St. Clair announced that the President would "voluntarily" hand over to the House committee copies of all tapes previously obtained by the Special Prosecutor's office.

Of course, these tapes were already on their way to the Congress in our "bulging briefcase." Nixon's tardy generosity could not hide the simple fact that he had been finessed by the grand jury.

Legal precedents unquestionably gave Judge Sirica the authority to transmit the grand jury's report to the House committee. Nevertheless, the judge kept us in suspense for nearly two weeks before ruling on March 18 that the report should go over. Nixon would have had at least a plausible legal case to block the report; Haldeman had none. The U.S. Court of Appeals summarily affirmed Judge Sirica's decision without calling for any arguments.

On March 26, nearly a month after return of the report, Judge Sirica formally turned it over to Judiciary Committee counsel John Doar and Albert Jenner in his chambers. Since that was the week the Watergate Task Force had chosen for a vacation, Jaworski's executive assistant Peter Kreindler went to the judge's chambers to be sure the report was complete—that each piece of evidence referenced in the road map was included. When the check was finished and the documents were being gathered up, Doar was unable to restrain his dry humor. With a twinkle in his eye he said to Kreindler, "You know, this is the most *organized* grand jury I've ever seen."

On March 7, another major indictment was handed down. John Ehrlichman and Charles Colson were charged with conspiring to violate the civil rights of Dr. Lewis Fielding, Daniel Ellsberg's psychiatrist, in the White House–sponsored raid on Fielding's office in 1971.

On March 9, the defendants in the cover-up case were arraigned in Judge Sirica's courtroom. Under a dull and blustery sky a huge crowd of onlookers, watched warily by a phalanx of jacketed Metropolitan Police, milled about restlessly. Some had come to gawk, others to demonstrate. Most of the placards assailed the President ("Jail to the Chief"), "Mr. Law and Order" John Mitchell, and John Ehrlichman. One demonstrator donned a giant papier-mâché head of Richard Nixon. As each of the defendants arrived and the police cleared a path to the courthouse door, the Nixon figure danced bizarrely on the fringe of the crowd, doing a "Watergate" snake dance. The mood, like the weather, was cold, gray and ugly—a portent of things to come.

Inside, Judge Sirica's courtroom had long ago been filled to overflowing. Some of the defendants pushed their way through the crowded courtroom, accompanied by their lawyers. Casually, a little nervously, they greeted each other. John Mitchell was the first to take his seat, appropriating the chair at the head of the long table reserved for defendants. Others stood by. When Haldeman and Ehrlichman entered the courtroom each greeted friends briefly. Then each approached Mitchell's chair and greeted him, as if paying homage to the Godfather. Ehrlichman and Haldeman eventually approached each other, chatted briefly but awkwardly, and separated.

Kenneth Parkinson, who had never met Haldeman or Ehrlichman, remained apart from all the other defendants, as he was to do throughout the trial, sitting with his attorney on a back bench. Haldeman inquired after Gordon Strachan's health. Colson and Mitchell indulged in a brief formal handshake and then ignored each other.

We tried our best not to act too curious. This was a remarkable assemblage of men, governing in the White House just a year ago, now gathered in the public dock. They had fallen from public grace, but they still exuded an aura of power.

We had met these men and their attorneys and interrogated them before the grand jury. In a peculiar way we knew them intimately: by their desk diaries, their handwritten notes, their tape-recorded voices. They held no awe for us. What fascinated us was the interplay of tensions among them. Thrown together now in a manner not of their own choosing, these were proud, arrogant and unforgiving men whose mutual dislike and distrust were manifest. John Mitchell had been screened away from the President by Haldeman and Ehrlichman. Then, when the cover-up collapsed, they had tried to save themselves by putting Mitchell forward to take the rap. Mitchell didn't respect Haldeman, but at least he had cordial relations with him. The mutual disdain of Mitchell and Colson was epic. Colson had campaigned long and hard to convince Nixon to use Mitchell as his scapegoat. Mardian was Mitchell's man, but would he try to disassociate himself from his discredited mentor, who had gotten him into this? Or would loyalty prove stronger than self-interest? Strachan might face the same choice vis-à-vis Haldeman. We wondered whether, when push came to shove, the defendants would abandon their uneasy cordiality in favor of finger-pointing.

After the arraignment, the defendants were taken to the basement of the Old Post Office Building, FBI field headquarters. There each was required to be photographed ("mugged") and fingerprinted. Some of them had tried to get out of it. Their lawyers had hinted subtly that this procedure was beneath the dignity of men who had been running the country just a short time before. The judge was unmoved by their pleas: the familiar front- and side-view mug shots were taken.

The Watergate cover-up and Fielding break-in indictments did not end the President's distress. In early March he had another accuser whose allegations were given considerable play by the media: none other than James McCord. McCord charged that Nixon's failure to report what he had learned about hush money to law enforcement authorities constituted a crime: "misprision of felony." Within a few days of McCord's charge, the President's counsel James St. Clair responded that Nixon did not have to report what he knew to "law enforcement authorities" because Nixon *was* "the nation's chief law enforcement officer." The same newspapers that had trumpeted McCord's charge (which was a perfectly valid one—it just seemed ironic coming from one who had been on the receiving end of the covert cash pipeline) appeared stunned by the elegant sophistry of

St. Clair's riposte. Had he rebutted McCord's charge, they wondered, or had he confirmed it?

On April 3, the Internal Revenue Service announced that President Nixon owed nearly $433,000 in back taxes, excluding interest and penalties. Much of it was due to an improper deduction he had taken on a gift of pre-Presidential papers to the National Archives, using a deed backdated to the legal cutoff date.

On April 5, the President's young, fresh-faced former appointments secretary Dwight L. Chapin was convicted of perjury on charges arising out of his supervision of dirty trickster Donald Segretti. His conviction was particularly damaging to Nixon since the White House PR machine had predicted that John Dean, one of the key witnesses in the Chapin trial, would be demolished in cross-examination. To the contrary, Dean emerged unscathed in the contest. The much heralded ammunition against Dean that the White House had promised to provide to Chapin's defense lawyer had turned out to be pure mush.

WHILE THE PRESIDENT was taking a highly visible public beating, less obvious but more ineluctable forces were being quietly set into motion—forces that would eventually drive Nixon from office.

During the winter we had asked the White House repeatedly but unsuccessfully for more tapes and documents. In order not to delay the return of our indictment with another court battle over a second grand-jury subpoena, we had decided to try for these tapes through the use of a *trial* subpoena after indictment. Once the indictment was voted, the task force wanted to move as quickly as possible with this strategy. Under the procedural rules, either party—not just the prosecution—can subpoena evidence for trial. The trial subpoena carries the force of law. Failure to obey can result in a citation by the trial judge for contempt of court, and thereafter potentially in a fine or incarceration.

The pertinent criminal rules provide that if the person subpoenaed objects to producing the items, the court may quash the subpoena only if it is "unreasonable or oppressive." But judicial rulings had made it clear that a trial subpoena will stick only if the material sought can actually be used as trial evidence. The additional tapes seemed certain to contain relevant evidence, so we felt sure that a subpoena to the President would be upheld.

As usual, the Special Prosecutor before resorting to subpoenas would give the President every opportunity to comply voluntarily with our requests for evidence. On March 12, Jaworski addressed a letter to St. Clair reminding him of our previous unanswered requests and asking for tape recordings and other documents relating to forty-four Presidential conversations, for use at the cover-up trial. From the White House there was only the familiar foot-dragging. St. Clair informed us that the President was considering a request from the House Judiciary Committee for forty-two tapes, and when he made up his mind about the committee's request we would get whatever the committee got—no more and no less.

It was the Judiciary Committee's demand for tapes that dominated the headlines. Since February 25, when the committee had first requested sixty tapes in all, no response at all had been forthcoming from the White House. Finally, on the afternoon of April 11, the Judiciary Committee voted 33–3 to subpoena the President's tapes— the first time a President had ever been subpoenaed in the course of an impeachment proceeding.

Setting aside the historical significance of the committee's subpoena, the problem was that it stood only a very slight chance of prying loose the desired tapes from the White House. The only means by which the committee could enforce its subpoena was to vote to hold the President in contempt of Congress for failing to comply. What then? Nothing. The House had no enforcement powers, no way to hold the President hostage to his legal duties. The contempt citation could be used as a basis for impeachment, of course, but if the President chose to defy the House this political remedy was the only one available.

Some had suggested that the House committee should go to federal court to enforce its subpoena, and thus avail itself of the court's power to compel production of evidence. Most of the committee members rejected this route: it would take more time than the impeachment schedule permitted. Besides, many on the committee believed strongly as a matter of constitutional principle that Congress should not have to piggyback on the power of the judiciary branch in order to enforce its own legal process. The committee's disavowal of judicial power struck a blow for congressional dignity but as a practical matter left the committee powerless to get the tapes it wanted.

Five days after the Judiciary Committee's vote, we filed legal papers asking Judge Sirica to issue a trial subpoena to the President for tapes and other documents pertaining to sixty-four Presidential conversations. In addition, we asked the judge to issue a protective order that would deter mishandling or erasure of the tapes while the issue was being litigated. In the past, the task force had pressed two Special Prosecutors unsuccessfully for permission to seek protective orders in disputes with the White House over tapes. The Presidential track record forced Jaworski to accede to our latest request. Almost immediately the judge issued a subpoena. He set the "return date"—the date on which the tapes were required to be produced in court—for May 2. Now the President was faced by two outstanding subpoenas for tapes.

The tapes we chose to subpoena were selected with meticulous care, but, in retrospect, the selection process illustrates the large role so often played by Lady Luck. Because we were concentrating on the main areas that would be the subject of the upcoming trial, the June 23 tapes that were fated to bring about the President's resignation were not included in early drafts of our subpoena. At the time, the use of the CIA to manipulate the FBI was an unlikely candidate for proof at trial. When the subpoena was in its final draft, Jerry Goldman passed around a hastily scribbled note suggesting that the June 23 tapes ought to be tacked on. The only way we could ever conclusively disprove the national-security justification for the CIA-FBI episode, he observed, was with tapes. Consequently, at the last minute, three recordings of Presidential meetings with H. R. Haldeman on June 23, 1972, were added to our subpoena and the entire list of subpoenaed tapes was retyped to include these additional items.

Nixon's response to the two subpoenas confronting him came on April 29, almost exactly a year after he had announced the resignations of Haldeman, Ehrlichman and Dean. Once again the President was trapped in a pincer movement, the criminal process crowding him on one flank and political pressures overtaking him on the other. Once again he was trying desperately to convey the impression of initiative. He had finally decided to do what we had expected him to do months before: give the public his *own* version of the Watergate tapes and, with a giant fanfare, proclaim that black was white—that they proved him to be innocent.

Shortly into the President's televised speech on April 29, the cameras swung to a prominent stack of looseleaf notebooks piled near the

President's desk. The President was giving the world "edited" transcripts not just of tapes that the prosecution and the impeachment staff already had obtained, but of dozens more—forty-six in all, nearly the entire complement sought by the House Judiciary Committee. Disclosure of these edited transcripts, the President said, would "at last, once and for all, show that what I knew and what I did with regard to the Watergate . . . were just as I have described them to you from the very beginning." Quoting a handful of exculpatory statements from the transcripts, Mr. Nixon concluded, "As far as the President's role with regard to Watergate is concerned, the entire story is here." These materials, he said, would "tell it all."

They didn't tell it all, not by a long shot, as we would discover a few months later. But even as he talked, we realized that quotations he was using from tapes we had painstakingly transcribed ourselves were selective, distorted, taken out of context. As it turned out, even his gestures were bogus: the stack of notebooks had been constructed solely for the purpose of inflating by five to ten times the supposed bulk of the transcripts he was releasing.

Moreover, the transcripts were riddled with deletions at inexplicable points, the parenthetical notes reading: "materials unrelated to Presidential actions deleted," or "unintelligible," or "inaudible," or "expletive deleted." When we eventually compared the transcripts with actual tapes in our possession we realized that many damaging passages were either omitted altogether or so obscured by poor transcription or exclusions as to be meaningless.*

As usual, the President's strategy was geared to the short term only. The self-serving claims of his evening speech and of a fifty-page "summary" (released in advance of the transcripts themselves) initially

---

* After the cover-up trial ended, an investigation was begun to determine who was responsible for these deletions and omissions. More than half a dozen long, incriminating passages later found to have been omitted altogether from the transcripts were the focus of the inquiry. In spite of a lengthy investigation, no criminal charges were brought. The Special Prosecution Force report, issued in October 1975, cited legal barriers to proving the requisite criminal intent necessary to charge the federal crime of obstructing a congressional investigation (an offense similar to that of obstructing justice). The investigation in fact developed considerable, though fragmented, information about those who had been responsible for this blatant effort to hoodwink Congress and the public, but the report did not make any of these findings public. The report's silence left those most intimately involved in making the deletions free, in later anonymous-source accounts, to put out a version of events absolving themselves from blame and pinning the rap on their former boss, the one man who could no longer be prosecuted for sponsoring the deletions.

dominated the headlines. Evidently the President had hoped that the sheer bulk of the transcripts would deter most people from reading them closely and that the summary would carry the day. Nixon was relying on the drama of his action to mask the fact that he was giving no *tapes* to the Judiciary Committee or the Special Prosecutor, thus defying both subpoenas. But even with the critical deletions, the orchestrated flimflam and the distorted transcription, the revelations that remained on Nixon's doctored transcripts were still too devastating for either ploy to succeed.

Based on the tapes we had already received, we expected that the new Nixon transcripts would contain a fair amount of material damaging to his case. But in fact they were far more explicit than we had dreamed, even with their frustrating gaps and deletions. We had even speculated that in the long run the President could help his case by making public those seven tapes he had initially been forced to supply to us under the grand-jury subpoena, rather than waiting for the prosecutors or Congress to do so. Yet when we saw the picture painted by the tapes we had previously received taken together with the new transcripts, we knew that the "blue book," as the bound compendium published by the Government Printing Office came to be known, had to finish him. What was in the President's transcripts would overwhelm any strategy that could be devised to hide or distort it. Richard Nixon, it seemed to us, had just committed political suicide.

The transcripts were harmful enough to the President's evidentiary case, but it was their tone that appeared to strike the deepest chord in most readers—just as the quality of the conversation on the March 21 tape had shocked us back in December even more than its substance. The transcripts showed that the President, Haldeman and Ehrlichman had talked incessantly of Watergate during April of 1973. They revealed that the sole concern of these three had been to limit the political and legal damage threatened by each day's developments.

Even among the conspirators the atmosphere was one of mutual mistrust and contempt. The matter-of-factness, the cynicism with which the President and his two closest aides plotted their course, and the hatred they voiced for their enemies—the "liberals," the Congress, cooperating witnesses and even some of their own comrades—destroyed any vestige of respect for Richard Nixon. Not that these conversations seemed diabolical: to the contrary, they revealed incompetent bumbling and an utter failure to comprehend what was happening in the real world. The level of discourse was appalling. Over and over the President would return to the same subject; often he had to be reminded by his aides of something he had been told minutes before. Occasionally the President would proclaim forcefully that he had reached a decision on some particular point, only to reverse himself a moment later at the prodding of Haldeman or Ehrlichman.

If the President had relied on the public's short attention span in releasing this mass of evidence, he was wrong. The public *wanted* to know what the transcripts revealed, and the media told them. Contrary to the President's hopes, there was a giant run on Government Printing Office copies of the "blue book." Two publishing companies rushed to print the entire volume of transcripts in easy-to-carry paperback editions, and they were on the street within days. The *Chicago Tribune*, a longtime Nixon fan, in a marvel of journalistic engineering carried every word of the transcripts in a special supplement; other papers serialized them widely. There were even reconstructions, "responsive readings" on late-night television with newsmen and actors talking the parts of Dean, Nixon, Haldeman and others. The massiveness of the material worked to the President's disadvantage, since it took most readers the better part of a week to get through it. Each day, embarrassing and incriminating new gaucheries were "discovered" in the transcripts.

The public's adverse reaction to the many "expletives deleted" in the transcripts, while perhaps unfair to the President (whether or not he used vulgar language in private was a false issue), can only be attributed to additional White House bungling. To maintain his prissy public image the President had ordered those who transcribed the tapes to remove swear words and embarrassing language from the transcripts. However, no guidelines were ever issued explaining what should be deleted. Consequently, as the public later discovered when prosecution transcripts of these same conversations were made public in the Watergate cover-up trial, most of the deleted expletives were words like "damn," "Christ," "God" and even less offensive phrases. Not that Nixon didn't use plenty of gross language, in a gratuitous rather than an earthy fashion: one of his favorite linguistic tricks was to refer to his political enemies, no matter who they were, by generic terms such as "the assholes." But the hundreds of "expletives deleted" in the newly published transcripts made the President's language seem a lot worse than it really had been. This was one instance where Nixon's hypocrisy had come back to haunt him.*

Close on the heels of the President's monumental public-relations misadventure, the President's lawyers embarked on a course of legal action that was to result in further embarrassment. On May 1, in court papers asking Judge Sirica to "quash" our trial subpoena, the White House argued not that the tapes were protected by executive privilege (as the President had claimed the last time around) but rather that the tapes could not be used as evidence at the cover-up trial because they would constitute "inadmissible hearsay." Thus, the President's lawyers proclaimed triumphantly, the subpoena did not meet the legal requirement that the material sought be "evidentiary."

Perhaps the argument that the tapes would not be admissible evidence was used because nobody could think of anything better. It would have been hard for the President's lawyers to stand on the confidentiality of many of the subpoenaed tapes, because the President himself had destroyed that confidentiality by publishing transcripts of them. More likely, the President's reliance on the argument that the tapes were "hearsay" was the result of a strategic calculation on the part of James St. Clair. An experienced trial lawyer versed in the rules of evidence, St. Clair undoubtedly had concluded that by failing to name President Nixon as an unindicted co-conspirator in the cover-up indictment Leon Jaworski had trapped himself: for if the President's taped conversations were not part of the charged conspiracy, then they would not be "evidence." But it was just this issue that had prompted the Watergate Task Force to press Jaworski so hard in January and February for permission to recommend the naming of the President as a member of the conspiracy.

Part of the President's miscalculation was undoubtedly based on our ability to keep the monumental fact of the grand jury's action secret for so long. The White House, attributing their own values to us, must have believed that if the grand jury had taken any action against the President we would have leaked it by now. The fact that wind of the grand jury's vote hadn't gotten out thereby proved to the

---

* This was the same Richard Nixon who, during his debates with John Kennedy in 1960, excoriated Harry S. Truman for his bad "language," promising that if he were elected, "whenever any mother or father talks to his child, he can look at the man in the White House, and whatever he may think of his policies, he will say, 'Well, there is a man who maintains the kind of standards personally that I would want my child to follow.'"

White House that Jaworski had declined to take any action. After all, who could conceive of the Nixon White House having such damaging information about an "enemy" and not leaking it?

We had anticipated that the grand jury's vote would remain a secret for many more months, until shortly before trial. Now St. Clair had outmaneuvered himself. By staking the President's case to avoid producing more tapes on the argument that they would not constitute "evidence" at the cover-up trial, St. Clair had all but compelled us to counter his argument by exposing the grand jury's action—now. For the jury's finding was the basis for the rule of evidence we would invoke to convince the court that the tapes were indeed properly "evidentiary." And in the bargain showing the court (and the nation) the true dimension of the cover-up conspiracy as the prosecutors saw it.

The President's legal papers were filed on a Wednesday; our written arguments in support of the subpoena were due the following Monday, May 6. All that week Leon Jaworski had been in Texas and was not scheduled to return until Monday or later. But Thursday afternoon the Watergate Task Force sat down with Deputy Special Prosecutor Hank Ruth and with several others. Bluntly, we told them that in order to make our best legal case in support of the tapes subpoena we would have to use the grand jury's authorization as an important component of our argument.

This was a decision only Leon Jaworski could make. The task force pressed Ruth to phone Jaworski in Texas and sketch out the situation to him. Would he consider our proposed course, and if so would he return to Washington on Saturday to discuss the decision with us? In the telephone conversation, the Special Prosecutor was noncommittal but agreed to meet with all of us on Saturday.

Meantime, the task force was working swiftly to complete a gigantic project: an exhaustive summary and analysis of the President's transcripts, all 1,293 pages of them. The President's lawyers had argued in their motion to "quash" our subpoena that the tapes weren't "relevant," that we really didn't need them. We intended to blast *that* argument by submitting to the court, under "seal," our interpretation of just what the transcripts really showed.

At 1 P.M. on Saturday, May 4, the task force and the Special Prosecutor's aides gathered in Hank Ruth's office to await Leon Jaworski's arrival. A brief discussion confirmed that the staff was convinced we had to go into court armed with the grand jury's vote. But would Jaworski agree? Although only two months had passed since the return of the cover-up indictment, these months had seen a significant shift in public opinion. First the effect of the indictment, then the other blows to the President's position. Impeachment seemed more of a reality than it had on March 1. Public reaction to the transcripts was already pouring in, all adverse to the President. Had things changed enough that we could reveal the grand jury's action without appearing to be too far out in front of the available evidence?

Probably. But this was to be only one factor in the Special Prosecutor's decision. More personal factors would also play a role. That afternoon, Jaworski arrived at the office in a dark-blue suit looking relaxed, fit and cheerful. He greeted us warmly and invited the assembled group into his office; then he closed the door. "Before we begin," he said, "there are certain matters I want to tell you about that will affect our decision here."

Jaworski's tone became grave. The previous Sunday he had received a telephone call at his Texas ranch from Alexander Haig. Haig had strongly urged Jaworski to meet with him at the White House. Haig would send a military airplane to Texas, within minutes, he said, to pick Jaworski up. So Jaworski heeded this unusual summons, came to the White House and met with Haig for an hour and a half. The President, Jaworski told us, had been at Camp David that Sunday afternoon.

According to Jaworski, Haig had "said some things I *interpreted* as threats." (Jaworski did not confide what they were, it was more Haig's tone than anything specific.) Much of Haig's wrath, Jaworski told us, had been directed at the Watergate Task Force, particularly against Ben-Veniste. Haig had accused us of manipulating the grand jury and hinted that our proof that the final payment of hush money had been delivered to Howard Hunt on March 21, 1973, might not "stand up." "Well, I went right into him then," Jaworski told us. Jaworski said he had refused to accept Haig's criticism and had told Haig that everything done by his staff was at his direction and with his knowledge. He had defended Ben-Veniste, obtaining Haig's concession that he had been treated fairly by Ben-Veniste during his own interrogation in the tapes hearings. Jaworski had told Haig that he thought the entire task force had done a professional job, and that as far as our proof was concerned it was "documented" (as indeed it was, nailed down beyond any doubt). We had been fair to the President, Jaworski had told Haig, but if the President now wanted to "lower the barriers" Jaworski was ready to do that. The tone of the conversation, as Jaworski recounted it, was evident from his response to another Haig remark. Haig had warned Jaworski that St. Clair would be "tough." Jaworski had retorted to Haig, "I've dealt with tough guys all my life," that St. Clair was hardly the type to scare him.

Then the real purpose of the meeting emerged. Haig had wanted Jaworski to read the President's fifty-page "summary" of the transcripts which he was about to release in his television speech the following evening, and which Haig said "proved the President was innocent." Not only that, he had wanted Jaworski to *comment on it*. Why Haig or Nixon believed that the Special Prosecutor might fall for such a ploy beggars the imagination. Haig was suggesting no less than that Jaworski join the President in an exculpatory public judgment on the transcripts without even reading them—on the basis of the President's own "summary"! The ultimate blurb for Nixon's "blue book." In any event, Jaworski would have none of it. He told Haig that he would read anything he was given, but he would not make any comments on it.

About this time, Jaworski recounted, Haig got very "nervous." Jaworski guessed that "Milhous must have been waiting for him up at Camp David on pins and needles." So Jaworski had returned to Texas.

Only a short discussion between the Special Prosecutor and the task force was needed. Jaworski agreed that we had no option but to press our best legal arguments in support of the tapes subpoena. That meant revealing the grand jury's authorization to name the President as an unindicted co-conspirator. The President himself, either unknowingly or thinking erroneously he had us trapped, had pushed us into it. Jaworski displayed no regret over this plan. Haig's "threats" had obviously rankled him, and he wanted to make it clear to the President and everyone else that Leon Jaworski was not going to be deterred from seeing the work of the office through, come hell or high water.

First, though, as always, the art of diplomacy. It seemed only fair, said Jaworski, to warn the President what we intended to do, and why. Moreover, Jaworski suggested, what we wanted more than anything else was to be assured of getting the tapes we needed for trial.

Perhaps with the ammunition available to us we could at one time promote a compromise, avoid prolonged litigation, and demonstrate that we had no desire to reveal the grand jury's action for political reasons, that we were doing this because our cover-up prosecution required it. Jaworski proposed that we select those subpoenaed tapes that were really key to the trial and agree to drop our subpoena for the rest if the President would commit himself to making the critical ones available immediately. If this compromise resulted in delaying the legal need for public disclosure of the grand jury's action, so be it. We would have to tell the President's lawyers, in all candor, that the grand jury's action would probably still come out in the end, as we would be required to reveal the names of the unindicted co-conspirators in the bill of particulars prior to trial.

While the task force began selecting the key tapes, Jaworski placed a call to the White House switchboard to reach Alexander Haig. Haig was on the West Coast with the President on a trip, but he called back within minutes. Jaworski asked to meet with him and St. Clair the next afternoon, Sunday, at the White House. Jaworski said nothing of the subject matter, but admitted it was of "considerable gravity." Haig agreed at once to the meeting. In all, we decided to ask for twenty tapes whose transcripts had just been published, and nineteen others.

At 3:30 P.M. Sunday, Jaworski, Ben-Veniste and Lacovara pulled up to a secluded White House entrance, where they were greeted by Haig's aide Colonel George Joulwan. With them they carried a transcription of the grand jury's action on February 25 authorizing the naming of President Nixon. Ben-Veniste, who was identified in the transcript as having presented the matter to the grand jury, was less than serene about this little Sunday visit. What would Nixon's reaction be to the bad news? The memory of the Middle East mobilization following the Saturday Night Massacre was very much in his thoughts. This was one hell of a way to walk into the lion's den.

Jaworski and Haig met privately for a few minutes while Joulwan entertained Lacovara and Ben-Veniste in the "Map Room" with tales of his service with Haig. Earlier that morning Haig had appeared on *Meet the Press* to warn that "excesses and distortions" in Watergate investigations might make the cure for Watergate worse than the illness. Just as Jaworski and Haig emerged, St. Clair rushed in, still out of breath from an appearance on *Face the Nation*, where he had just finished telling a nationwide television audience of the President's "final" decision to provide no more tapes to anyone. Joulwan was excused. Ben-Veniste handed the transcript of the grand-jury vote to St. Clair. As St. Clair read it, his face and neck flushed with color. At first, he seemed to think that what the grand jury had done was to *indict* the President in secret, and that a "sealed indictment" was at that very moment lodged in a package in Judge Sirica's courthouse safe. Briefly the facts were explained to him, but the explanation hardly decreased his agitation. Haig, on the other hand, seemed calmer. It was evident that he appreciated the fact that we had been able to keep this totally unexpected development secret for months, despite the national preoccupation with impeachment and the hothouse atmosphere of Washington.

The prosecutors reiterated that they did not want to harm the President unnecessarily, but that we were committed to the legal process. If the President forced us to litigate for the tapes, he would have to suffer the consequences. St. Clair's face now betrayed his miscalculation.

After a few minutes of discussion, Jaworski broached the subject of compromise. He showed Haig and St. Clair a list of the tapes we felt were key to the trial. If the President would hand over those tapes, he said, we would drop our subpoena; there would be no need at the present to reveal the grand jury's action. This list, however, represented our bottom line.

Jaworski made it clear during this discussion that the grand jury's action would probably come out later, compromise or no: if we needed to assert the President's status as a member of the conspiracy at trial in order to get the tapes into evidence, we would do so.

Haig asked for time. Jaworski agreed to delay the filing of our legal papers two days, from the next day (Monday) till Wednesday. The next morning St. Clair phoned: the President wanted an extra couple of days, until Friday, to think it over. We agreed.

Monday morning we met with attorneys for the defendants in Judge Sirica's chambers. A few days earlier we had asked Judge Sirica to approve disclosure, in our court papers dealing with the tapes subpoena, of "some grand jury evidence necessary to support our arguments." (We had not told him of the grand jury's action.) The judge suggested that instead of making the information public, we file our brief *in camera,* with copies only for the court and for other attorneys.

Meanwhile, in an abrupt about-face from its position of a few hours before, the White House announced that the President was considering turning over some tapes to the Special Prosecutor. Judge Sirica approved our request for a delay in the litigation citing "discussions leading to possible compliance" with the subpoena. Unbeknownst to us, the President had begun listening to the key tapes on our compromise list on Sunday night and was continuing all day Monday to make his damage assessment. He had until Friday to decide, but apparently by Tuesday morning he had heard enough. On late Tuesday afternoon St. Clair issued a statement saying the President declined to comply with the subpoena: no compromise was possible.

Happy thoughts cannot have been in the President's mind as that week wore on. On Wednesday night he took an evening cruise on the Presidential yacht the *Sequoia,* accompanied only by Alexander Haig. The next day, the press began to report vague rumors that the President might resign. The evening after that, the President again sailed on the *Sequoia,* this time with his family. On May 9, the *Chicago Tribune* called for the President's resignation in a harsh editorial charging that the transcripts showed the President to be "immoral." They, and his scandalous tax returns, "stripped the man to his essential character," the *Tribune* said, "and that character could not stand that kind of scrutiny."* The resignation reports mutliplied, and two White House spokesmen had to issue denials. The President would stay and fight, vowed Ron Ziegler. He would not resign.

The President must have realized that quick disclosure of the grand jury's action was now almost inevitable. Having suffered the worst that he stood to suffer from Leon Jaworski's hand, the President no longer had anything to gain by courting the Special Prosecutor. It was going to be gloves off for the rest of the journey.

During the same week James Neal returned to active duty to serve as chief trial counsel for the cover-up trial. Jim's arrival added another element to our feverish work in preparing our legal brief that would analyze the President's transcripts. Neal had had no access to the tapes received by the grand jury and had had little chance to study the President's newly released transcripts. Psychologically, he was unprepared for the massive evidence of Presidential guilt. His assumptions were still those of October 1973, when we had scant evidence of criminal conduct by the President. As the task force worked to com-

---

* Gerald Ford said, on May 13, that he had read the transcripts and that the "overwhelming weight of the evidence" proved Nixon "innocent of any charges."

plete our legal papers, we also strove to prove to Jim how strong the evidence really was. By Thursday, his trial-lawyer instincts had overcome his innate reluctance to believe that the President of the United States not only could be but was a crook. The evidence was there. Nonetheless, Neal's skepticism played an important role in the shaping of our brief, because he challenged us at every step to be sure of our facts and to separate argument from evidence. On Friday morning, Neal told Jaworski that he approved of our legal papers, though he warned him that we might get roasted for doing what we were doing. Jaworski signed the brief, and it was filed. We were committed.

MEANWHILE THE President's lawyers unveiled for the first time a new legal argument to contest our trial subpoena. Relying on the constitutional limitation that the federal courts may decide lawsuits only when a genuine "case or controversy" is presented, they claimed that since the Special Prosecutor was an employee of the executive branch and thus of the President, there was no legally recognizable dispute involved. Rather, the tapes subpoena represented a mere intramural squabble within the executive branch of government. In the President's role as the Special Prosecutor's superior, his lawyers argued, he had the unquestioned right to make the final decision whether his employee, Jaworski, would get the tapes for trial. The President had decided he would not; the dispute was therefore definitively settled, and the courts had no right to take jurisdiction over Jaworski's complaint that his superior had overruled him.

The President's defense was one that had been batted around by legal theoreticians for some months after it was first raised by a Yale law professor, Alexander Bickel, in a magazine article in late September of 1973. The defense had not been useful to the President in his battle to avoid the earlier tapes subpoena issued by the grand jury, because that body had a unique and independent status derivative of the judicial system. Nobody could have contended that the grand jury was an employee of the President. Our trial subpoena, however, was issued solely at the behest of the prosecutors.

The trouble with the argument, even now, was that it was more abstract theory than tangible reality. In the first place, the spirit of the Constitution's "case or controversy" limitation (designed to insulate the courts from artificial test cases and "advisory" opinions) hardly seemed applicable. It would be difficult to imagine a more genuine "controversy," or one more apt for judicial-type resolution. Constitutional interpretation should be flexible enough to recognize that the enormous executive branch of the federal government is no "monolith" with a single purpose and personality. Indeed, creation of a Special Prosecution Force was intended to vindicate public confidence that ordinary criminal procedures could bring to justice the most powerful figures in the government even though those procedures were supervised by public servants within the executive branch itself. If that turned out to be impossible because the President could resist legitimate demands for evidence on a legal technicality, confidence in the law, and in the Constitution itself, could only suffer.

More to the point, Congress and the President himself had recognized the problems inherent in such an arrangement and used the processes of the law to provide for them *in advance*, when the Special Prosecution Force was created. By his charter, reissued when Leon Jaworski was appointed, the Special Prosecutor was given certain legal powers, including the express power to contest in court any resistance by the President to the prosecutors' quest for evidence. The charter was a legal regulation of the executive branch and still in force. Thus the President had taken formal, legal steps to cede his power of control over his "employee," the Special Prosecutor, in this instance. That these regulations were legally binding on the President had been emphasized by the ruling of a federal court that Nixon's firing of Cox without just cause—plainly contrary to the regulations—had been "illegal." Now the President's lawyers were saying that the regulations were no longer binding on the President.

The President's move demonstrated how desperate he had now become to escape the tightening grip of the legal process and to avoid disclosure of more tapes which he knew (from his recent review of them) would prematurely terminate his tenure in office. Once before the President had used naked power to emasculate his Special Prosecutor. Now the President could no longer use this power without incurring certain and swift impeachment. Instead, he was attempting to accomplish the same goal, to put himself above the rule of law, through the guise of a sleight-of-hand legal trick.

Jaworski moved boldly to expose the President's action for what it was. In written legal papers filed with Judge Sirica we asserted that the President's invocation of the "no jurisdiction" argument was a blatant and illegal interference with the Special Prosecutor's autonomy. Jaworski himself took the issue publicly to the congressional leadership and to the Senate Judiciary Committee that had confirmed him. The President's position, Jaworski told Congress, would make a "farce" of his role as Special Prosecutor.

On May 20, Judge Sirica agreed with us that the President's position was untenable and ruled that the subpoena should be enforced. The next day, the Senate Judiciary Committee voted to support us, too, proclaiming that the Special Prosecutor was "acting within the scope of the authority conferred upon him."

Even before Judge Sirica's favorable ruling on the tapes subpoena, we had been calculating the chances that the cover-up trial could still begin as scheduled, in early September. It was inevitable that the President would appeal any adverse decision in the tapes case all the way to the Supreme Court. Remembering how the Court of Appeals had dragged its feet the previous fall, we decided on a new strategy.

In cases that present important and novel constitutional issues, a special procedure exists for bypassing the Court of Appeals and going directly for resolution from the trial court to the Supreme Court. Ordinarily, only the losing party wants to avail itself of this procedure, but legal requirements impose no such limitation. So, as soon as Judge Sirica ruled in our favor, we appealed to the Supreme Court to take the case immediately. The President's lawyers fought this suggestion tooth and nail, for delay was now a key element in the Nixon impeachment defense. But the Court agreed not only to hear the case directly but to convene in an extraordinary summer session on July 8 to do so.

Events of May and early June confirmed the unique and critical role the criminal-justice process was playing in extracting critical Watergate evidence—and highlighted the importance of preventing the President from blocking that process. On May 23, the U.S. Court of Appeals refused to enforce the subpoena for tapes served on the President way back in July of 1973 by the Ervin Committee. That case had been slowly progressing through the courts with noticeable lack of success on the committee's part. The new ruling killed it. The Ervin Committee, the Court of Appeals ruled, had had only a "marginal" need for the tapes.

The House Judiciary Committee too was manifestly unhappy with the President's refusal to honor *its* impeachment subpoena with anything more than transcripts. Counsel Doar and Jenner announced on May 13 that the transcripts alone were "inadequate and unsatisfactory," that they were no substitute for the tapes themselves. Yet when the President repeatedly made it clear that tapes would not be forthcoming, the Judiciary Committee showed no sign of moving to the courts to enforce the subpoena and eschewed any formal attempt to hold the President in contempt. The only remedy was political: the committee warned the President that his failure to comply might become the basis for an article of impeachment. These developments underlined the fact that while congressional inquiries and the media could play key roles in educating the public about Watergate abuses, only through the criminal-justice system were Congress and the public going to get crucial evidence on which an accounting could be rendered for these abuses.

Despite overwhelming evidence, the outcome of a full House vote on impeachment was still very much in doubt. It appeared likely that the Judiciary Committee would vote along party lines to recommend several articles of impeachment, but the vote in the full House was thought to depend in large part on a strong bipartisan recommendation by the committee. Many congressmen seemed stubbornly unwilling to recognize the indisputable evidence before their eyes of criminal conduct by the President. The votes of most of the Republican members of the Judiciary Committee—and a handful of Southern Democrats—stayed uncommitted until the final days of the committee's deliberations.

To some degree, the committee's apparent lack of progress or consensus was attributable to a strategic decision by Chairman Peter W. Rodino and his counsel, John Doar. The best way to assure eventual bipartisan support for impeachment within the committee, they concluded, was to keep the staff work scrupulously neutral and objective as long as possible, thus avoiding attack on the basis of any "unfairness." In practice, this technique meshed perfectly with Doar's personality and his "filing-system" approach to the inquiry, the gathering and assembling of every "fact" having any conceivable relation to the events under consideration.

On May 9, the Judiciary Committee staff began presenting "raw evidence" to the committee four or five days a week in closed sessions. The presentation consisted of reading aloud to members of the committee thousands upon thousands of pages of facts in the form of "statements of information" organized and numbered in precisely the same format as the grand jury's report to the committee of March 1. The contents of the Doar filing system were thus systematically poured out to the committee over six long and crucial weeks, ending on June 22.

The Rodino-Doar strategy successfully robbed diehard Nixon supporters of any basis for charges of unfairness, and undoubtedly cemented confidence in Doar's own probity and judgment. Moreover, the very mass of the evidence obviously made a considerable impression on many members. On the other hand, there were drawbacks in the execution of the strategy. The staff's "statements of information" contained voluminous material unrelated to the President's own action or to impeachment—the distinction between information and evidence was often blurred. In fact, from our contacts with the staff it seemed to us they had set out to redo every Watergate investigation from the bottom up, when what was needed was a cogent assembly of the evidence dealing with the President's personal role.

While the committee staff plodded down this high (and sometimes boring) road, the Nixon White House launched an unremitting and often vicious attack on the committee, its members, the staff, and other forces now perceived by the President to be arrayed against him. White House publication on May 4 of a thirty-two-page memorandum charging John Dean with "misstatements" in the Ervin Committee testimony signaled the beginning of this offensive. What came soon after was no less than an orchestrated attack on the motivation and character of the inquiry and of its leaders.

The Judiciary Committee's "objective" approach might have blunted some of this criticism, but unfortunately the committee leaked like a sieve. Though the evidence was presented in closed session, each day's adjournment saw committee members rush to seek out their favorite press and television reporters to discuss the highlights of the day; the resulting reports appeared on that evening's programs and in the next day's newspapers. The torrent of leaks gave Administration spokesmen the issue they were looking for, and they utilized it skillfully to provoke the partisan wrangling within the committee that the Doar approach had been designed to avoid. As early as May 16, for example, St. Clair complained that leaks were prejudicing the President's "fundamental rights." White House PR man Ken W. Clawson accused a "clique of Nixon-hating partisans" of leaking documents and demanded that the committee cease its "trial by innuendo." Nixon speechwriter Patrick J. Buchanan charged that those leaking the information were "nameless, faceless character assassins." Clawson later complained that staff memoranda were designed for the purpose of "slandering" the President and suggested they had originated with the "dirty tricks" division of the Judiciary Committee.

The most scurrilous episode in the Nixon counteroffensive was an article by the same Buchanan in the *New York Times* on June 14 apparently intended as the President's response to the grand jury's authorization to name him as a co-conspirator. The jurors, Buchanan wrote, were drawn from the most "anti-Nixon" city in the United States. Not content to stop there, he made the implicit racism of this thought brutally explicit. Seventeen of the twenty-three jurors, he said, were black. That proved something because blacks had voted "upwards of 10–1 against the President" in the 1972 elections. This was quintessential Nixon, revealing the same fundamental misunderstanding and contempt for the legal process that had created the climate in which Watergate became a reality. In Richard Nixon's eyes the administration of criminal justice became truly a politically partisan vehicle capable of being manipulated for political ends by whoever was powerful enough to control it.

The Nixon assault was having its effect. On June 22, when the House Judiciary Committee staff had finished its presentation of evidence, a party-line political split immediately developed about how the committee should deal with testimony of live witnesses. In truth, the whole idea of live testimony was redundant at this point, but the Nixon supporters wanted to give St. Clair an opportunity to cross swords with John Dean and some of the others who would be important prosecution witnesses in the cover-up trial. After agreeing to public debate on articles of impeachment beginning July 9 and a vote the week after that, the committee decided to hear five live witnesses. A Nixon-sponsored proposal to hear twice as many failed by a tie vote of 19–19; the committee was becoming even more polarized. As the President departed for a visit to the Soviet Union, St. Clair began on June 22 to present his "defense" of the President. There was considerable irony in this, since no case for the "prosecution" had yet been permitted to see the light of day.

In May the Watergate Task Force began to have occasional substantive contacts with the impeachment staff. Everyone in the office was extremely sensitive about these meetings lest they result in charges of partisan collusion against the President. The developing White House political attack on the Judiciary Committee intensified our concern. But the committee was, it seemed to us, certainly entitled to whatever evidence we had gathered concerning the President's role in Watergate that was not required to be kept confidential by the rules of grand-jury secrecy.

The contacts began with a meeting in our offices with Jenner and Doar and continued primarily with two exceptionally able Doar aides who had been assigned principal responsibility in the Watergate cover-up area, Bernard Nussbaum (a former alumnus of the U.S. Attorney's office for the Southern District of New York) and Evan Davis. At first we were taken aback by the triviality of some of the items of information being sought by Doar's staff and their focus on events that had nothing to do with the President's own knowledge or action. As time went on, members of the task force meeting with Doar's aides tried to provide additional information and points of view that would encourage them to devote more of their time to the evidence directly applicable to Nixon.

Personally, the task force prosecutors feared that the impeachment staff might not get around to the critical (and time-consuming) job of putting their case together in "prosecutorial" form until it was too late. Gently we hinted to them on one or two occasions that their search for evidence might be clarified if they had a better idea what kind of case they were going to make. For example, was their plan to propose impeachment articles in the form of criminal statutes? Or would the staff keep away from alleging outright crimes and try to focus on more widespread patterns of abuse?

Doar and his aides simply were not in a position to address these questions. They repeatedly explained their political problems to us: any attempt by the staff to organize the evidence supporting a particular charge in a prosecutorial format would subject them to harsh and immediate attack for "unfairness." Of course that was what they *should* be doing, but the climate created by the White House made it politically impossible.

In mid-June Hank Ruth suggested to Frampton that it would be a good idea to have in hand a comprehensive, up-to-date prosecutive memorandum laying out all the evidence against the President. The document should integrate the previous prosecutive report prepared in January with the evidence provided by the President's newly published transcripts. By the twenty-eighth of June Frampton had completed a concise sixty-four-page prosecutive summary. It demonstrated, among other things, that the President's participation in a criminal conspiracy was proved by much more than just the payment of hush money on March 21—the issue that almost exclusively had occupied the Judiciary Committee and commentators in debate over Nixon's culpability. The memorandum considered each phase of the conspiracy charged in the cover-up indictment and cited the most important evidence available to show the President's participation in similar activities. Specific statutes under which the President might be charged were listed. In short, this document was the summation of evidence a good prosecutor would give the House Judiciary Committee in support of the argument that President Nixon should be impeached and tried in the Senate for violation of a number of federal criminal statutes.

Within a few days John Doar became aware of the existence of this memorandum. Doar demanded the document and told the Special Prosecutor and his deputy that he would recommend to the full Judiciary Committee that it be subpoenaed if necessary. Doar was told, in response, that we believed it would be unwise to have a copy of this document go to the committee physically, as it was an internal prosecution document. Since it was obviously relevant to the impeachment inquiry, however, Doar would be permitted to examine it in our offices if he agreed to withdraw the "threat" of a subpoena. Several late evenings that week Doar pored over the memorandum in Ruth's office, taking copious notes.

After more than six months of assembling and presenting the "raw evidence" relating to the President, Doar presented his own 306-page "summary of information" concerning that evidence on July 19, the Friday before the Judiciary Committee's scheduled week-long debate. He and minority counsel Albert Jenner then joined in urging approval of articles of impeachment on five central impeachment charges. Two of them were obstruction of justice in the Watergate case and failure to adhere to the constitutional duty to "take care that the laws be faithfully executed." The prodigious and careful work of Doar and his staff would now bear fruit.

The next week, as the formal committee debate began, a bipartisan group of committee members consulting with Doar gradually fashioned the language of two articles of impeachment that a large majority of the committee could support. As we had expected, the Watergate cover-up article gradually came to look more and more like a criminal indictment for conspiracy to obstruct justice: it accused President Nixon of engaging in a "course of conduct" designed to "obstruct justice" in the Watergate case. As the committee members came to realize what we had known for months, that the available evidence supported an outright criminal charge, the long-standing debate about whether impeachment could be based only on commission of a serious crime became moot. On July 27, the committee adopted this article by a vote of 27–11. Two days later, it voted 28–10 to charge the President in a second article with "abuse of power," and on July 30 the committee adopted its third and final article accusing the President of unconstitutionally defying its subpoena for evidence.

The Judiciary Committee's final days of debate were carried live on national television and radio by the major networks and replayed on the national public television network in the evenings. These unprecedented and historic sessions played a key role in preparing the American public for the cataclysm of Presidential resignation, despite the fierce arguments by Mr. Nixon's Judiciary Committee supporters. Not that the evidence cited by speaker after speaker was new. Much of it had long been public—in the transcripts, released months before, and in the voluminous catalogues of information published over the past weeks by the Judiciary Committee. There was little to surprise careful followers of Watergate. For the first time, however, the American public was hearing this evidence from an unaccustomed source, out of the mouths of its own elected representatives, a cross section of the nation. The congressmen and congresswomen the public was now seeing on television were not the usual media superstar senators and "influential" legislators the public ordinarily sees and reads about on the largest national issues. Many of these were people who seemed to have been thrust into the role of "constitutional jurors" against their will, almost by accident. The pain, the eloquence, the uncertainty expressed by the committee members as they explained the evidence to their constituents on the television screen was unmistakable. Without these few days of nationally televised hearings the public reaction to the President's withdrawal from office two weeks later might well have been profoundly different.

If the Judiciary Committee's televised debates laid the groundwork for the President's resignation, the events that were to precipitate that event directly—the final meshing of the criminal process in its quest for evidence—had begun just a few days earlier. On July 8, the Supreme Court had convened in historic special session to hear three hours of oral arguments in the tapes subpoena case. Special Prosecutor Jaworski, arguing first, framed the ultimate question: "When boiled down, this case really presents one fundamental issue: Who is to be the arbiter of what the Constitution says?" If the President can place his own interpretation on what the Constitution demands of him, Jaworski asked the justices, "what then becomes of our constitutional form of government?"

James St. Clair followed Jaworski in oral argument, urging the Court to find that the dispute before it was a "political question" in which the Court ought not interfere, and reiterating the President's claim that the dispute was internal to the executive branch and thus not cognizable by the courts. The President, St. Clair argued, possesses an absolute privilege which protects even Presidential conversations relating to criminal conspiracy from disclosure. Phil Lacovara concluded the argument by rebutting St. Clair in what observers unanimously agreed was the best presentation of the day.

On July 24, three days before the Judiciary Committee's vote to adopt its first article of impeachment, the Court ruled. In an opinion by Chief Justice Warren Burger joined by all of the other seven justices participating in the case, the Court rejected each of the President's arguments. His obligation to obey the courts, the Chief Justice wrote, was absolute; even the President must obey the law. Recognizing explicitly for the first time the doctrine of executive privilege, the Court nevertheless held that that privilege must give way to the need of the criminal-justice process for evidence.

The President was in San Clemente on July 24 when the news was flashed to him that the Supreme Court had ruled against him unanimously. It must have been a bitter blow, not only because he had convinced himself that he would prevail but also because he, more than anyone else, knew the consequences of what he had now been ordered to do. As the day wore on, there was no word from the Presidential compound to confirm that he would obey the Court's order.

But there could be little question. Just as public reaction had curtailed his desire to finish off the Watergate investigation in the Saturday Night Massacre, now the President's further deteriorated position made it politically impossible for him to defy the Supreme Court's ruling. At 7 P.M. Washington time, James St. Clair announced that the President would comply with the Court's mandate.

CHAPTER **13** **Resignation and Pardon: President Ford Adopts the Monkey**

ON THE AFTERNOON of August 5, the White House released to the press partial transcripts of three subpoenaed conversations between the President and H. R. Haldeman on June 23, 1972. The White House transcripts proved that the President himself had directed the manipulation of the CIA in order to obstruct the FBI's Watergate investigation. Under federal statutes this was an outright criminal obstruction of justice.

Three days later, his already meager public and congressional support shattered, Nixon told the nation in a televised address that he would resign the following day. By the time his resignation became effective on August 9, he had already fled Washington with the bulk of his personal belongings on a jet flight bound for San Clemente.

Almost a month later to the day, on September 8, now President Ford hurriedly summoned the White House press corps to an unusual Sunday-morning meeting. To the startled reporters he announced that he had just granted Richard M. Nixon a "full, free and absolute pardon" for everything with which Mr. Nixon might be criminally charged in connection with his Presidential years. Thus in the end only Richard Nixon himself grasped the brass ring of executive clemency that he and his co-conspirators had so often during the Watergate cover-up held out to others as a powerful incentive to their continued silence.

Our office protested that we had nothing to do with the pardon of Richard Nixon. In the sense of our having a formal role, there is no concrete evidence to the contrary. Nevertheless, the attitudes and actions of our office during that critical month between August 9 and September 8 contributed significantly to the atmosphere that made the pardon a reality.

THE JUNE 23 TRANSCRIPTS released by the White House were accompanied by a written statement from President Nixon that was tantamount to an admission of guilt. The statement acknowledged that when Nixon approved an attempt to halt part of the FBI's Watergate investigation, he did not do it solely for national-security reasons as he had formerly claimed but "was aware of the advantages this course of action would have with respect to limiting possible exposure of involvement by persons connected with the re-election committee." In other words, he had sought to obstruct justice. And, the statement conceded, the new tapes "were at variance with certain of my previous statements." In other words, Nixon had not only sought to obstruct justice, he had subsequently lied about his actions to the public.

Unknown to us, some of the President's closest advisers had learned about the June 23 tapes more than a week before. On the morning before they were made public, James St. Clair telephoned Leon Jaworski and disclosed that three of the subpoenaed tapes about to be turned over to Judge Sirica pursuant to the Supreme Court's decision were very harmful to the President. St. Clair told Jaworski he had not known about these tapes and had had no role in suppressing them. When he discovered what was on them, he said, he had demanded that Nixon disclose their contents to the Congress and the public immediately. St. Clair's call signaled the imminent demise of the Nixon Presidency. Not only were the President's closest advisers convinced he was finished, they were beginning to be concerned about their own reputations and perhaps even potential legal problems.

The transcripts created an instant public sensation. Within about twenty-four hours, all ten Republican congressmen on the House Judiciary Committee who had voted against President Nixon's impeachment switched their positions and abandoned him. The news media and a flood of public reaction called for Nixon's immediate resignation. The "smoking pistol," several legislators said, had been found. Others pointed to the new tapes as plain and incontrovertible proof that the President had lied to the American people about Watergate.

In fact evidence already available to the public through the Judi-

ciary Committee's televised debates was more than sufficient to implicate the President in federal crimes and to prove he had lied about
Watergate. The alleged absence of the smoking pistol had always
seemed to us primarily a political ploy developed by the President's
supporters to obfuscate that evidence. Now, perceiving that the public
simply would not tolerate one more incriminating surprise, Nixon die-
hards seized on the June 23 tapes as the type of proof that had been
lacking all along and promptly switched sides.

The new transcripts proved that Haldeman had been fully briefed
on the background of the bugging and on plans to cover it up within
days of the Watergate arrests—just as John Dean had testified—and
that Haldeman had passed along his knowledge to the President.

From an evidentiary point of view, the transcripts were pure gold.
Haldeman explained to Nixon, in their first meeting on June 23, that
"on the investigation" they were "back to the—in the, the problem
area because the FBI is not under control, . . . their investigation is
now leading into some productive areas, because they've been able to
trace the money . . . through the bank . . . And it goes in some directions we don't want it to do. . . . [T]he only way to solve this, and
we're set up beautifully to do it . . . is for us to have Walters call Pat
Gray and just say, 'Stay the hell out of this, this, ah, business here, we
don't want you to go any further on it.' "

Haldeman also told the President that the money found on the
Watergate burglars, which had been laundered through a Mexican
bank, was "directly traceable" to CRP through a number of Texans
and a Minnesota campaign official named Dahlberg. Nixon suggested
that perhaps these people could be convinced to give the FBI a false
story. Haldeman demurred: "Well, if they will. But then we're relying
on more and more people all the time."

Haldeman pressed instead for the CIA ploy. Nixon: "All right, fine.
. . . I'm not going to get that involved. . . . You call them in. . . . Play it
tough." Later he instructed Haldeman to have the CIA "call the FBI
in and say that we wish for the country, don't go any further into this
case, period."

During a second conversation on June 23 the President cautioned
Haldeman: "Just better tough it and lay it on them. . . . I don't want
them to get any ideas we're doing it because our concern is political.
. . . And at the same time I would not tell them that it is not political."

The transcripts exposed the previous Haldeman-Nixon version of these events and the national-security justification for calling in the CIA as fabrications. Use of the CIA had had nothing to do with legitimate CIA or national-security interests. The conversations on the tapes and the intentions they laid bare were so unequivocal that there was no way Haldeman or Ehrlichman (who had participated with Haldeman in meeting with top CIA officials on June 23) could walk away from the plain implications of this evidence.

In the statement accompanying release of the June 23 transcripts, President Nixon excused his previous lies by saying they had been "based on my recollection at the time." What made this lame excuse incredible to us—and what apparently convinced Nixon and his advisers that he was trapped—was the fact that he had reviewed those same June 23 tapes in early May of 1974, just three months before. At that time the House Judiciary Committee was gearing up for its impeachment hearings and debate. In spite of his review, Nixon had continued throughout the impeachment inquiry to adhere to his earlier, false version of the June 23 events. We had proof that Nixon had reviewed the June 23 tapes, and he knew that we had it. Nixon realized that should he attempt to deny his familiarity with them we would make certain the House Judiciary Committee knew of his duplicity in short order.

As part of our inquiry into the eighteen-minute gap, in early June we had summoned White House aide Steve Bull to tell us what he had done for the President lately. Disenchanted with his role as Nixon's tape boy, Bull was still smarting from the roasting he had taken during the tapes hearings before Judge Sirica the previous winter. Moreover, he felt that the White House team of Haig and the Nixon lawyers had treated him poorly; all the more reason not to be thrust into the position of scapegoat for missing tapes. Bull told us he had a detailed list of the tapes to which Nixon had listened on May 5 and 6, when the President was trying to decide whether to compromise with us over the tapes subpoena. Bypassing White House political channels which required that all prosecutorial requests for evidence be screened by St. Clair and Buzhardt, Bull presented us his notes directly. They showed that Bull had cued up the June 23 tapes for Nixon on May 5 and that "P listened."

At the time, of course, we could not appreciate how important it would later become to prove these events. Now, on August 5, reading the fateful White House transcripts, we realized why the President had been foreclosed from claiming that the June 23 tapes were "missing" even had he been so inclined. And why he was prevented from arguing to his own lawyers and staff and to congressional supporters that he had simply had a horrible slip of memory in constructing his impeachment defense. The reason was Steve Bull and his May 5 notes, "P listened."

ON AUGUST 7, in the late afternoon, the President received a congressional delegation of Senator Goldwater, Senate Republican leader Hugh Scott and House Republican leader John J. Rhodes. The handwriting was on the wall. Leon Jaworski, who was at his ranch in Texas, notified the staff that he was on his way back to Washington and would arrive that evening. Might the President be about to approach Jaworski with a deal—resignation in exchange for a pledge of no criminal prosecution? Might Nixon be thinking of going to Congress for immunity?

We knew that Jaworski, for his part, saw his principal public responsibility vis-à-vis the President as insuring that Nixon did not remain in office in light of the evidence of criminal wrongdoing. Furthermore, Jaworski had a strong, adverse emotional reaction to the idea of Nixon being prosecuted as an ordinary citizen—a reaction undoubtedly shared by a substantial segment of the public. The prestige and symbolism of the Presidency that Nixon had gathered to him in the White House would not fall away altogether as soon as he ceased to be President. We felt sure many people shared the Special Prosecutor's instinct that the public interest would be better served by getting the man out of office and saving the country further political turmoil than by worrying about abstract principles such as the vindication of the criminal-justice system. From Leon Jaworski's vantage point, we believed, an offer from President Nixon to resign in exchange for immunity from prosecution might be an offer he couldn't refuse.

As our disquiet grew, task force heads met to outline a "staff policy" that would tend to discourage the Special Prosecutor from rushing into any deal with the President. All agreed that our office should take no action pledging non-prosecution of Nixon in exchange for his resignation, at least not without some concrete expression of congressional policy favoring such a course. Moreover, we ought not to acquiesce even in congressional immunity for Nixon except under certain conditions—including his agreement to leave his tapes and White House documents intact for investigators, and his willingness to admit complicity in the cover-up.

On the morning of August 8 Alexander Haig phoned and asked Jaworski to meet him for lunch—at Haig's home, not at the White House. According to what Jaworski reported upon returning from lunch, Haig informed Jaworski as a courtesy that President Nixon would announce his resignation that night in a speech of about ten minutes' length. Haig made no mention of immunity for Nixon. But he did say that, as he understood it, Nixon would not pardon the defendants in the cover-up case, nor would he pardon himself, before leaving office. Haig related to Jaworski, though, that both Haldeman and Ehrlichman had "been around" asking for pardons for themselves before Nixon departed. Haldeman had approached Haig directly; Ehrlichman had contacted Rose Mary Woods. Haig intimated that on Haig's initiative these entreaties had not been permitted to reach the President's ears. Ben-Veniste commented that it would be the final irony if the last pleas for mercy from Nixon's old "Berlin Wall" were prevented from reaching Nixon by his new gatekeepers.

If indeed Haig had been sent by his boss to extract from the Special Prosecutor some expression of disinterest in prosecuting Nixon after his resignation, the mission failed, according to Jaworski's account. The Special Prosecutor reported to us he had told Haig at the outset of their meeting that he could make no commitments.

We were heartened by Jaworski's account of his meeting with Haig, but our anxieties were hardly allayed. Would President Nixon really leave office without making any provision for protecting himself from the criminal process, throwing himself on the mercy of public opinion and the Special Prosecutor? It was not like him. Even if what Haig had told Jaworski were true, Nixon could change his mind and pardon himself and everyone else in the dying moments of his Presidency. Or Nixon could be holding out on Haig.

It was not until the President's televised speech that evening announcing his resignation—and a statement issued by our office at Jaworski's instruction saying that no deal had been requested or offered—that the Special Prosecutor's staff began to feel some relief. When the President's resignation became effective at noon the next day, we still had six defendants to try in the cover-up case and, to all appearances at the time, an additional potential defendant.

ALTHOUGH THE COVER-UP TRIAL was still scheduled to begin in a month, September 9, that date now seemed unlikely. In thirty days we could not hope to finish transcribing and reviewing the sixty-odd new White House tapes, in spite of a round-the-clock operation we had established, using skilled FBI clerks to make first-draft transcripts for revision by the trial team. The defendants too were complaining that they did not have enough time to evaluate this new evidence prior to the September 9 trial date.

Moreover, President Nixon's release of the June 23 transcripts and his resignation had created a new flood of nationwide publicity. The defendants had already filed legal papers asking for a "continuance" in the trial based on the publicity generated by the televised House Judiciary hearings on impeachment. The new publicity would strengthen their argument that it was impossible to find unbiased jurors for a trial beginning in the near future, because recent events were in the forefront of the public's mind.

Thus we now faced two problems that were interrelated: whether to indict Nixon, and whether to agree to a substantial delay in the beginning of the trial of his aides.

The trial team was split on what position we should take with Judge Sirica in answer to the defendants' pleas for a six-month postponement of the trial. Some of us thought six months was a reasonable delay in light of recent publicity, but we eventually agreed to acquiesce in a continuance of only six weeks. Jaworski, however, was reluctant to agree to any delay. Only after considerable persuasion did he permit the trial team to tell Judge Sirica that a short postponement of a few weeks might be in order. Nonetheless, to our consternation the judge promptly ruled against both sides that the trial would go off September 9 as planned. The defendants won the assistance of the Court of Appeals, which "suggested" that Sirica set a three- to four-week delay. The judge accepted the suggestion and set the new trial date for September 30.

Many of us, assuming that Jaworski would favor trying Nixon together with his aides if at all, feared that the Special Prosecutor's eagerness to rush to trial against Haldeman *et al.* was in effect an attempt to finesse any decision to indict Nixon. By traditional prosecutorial logic a joint trial offers the best shot at conviction of all the defendants. However, if the grand jury returned a "superseding indictment" adding Nixon as a defendant in the cover-up case, a new trial date would have to be set. It might be six months or a year before a joint trial. Jaworski's thinking may have paralleled that of Ben-Veniste and others who believed it made more sense to indict Nixon separately and try him at a later time. Why not go forward against Nixon's lieutenants immediately, Ben-Veniste argued, rather than wait a year to try them together with their former boss? Then Nixon's case could be presented separately to the grand jury as soon as the trial jury at the cover-up trial was chosen and sequestered.

Naturally, there were personal factors that came into play in this calculus, including Leon Jaworski's eagerness to return to Texas. A decision to press on with the cover-up trial and not to indict Nixon would permit Jaworski to depart quickly. Any other course might require him to stay, to help find someone of similar stature and national reputation to replace him.

Trial tactics were also involved, since we would prefer to have Nixon appear at any trial as a defendant rather than as a witness. Then we could bring out his knowledge through aggressive cross-examination, and his credibility could be impeached by his false public statements.

Finally, there were institutional considerations: Where did ultimate responsibility properly lie for deciding whether to prosecute the former President? With us? The grand jury? The Congress? Public sentiment? Should we as prosecutors proceed strictly according to the evidence? Or should we try to take into account the "public interest" and decide in our own minds whether it would be too divisive for the country to have Nixon indicted, thus prolonging the agony of Watergate?

There was strong feeling among the staff that the latter approach would be wrong. A decision not to prosecute Nixon in order to save the country further Watergate anxiety, we believed, should be made if at all by a more representative body, namely Congress. If the country didn't want us to pursue Nixon, better for that consensus to be expressed through legislation or congressional resolution than by the lone decision of one prosecutor not accountable to the electorate.

Then there was the grand jury, which of course had the final say in indicting Nixon (though it could not make an affirmative decision to indict without the Special Prosecutor's concurrence). Some suggested leaving the matter up to the jurors altogether: going to them without any recommendation. Others termed this a copout, for we felt morally certain the grand jurors would want to indict. Nonetheless, leaving the matter to the jury offered the opportunity to put the institutional onus for indicting Nixon on a body somewhat more representative of the community than the Special Prosecutor.

The issue of who should properly share in the Nixon prosecutive decision—to put it bluntly, who should shoulder the responsibility and take the heat—was bruited about in our office as the "monkey problem." On whose back was the monkey going to end up: the prosecutors, Congress, the White House, the grand jury, the court? Shortly after Nixon resigned, large publicity posters for the old film *King Kong* appeared mysteriously on walls near the offices of the trial team (silent courtesy of Ben-Veniste). The posters featured, of course, the world's largest monkey and aptly symbolized our dilemma. The younger prosecutors joked constantly about the daily habits of the monkey. When President Ford answered a reporter's question about prosecuting Nixon we observed that the monkey had spent an evening at the White House. When there was a move for congressional action we noted that Leon Jaworski had apparently sent the monkey up to the Hill and locked the door of his cage behind him. Prior to Nixon's resignation, when the primary responsibility for dealing with the President still resided with the Judiciary Committee, Leon himself had once remarked to us at the suggestion that he take some action relative to Nixon, "Oh, no, the monkey is on John Doar's back—I'm not going to adopt that monkey now."

Shortly after Nixon's resignation Neal had met with Jaworski and reported back to the trial team that Jaworski's mind was still open on the question of prosecuting him. Neal acknowledged that "every inclination and instinct in Leon's bones" rebelled at indicting the former President, but he thought the Special Prosecutor was inclined to see how public opinion flowed. If Congress did nothing to take the monkey off Jaworski's back, and if public sentiment seemed to favor indictment, then the Special Prosecutor might be driven to take that course, Neal predicted.

A few days later, though, Jim Vorenberg told the trial team that Jaworski was considering another plan—to present to the grand jury all the reasons why Nixon should *not* be indicted and encourage it to issue a report making clear its belief that while Nixon was guilty his indictment would be contrary to the public interest. At our urging, Vorenberg agreed to make a counterproposal to Jaworski. We believed Jaworski should agree to present all the evidence of Nixon's conduct to the grand jury and, if he wanted to, recommend that it not indict. But he should leave the final decision up to the jurors. If they voted an indictment, then Jaworski should agree to sign it.

In the meantime, Phil Lacovara had been preparing a lengthy memorandum to Leon Jaworski setting out his views on prosecuting Nixon. The memorandum recommended that the Special Prosecutor move quickly to indict Nixon and consolidate the case with the prosecution of his aides. Careful, complete and articulate, this memorandum must have represented to the Special Prosecutor a fact of some consequence with which he would have to reckon: his own counsel had now gone on record and had ably countered most of the available arguments for declining Nixon's prosecution.

Lacovara discussed at length the question of what weight a public consensus on the issue of indicting Nixon ought to have and concluded that it should be discarded for more objective factors. The public was entitled to a definitive resolution of the charges that had been made against the former President, Lacovara pointed out. He called it "extraordinarily unjust" that Nixon's subordinates faced jail sentences and personal and professional ruin while Nixon himself retained the not inconsiderable perquisites of a former President who had left office honorably.

Finally, Lacovara's memorandum argued that the extensive publicity that had surrounded Nixon's role in Watergate would not make it impossible for him to get a fair trial in the reasonably foreseeable future.

THE QUESTION of prejudicial publicity addressed by Lacovara was a peculiar one that had suddenly become very important. On August 27 we learned that Nixon had engaged Herbert J. Miller as his personal attorney.* Jack Miller and Jaworski had several private meetings.

---

* In a bizarre but humorous sidelight to Miller's retention, Miller had a telephone conversation with his old friend Jim Neal just a few minutes after Miller had informed Jaworski he now represented Nixon. Jaworski, however, had not yet informed Neal, though Miller obviously assumed he had. A jocular discussion ensued between Neal and Miller about Miller's "bringing his client in on a misdemeanor." Neal assumed

During these meetings they discussed whether the publicity generated by the House Judiciary Committee hearings had been so prejudicial to Nixon that it would never be possible to find a truly unbiased
jury. If this were true, the argument went, it would be better for
Jaworski to decline to indict Nixon than to subject him to what
would inevitably be judged by a higher court an invalid and unconstitutional trial.

The prejudicial-publicity argument for non-prosecution of Nixon
was not entirely lacking in respectability, but there was absolutely no
legal precedent for it. There are many legal techniques available to
vitiate the effect of massive publicity: long delays in selecting juries,
court orders to prevent parties from discussing a case in public, careful
individual questioning of prospective jurors, a willingness to interview
a large enough pool of prospective jurors to find twelve who will be
objective, and transfer of the trial to a location where the publicity
has been less pervasive. Up until now, courts had consistently held
that the way to deal with publicly celebrated cases was to use these
techniques in attempting to select a jury. To do otherwise here was
to admit that the enormity of Nixon's crimes and the importance of
his office automatically guaranteed him immunity from prosecution.

The Watergate trial team believed the prejudicial-publicity argument for non-indictment of Nixon to be a spurious one. The curious
thing is that Jaworski himself, rather than Miller, was the one who
originated it. Long before Jaworski knew that Miller had entered the
case the Special Prosecutor mentioned his concern about publicity to
the staff. In fact, he badgered press officer Jim Doyle to compile for
him a complete set of press clippings surrounding impeachment and
resignation that carried information or comment adverse to Nixon.
This was an onerous task; some of us wondered what the point of
it was.

Jaworski also asked Peter Kreindler to research the issue of whether
any case had ever been thrown out of court altogether on account of
overwhelming pretrial publicity. Kreindler's answer in the negative
was delivered to the Special Prosecutor before Miller came into the
case. Jaworski was not pleased by Kreindler's conclusion. He told him

---

they were talking about one of a number of other clients represented by Miller.
Miller assumed Neal was talking about Nixon. Neal was rather taken aback when informed by others sitting in his office as he hung up the phone that Miller obviously
assumed they had been talking about Nixon.

that although his memo was a good one he had "let his bias show."

Jim Vorenberg also had a go-round with the Special Prosecutor on this same subject. Vorenberg told Jaworski that the publicity rationale for declining to indict Nixon was a lame excuse. If prejudicial pretrial publicity really presented a serious barrier to a fair trial of the former President, the courts should decide upon the matter subsequent to indictment. Jaworski retorted, "That's the worst argument I've ever heard," a comment we decided could be fairly described as letting one's bias show.

In spite of the conclusions drawn by Lacovara and Kreindler, and in spite of Vorenberg's arguments, Jaworski on his own initiative invited Jack Miller to submit a legal memorandum to our office laying out the prejudicial-publicity argument for non-indictment from Nixon's point of view. Miller was only too pleased to oblige.

The trial team was concerned about Jaworski's preoccupation with the prejudicial-publicity rationale for declining to indict. Unlike arguments going to the public interest generally, the publicity argument had the appearance of a legitimate legal doctrine—the kind of thing prosecutors are accustomed to deal with every day. Here was something a prosecutor might hang his hat on if he were searching for a plausible reason to justify avoiding an indictment.

On August 27 Jim Neal gave Jaworski a short memorandum setting forth his views on the Nixon prosecutive decision. Neal observed that he "personally leaned" to the view that "it would not be in the country's best interest to prosecute." He mentioned that many people felt Nixon had been punished enough; that Nixon did not initiate but only aided the cover-up; and that it might be difficult for him to receive a fair trial in the near future. Indeed, Neal noted that a trial of Nixon could lead to a "tragic event" (presumably assassination) and that "such a prosecution would divide the country for a considerable period of time." Neal went on to say, however, that irrespective of his personal feelings, he believed firmly that the "manner in which this issue is decided is more important than the decision itself."

Neal then proposed that Jaworski appear before the grand jury personally, let it review the new tapes, again offer Nixon the opportunity to appear or make a statement to the grand jury, advise the grand jury of Jaworski's own opinion, and then agree to abide by the grand jury's final decision on the matter. If the grand jury agreed with Neal's view that it would be better not to prosecute, Neal suggested that a "report" be made announcing the sense of the grand jury. Neal also suggested that if Nixon were indicted his trial be consolidated with that of Haldeman, Ehrlichman and Mitchell.

That same evening Jaworski sent each prosecutor in the office a short memo in a plain white envelope stamped with a recently acquired rubber stamp "PERSONAL/CONFIDENTIAL." The memo invited each of us to give him a memo within "the next few days" on what we thought should be done about Nixon. Jaworski's memo said he considered this course "far superior to the holding of staff conferences because in this manner I will be able to give study to any views that are expressed."

Two days later, on August 29, Jaworski wrote a short note in memo form to Neal thanking him for his memorandum on the subject and saying "there is only one point from which I probably will depart." That was that Jaworski did not want to delay or possibly "contaminate" the *Mitchell* trial. He was eager to have that trial go off on September 30, wait until the jury was sequestered, and then announce a decision about Mr. Nixon. In other words, if he were to urge indictment it would be a separate indictment and trial. Jaworski's memo also observed: "Mitchell and the others are not apt to plead if they know that there will be months of delay and ample time for deferring a decision involving a plea." The Special Prosecutor was still harboring the hope that as the trial date approached, one or more of the Big Three defendants in the cover-up case would break and decide to plead guilty rather than face trial.

Neal's "personal leaning" undoubtedly reflected the views of a large segment of the American public. In fact, at just about this same time, the press reported that a Gallup poll taken shortly after Mr. Nixon's resignation disclosed that fifty-five percent of those interviewed thought that Mr. Nixon should now be "left alone" rather than brought to trial.

In response to Jaworski's invitation, each of the prosecutors on the trial team submitted a memorandum to him. Each (with the exception of Neal) recommended that Nixon be indicted, a sentiment we had all shared with some depth of feeling from the date of President Nixon's resignation. The language and reasoning of our memoranda varied, but in general the reasons cited by each for his or her conclusion were the same.

By ordinary evidentiary standards there was clear and compelling evidence that Mr. Nixon had acted criminally. Moreover, the offenses he had committed were major ones. They represented an attack on the democratic system itself and on the principle of rule by law. They involved high costs to the nation by undermining confidence in public, democratic institutions.

It was clear, many of us wrote, from the text and history of the Constitution that the Framers explicitly contemplated criminal prosecution of a President who left office or was removed from office by impeachment. Prosecution was vital to affirm the principle of equal justice for all, to prove what we had been saying in our legal papers: that no man was above the law. More than in any other decision the Special Prosecutor had faced, there was involved here the public perception of the evenhandedness of justice. Indeed, the specter of Mr. Nixon's subordinates and agents trooping off to jail, suffering the humiliation of trials and guilty pleas, losing *their* livelihoods and liberty while he lived in remote splendor with his ex-President's perquisites intact was morally repugnant; it reeked of the most basic unfairness.

Nixon could not rationally be distinguished from his former aides on the basis of complicity, lack of responsibility, or quality and quantity of what was personally at stake in being prosecuted. Some of us cited the detrimental effect on the *Mitchell* trial if the jurors knew that the top man had received a "walk" while his subordinates suffered. Mr. Nixon's resignation alone could not be considered adequate "punishment," and in any event the purpose of prosecution was hardly to "punish" him but rather to vindicate the system his crimes had sought to undermine. Prosecution, we noted, obviously did not necessarily mean a jail term.

Nor did Nixon's resignation vindicate either the criminal-justice system or the integrity of the congressional remedy of impeachment: the public and history were still entitled to a definitive resolution of the issue of Nixon's involvement in the Watergate cover-up. Who could say, without such a resolution, what ambiguities historical analysis might later bring to this controversy? Nixon himself, if not prosecuted, would be free to write and lecture, to maintain his innocence, to claim he was hounded from office. What if history eventually came to regard the invocation of impeachment and the voting of articles of impeachment as a mere political witch-hunt?

Most of us took pains to rebut the argument that the indictment of Nixon would be too "divisive" for the country, that a trial would continue to drag the sordid aspects of Watergate before the public at a time when the country should be getting on to more positive business. We argued that the cost to the credibility of our institutions and government would be much greater if we *failed* to prosecute than if there were some public dismay over an indictment. As Carl Feldbaum said of this issue, "Many young Americans like myself believe that this nation is a mature democracy that can stand to abide by the letter and intent of its Constitution and laws."

In submitting our memoranda to the Special Prosecutor, most of us had little confidence he would be swayed by our views. What none of us could know was that events were rapidly overtaking us.

IN A PRESS CONFERENCE on August 28 President Ford said that he believed it to be the view of the American people that Mr. Nixon would now find peace for himself, and that he himself concurred in that view. Ford emphasized that he was keeping open the option of a pardon for Nixon. But he implied that it would be inappropriate to act immediately, since "there has been no action by the courts, there has been no action by any jury, and until any legal process has been undertaken I think it is unwise and untimely for me to make any commitment." Asked whether the Special Prosecutor could in good conscience proceed on this basis, Ford answered that Jaworski had "an obligation to take whatever action" he saw fit "in conformity with his oath of office and that should include any and all individuals . . ." Asked again, specifically, if he would grant a pardon before a trial took place, Ford said, "Until the matter reaches me, I am not going to make any comment during the process of whatever charges are made."

On its face, Ford's promise not to interfere at least until Nixon were to be formally charged meant we had a clear shot at indicting Nixon in six weeks when the trial jury would be sequestered.

But there was another way of interpreting Ford's remarks: looked at from the point of view of a prosecutor reluctant to take responsibility for the Nixon decision entirely upon his own shoulders, Ford's statement *could* have been perceived as an opportunity to resolve that predicament. For Ford had now opened the door to taking the responsibility—the monkey—on his own back.

A private memorandum sent by Phil Lacovara to Jaworski the

next day, August 29, sounded this very theme. Lacovara declared that Ford had now placed Jaworski in "an intolerable position by making his public announcement. I see no reason why the matter should not be put squarely to him now whether he wishes to have a criminal prosecution of the former President instituted or not." Lacovara went on:

> Since President Ford is now publicly on record as having expressed willingness to assume the responsibility for the exercise of the ultimate constitutional powers that are his, I believe he should be asked to face this issue *now* and make the operative judgment concerning the former President, rather than leaving this matter in the limbo of uncertainty that has been created.

Why had the situation become "intolerable"? Why was it suddenly incumbent upon Ford to tell the Special Prosecutor whether he "wished" a criminal prosecution to go forward? Ford's mention of the pardon power injected no new element into the problem of whether to indict Nixon *except* from the point of view implicitly reflected in Lacovara's memorandum: that Jaworski should not have to take the heat for a decision to indict (or not to indict) if he could possibly avoid it.

"Soon" after his press conference on the twenty-eighth Ford (by his own account) suddenly and inexplicably decided to consider an immediate pardon for Nixon, a complete reversal of the position he had taken publicly only a day or two before. He asked his counsel, Philip Buchen, to research the pardon power and also to find out from Leon Jaworski what charges might be brought against Nixon and how long a trial of Nixon would last. Buchen says Ford did not approach him until late afternoon on Friday, August 30. This was the day *following* Lacovara's memorandum to Jaworski urging that the immediate exercise of the pardon power be "put squarely" to Ford.

Did Jaworski talk to Buchen in the interim and act on Lacovara's proposal, thus prompting the President's action? Is it possible that Jaworski chose a more roundabout way to do the same thing, notifying Nixon's lawyer Jack Miller that if Ford intended to act he should act now?

One thing is sure: the source of Ford's abrupt change of mind following his August 28 press conference has not yet been explained.

Ford himself has said only that after the press conference he began to think on the matter. On the record, we are apparently asked to believe that the questions posed by the press on August 28 for the first time triggered Ford's interest in this matter, and as a result he decided he would reverse his prior position, deciding in favor of an immediate pardon, before the Special Prosecutor made any determination whether to indict Nixon.

In any event, it appears that by the following Tuesday, September 3, Ford had tentatively decided to grant a pardon, subject to two conditions being fulfilled by Nixon. One was that Nixon sign an agreement supposedly preserving the tapes and documents sought by the Special Prosecutor. The other was a statement of contrition or admission of guilt by the former President. Buchen recalls that Ford told him to communicate to Nixon's lawyer the intention to grant a pardon on Monday; Ford believes it was the following day, Tuesday.

In retrospect, it seems unlikely that Ford would have gone ahead in negotiations with Nixon's counsel without some indication that Special Prosecutor Jaworski would not stand firmly against a pardon.

Meanwhile, negotiations between emissaries of Ford and Nixon plunged ahead. Buchen had phoned Jack Miller on Friday concerning an agreement on White House tapes. By Tuesday or early Wednesday Miller had completed the draft of an agreement Nixon might sign. On the fifth, Miller and Buchen went over the agreement in Buchen's residential hotel suite in Washington and Miller then flew to San Clemente that evening together with a Buchen aide, Benton Becker, to confer with Nixon and Ron Ziegler about the pardon and the tapes agreement.

Before Becker and Miller went out to San Clemente the White House had been able to assure itself that Special Prosecutor Jaworski would not stand in the way of a pre-indictment pardon. Jaworski met personally with Buchen on the morning of Wednesday, September 4—alone, and without informing any staff member of his mission.

At the meeting, Jaworski gave Buchen two items previously requested by Ford's lawyer. First, there was a two-page letter concluding that it would be "from nine months to a year, and perhaps even longer" before Nixon could expect to receive a fair trial, on account of the prejudicial publicity that had occurred. This was a judgment upon which Ford was to rely very heavily in defending the pardon. Second, Jaworski gave Ford a list of areas outside the Watergate cover-up in which Nixon might conceivably have some criminal liability.

Precisely what was said between Ford and Buchen that morning is unclear. What evidence there is indicates that Buchen advised the Special Prosecutor that a pardon was in the offing, and that Jaworski —by words or silence—intimated that as long as the pardon was based on the premise that prejudicial publicity made it impossible for Nixon to get a fair trial, Jaworski would not oppose it.

The day after Jaworski's meeting with Buchen, Lacovara wrote Jaworski another memorandum amending his proposal of the week before. Lacovara now suggested that Jaworski recommend that any pardon issued by Ford be conditioned upon a formal acknowledgment of guilt by Nixon and an ironclad agreement protecting the tapes. Jaworski immediately fired back a somewhat angry memorandum to Lacovara telling him in so many words that it was already too late to have second thoughts about this matter.

Jaworski stated that Ford had not sought the Special Prosecutor's advice on the matter of a pardon but that "the comments made to me—all by President Ford's counsel—indicate that the President has reached some decision on the matter, and I have not been advised of the terms or conditions." Since

> we have been excluded from any discussions on terms and conditions I believe it would be highly presumptuous, in fact, improper, for me to impose my thoughts on his action. . . .
>
> The one conference I had with Buchen was *a follow-up on your memo to me*, dated August 29. The meeting was on Wednesday morning, September 4th following my return [from Texas] on the afternoon of the 3rd. *I followed the recommendation as outlined in your August 29 memorandum* [that Jaworski urge Ford to pardon Nixon immediately if at all]. I regret that I cannot follow your recommendation of the 5th which I did not receive until this morning, the 6th, because, if conditions were to be mentioned, this should have been done at the Buchen meeting on the 4th, if at all. But I would consider it inappropriate to have done so at that time, because our counsel was not sought. . . . [Emphasis added.]

In other words, the fat was in the fire. Henry Ruth, who received a copy of this latter memorandum, was surprised by revelation of the Jaworski-Buchen meeting. He asked Jaworski if it was true that he had told Buchen that Ford should act now to pardon Nixon or not at all. Well, Jaworski replied, he did not really mean to have said that in his memo to Lacovara. Jaworski quickly dictated another "clarifying" memorandum for the files. In this second memorandum he said that in his remarks to Buchen on September 4 he had limited himself to saying that Ford's threat to use the pardon power put the Special Prosecutor in a "peculiar position."

WE LEARNED that Ford had pardoned Nixon about noon on Sunday, September 8. Maureen Dean heard the news on the radio and phoned our office, where we were closeted with her husband, to find out if he too had been the beneficiary of Ford's largesse. He hadn't.

The first wire-service story on our ticker reported the reaction of Barry Goldwater to the pardon. He was quoted as saying that Leon Jaworski had serious doubts whether Nixon could ever receive a fair trial, and that Ford's decision was therefore a wise and courageous one.

In announcing the pardon to the press that morning Ford stated two reasons for his action. First: national reconciliation. The problem of massive prejudicial publicity made an early pardon mandatory, Ford said, in order to write an end to "an American tragedy in which we all have played a part." Ford then said, "I have been advised and I am compelled to conclude that many months and perhaps more years will have to pass before Richard Nixon could obtain a fair trial by jury." In the meantime, Ford claimed, Nixon would be "penalized," passions would be aroused, the populace would be polarized, and the credibility of our institutions would be challenged. Ford concluded on a note that was only too familiar to us as a reincarnation of the "prejudicial-publicity" argument: "In the end, the courts might well hold that Richard Nixon had been denied due process and the verdict of history would even more be inconclusive with respect to those charges arising out of the period of his presidency of which I am presently aware."

Second, Ford said that "President Nixon and his loved ones" had suffered enough.

That same afternoon, counsel Philip Buchen held a press briefing to elaborate on Ford's action. Buchen quoted extensively from Jaworski's letter of September 4. At the briefing Buchen also announced the agreement that had been reached between the Administration and Nixon to "preserve" Nixon tapes and documents for the Special Prosecutor. Of course our office had never been consulted about this agreement and would never have consented to it, since it not only recognized Nixon's ownership of all the tapes and documents, and turned them over to him subject to certain conditions, but also granted him personally the right to withhold anything subpoenaed by our office pending time-consuming litigation. In our view, the agreement was nothing more than a giveaway motivated by President Ford's desire to remove himself from the controversy over his predecessor's files.

That same day, former President Nixon's "statement of contrition" was issued at San Clemente. The statement admitted only to "mistakes" and "misjudgments," saying that he was wrong only in "not acting more decisively and more forthrightly in dealing with Watergate."

Jaworski instructed press officer Jim Doyle to issue a statement on his behalf saying that in view of the upcoming trial, our office would "not discuss" the pardon and there would be "no further comment on that subject from this office."

Frampton was appalled by the pardon, coming as it did in time to cut off any possibility of a resolution of the issue of Nixon's culpability through the criminal-justice system. He believed that Ford's action flew in the face of what we had been fighting for as members of the Special Prosecution Force: the credibility of the criminal-justice system and the reality of equal treatment for all. His reaction, one of anger and disgust, was shared by most of the young prosecutors within the office.

Ben-Veniste was deeply disturbed by the behind-the-scenes maneuvering which apparently contributed to Ford's precipitous action. If we had had the time to bring an indictment against Nixon (as Ford implied in his August press conference), then it would have been up to Nixon to accept Ford's pardon or fight the charges in court. By forcing Ford's hand, Ben-Veniste thought, we had abdicated our responsibility to see that formal charges outlining Nixon's conduct were presented. As for the decision to pardon Nixon, that was a political judgment within the bounds of Ford's constitutional authority. Ben-Veniste believed that strong public sentiment against pursuing Nixon through criminal channels, and the possible public reaction to a protracted trial of a former President as the country moved into its Bicentennial year, were factors that Ford could legitimately take into account in exercising his constitutional authority. If the decision to grant a pardon was wrong, then Ford would be made accountable for his political decision in the political process, at the polls.

Ford's decision was criticized by much of the media in bitter terms. The *New York Times* called it a "profoundly unwise, divisive and unjust act. . . . This blundering intervention is a body blow to the President's own credibility and the public's reviving confidence in the integrity of its Government." The *Washington Post* observed that Ford's action was of a piece with Nixon's efforts to abort the legitimate processes inquiring into Watergate and seeking a full public accounting—another chapter in the cover-up.

THE NEXT DAY, Monday, was the day the Watergate cover-up trial was originally to have begun. The prevailing attitude in the Special Prosecutor's office was one of frustration. Phil Lacovara had drafted a letter of resignation. We had written in our Supreme Court briefs, Lacovara noted, that ours is a system of equal justice, where no man is above the law. The prosecutors, the grand jury and the courts had all done *their* part during Watergate to realize that ideal. Ford's action, however, worked to undermine their efforts. Lacovara did not want to be part of a prosecution of Nixon subordinates whose guilt was also subordinate to that of their pardoned chief.

Many on the staff regarded Lacovara's quick resignation quizzically, as he had been planning to leave anyway and would have had nothing to do with the cover-up trial. Indeed, Lacovara was protesting action which was fully consistent with his own earlier advice to Jaworski—a fact which made the Special Prosecutor most critical of Lacovara's flip-flop. But Phil's letter summed up precisely how many of us felt. Noting Lacovara's invocation of the principle that no man is above the law, Carl Feldbaum remarked that he really hadn't believed it when he was hired for the Special Prosecutor's staff, and now he would be leaving the office still in disbelief. But there had been a point in the past year, he said, when he really thought it was true.

The long-run public reaction is more difficult to judge. The initial response was overwhelmingly negative. The country's honeymoon with Honest Jerry, the man who toasted his own English muffins, was at an abrupt end. Polls showed that substantially over half those questioned believed that the pardon was a mistake. Ford's popularity began a long-term precipitous decline. However, it also seems likely that a very large segment of the public—whatever their views on the pardon—may have breathed a large sigh of relief that the nation would not have to be put through another, final, disgraceful Watergate chapter in which the former President himself occupied the criminal dock.

The Ford-Jaworski argument that Nixon might never be able to get a fair trial—that massive publicity might tie up the process of justice for years—obviously played a key role in supporting the pardon. Buchen told the press on September 10 that Jaworski's conclusion that delay of "a year or more" would ensue before a Nixon trial was possible was a "significant factor" in Ford's decision. Buchen also leaned heavily on Jaworski's September 4 letter and released Miller's memorandum of law arguing that Nixon could never receive a fair trial on publicity grounds.

After the pardon, some of those on Jaworski's staff speculated that the Special Prosecutor had finally found a way to "share the monkey" of a non-prosecution decision with the President: in a situation where neither Jaworski nor Ford was willing to quite stand up straight to letting Nixon off, they had managed it by leaning on each other— in such a precarious way that if either one didn't lean quite right both would fall over. Others believed that in effect Jaworski had "faced down" the new man in the White House, making him adopt the monkey. According to this theory, the Special Prosecutor let the White House believe that Jaworski was about to indict Nixon and that once an indictment came down Ford could not afford politically to intervene with a pardon; Ford, in short, had to act right away or not at all. At the same time, Jaworski let Ford know that if Ford employed the argument that Nixon could never get a fair trial, then Jaworski would help him out with that argument and would not oppose a pardon. In any event, Jaworski achieved the result he favored emotionally, non-prosecution, without having to make the decision himself.

The Nixon pardon compounded our trial problems. Was it unfair to pursue Nixon subordinates when Nixon himself could not be brought to justice? Would jurors vote to convict Nixon's lieutenants, knowing that the boss had gotten away scot free? Would Nixon appear at trial as a live witness? Should we now try to have admitted into evidence all the not-yet-public tapes that showed Nixon's personal involvement in the cover-up, regardless of whether they helped our case against his aides?

Worse was the pardon's effect on the momentum of other investigations in the Special Prosecutor's office that focused on close Nixon associates. Who could be enthusiastic about pursuing those who had done Nixon's bidding when the top man was never going to be held accountable? Defense lawyers knew our plight, and knew that the pressure on their clients to admit guilt and finger higher-ups —especially Nixon himself—had lessened. The pardon guaranteed that many investigations would wither and die on the vine. In practical effect, our office was emasculated the day Nixon was pardoned.

One remaining question was whether anything could or should be done to challenge the pardon. Its legal validity was hotly debated within our office, but everybody knew Special Prosecutor Jaworski's views. If he had not actually invited the pardon, he had certainly welcomed it. And he believed strongly that Ford's action was well within the President's legal powers. Jaworski had already given notice that he intended to return to Texas as soon as the cover-up trial got under way. No one seriously thought there would be any challenge to the pardon from Leon Jaworski.

Anyway, the state of the law was not propitious to a challenge. Some commentators claimed that a pardon could not be granted before indictment and conviction. But in fact there was considerable historical precedent for Ford's early timing. A more convincing argument advanced against the pardon was that the President was bound by the Special Prosecutor's charter not to exercise his constitutional powers, including the pardon power, to interfere in our independent handling of the Watergate case.

Before leaving the office Phil Lacovara sent Jaworski a memorandum outlining this argument and concluding that a challenge to the pardon along these lines stood some chance of success in the courts. But Lacovara did not recommend that course. The only way to present legal objections to the pardon was to indict Nixon. Given the uncertainty of the matter, even some of those who thought the pardon was illegal had serious reservations about proceeding in that manner. The time to have acted was *before* the pardon, not now.

Jaworski himself strongly disagreed with the proposition that his charter in any way limited President Ford's pardon power, as he made clear when he submitted his resignation in a letter to the Attorney General on October 12. Moreover, Jaworski wrote that to indict Nixon "for the sole purpose of generating a purported court test on the legality of the pardon" would be "spurious," unprofessional and violative of his responsibility as an officer of the court.

The pardoning of Richard Nixon by Gerald Ford left many unanswered questions. Chief among them: Was there a deal? Did Nixon resign the Presidency without taking steps to protect himself from the criminal process, secure in the understanding that the man who inherited his power would take those steps for him if necessary? Ford denies that there was any deal with the former President. Ford's subsequent testimony before the House Judiciary Committee revealed, however, that President Nixon in his last days in the White House was preoccupied with taking steps to immunize himself from future criminal action.

On August 1 Alexander Haig had met with Ford and informed him that the new evidence in the tapes was devastating. Nixon, Haig told Ford, was considering a number of options. One of these options was to pardon everyone else involved in Watergate, then pardon himself, and then resign. Another was resignation followed by a pardon from President Ford—precisely the course eventually followed. The proposal that Nixon pardon his chief aides and then himself before resigning had also been raised in a written memorandum submitted to the White House by H. R. Haldeman. Haldeman went so far as to draft Nixon's resignation speech announcing the pardons.

At the meeting between Haig and Ford on August 1, Haig was seeking advice and perhaps Ford's support in convincing Nixon that resignation was now the only possible course. Ford claims he took no position and made no commitment. However, sometime later Ford decided he had better call Haig on the telephone to reiterate his position and make *sure* Haig understood that Ford had taken "no position." He told Haig that "nothing we had talked about the previous afternoon should be given any consideration in whatever decision the President might make."

Obviously, Ford believed that something he had said or intimated to Haig might have led Haig to conclude otherwise. Moreover, Ford volunteered at the very end of his House Judiciary Committee appearance that on August 8, the day President Nixon announced his resignation, Ford and Nixon met for an hour-and-a-half private meeting. Had there been an aggressive prosecutor on the House Judiciary Committee he doubtless would have asked why Ford was afraid that Haig might have misunderstood Ford's position on Nixon's "options," and what Ford and Nixon talked about on August 8. But these questions went unasked.

It is certainly unlikely—and no one has seriously contended—that there was an explicit agreement between Ford and Nixon. The real question is whether Ford subtly let it be known to Haig or Nixon that once he became President he would look favorably on exercise of the pardon power if Nixon resigned without pardoning himself. In this case, just as in the case of the Special Prosecutor's contribution to Ford's decision to grant a pardon, subtle attitudinal signals may well have played a far larger role than the public will ever know.

THE CRUCIAL BUSINESS of selecting a jury began October 1 in the
packed ceremonial courtroom on the sixth floor of the U.S. Courthouse. We were confident of the strength of our case, but an error in
judgment at this stage could still render worthless all our past efforts.
The trial lawyer who, out of eagerness to get started with the presentation of evidence, is less than diligent in screening potential jurors
often discovers sadly that he has plenty of time later to lament his
error. Only five of the seven original defendants would be going on
trial. Back in June, the Special Prosecutor had accepted a plea of
guilty from Charles Colson to obstruction of justice in the Fielding
break-in case. As part of the plea bargain, the charges against him
were dropped. Gordon Strachan had been granted a separate trial, on
the prosecution's motion, because of the unique legal problems posed
by his having testified before the Ervin Committee under formal
immunity.*

Our task in selecting the jury in the cover-up case would be more
onerous than in the usual criminal prosecution because Judge Sirica
had tentatively ruled that the defendants would be permitted more
"peremptory challenges" than the number to which they were statu-
torily entitled, while the prosecution would be held to its statutory
minimum. Peremptory challenges are exercised in the final stage of
jury selection for any reason to eliminate potential jurors a party
thinks may be unsympathetic to his case. Under the federal rules of
criminal procedure the prosecution is normally afforded six peremp-

* Strachan's lawyer, Jack Bray, played the nuances of the immunity laws with the
skill of a concert violinist—eventually all charges against Strachan were dropped.

tory challenges, the defense ten; but the trial judge may in his discretion grant the defense additional challenges. Here, the defense would have fifteen challenges to our six. The disparity could prove significant in the tactical duel that occurred when both sides exercised their peremptory challenges against the array of potential jurors, each side trying to select the best possible jury.

The pardoning of Richard Nixon infused further complications into the selection process. Even jurors customarily inclined to decide the case strictly on the evidence presented at trial might feel it was unfair to proceed against the henchmen when the ringleader had been excused.

As in any criminal case, a unanimous verdict would be needed to convict. Here, after a three- to six-month trial, a hung jury that could result from just one juror holding out against a guilty verdict would spell victory for the major defendants. The issue of whether pretrial publicity would delay or prevent us from even having a trial had been a close question up until now. After one highly publicized trial ending in a hung jury, the chances of being able to select another jury for a second trial in the foreseeable future were remote. Consequently, while the prosecution would be burdened with selecting twelve jurors who would be willing to decide the case our way, the defense in effect had only to find *one* juror who would be sympathetic to them despite the evidence.

Unless there was unfairness or major error in the trial, the claim of prejudicial publicity would be the defendants' strongest issue on appeal from any convictions. The primary remedy for extensive pretrial publicity is scrupulous screening during the jury selection process to exclude potential jurors who have biases they cannot set aside or who have been subjected to overwhelming prejudicial publicity. Consequently our task during jury-selection would be twofold: to eliminate those who were unwilling to decide the case in our favor if the evidence warranted it; and to make sure that the selection procedure itself worked properly to exclude those biased against the defendants, to prevent injustice and to avoid any chance that hard-won convictions would later be overthrown by an appeals court.

In preparation for the selection process the members of the trial team with little previous trial experience were reminded that from here on all our actions would be subject to the scrutiny of the twelve men and women who would eventually render a verdict in the case.

Just as we would soon be sizing up the prospective jurors, so too would they be assessing us—not only on the basis of what we said in the courtroom but also by how we looked and acted, by our mannerisms and facial expressions. Until the jury was picked and sequestered, any foolish conduct by anyone connected with the trial team might be observed, noted, and ultimately held against us consciously or otherwise by one of the jurors—and until the final panel was selected it was possible to encounter prospective jurors not only around the courthouse but on a bus, at the supermarket or in line at a movie theater.

It is surprising that some affluent defendants and counsel think nothing of arriving at and departing from a courthouse in chauffered limousines in full view of those who will ultimately judge their case. More cautious defense lawyers minimize the chance of offending jurors with any ostentatious show by alighting from the Caddy a prudent distance from the courthouse, bidding the driver farewell, and hoofing it the rest of the way—modest sacrifice when a resentful juror might spell the difference between victory and defeat.

As we arrived that day at the courthouse the scene that greeted us was one to which we had become accustomed during the year before and which would continue throughout the trial: scores of photographers and film crews grinding away, whether or not anyone seemed disposed to pause for a comment. A prudent investor seeing this profligate and wasteful use of film each day would undoubtedly add Kodak or GAF to his portfolio. The assembled spectators outside, waiting for a glimpse of the trial proceedings, were orderly and friendly, craning their necks to see who it was the film crews were scrambling to photograph.

Unknown to us, after we entered the courthouse that morning John Ehrlichman, running the same gauntlet of press and spectators on his way to stand trial, was spat upon by a shaggy demonstrator in a denim jacket. Andrew Hall, the aggressive and indefatigable assistant to Ehrlichman's counsel William Frates, lunged after this cretin—who was considerably bigger than Hall—but the assailant's courage evidently matched his intelligence, and he darted for cover. To us, this was a very bad omen. Beyond the dismay felt when an accused person is subjected to such outrageous conduct on the courthouse steps, we knew that the chances of being able to select an unbiased jury panel would be sufficiently difficult without the existence of a carnival atmosphere on the doorstep of the courtroom.

By the time we entered the cavernous courtroom the 155 citizens summoned for jury duty that day were already occupying two of the three sections comprising the gallery. The remaining section was reserved for press and the few spectators who could wangle their way past the legion of federal marshals guarding the portals. Through the hustle and bustle of handling this crowd chief clerk James Davey remained cool and collected, vital statistics at his fingertips.

We found our way to the table assigned to us at the far right side of the courtroom facing the bench. The seats and other courtroom furniture were of blond wood—1930s WPA chic—the walls of marble. Peering down ominously at the assemblage from their perch well above the bench were the larger-than-life statues of the venerable law-givers Moses, Hammurabi, Justinian and Solon. Four of the five defendants and their lawyers exchanged greetings and pleasantries in small clusters prior to being seated at their designated tables. The one exception was Kenneth Parkinson, who sat quietly apart with his attorney, Jacob Stein, in the first row behind the defense tables. Stein's courtroom acumen was beginning to show right from the start: if your defense is going to be that your bird's feathers put him in a different flock from the rest, then you ought not to have him seen roosting in the same nest as Haldeman and Ehrlichman and Mitchell, in full view of 155 prospective jurors.

To the left of our table appeared to be a good forty-yard dash to the other side of the courtroom. We were glad that the trial would not be held here. With the lack of intimacy and the reverberating acoustics it would be extremely difficult for the jury to concentrate fully on the evidence. And any distraction would enure to the benefit of the defense.

As the minutes began to tick off before the nine-thirty opening of court Leon Jaworski, looking fit and dapper, joined our table, the only occasion he was to do so during the trial. Last-minute greetings were exchanged between us and the defense lawyers. With the culmination of more than a year of investigation, plus months of pretrial maneuvering and scrapping all behind us, they were as nervous as we were to get on with the main event.

At 9:29 A.M., as if unable to wait out the final minute, Judge Sirica strode deliberately into the courtroom to his position on the bench, elevated well above the assembled throng. He waited patiently as his bailiff James Capitanio slowly intoned the ritualistic words summoning all those having business before the United States District Court for the District of Columbia to draw near and give their attention to the presiding judge, the Honorable John J. Sirica. The case of *United States v. John Mitchell et al.* was called and the defense attorneys answered "Ready" on behalf of their clients, as did Jim Neal on behalf of our client, the people of the United States. Whether or not they were psychologically, emotionally or intellectually ready for what was to come, and whether they liked it or not, the men who had been closest to the thirty-seventh President of the United States were now going to have their day in court.

All eyes focused on Judge Sirica as he began by explaining to the veniremen that this would be a criminal case and briefly summarized the charges contained in the indictment. Prior to asking the prospective jurors any questions, Judge Sirica, who himself had had many years of experience as both a prosecutor and a defense lawyer, took the unusual step of admonishing the jurors that they must be truthful in their response to all the questions propounded to them by the court during the selection process. Knowing that an entire trial can go for nought if a juror lies on an important question, the judge warned that any juror who was purposefully untruthful could well expect a jail term for contempt of court.

The first order of business was to hear the explanations of those who felt they could not serve, particularly in light of the hardship that would be caused by sequestration of the jurors over some months away from their families and jobs. The initial jurors to approach the bench betrayed obvious nervousness not only by reason of finding themselves suddenly involved in Watergate but also at being called upon to explain to Judge Sirica why they could not shoulder their burden of jury duty. Many spoke in such inaudible, self-conscious tones that the lawyers and court stenographers clustered around the bench could barely make out more than an occasional word. Unbeknownst to us, one juror became so agitated he fainted dead away in the corridor. Jim Davey politely thanked the man for having done it outside the courtroom and with that excused him. To remedy the situation we adjourned to the large conference room behind the courtroom, where both we and the jurors could discuss their problems in comfort.

The initial group of some ninety jurors who answered that they could not serve on a sequestered jury without substantial hardship fell into three broad categories—those with young children to care for, those for whom it would be disastrous economically, and those with disabling medical problems. Many had to hold down two separate jobs just to make ends meet in raising a family. Thus, the first day was spent listening to accounts of high blood pressure, dizziness, hemorrhoids and the like. One prospective juror claimed she had a bad pancreas and was "under the doctor," another suffered from phlebitis, the same malady plaguing the former President.

Although surprisingly few potential jurors were acquainted with any of the score of Washingtonians whose names had come up in Watergate, one attractive young woman announced that she had been a secretary to David Young, former member of the notorious Plumbers unit who had been named an unindicted co-conspirator in the Fielding break-in indictment. Though Mitchell's lawyer Bill Hundley admitted he would be "crying" over the decision, it was agreed that she should be disqualified from service.

The second day of jury selection got off to a tumultuous start. As the question of the number of peremptory challenges had not yet been finally settled, John Wilson began by arguing that the defense should be granted an increased number, from ten to twenty-five, with the government's challenges remaining at six. When Jim Neal voiced a vigorous objection, Wilson, casting his eyes over the array of prospective jurors, stated that he was prepared to make an "off-the-record" statement to all those at the bench but that he wouldn't want it perpetuated by the court reporter. "Neal doesn't know this town," Wilson exclaimed. "We have a certain strategy . . ." Ben-Veniste, smelling the possibility of some "gentlemen's agreement" percolating in Wilson's mind, demanded that any statement be made on the record or not at all. Wilson bristled and, accusing Ben-Veniste of "always trying to put a lawyer on the spot," denied that he was referring to the racial makeup of the venire. Judge Sirica quickly quelled the argument. Weeks later John Wilson explained that his earlier reference had been to the political affiliations of the prospective jurors.

An eccentric lady in a red hat was quickly excused from service after we disclosed that the previous day she had approached Leon Jaworski with the news that she thought he was the finest man in America.

By the end of the second day's work 171 jurors had been excused by reason of their inability to be sequestered for a three- to six-month trial, leaving us with a pool of 144 potential jurors from which to select a jury of twelve and six alternates whose minds had not been swayed by the enormous publicity that had surrounded Watergate.

Now that the first phase of selection had been concluded and those unable to be sequestered had been weeded out, it was time to question the individual jurors at length to determine the nature and extent of any bias they might have as a result of this publicity or from other causes.

The problem of prejudicial pretrial publicity is posed by the competing values of a free press and of the right of defendants in a criminal trial to receive judgment from a "fair and impartial jury." Pertinent Supreme Court decisions defining the constitutional right to an impartial or "unbiased" jury do not require that the jury be composed of persons who have had no exposure whatever to publicity about the case, or even that it be made up exclusively of those who have never held opinions about the matter. It would, after all, be intolerable for the legal system to allow an accused to escape trial simply because the alleged crime with which he is charged was exceptionally notorious. At the same time, the ends of justice would not be served by having to impanel a jury composed entirely of hermits, defectives and others who had totally insulated themselves from the world at large.

What *is* required by Supreme Court rulings is either that qualified jurors have formed no opinion on the question of the defendants' guilt *or,* if they have at one time held some opinion, that they can now conscientiously put that opinion aside and render a verdict based solely on the evidence presented in court and the law as explained by the trial judge. Prospective jurors who have formed firm opinions that would affect their judgment of the case or who are not sure that their opinions might not influence them in some way are challengeable for "cause" and, if challenged by either side, should be excused by the trial judge.

Theoretically there is no limit to the number of jurors who can be excused for "cause"—either because the publicity has made it impossible for them to render a fair and unbiased judgment of the case or because they are incompetent to serve for a variety of other reasons (e.g., they may have some personal relationship with the case or the participants or attorneys connected with it). If a competent and un-biased jury cannot be assembled, then a continuance in the trial may occur or the venue (locale) of the trial may be changed. On the other hand, if a sufficient pool of jurors deemed legally qualified to serve under the Supreme Court guidelines governing bias and prejudicial publicity could be found, then we would pass on to the final stage of jury selection, at which time each side would exercise its peremptory challenges, the challenges that may be used for any reason at all in the discretion of the party and require no explanation.*

The procedure now adopted was for us to proceed down to Judge Sirica's second-floor courtroom, where the trial would be held. With the courtroom sealed off from the press and the windows covered over with brown paper, Judge Sirica would be able to question the jurors individually from scores of questions suggested by the lawyers. The questions were designed not only to elicit the extent and nature of the exposure the jurors had to Watergate publicity and the effect it had on them, but also to get enough information to use later on in exercising peremptory challenges. Thus we would be listening care-fully not only to judge whether a juror was challengeable for cause but also to observe everything about him that could help us assess whether he would be the type of juror we wanted on the final panel. The exercise of the later peremptory challenges in particular would test our abilities to evaluate all the data brought out by this interro-gation, including the subtleties of the jurors' responses and their demeanor.

Significantly, none of the parties chose to employ a psychologist or a body-language expert to analyze the prospective jurors' responses. That was no rejection of the concept that much can be learned from the mannerisms, gestures, choice of words and tone of voice used by

---

* In fact Supreme Court guidelines are more stringent than this procedure implies. If a substantial majority of those questioned have formed strong opinions they cannot set aside and hundreds of prospective jurors have to be questioned to find a few who claim to be impartial, there may be a presumption that those few have been less than candid about their impartiality. The small pool, however theoretically pure, is pre-sumed poisoned because it was "drawn from a poisoned well." Similarly, courts have not looked kindly on juries composed entirely of those who admitted to having formed opinions but said they could set them aside. If either of these situations develops in individual questioning, a trial judge is justified in concluding that an impartial jury cannot be impaneled. Neither appeared to arise in our case.

jurors in responding to questions. Rather, it was a tacit judgment that in evaluating those factors the combined knowledge of experienced trial lawyers in sizing up their fellow human beings would provide the most accurate assessment, however approximate that would have to be.

Attention was rapt and the concentration of the lawyers during the four days of individual questioning was total. There was no question that negligence at this stage of the proceeding—a missed nuance in a juror's demeanor, say—could mean the difference between victory and defeat. The concentration was particularly exhausting because on the surface no action seemed to be taking place. Hour after hour the lawyers would furiously scribble down notes of another prospective juror's answers to Judge Sirica's same questions. The action would not come until the final stage. But the facts on which quick decisions would later be made had to be accumulated now.

The interrogation began slowly as questions and procedures were initially refined to meet problems as they arose. It was at once clear that it would take well over a week before actual selection of a jury would be possible. As with trial practice in general, there were many surprises to greet us as we listened to members of the community, randomly selected by the court clerk's computer, share with us the facets of their lives which would bear on their suitability to serve as jurors.

One reaction by several housewives was that the televised Senate Watergate hearings had roused their ire by preempting their favorite programs—the daytime serials and soap operas that enjoy a popularity few of those connected with the case had appreciated with the probable exception of former ad man Haldeman.

One awestruck juror asked to be excused on the simple ground that she had never experienced anything like this before. Judge Sirica briskly replied, "*Nobody* has experienced anything like it."

A harrowing insight into the potential perils of Washington's planned subway system was provided by a woman whose husband was a construction worker on Metro. When the judge breezily inquired as to whether she had been keeping current by reading newspaper articles on Metro construction, she matter-of-factly replied that she had no interest in doing so since after she had discussed it with her husband there was no way anybody was going to get her to ride on it.

One gentleman who had made it through the initial screening volunteered that he had a hearing problem resulting from being hit on the side of his head by a train. It would not be long, we knew, before the jurors who were selected would experience a sensation similar in nature if not in degree when they would be obliged to listen to the conversations faithfully recorded by the Presidential taping system.

On one occasion Judge Sirica, addressing a particularly obtuse potential juror, made several references to the defendants as "these fine gentlemen." The judge's phrase did not escape the sharp notice of Jim Neal, who took polite exception. When Judge Sirica explained that the defendants were *presumed* to be fine gentlemen under the law until proven guilty Neal replied that they were presumed to be *innocent*, not fine gentlemen.

The degree of trauma and confusion the nation had recently undergone in the attrition rate of high officials to the criminal-justice system was borne out by an elderly juror who described her occupation as having gone from a hotel maid to a maid in her own home. In the course of the questioning she advised the judge that the pardoning of the Vice President was grounds for everyone getting a pardon. No, we thought, the *Vice* President had merely received a suspended sentence, and so had the former Attorney General, Richard Kleindienst; only the President himself had gotten the real McCoy.

The lack of education and sophistication demonstrated by some of the prospective jurors was the cause of occasional snickering and *sotto voce* commentary by the Haldeman defense table, the one in closest proximity to ours. Most of it came from the defendant himself and from one of John Wilson's assistants. It appeared that the concept of being judged by ordinary people might be a trifle disquieting to the palace elite.

As the selection process went on beyond the first week and individual questioning continued it seemed apparent that it would be possible to extract from the group of potential jurors originally summoned a sufficient pool of impartial jurors to proceed to the final stage. The knowledge that there *would* be a trial served to heighten the tension in the screened-off courtroom. At the end of another nine-hour session on October 10, nerves were frayed and each of the participants was showing fatigue. Judge Sirica looked up to find Haldeman shaking his head in response to the court's ruling on the previous juror. The seventy-year-old jurist scolded the imperious Haldeman, "You may not like it, but I'm the judge and you're the defendant." There was to be no mistake about who was who in Judge Sirica's courtroom.

By Thursday evening, October 10, after interviewing 315 jurors over eight days, we had accumulated some forty-five jurors who satisfied the Supreme Court's criteria for impartiality, more than enough to pick twelve jurors and six alternates even if all the peremptory challenges accorded both sides were exercised.

The next morning, Friday, we would come to the final stage, the choosing of those twelve jurors who would sit in judgment on our case. Compared to the wearying days of questioning that lay behind us, the next step would be short, swift and action-packed. Peculiarly, federal trial practice prescribes no one way to structure the exercise of peremptory challenges; different courts and judges are accustomed to different procedures. In our case the selection process would begin with twelve of the forty-five prospective jurors taking their places in the jury box. Peremptory challenges would then be exercised first by one side, then by the other. (They would exercise two at a time; then we would exercise one.) Each time a juror was "struck" by exercise of a peremptory he would leave the jury box and be replaced by the next juror from the top of the list of those thirty-three remaining.

Under the procedure designated by Judge Sirica the order of the list of thirty-three was known to both sides in advance. Thus the order in which new jurors would fill the places of challenged jurors was predetermined, rather than a new juror being chosen at random from the remaining pool each time a juror in the box was struck. Consequently, there was no "risk" to the party exercising a challenge of getting an unknown commodity, and the defense could fully exploit its three-to-one advantage in challenges. We had previously engaged in more than a little legal skirmishing over this procedure, with the prosecution bidding for a random-selection procedure so that it would be more difficult to manipulate the entire selection process. But the judge had rejected our plea. With the procedure planned, complicated calculations could be made about the ultimate outcome, just like planning all the "combinations" for the first fifteen moves of an opening in a chess game.

By the time court adjourned for the day on Thursday and we returned to our offices on the top floor of the courthouse, where we would be installed for the duration of the trial, it was nearly 7 P.M.

A long night of deliberation and analysis was in store for the trial team, which was beginning to show the wear and tear from the concentration of the past two weeks.

In some respects the usual notions of what the prosecution regards as desirable traits in a potential juror in a federal criminal case would be qualified in this case. For example, because of the sustained Nixon PR campaign about crime in the streets any juror who appeared to be strong on "law and order" might also tend to favor John Mitchell and the other Administration stalwarts. Similarly, while the prosecution ordinarily seeks persons with a stake in the community, and although we would of course be contending that the Watergate defendants had corrupted the community, nonetheless we would have to take care that no rock-ribbed Republican types who still believed Watergate to be a political witch-hunt got on the jury if we could help it.

We were confident that an impartial jury of citizens who would consider and decide the case on the evidence would be unanimous for a guilty verdict against the major defendants. We approached the selection process accordingly. What we desired most was to pick at least one or two jurors who, due to their intelligence and personal demeanor, would naturally evolve as leaders when it came time for the jury's deliberations. Beyond that, it was important to insure that the individual jurors would be able to get along amicably with one another during their months of confinement. The jury process is a *group* process. Often personal differences exacerbated by circumstances over a long trial can play as great a role in the dynamics of the jury's deliberations as philosophical differences or differing views of the evidence. We didn't want any jurors whose function would be primarily to upset the apple cart. Consequently, we wanted to challenge any juror who seemed to have the potential for alienating the others, even if he or she appeared sympathetic and receptive to the prosecution's position intellectually and emotionally.

Despite the six alternates, we would want to take the precaution of having younger, healthy jurors with good hearing ability so that they would be able to make out what was on the Nixon tapes.

Our first order of business was to print on a large cardboard chart the names of the forty-five prospective jurors in the order they would be called into the jury box. Then, long into the night, we went through the various moves and countermoves, the permutations and combinations that might result from the exercise of challenges against these forty-five. Because the defense or the prosecution could waive any number of their challenges the variations were substantial. At one point we sent back to 1425 K Street for our computer expert, to make sure we understood all the mathematical combinations. One thing was certain. Unless we got lucky and the defense miscalculated, the best we could hope to do with our six challenges was to block the most undesirable jurors from sitting or to excuse a few mediocre jurors in the hope of seating more desirable jurors farther on down the list.

As we filed into Judge Sirica's packed courtroom just before 9:30 A.M. on Friday, October 11, the air was electric. The press and the public, who had been excluded from the jury-selection process up until now, were crammed into one section of the modest courtroom, while the other section was occupied by the forty-five prospective jurors, who nervously chatted with each other in subdued tones as they waited for the judge's entrance.

The five defendants sat at their individual tables along with a total of twelve defense lawyers. The gleaming trays on each table containing water pitchers and glasses, unusual accouterments in a time of judicial economies, testified to the singular importance of the case— as did the inconspicuous round junction boxes perched on each counsel table into which headsets would eventually be plugged for listening to the Nixon tapes. At least a dozen federal marshals were on hand, nattily dressed but each sporting the telltale bulge on his hip.

Despite our marathon strategy session it was impossible to foretell what the defense would do and which of the jurors would survive the combined exercise of challenges. Immediately, our intricate calculations became obsolete as two of the forty-five jurors, both high up on the list, reconsidered the onerous tasks ahead for the jury and asked to be excused on grounds of hardship. We were quickly sobered by the fact that it was a young, intelligent black juror who we thought would be quite acceptable to us who had as his excuse that he could not take the "pressure" of having to make a decision he would have to live with for the rest of his life.

The first twelve names were called and the jurors filed self-consciously into the jury box. Only one third of those first seated were to survive the challenges. As we had predicted, the first defense challenge removed Gordon Roth, an older white juror, highly educated, who was a specialist in international development at the Agency for International Development (AID) and was also teaching a course at

American University. Our only other shot at an obvious intellectual leader was Ruth Gould, a mature, articulate, well-groomed woman far down the list but brought to within reach by the unexpected attrition of the two jurors earlier that morning. With the exception of striking one juror who gave us a substantial chill, we used our peremptory challenges to excuse the jurors we liked least on the panel simply in the hopes of reaching far enough down on the list to seat Mrs. Gould.

The one juror we found it essential to strike was a middle-aged man who related that in his job as a school superintendent his supervisor had once told him, "Anything I tell you to do, you do it, and if anything comes up I will take responsibility." "If you work for somebody, like me, you do what your boss tells you," this juror had told the judge. If this weren't bad enough, this potential consumer of the just-following-orders defense had gone on to say that he thought that if Nixon was pardoned then "all the guys who worked for him should be pardoned." Judge Sirica had denied our challenge for cause to this juror; thus one of our six peremptories had to be expended on him.

It became apparent that the defense strategy was in a sense compatible with ours in that they were trying to use all *their* peremptories as well in order to reach a retired park police officer named John Hoffar, whose name came up immediately after Gould's on the list. Thus, instead of forfeiting enough of their challenges to foreclose the possibility of our reaching Gould, they were exercising each of their strikes, thus enabling us to reach our objective. Only one serious deviation occurred from what we had predicted the defense would do, and that nearly forced a change in our strategy. A pale, gaunt thirty-six-year-old government worker, about six feet four inches tall with stringy shoulder-length blond hair and a piercing gaze—in appearance, the antithesis of all the Nixon Administration held dear—took his place in the jury box after the second round of challenges. In our strategy session the night before we all agreed that he would be bounced by the defense faster than you could say "Abbie Hoffman." Yet the third and fourth rounds passed with the defense using their challenges to strike other jurors, leaving our long-haired juror in the box. After the fourth round of exercising challenges, we asked the court for a short recess and repaired to our sixth-floor offices to thrash out this new problem. Had the defense zeroed in on our friend to play the role of sore thumb, hoping he might be personally incompatible with the rest of the jurors and thus become an irritant and an antidote to jury solidarity? All they needed was one holdout for a hung jury; that would be a substantial victory for the defense. We recalled that the long-haired gentleman told the court he had spent four years in the Air Force in a highly "classified" assignment. Did the defense have some inside information about him?

Ben-Veniste called for a change in the original strategy, which had been to use our sixth and final challenge to prevent a juror named Chase from being seated. Mr. Chase followed immediately after John Hoffar on the list. During the court's interrogation, Chase had allowed as how he had high respect for the defendants, whom he found to have conducted themselves before the Ervin Committee in a "beautiful" manner, enjoying their "photogenic" quality and their fine diction. Ben-Veniste argued that we ought to use our last challenge on the longhair rather than on Chase, if necessary. But Chase had caused such bad vibrations during his interrogation that we faced a real Hobson's choice. We decided to use our fifth challenge, as planned, to strike a woman employee of the Defense Department who had contributed to the 1972 Nixon campaign and who "hadn't paid much attention to Watergate," and hope the defense, in this game of bluff, would use one of *its* remaining challenges to strike the longhair.

Above all, what we had to do was maintain a confident air about having him on the jury when we returned to the courtroom. Apparently, the specter of being in the company of our friend for the next three months outweighed his potential for disruption on the jury, for the defense struck him in the fifth round. The sigh of relief from the prosecution table must have been audible. Our sense of deliverance was reaffirmed a couple of days later with the report that the long-haired juror had been spotted on the sidewalk outside the courthouse having an animated conversation with himself.

Despite the fact that as we reached the last stages of this process the defense had five remaining challenges to our one, they did not strike Mrs. Gould from the jury. Perhaps it was her sympathetic demeanor and her opinion that it would be unfair to prosecute the defendants in light of the pardon that gave the defense confidence. We were willing to accept the burden of changing her opinion in return for the knowledge that she would be helpful in comprehending and explaining some of the complexities of the case to the rest of the jury panel. As the trial unfolded it became apparent that our analysis had proved correct. Mrs. Gould immediately assumed the role of leader and spokeswoman for the jury, communicating articulately to the court about various logistical matters of concern to the sequestered jury, such as hotel accommodations and scheduling.

The defense, for its part, was delighted and surprised that John Hoffar, the retired Park Services policeman, was not the subject of our last remaining challenge. It was either Hoffar or Chase, and we gambled that Hoffar would not be the pro-Mitchell law-and-order extremist for which the defense was hoping, but would give us a fair shake and base his decision on the evidence. From time to time during the trial John Mitchell's chief trial counsel, Bill Hundley, would twit us that Hoffar had sent home for his uniform and his horse.

A sigh of relief and anticipation swept the courtroom when both sides acknowledged by the ritualistic incantation "We are content with the jury" that they had done their best to implement their respective strategies and could do no more.

Despite all the arguments that it was unfair to prosecute this case in Washington, D.C., and that any jury selected would be biased in favor of conviction, we found ourselves with some interesting statistics. While some jurors who qualified for the pool had told the judge under interrogation that they had an opinion about the defendants' guilt (they qualified when they swore they could put their opinions aside and decide the case on the evidence), *none* of those prospective jurors was on the final panel we had just chosen. On the other hand, five of the twelve final jurors had expressed the opinion that it was *unfair* to prosecute the President's subordinates in light of the pardon—one of them describing her opinion as so firm she couldn't "guarantee" a fair verdict. Another on the panel had stated that she had doubts whether the defendants should even be on trial.

As we began the selection of six alternate jurors who would participate in the jury's deliberations only if one or more of the regular jurors became seriously ill or was otherwise excused, we were at least confident that we couldn't be bullied by the defense: each side had three peremptory challenges for alternate jurors. Yet we were mindful of the importance of the alternates during a long and onerous trial. Indeed, it had been the first alternate at the trial of John Mitchell and former Commerce Secretary Maurice H. Stans in the Vesco case in

New York, a middle-aged bank executive, who after replacing a sick regular juror had become a strong exponent for acquittal and brought many jurors around in the final deliberations.

Our caution was shown to be well founded. On the very first day of trial one of the jurors had to be excused and the first alternate took her place. Fortunately there was no further attrition of jurors during the trial.

The jury that would decide our case was predominantly middle-aged, middle-class, black and female. Of the twelve regular jurors, ranging in age from twenty-seven to sixty-eight, nine were women; all six alternates were also women. Eight of the twelve regular jurors were black.

Besides Hoffar and Gould, the jurors were:

Roy Carter, twenty-seven, a logistics coordinator at George Washington University, the youngest person on the jury and an enthusiastic worker in the Big Brothers organization.

Marjorie Milbourn, fifty-five, a retired international-relations specialist originally from Kansas, who had been educated in Geneva and worked in the State Department for many years. We regarded her as a close competitor to Ruth Gould for de-facto leadership on the jury.

Jane Ryon, sixty-three, a retired former Justice Department secretary.

Thelma Wells, sixty-eight, a dignified-looking woman who we later learned was a registered Republican interested in Eastern religion. As the trial wore on, her inscrutable expression, which never changed day after day, would give us cause for concern.

Gladys Carter, forty, a hospital machine operator.

Dock Reid, sixty, a longtime hotel doorman.

Sandra Young, twenty-eight, a pharmacist's assistant at a drugstore operated by the National Retired Teachers Association in Foggy Bottom, near the State Department.

Anita King, fifty-seven, a matron at a D.C. public school.

Helen Pratt, sixty-three, the retired maid.

Vanetta Metoyer, forty-nine, a sales clerk at a local Kresge's store.

When the jurors and the alternates were sworn in, the mood of the lawyers lightened. For better or worse, there was nothing more that could be done about the jury now; attention turned to the trial itself.

CHAPTER **15** "Truth . . . T-r-u-t-h . . . Truth"

THE NEWS MEDIA HERALDED the cover-up trial as the ultimate Watergate forum. Commentators told the public that the trial would "get out the whole truth of Watergate."

But the purpose of a criminal trial is not to fully air all the facts—it is much more confined. The prosecutor's power is too heavy a weapon to be used in aid of a generalized inquest into wrongdoing. The trial process is narrowly focused. Rules of evidence limit the kind of proof that can be used to establish the defendants' guilt. Some rules even exclude proof that common sense tells us is highly relevant to the jury's decision—because it is deemed to be insufficiently trustworthy or more inflammatory than probative of guilt.

Even within these limits "all the facts" are seldom brought out. The trial is an adversary proceeding, a contest of persuasion in which facts are the ammunition. Each side naturally wants to exploit only those facts that will convince the jury to decide the case in its favor.

The audience in this contest is the jury. What most trial observers—and many inexperienced trial lawyers—don't appreciate in a case that has received great publicity is that the jurors will be hearing the facts virtually for the first time. Their task is not an easy one. Sometimes only fragments of proof are allowed into evidence. The jurors cannot take notes and usually they do not receive the facts in a way that makes it easy for them to comprehend the whole.

It is the lawyers' job, therefore, not so much to bring out all the available facts as to dramatize the evidence, to breathe life into it, to fashion some coherent impressions about the defendants' conduct that can be communicated to the jury within the legal constraints imposed on the trial process.

During pretrial conferences Judge Sirica had warned the lawyers in no uncertain terms that the courtroom proceedings in the cover-up case would be conducted with dignity and decorum. His stern attitude suited us fine. We wanted the evidence to be laid out for the jury as smoothly as possible. At the same time, we wanted the trial to be good theater.

To say that the trial of a criminal case is an exercise in theater is not to reduce courtroom practice to lawyers' histrionics any more than it is to say that melodrama, slapstick or burlesque is the heart of effective drama. Prosecuting has a good deal in common with staging a play. The prosecutor must organize his material in order to make a clear statement to his audience the jury. He must prepare his witnesses carefully. When the trial begins, his first task is to establish a rapport with the jurors and win their confidence. And not just by personal demeanor—a jury evaluates a prosecutor by the program he lays out in his opening statement, the witnesses he calls, and the selectivity he exercises in presenting evidence.

A successful prosecutor has to have a good sense of timing and an ability to highlight critical facts. He must establish a tempo that will keep the jury alert, interested and involved. And he must put himself into the jury's shoes to gauge the impact the evidence is making on them as the trial proceeds. Perhaps this is the reason that the best criminal trial lawyers, like good actors, are always "on stage": acutely aware of nuances in the courtroom, conscious of gesture and mannerism, they can communicate more by their tone, demeanor and emphasis in asking a question or raising a legal point than later appears from the cold printed transcript.

From the perspective of good theater, of making our point to the jury, the greatest danger to the prosecution was precisely that we might succumb to the temptation to "bring out all the facts," to dump into evidence everything we had learned about Watergate, and thus hopelessly overtry our case. The overtrying of a case is an affliction which frequently plagues prosecutors in celebrated lawsuits. Some fear that if they leave something out and later lose the case they will be second-guessed for the omission. Others simply confuse quantity with quality—failing to accord juries their due in being able to discriminate—and throw in the kitchen sink. Sometimes the affliction can be fatal. In a long, complicated case like ours we would be lucky if the jury, when it went out to deliberate, remembered ten percent of all the evidence introduced at trial. Our problem was to make sure they remembered *our* ten percent. It was our decision to try as lean a case as possible.

The Nixon tapes presented a special temptation. There was no question that they constituted our most potent evidence. However, the jury—unlike the prosecutors—would not have the opportunity to listen to them again and again, to study them, to analyze the conversations with reference to other evidence. During the presentation of evidence, the jury would hear the tapes through only once.

Besides, introducing the tapes into evidence was going to be a nightmare. Legal requirements obligated the government to present formal proof in front of the jury that every tape we offered was an "authentic and accurate" record of the Presidential conversation that it purported to be. Obviously, the mishandling of the tapes at the White House before they were subpoenaed—the same abuses we had brought out almost a year earlier in the tapes hearings in Judge Sirica's courtroom—would make this proof a headache for us. We would also have to show that our transcripts were accurate. All of this technical proof would be confusing to the jury. Thematically, it would be a diversion from the main part of our case. Each additional tape we sought to introduce in evidence meant a marginal increase in the distraction of the jury from the real issues.

Then there would be mechanical and logistical problems in playing the tapes, especially when we wanted to play only a small part of a long tape or to skip fragments of conversation that seemed unduly prejudicial. Neal and Ben-Veniste both had experience with the playing of tape recordings at trials. They warned the rest of the trial team that the potential for screw-ups was high. Even in short trials where a few tapes were played, they brooded, the process almost never went smoothly, because of the myriad of technical and legal obstacles.

Jim Neal was convinced that the defense lawyers were banking on our inability to resist making a public statement of everything that had happened in Watergate over the past two years. The jury might just be so confused by such an overdose of detail—especially if it were accompanied by logistical bumbling on the prosecution's part—that the defendants would escape. The greater the bulk of our case, the more likely too that we'd commit silly mistakes.

Neal was right. As Haldeman's chief counsel, John Wilson, admitted to us after the trial, he was basing his defense on the tried and true premise that the prosecution would lose its case, if at all, through its own errors. There was, in fact, little that Haldeman could do to rebut the strong evidence against him. Wilson was hoping merely to return our strokes and wait until we hit the ball out of bounds.

Our trial strategy was to retrace the basic outline of the cover-up as many times as possible early in the trial. Ben-Veniste would use his opening statement to the jury to give a detailed, factual account of the cover-up. John Dean, who could tell more of the story on the stand than anyone else, would be the lead-off witness for the government. Right away, within a day or two of Ben-Veniste's opening, the jury would hear the story again, this time from the mouth of Dean. While Dean was still on the stand we would play the tapes of his conversations with President Nixon. The tape of Dean's famous conversation with Nixon on March 21, 1973, in which he laid out the history of the cover-up, echoed Dean's trial testimony. By the time Dean got off the stand, a few days into the trial, the jury would have heard our story through three times. Dean would be the best-corroborated witness in history—and rightly so, for his testimony before the Ervin Committee had occurred *before* the secret of the White House taping system had been blown by Butterfield. Jeb Magruder, the second government witness, would tell a considerable portion of the story for a fourth time. Then we would follow with testimony about misuse of the CIA and about hush money, and finish our case with a barrage of tapes.

One mistake we wanted to avoid was forcing John Dean to carry too much water. This had been a problem in the Vesco case in New York in which John Mitchell and Maurice Stans were acquitted. Because that was Dean's first appearance on a witness stand in court, the importance of his testimony was blown up out of proportion. In preparing Dean for trial, Jim Neal kept telling him, "John, if you're not absolutely sure about it, if your recollection isn't clear—to hell with it. We won't go into it at all." Each witness, Neal told Dean, was going to carry his own pail of water in this trial.

All but one. Jeb Magruder, we decided, had the potential for being a miserable trial witness. In hopes that he could carry less than a full pail, Neal kept after Jill Volner to narrow the testimony she would elicit from Magruder on direct examination to a few critical areas. We wanted to get him off the stand as soon as possible.

ONE OF THE TWO BIG QUESTION MARKS in the trial, from our point of view, was Judge Sirica. The son of a modest itinerant Italian barber, the judge remembered poverty well. He had never attended college and had graduated from Georgetown Law School in Washington only after twice dropping out. During and after law school he worked as a boxing coach, a sparring partner and a sometime local fighter. As prosecutor and private attorney he had long been active in Republican politics and was appointed by President Dwight Eisenhower to the federal district court in the late 1950s. His pro-government decisions on the bench in criminal cases had earned him the local nickname of Maximum John.

This was going to be a long trial, officially estimated at three to four months (though we were hoping to keep it closer to two and a half). At seventy, the judge wasn't getting any younger—even if seventy-three-year-old John Wilson did occasionally refer to Sirica fondly as "Johnny" Sirica in recalling their younger days together. Fatigue, on the part of the lawyers as well as the judge, threatened to be a potential factor in the outcome.*

The judge had adopted an aggressive posture during and after the original trial of the Watergate burglars—in fact, it was his role that helped trigger the collapse of the cover-up. He had, for example, taken it upon himself to question some of the witnesses in that case, in tones clearly evidencing his disbelief of their testimony. Arguments had been made that his actions deprived the burglars of a fair trial, and the Court of Appeals had not yet ruled on those claims when our trial began. In the cover-up trial, we wanted nothing to jeopardize the clear weight of the evidence. So long as the judge's legal rulings and instructions to the jury were fair we had nothing to fear from the appellate courts. One technique we planned to achieve this goal was to be unusually well prepared with research for every important legal point at trial, however fundamental. Well before trial we began to shower the court and the defendants with legal memoranda prepared by Peter Rient and by other members of the trial team. When our flood of legal memoranda began to descend on him, the judge remarked at a bench conference, "You memo me to death." Undeterred, Ben-Veniste chipped in, "That's a good title for a tune, Judge." We also planned to be very conservative in pressing evidentiary and other tactical points, lest we ask for more than we deserved and be granted

---

* Thirteen months after the verdict was returned, the judge was stricken with a massive heart attack—a grim reminder of what might have been.

it by Judge Sirica, only to have the Court of Appeals later decide we had been wrong.

At the same time, we had to watch out for our interests. In pretrial legal maneuvering to remove Judge Sirica from the case, the defense lawyers had vocally alleged that he would be biased against their clients. The judge was extremely sensitive to these charges and had repeatedly assured the defendants that they were going to receive a scrupulously fair trial at his hands. Of course, the defendants were hoping to intimidate the judge by marshaling past criticism into a backlash against the prosecution. Undoubtedly there would be a tendency for him to lean over backward on some points to avoid any imputation of prejudice. That tendency might boomerang against us unexpectedly.

The other big question mark was Richard Nixon: What role would he play in this trial? The presence on the jury of quite a few individuals who believed it was unfair to prosecute the defendants in light of their flag bearer's escape from criminal charges made particularly acute the question of the former President's personal appearance at trial. Nobody could predict how the jurors would react to being reminded of Nixon's immunity from prosecution by seeing him in the flesh.

We were not eager to sponsor the testimony of the pardoned ex-President as a government witness. Predictably, he would try to exculpate himself and his subordinates as well. In an ordinary situation we would have welcomed the opportunity to get him on the stand as a defense witness or a "court witness"—an individual called by the judge for whose veracity neither side need vouch. Then he could be vigorously cross-examined and his credibility impeached by his false public statements about Watergate. Despite the deferential courtesies the former President would receive, his deep conspiratorial involvement in the cover-up would make him a sitting duck.

Yet the worse we made Nixon look the more unjust it might appear to some jurors that his aides were being forced to take the rap for him. All in all, we preferred Nixon's candid admissions recorded on tape to the live denials we could anticipate from any court appearance.

By the time the jury was sworn, it looked as if Nixon's health might prevent any live appearance by the former President in Judge Sirica's courtroom. A recurrence of the vein disease, phlebitis, that he had first suffered ten years before and that had flared up the previous spring had again struck him. A brief hospitalization resulted in a report from his doctors of a blood clot in his lung. Nixon was soon released, but his longtime personal physician told reporters that Nixon would have to have a "restricted convalescence" and would not be medically fit to travel to Washington for "one to three months"—a period that just happened to coincide with the projected length of our trial.

On Sunday, October 13, two days after the jury was sworn and sequestered, Leon Jaworski announced his resignation as Special Prosecutor, saying in a written statement that the "bulk of the work" entrusted to his office had "been discharged." His decision didn't surprise us a bit. We all knew Leon was straining at the bit to return home to his Houston law practice and beloved ranch, and that he was simply waiting for the trial to get off the ground before he departed. Indeed, Jaworski had been under so much pressure for so many months that the first thing the distinguished and mannerly Texan did when he got home was drive his jeep to the farthest reaches of his ranch and let loose with a howl at the moon! But the public seemed taken unpleasantly by surprise. Editorialists castigated Jaworski for leaving office with important matters unresolved. A particularly vivid Herblock cartoon showed the Special Prosecutor as a misguided football player aborting a successful touchdown run by darting out of bounds at the twenty-yard line, the ball nonetheless held triumphantly if mistakenly over his head to signal success.

Some of the criticism may have been justified, but in our area of responsibility it was misplaced. Having someone as tough and seasoned as Leon in the wings to render support and advice would, naturally, have been a comforting note if the going got very rocky at trial. However, Leon had played no active role in formulating trial strategy or in trial preparation, and it was never intended that he would participate in the trial itself. The Watergate Task Force had been mostly independent in drafting the indictment and then in bringing the case to trial, wth the exception of decisions relating to the President and his tapes. Jaworski's departure just meant that we would be that much more out front during the ensuing weeks.

October 14, the day set for the government's opening statement to the jury, was our first chance publicly to present an outline of what we had learned about the Watergate cover-up. When Ben-Veniste told the jury it was his "honor and privilege to represent the government" in this criminal trial it seemed hard to believe that this was the same government that had recently been run by an oligarchy of the defendants and their co-conspirators. In the first minutes of his statement, Ben-Veniste seized the opportunity to make clear to the jury our theory that Richard Nixon was a central figure in the cover-up. Then, emphasizing the hush-money phase of the conspiracy, Ben-Veniste asked the jurors to keep asking themselves as they heard the evidence unfold *why* the defendants, while publicly proclaiming that the White House and CRP had no connection with the break-in, found it necessary to deliver surreptitiously almost half a million dollars in currency to the Watergate burglars—unless the secret payments were intended as a quid pro quo to keep the burglars from spilling the beans.

The importance of the tapes in corroborating our theory was stressed, but Ben-Veniste urged the jury not to hold the locker-room language against the participants in the conversations, as many media and political critics had done. There was enough hypocrisy in the world without suggesting that nice Presidents don't use nasty language.

Counsel for Mitchell and Haldeman opted to make their opening statements to the jury after the government had completed its case, as was their prerogative. That put Ehrlichman up to bat first for the defense. His attorney, William Frates, a Miami lawyer who had done legal work in the past for Nixon's friend Charles G. (Bebe) Rebozo, strode to the podium and in stentorian tones unveiled Ehrlichman's line of defense: Ehrlichman was going to place the blame squarely on his former employer—just as he had warned Nixon on one of the tapes that he might have to if the cover-up collapsed. Ehrlichman was merely an innocent pawn, Frates declared. Nixon "deceived, misled, lied to and used John Ehrlichman to cover up his own knowledge and his own activities" in Watergate, "to save his own neck." These were the harshest accusations leveled against Nixon so far by any insider, even John Dean.

Citing the June 23 tape, the "smoking pistol," Frates argued (to the obvious discomfiture of H. R. Haldeman, who tried not to look at Ehrlichman in the courtroom as Frates was speaking) that Nixon had misled Ehrlichman by sending him to meet with CIA officials shortly after the break-in without briefing Ehrlichman on the facts as Nixon knew them. Of course, this meant that Haldeman had also duped Ehrlichman, but Frates stayed away from that one—as he was to do through the balance of the trial. A gentlemen's agreement apparently had been struck: the three major figures would refrain from pointing a finger at each other and concentrate only on those who had either turned state's evidence or were unavailable to be called as witnesses.

The barrel-chested Miami lawyer then told the jury, "The tapes might have done some people harm, but they're the greatest thing that ever happened to John Ehrlichman." If the tapes were the "greatest thing," the mind boggled at what the worst might have been.

Payments to the burglars, Frates told the jury, were simply a "humanitarian gesture." This was a welcome surprise to us. Nixon, Haldeman and Ehrlichman had kicked around such a justification in a taped conversation back in April 1973 and had apparently discarded it, for obvious logical reasons.

Much more troublesome would have been an assertion that the payments were made as the result of out-and-out extortion by the burglars, who, it might have been claimed, were prepared to falsely accuse Administration officials of sponsoring the break-in, unless they were paid off. This was a potentially effective defense that we had worried about for almost a year and had spent a good deal of time preparing to rebut; as it turned out, the claim would never be advanced during the trial by any of the defendants.

Predictably, both Mardian's lawyer, David Bress, and Parkinson's attorney, Jacob Stein, stressed the relatively minor roles allegedly played by their clients in the Watergate drama—but with very different styles. Bress's opening statement foreshadowed in tone and substance Mardian's aggressive, angry defense, a defense that would be heavily colored by moral outrage and bitterness toward the prosecutors. In this, Mardian's case strongly echoed his own personality. Bress used nearly three hours to denounce Mardian's indictment, claiming that the government "did wrong" to name him as a defendant. Rapping his fist on the lectern, Bress charged that Mardian was "dragged in at the tail end of a conspiracy indictment simply because of suspicion."

The tall, urbane and scholarly-looking Jacob Stein immediately took the opposite tack, telling the jury in soft, controlled, soothing tones that "Ken" Parkinson had had nothing to do with the politics of the Nixon Administration and was simply acting as hired counsel for CRP in the lawsuit brought against it by the Democratic National Committee. He had no motive for joining a cover-up and no interest in doing so, Stein argued. It was one of the few times the jury would hear Stein speak during the first two months of the trial—all part of his strategy to lower his client's profile and set him apart from the other defendants. To the jurors, he must have seemed an anomaly in the courtroom. From his elegant dress (Stein was habitually attired in a stylish black suit of European cut, a heavily starched white shirt and a waistcoat), his well modulated voice and his learned air the casual observer would have guessed him to be a visiting Eastern European count or a professor of Romance literature at the Sorbonne long before tabbing him as a Washington trial lawyer.

The conclusion of Stein's low-key opening statement set the stage for our star witness, John Dean. Dean had continued to amaze us with his ability to recall remote facts, and he was the most conscientious witness anyone connected with Watergate had ever seen. He checked and cross-checked even the most minor points, using whatever documents we could give him to jog his remarkable recollection into further service. And he was probably one of the best-prepared witnesses ever to come down the pike. Jim Neal had spent hours and days with Dean, shuttling him back and forth from prison via contingents of federal marshals, testing his version of the facts, challenging motives. Much of the preparation was devoted to cross-examination, with Neal and others on the trial team throwing every question we could think of at Dean, accusing him, shouting at him. Dean was later to find that his cross-examination at trial was mild in comparison.

Dean took the stand, and, raising his left hand, surveyed the audience: his former associates at the White House, their lawyers, the judge who had sentenced him to four years' imprisonment—only a year less than the maximum allowed under the law—on his one-count plea of guilty, the Watergate Task Force members he had come to know, the fearsome Washington press corps and the packed gallery of spectators. For personal reasons, his wife, Mo, was unable to attend the first day's examination. Dean placed his right hand on the Holy Scriptures and swore to God that he would tell the whole truth and nothing but the truth.

Dean was no more nervous than the rest of the combatants. After all, he was becoming an old hand at testifying—first the Ervin Committee, then the Vesco trial in New York and next the perjury trial of Nixon aide Dwight Chapin. No one had laid a glove on him yet.

Jim Neal's first questions were routine—the type asked of any witness in a criminal case. The answers told the national and personal tragedy of Watergate.

> NEAL: You are Mr. John W. Dean?
>
> DEAN: Yes, I am.
>
> NEAL: Mr. Dean, what is your present employment status and residence?
>
> DEAN: Mr. Neal, I am presently serving a prison term at Fort Holabird, Maryland.
>
> NEAL: A prison term for what offense?
>
> DEAN: Conspiracy to obstruct justice.
>
> NEAL: In connection with what?
>
> DEAN: With my involvement in the Watergate cover-up.
>
> NEAL: What was your last position prior to being in a federal prison?
>
> DEAN: The last position I held was that of counsel to the President of the United States.
>
> NEAL: What was the President's name?
>
> DEAN: Richard Nixon.

At Neal's direction Dean began to identify the various defendants for the record, describing their clothing and where they sat in the courtroom. No one in the courtroom seemed to notice a slip when Dean pointed to Haldeman, who was wearing a narrow-lapel green suit, and identified him as the man in the brown suit. Except Ben-Veniste. Earlier Ben-Veniste had noticed Dean wearing a green tie with a blue shirt; while he hadn't been sure of such a combination, it looked pretty good on Dean, so he had tried the match-up himself. Now he wondered if he had been taking a fashion tip from a man who was color blind.

Dean's direct testimony went in smooth as silk. He was the earnest young man gone wrong, repentant and eager to help the jury understand what had happened. His tone, although conversational, was flat and unemotional. His wry sense of humor found no outlet in this serious business. There were no surprises for the press; although better organized and more detailed, this was the same basic story Dean had told before national television cameras during the Ervin Committee hearings. But now there were tapes.

On the second day of Dean's testimony the trial team rolled out several grocery carts filled with stereo headsets. Each set was wrapped in a small white plastic bag. The bags were designed to keep the headsets clean while in storage and keep their cords from getting tangled up together, so that they could be distributed quickly. In the carts, the mounds of wrapped headsets looked like frozen chickens heading for the meat counter.

The system for playing the tapes allowed every person in the courtroom to listen through his own personal headset. On a small table in a front corner of the courtroom, partly obscured by the defense tables and a large blackboard, sat a sophisticated tape player and attached audio filter equipment. From the table, wires ran discreetly out all over the courtroom, taped to the floor and under tables and benches, ending in over eighty junction boxes. Each box could accommodate the plug-in cords for two headsets and had its own volume control.

Dean had just testified to his meeting with Nixon and Haldeman on September 15, 1972—the date the original Watergate burglars were first indicted. Dean told the jury that Nixon congratulated him on keeping things contained and was elated that nobody higher than Liddy had been indicted. Tape transcripts were handed to the marshal who had charge of ushering the jury into and out of the courtroom; he in turn distributed them to the jurors. It was a sight that few present would ever forget, as everyone in the courtroom simultaneously donned a headset and prepared to tune in on the electronics that had brought down an American President. The visual parallel to the Nazi war crimes trials—where similar headsets were used for simultaneous translation—was not lost.

The public, of course, was already familiar with the transcripts of tapes of most of Dean's meetings with the President—they had been released first by the White House the previous May and then in more accurate form by the House Judiciary Committee. But very few people had actually heard the President's voice on tape. As we knew from our first listening almost a year before, transcripts could never capture the drama and the nuances of the real thing, of the President's low, hesitant voice with its jerky cadence telling Dean, "Well, the whole thing is a can of worms—as you know, a lot of this stuff went on. And, uh, the people who worked [inaudible] are awfully embarrassed. And uh, the uh, but the way you, you've handled it seems to me very skillful—just putting your fingers in the dike, and the leaks that have sprung here and sprung there."

So it went for nearly four days. After Dean testified about a conversation with the former President, we would play a tape of the same conversation. The defense lawyers fumed. They knew that the tapes were cementing Dean's credibility with the jury, but there was nothing they could do about it. Dean had paid a heavy price for his Ervin Committee testimony. For fifteen months he had been the one out front against Richard Nixon, the President's public accuser, while others could doubt or chip away at his story. Now, with all the major participants in his taped conversations except Nixon sitting in the courtroom and listening with him to the tapes, Dean was harvesting the vindication due him for his decision to testify truthfully before the Ervin Committee.

When it came time for Dean's cross-examination, the defense camp agreed that John Wilson would have the first crack at him even though the regular order by the names listed in the indictment would call for Mitchell's lawyer to precede Haldeman's. "Boy," said the crusty Wilson to Mitchell's lawyer, William Hundley, "let me tear the ass off that kid Dean first."

However, far from confronting Dean or attempting to chew him up, Wilson was wary and respectful. The canny old lawyer's demeanor and his line of questioning set the tone for the entire Dean cross-examination. Wilson's approach was to nick Dean a little around the edges, to feel him out, before moving in for the kill. But when Dean showed no vulnerability, Wilson withdrew. The defense lawyers obviously regarded Dean as a dangerous witness, someone who might well do them far more harm on cross-examination than good.

John Mitchell's lawyer, Hundley, also approached Dean obliquely, but with a different purpose in mind. Hundley's idea was to use Dean's cross-examination as a vehicle for throwing blame on a *third* person, Charles Colson, Mitchell's old rival, who had pleaded guilty in June to obstructing justice in the Ellsberg case as part of a plea bargain in which the cover-up charges against him were dropped. Hundley tried to get Dean to tell as much as he could about Colson's involvement in Watergate, hoping to convince the jury that Colson was the mastermind of Watergate. A rather slender reed, but then Mitchell was not the world's easiest man to defend.

Ehrlichman's lawyer, William Frates, was next to the lectern. His booming voice, clearly his most notable asset, was in marked contrast to Dean's low measured tones. Indeed, as the trial wore on, Frates's volume, particularly in the morning, began to be a bit much to take. It made no difference what was happening, Frates's decibel level remained constant. The prosecutors discussed buying him a Midas muffler for Christmas. Dean stayed cool and confident despite Frates's bombast. As the days of his testimony mounted he seemed to get stronger and stronger. He had never wavered in linking all five of the defendants to the conspiracy. The defense lawyers obviously had given up trying to break his story. Their only hope was to sully his character as best they could and get him off the stand, hoping the jury would forget the damaging quality of his testimony over the coming weeks before it began its deliberations.

After seven and a half days of Dean's presence on the stand our trial strategy seemed to be working.

WITH DEAN ON THE STAND day after day, Judge Sirica had been doing well in controlling the courtroom and quieting the ever present squabbling among the lawyers. But he sometimes seemed weary and irritable. Toward the end of Dean's testimony his penchant for speaking his mind began to get him in trouble.

One morning the judge excused the jury for lunch and, noticeably weary from the tension of the morning's events, commented on the presentation of Liddy's intelligence plan to John Mitchell, "Maybe I shouldn't say what is on my mind. . . . It is too bad that Mr. Mitchell didn't say, 'Throw them out of here, get them out fast,' and you wouldn't even be in this courtroom today. It is too bad it didn't happen that way. Anyway, it is not for me to say what should have been done."

The jury, of course, well on its way to the cafeteria, didn't hear the remark. Nonetheless, it was injudicious; had it been made in front of the jury it could have been grounds for a mistrial. The judge's off-the-cuff comment produced screaming headlines and legal motions from counsel.

The next day the judge, perhaps seeking to mend fences, asked a defense lawyer if the purpose of a particular question was to make Dean out to be a liar. Without waiting for an answer, the judge volunteered that the defense had all "done a pretty good job" on Dean in that regard. Obviously regretting the remark, the judge immediately told the jury he did not mean to imply that he thought Dean was lying. Nonetheless, Jim Neal objected vigorously. After a short recess, Judge Sirica read a prepared statement to the jury saying contritely that he had expressed no opinion about Dean and that assessing Dean's credibility was solely their job.

The judge's remarks and his apparent weariness initially caused some disquiet on the trial team, but as it turned out we could have saved ourselves a lot of worrying. From that point on, Judge Sirica settled down and ran the trial admirably and fairly, seeming to get stronger as time went along. One factor in the judge's superb performance was undoubtedly the ruling of the Court of Appeals upholding the Watergate burglars' conviction, which came about ten days after Dean left the stand in the cover-up trial. In its written opinion, the Court of Appeals firmly and explicitly upheld Judge Sirica's questioning of witnesses on his own initiative during the first trial and called the practice well justified when done out of the presence of the jury and in aid of justice. Judge Sirica, the Appeals Court declared, had acted "in the highest tradition of his office as a Federal judge."

The judge seemed to take strength from this ruling. From the beginning of the cover-up trial he had made it clear that he was the boss in his courtroom and that he would tolerate no backbiting among the lawyers or disobedience of his own orders. Yet he was tolerant in separating the attorneys when the inevitable petty wrangles broke out and personal bickering occurred in front of the jury. Acting like an amused but firm father separating a bunch of overly ambitious boys, he would tell us to quiet down, cut it out and get back to business. He seemed to be making a special, almost Solomonic effort toward evenhandedness, awarding one close point to the government and the next to the defense. Repeatedly he instructed the jury throughout the case that *they* were the sole arbiters of the facts: they would infer nothing from his legal rulings or his tone of voice about his own views of the evidence. That was their province alone.

More than once Judge Sirica admonished the jurors and the attorneys that the purpose of the trial was to get out the truth, and once he spelled it out: "T-r-u-t-h . . . truth, that's what this is all about," he said. It was their job, he told the jury, to ascertain the truth when the evidence was all in.

The judge's repeated reference to the jury's role in determining the "truth" served to emphasize to the jurors that they should not infer any view of the case that the judge himself might hold from his legal rulings or comments to attorneys. Thus his remarks were not only proper but helpful in insuring that the defendants received a fair trial. But the judge got a bad rap from the press when, on one occasion, he coupled his reference to "truth" with the unfortunate comment that he didn't intend to try the case by the "strict rules of evidence." Protests from editorial writers and law professors who took the remark out of context largely overlooked the fact that the judge had made it *in favor of the defense*, permitting Hundley extra-wide latitude in his cross-examination of John Dean. As the overall record of the trial would demonstrate, Judge Sirica's declared intention was not in fact borne out in the way the trial was actually conducted. Though "a little latitude" was given both sides in cross-examination of witnesses, especially the defense side, this was hardly unusual in a long criminal trial and not at all inconsistent with the rules of evidence. *

During Dean's testimony, we had been working behind the scenes to precipitate one of the few real surprises in the trial. Former CIA agent Howard Hunt had been lying to us for a year. We were prepared to ask Judge Sirica to declare Hunt a "court witness" and then cross-examine him mercilessly. Hunt knew that the examination was going to be plenty rough—he and Ben-Veniste had tangled on several occasions over the past year, giving him a good preview of what to expect. An effort by him to avoid testifying at trial altogether was quickly rejected.

A few days before trial Hunt's new lawyers, William Snyder and Thomas Koons of Baltimore, approached Frampton. "Why is Ben-Veniste so rough on Howard?" they said. "Maybe Hunt could be more helpful if personalities were deemphasized." Frampton relayed the message to Ben-Veniste and suggested that perhaps a truce was in the offing. Within days, Ben-Veniste and Frampton met with Hunt in our railroad-car suite of offices on the top floor of the courthouse. A change in Hunt's demeanor was visible—no longer was he the pedantic schoolmaster seeking refuge behind an arcane (and sometimes malapropos) vocabulary. He seemed sadder and resigned. His lawyers told us he was now prepared to tell the truth.

For the first time, Hunt now admitted to us that he had lied repeatedly under oath about the involvement of others after being granted immunity. More important, he also admitted that the cash received from CRP and the White House *was* a quid pro quo for silence. But, there was still a big question as to whether he would follow through on the witness stand with what he was telling us now in the office. Hunt could be plenty treacherous; indeed, in the galleys

---

* In their eventual appeals, the four defendants convicted in the cover-up trial assigned very few evidentiary errors as marring the trial; they made no claim whatsoever that Judge Sirica was biased or prejudiced in his handling of the courtroom proceedings.

of a book just about to come out he had written that Ben-Veniste had
tried to suborn his perjury (concerning the very matters to which he
was now admitting) and steadfastly denied any quid pro quo or
receipt of clemency offers. So we decided to persist in our course of
seeking to call Hunt as a "court witness."

The night before Hunt was to take the stand he appeared in Ben-
Veniste's office for a final run-through of the subject matter. Ben-
Veniste was nonplussed by Hunt's tie, which featured a pattern of
little gold scales of justice. "Howard, I can't believe you're wearing
that. Don't you think you're laying it on a bit thick?"

"What do you mean?" asked Hunt, taken aback.

"Your tie—the scales of justice. I mean *really*, Howard."

"Oh, the *tie*," said Hunt, "I'm a Libra, someone gave me this tie as a
present. I never thought about the scales of justice."

"Do me a favor, Howard," said Ben-Veniste. "Please don't wear it
to court."

The most dramatic moment in Hunt's testimony came as he described how he had repeatedly lied under oath before the grand jury,
in office interviews with us, and even in his about-to-be-published
memoirs, appropriately entitled *Undercover*. When had he finally decided to come clean? asked Ben-Veniste. "The past month, sir." And
what had brought him to that decision? Hunt explained how he had
read the contemptuous references "to those of us who had gone to
prison" contained in the Presidential transcripts released the previous
spring; the White House gang he had been protecting, he realized,
was no longer "worthy of my continued or future loyalty." His new
lawyers, who had taken over the case from William Bittman, urged
him to make truthful disclosure. Even his children, Hunt related, had
doubts that his story about Watergate "was in all respects factual and
candid."

> HUNT: . . . So as a result of all those factors I decided to make the hard
> decision to testify to the entire truth.
> BEN-VENISTE: Have you done so in this courtroom today, Mr. Hunt?
> HUNT: I have.
> BEN-VENISTE: To the best of your ability?
> HUNT: I have.
> BEN-VENISTE: No further questions.

It was the end of the day, and the jurors quietly filed out of a hushed courtroom. Our anxieties about a double-cross were laid to rest; Hunt had crossed over the line into the world of truthful witnesses.

The next day the defense lawyers could do little more than harangue Hunt about his prior perjuries and the false statements contained in his new book. Hundley zeroed in on whether Hunt's demand for $75,000 in March of 1973 was not blackmail, since Hunt threatened to disclose the "seamy things" he had done for the White House unless the sum were paid.

"No, sir," replied Hunt.

"What did you consider it, investment planning?" shouted Hundley.

"I considered it, if you will, in the tradition of a bill collector, attempting to get others who made a prior contract to live up to it."

WHILE SEVERAL OF THE DEFENDANTS bore unambiguous feelings about our next witness, Jeb Stuart Magruder, none of them was more eager to be rid of him than Jill Volner. Volner had been given the responsibility for preparing him as a trial witness and had spent considerably more time with him than any of the other task force lawyers. It was our clear consensus that to know Magruder was to dislike him. While John Dean obviously appreciated the effect of his disclosures on the course of American politics in the seventies, Magruder was seemingly oblivious to the more global features of what was going on; in fact, he well resembled the typical cooperating defendant in a securities swindle, totally absorbed in Number One.

Nevertheless, Magruder was an important witness to the involvement of Mitchell in authorizing the break-in and to the early workings of the cover-up. His surface appeal as a witness could not be understated. Indeed, while he was perjuring himself in the trial of the Watergate burglars as part of the cover-up plan, presiding Judge Sirica took hapless CRP treasurer Hugh Sloan to task for inconsistencies between his testimony and Magruder's! While we may have shared the defense camp's low opinion of Magruder as a person, he was our witness by *necessity*—he had been the defendants' partner in conspiracy by *choice*.

On the stand, Magruder performed far better than we had expected. Nervous at first, he had trouble answering Jill Volner's questions loudly enough for the jury to hear him distinctly. We noticed that it was awkward for the tall, somewhat gaunt Magruder to lean forward and talk directly into the low microphone sitting on the witness stand in front of him, so we suggested that some handy object be found to prop up the mike. The judge's bailiff had the answer: several Bibles kept on hand for use in administering the oath to witnesses. Ironically, the confessed perjurer became the first Watergate witness literally to tell his story on a stack of Bibles.

Aside from placing Mitchell and Mardian squarely in the cabal which fomented the cover-up immediately after the June 17 arrests, Magruder gave the first seriously damaging testimony about CRP attorney Kenneth Parkinson. Indeed, the cross-examination of Magruder by Parkinson's attorney Jacob Stein constituted the one flaw in an otherwise brilliant defense. Up to this point Parkinson's name had been mentioned about half a dozen times, and the jury must have wondered what the prim-looking fellow with the horn-rimmed glasses was doing sitting in the courtroom. Stein had done nothing to disabuse the jury of this notion; indeed, he had encouraged it by keeping Parkinson apart from his co-defendants and had himself maintained a low profile. But there was something in Magruder that got to the reserved, scholarly trial lawyer. Stein decided to take Magruder on. It was a mistake.

Stein's attack was designed to show that Parkinson had always been skeptical of Magruder's cover story for the Liddy budget—didn't Parkinson question Magruder about embezzling CRP funds? At Stein's prodding, Magruder remembered that Parkinson had indeed asked Magruder about his financial status and his net worth. But, Magruder retorted angrily, he had regarded that as a friendly inquiry about Magruder's ability to finance a criminal defense should he be indicted. Now, he lectured Stein, he realized that it had been a "set-up conversation." Lashing out at each of Stein's questions, growing more outraged by the minute, Magruder insisted on emphasizing over and over to the jury that he had been tricked by Parkinson's false sincerity into revealing intimate personal financial information.

Magruder got more and more sure of himself as the time he logged on the stand increased. He learned how much leeway he would get in answering questions and began peppering his answers with self-serving speeches. Magruder's cross-examination provided a good analogy to why the Spaniards do not permit a bull to fight more than once in the *corrida de toros*. One time is all the bull needs to learn how to use his horns against the deceptive red cape of the matador; were he allowed to rest and fight again he would surely kill his next adversary. As Jim

Neal was to remark to Judge Sirica, "I'm not objecting to Mr. Stein's questions—he's making this boy appear a victim."

By THE TIME we entered the month of November, the daily routine of the trial had become well established. The defense camp was head-quartered in a large suite on the second floor of the courthouse, down a side corridor from Judge Sirica's courtroom. Mitchell was conveyed to the trial each morning in a chauffered limousine from his plush mid-town apartment at the Jefferson Hotel. The other defendants and lawyers, with the exception of John Wilson and his partner Frank Strickler, depended on less ostentatious transportation.

In the defense suite Haldeman and Ehrlichman hung their hats in one room, which came to be called "the White House," while Mitchell, Mardian and Parkinson shared another large room, designated "CRP." A WATS line was installed, allowing the defendants to make unlimited long-distance calls to old friends and associates. Around the corner in a vast, dim marble corridor, spectators, lined up for a much prized seat in the courtroom, craned their necks for a glimpse of one of the famous defendants as they waited patiently for the courtroom doors to open. Surprisingly, the Big Three were quite willing to sign autographs—often on the flyleaf of Bernstein and Woodward's *All the President's Men*. One long-haired autograph seeker got Mitchell's autograph and asked the former Attorney General what nefarious deeds he expected to perpetrate on young demonstrators like himself once he got them kidnapped. "You better ask Liddy," replied Mitchell tersely. "It was his plan, not mine."

Shortly after nine o'clock every morning the prosecution team maneuvered two mobile file cabinets containing our trial evidence out of our sixth-floor offices, into a back elevator reserved for court personnel, and down to Judge Sirica's courtroom. The open-topped file cabinets sat next to the government table throughout each day of the trial. The defendants and their lawyers would begin to drift into the courtroom, and at 9:30 A.M. promptly Judge Sirica appeared and court was called to order.

At recesses we scuttled upstairs to our offices while defense counsel chatted with the press outside the courtroom. The side corridor con-taining the defense suite was separated from the public area of the courthouse by a sign reading "MEMBERS OF THE PRESS AND GENERAL PUBLIC NOT ALLOWED." At every recess dozens of reporters pressed up to the sign. The naturally gregarious defense lawyers loitered just on the other side of it, sipping coffee from plastic cups or smoking a cigarette and trading quips with their favorite reporters. (It was rumored that strong drink could be obtained in the inner reaches of the defense suite, and on more than one occasion when John Wilson repaired there "for a cup of hot soup" he was chided merrily by Hundley for reappearing "with ice on his vest.") At lunchtime, both prosecution and defense imported sandwiches from Barney's kosher delicatessen. Mitchell's chauffeur often picked up the sandwich order for the defense.

In the courtroom each of the defendants, together with his lawyers, occupied a separate table. The most forthrightly cheerful of the lot was Haldeman, whose table was nearest to that of the prosecutors. Always the most conscious within the White House hierarchy of matters involving image, the former advertising executive had let his brush cut grow to a slightly more fashionable length. His sleek new razor-cut, meticulously combed and modest sideburns softened the stern, almost military appearance he had presented before the Ervin Committee. Late in the trial we played for the jury on an oversized screen a color videotape of Haldeman's testimony before the Ervin Committee that was alleged in the indictment to be perjurious: "but it would be wrong." It was something of a shock—and a reminder of how far we had come in Watergate in fifteen months—to see the videotaped Haldeman in his prior, less hirsute incarnation. The familiar American-flag pin, however, still appeared daily in the lapel of the neat dark suits Haldeman wore to court.

As civil and polite as Haldeman was to courtroom spectators and to the prosecution team, his former associate John Ehrlichman was just as hostile. Arrogant, prickly and bitter, Ehrlichman made it perfectly clear that he had no use for any of the prosecutors. Several weeks before trial both Haldeman and Ehrlichman had appeared at the Special Prosecutor's offices on the same day to review subpoenaed Nixon tapes. When Ehrlichman was finished with his review of tapes, he was in a characteristic bad humor. Brushing past Frampton on his way to the door, he said bitterly, "When are we going to get to listen to the ones that are *exculpatory?*" Haldeman and Wilson, on their way out, stopped to chat pleasantly with Frampton in an inner hallway. Haldeman was eager to relate a "Polish joke" he had just heard that he thought was rather funny. "Do you know how Poland would have handled Watergate?" he asked Frampton. "Just like Nixon." He and Wilson chuckled.

The incident symbolized the respective attitudes of the two defendants toward us in the courtroom. Ehrlichman, somewhat slimmed but still hefty, habitually presented his large back squarely to the press and the spectators. Dressed every day in either a baggy blue suit or a green sport coat, he constantly sketched on a yellow legal pad, seldom seeming to pay much attention to the testimony. He refused altogether to speak to anyone from the prosecution table. When Frampton and Frates were discussing a legal point during recess and Ehrlichman had something to offer he would not look Frampton in the face; instead, he would say to Frates in a loud voice, "Tell Frampton here such and such." It was a childish performance. On one occasion when Frates and Jerry Goldman were haggling before court about whether the government would acquiesce in Frates's introducing some defense evidence, Ehrlichman abruptly asked Goldman (an honor graduate of Harvard College and Law School, *Harvard Law Review* editor and former law clerk to Supreme Court Justice William J. Brennan, Jr.) what night law school he had attended.

Mitchell seldom chatted with us or with the other defendants. When he was seen in company it was usually that of his lawyers. Outside courtroom hours Mitchell secluded himself. Thinner and somewhat more pallid than we had seen him over the past year, Mitchell sat implacably at the table farthest from the jury (a table cleverly seized upon by his lawyers the first day of trial). His dour expression only occasionally was lit by a grin at an improbable reference to him made by a witness or on a tape.

Robert Mardian, the only other defendant still friendly with Mitchell, had arrived at the trial sporting a healthy-looking Arizona tan, but it soon faded, as though consumed by Mardian's restless impatience and self-righteous energy. Often bored when not whispering excitedly to his attorneys or scowling at something that had been said about him, Mardian was even more hostile to the prosecutors than was Ehrlichman.

The mild-mannered Kenneth Parkinson, in the meantime, his anonymity so far undisturbed except by his lawyer's unfortunate cross-examination of Jeb Magruder, sat quietly at the table nearest to the courtroom spectators through the bulk of the testimony and evidence that hardly touched on him at all. Parkinson's personal situation was particularly tragic because shortly after the trial began one of his young sons had been terribly burned when a gasoline can ignited during a prank. After court each day Parkinson and his wife would visit their son in Children's Hospital, where he was undergoing skin-graft treatments.

Perhaps more important than the defendants, as far as the jury was concerned, were their lawyers. During the prosecution's case the defendants themselves never spoke or acted; counsel were, literally, their clients' mouthpieces. Later, each defendant would be on the stand for a day or two at most. But every day for months the jury heard defense lawyers arguing the defendants' cases, cross-examining witnesses and making objections. It seemed inevitable that the jury would come to view the defendants primarily through the personalities of their lawyers.

Three of the five chief defense lawyers were themselves former prosecutors. There was feisty, cantankerous old John Wilson, once a federal prosecutor for nearly a decade, the only lawyer in the court-room with the audacity to trade barbs with Judge Sirica. Indeed, Wilson's early tone of aggressive familiarity with the judge made courtroom observers hold their breath, but Judge Sirica remained unruffled. Wilson, as one observer put it, typified the "old-curmud-geon school of courtroom practitioners." * He won our respect early not just for toughness but also for integrity. Wilson was a scrapper, he could be expected to take every single legitimate advantage available to him, but he was fair and his word could be trusted.

Then there was William Hundley, former head of the Justice Department's Organized Crime Section under Robert Kennedy, whose spontaneous humor, ruddy face and snappy plaid suits made him look like a man who was always just on his way to the racetrack.

Mardian's original chief counsel, David Bress, partner in a well-known Washington firm and former United States Attorney in Washington, had had to withdraw after the first weeks of the trial because of serious illness. Bress's assistant, thirty-three-year-old Thomas Green, had been working with Bress since the indictment and took over the representation. Although Mardian complained vociferously

---

* Wilson's appreciation of his senior status was demonstrated on one occasion when Mitchell's lawyers asked that the former Attorney General be excused from an "onerous" court appearance because he was sixty years old. The seventy-three-year-old Wilson looked up from his papers and remarked to the seventy-year-old judge, "Sixty years old? A mere boy!"

to Judge Sirica that he should be granted a new trial because of this unexpected development, we felt that Mardian was doing just as well with Green as he had done with Bress, if not better. Nonetheless, Jim Neal told Judge Sirica that the prosecution would not oppose a severance. The judge, however, ruled that Mardian should proceed with Green.* If the ruling disappointed Mardian, it did not exactly bring joy to Green's heart either. Mardian appeared to be one of the world's worst clients, constantly badgering Green about Green's performance and about tactical points. The youngest defense lawyer in the courtroom, Green lacked the clout to contradict his client, so he had to bear Mardian's abuse stoically for the rest of the trial.

Then there was the inexplicable William Frates. His basso profundo voice constantly filled the courtroom. But his complaints seldom made any rational sense, even when the tortured syntax and mispronounced words could be unscrambled. The prosecution team had no idea what to make of Frates. There seemed to be no method to his "defense." His fellow defense counsel began to refer to him as "W. C. Fritos."

As the trial wore on, the lawyers (both prosecution and defense), the press and even some of the defendants developed a genial relationship—sort of a foxhole camaraderie—during breaks and recesses, born of a combination of necessity and boredom. Thrown together every day for six to eight hours, we thought of very little besides the trial and saw no one but one another. We were all adversaries, but we had to have *somebody* to talk to. We began to think of the courtroom as a space capsule with its own little daily reality, replaying the events of a year or two before as though in a time warp.

The climate allowed some degree of lighthearted banter. During a recess one day Ben-Veniste observed a bizarrely dressed woman approach the well of the courtroom from her seat in the spectators' section. She wore what appeared to be a Russian army greatcoat to which dozens of slogan buttons were pinned, matched with fluffy blue bedroom slippers; her hair might have served as a refuge for migratory birds. Rounding out her ensemble was an enormous shopping bag crammed with mysterious objects. At the dividing rail she en-

---

* Mardian's legal argument was borne out when the Court of Appeals reversed his conviction, holding that Judge Sirica should have "severed" his case and granted him a separate trial. On January 18, 1977, Charles F. Ruff, the fourth Special Prosecutor, announced that in lieu of a retrial, charges against Mardian would be dropped.

gaged H. R. Haldeman in a short conversation, after which she threw what appeared to be a crumpled dollar bill at Haldeman's feet. The former chief of staff deftly scooped up the bill, tossed it back over the rail and turned on his heel.

This game of volleyball proved too much for Ben-Veniste to bear in silence. "Who was that woman, Bob? Do you really think you ought to keep meeting her here like this?"

Haldeman reddened. "I've never set eyes on that kook before," he snapped. "Can you believe she wanted me to give that dollar bill to Ehrlichman? I've seen a lot of crazy things happen in Watergate, but I'll be goddamned if I'm going to start being a bagman for Ehrlichman!"

Before long we developed a healthy respect for the abilities of most of the defense counsel—Wilson's tenacity, Hundley's able attempt to picture Mitchell as a victim of the White House gang, Green's intelligence, Stein's low-key subtlety. Even John Wilson himself began to express grudging but genuine admiration for the efficiency of the prosecution team. All the defense counsel especially liked and admired Jim Neal and were somewhat in awe of his abilities. After the trial John Mitchell gave Neal an autographed copy of Bernstein and Woodward's *All the President's Men.* On the flyleaf the convicted former Attorney General wrote: "To one of the nicest guys I know, unfortunately cast in the wrong spot at the wrong time." Wilson gave Neal an autographed picture of himself reading: "To the best trial lawyer I have ever met."

The friendly out-of-court posture of the lawyers did not, however, get in the way of in-court squabbling, jibing and sometimes yelling. A certain amount of it—and it had its calculated purpose on both sides—went on in front of the jury, but the level of bickering always seemed to pick up in the late afternoon after the jury had been excused, as though the lawyers needed a short session of picking fights with one another after each day's proceedings to let off some steam.

When there was humor it invariably involved the irrepressible Hundley. One morning Frates complained that he was being taken by surprise when the government called three witnesses. Neal told Judge Sirica that we'd informed Hundley, as "liaison counsel" for the defense team, well in advance that these witnesses would be up soon; Hundley was supposed to tell Frates. Hundley promptly volunteered to resign as liaison counsel. "I sure would like to play out my option,

Judge," he told Sirica. With Hundley's help, Frates won this particular point. At a bench conference called by the judge to discuss names of doctors who might be appointed to examine Richard Nixon, Hundley suggested P. M. Palumbo, the physician for the Washington Redskins football team. "Dr. Palumbo'll get him back in the game, Judge," Hundley crowed. On one occasion when other defense attorneys complained that the jury might be influenced by courtroom spectators laughing at passages on the tape recordings, Hundley (whose client was not adverted to favorably on the tape) piped up, "Can we cry, your honor?"

From the beginning of the trial it was evident that the major defendants' strategy, in addition to hoping for prosecution mistakes, was to hope for mistakes by the judge as well—for some judicial error so egregious and so prejudicial to the defendants' rights that it would upset the trial or any conviction on legal grounds. John Wilson announced early on that he was keeping an "error bag" for the Court of Appeals. Every time Judge Sirica ruled against him Wilson proclaimed, often gleefully, that he had another item for his error bag. Judge Sirica, too seasoned to be intimidated by Wilson's ploy, remain relaxed about his error bag, referring to it on occasion as Wilson's windbag. After a while the sly old defense lawyer's gambit brought Jim Neal to his feet waxing reminiscent in his best good-old-boy style. "Mr. Wilson's error bag reminds me of something that we call a ferty bag back home in Tennessee. That's where you got two pounds of manure in a one-pound bag."

HOWARD HUNT'S ABRUPT DECISION to come clean touched off a behind-the-scenes drama that began while Jeb Magruder was still on the stand. Hunt had admitted for the first time that in late November 1972 he prepared a memorandum summarizing the facts of Watergate that was designed to spur payment of more funds to the burglars. Hunt said he had delivered the memo to his lawyer William Bittman; Bittman, in turn, was supposed to pass it on to CRP lawyer Kenneth Parkinson. All through our investigation Bittman, a former federal prosecutor, had repeatedly denied ever knowing that there had been a quid pro quo in return for the cash payments he knew Hunt was receiving. Jim Neal, who had worked closely with Bittman in Robert Kennedy's Justice Department, believed his old friend.

Two days after Hunt finished testifying we received word that a group of lawyers at the hundred-man firm of Hogan and Hartson, where Bittman had been a partner during his representation of Howard Hunt, were hurrying over to our offices. It seemed that *they* had in fact learned from Bittman of the existence of such a memo back in May 1973. Indeed, they had ordered that all of the "Hunt files" be microfilmed and inventoried; this particular memo had been catalogued. Bittman had since left the firm. When, after reading about Hunt's trial testimony in the newspaper, they had tried to locate the memo, it was missing. Alarmed about the state of the record and convinced that Hunt's attorney-client privilege with Bittman did not shield their information, the firm decided to come forward and make a disclosure to us about what they knew. Jim Neal, choking with rage and frustration, repeatedly told them how totally shocked and betrayed he felt, as he had always given Bittman the benefit of the doubt. Neal confided to Ben-Veniste (who had been more than skeptical about Bittman's candor) that he just hadn't been able to accept the fact that Bittman would lie to him.

The next day, Saturday, November 11, Bittman, a stocky pompadoured bear of a man, came to our courthouse offices with a photocopy of a two-and-a-half-page memo dated November 14, 1972, and entitled "Review and Statement of Problem." He had taken the copy with him when he left the Hogan and Hartson firm months before. It was even more explosive than we had imagined.

The memo began by saying that the seven men then currently under indictment "and others not yet indicted," including Jeb Magruder, had bugged the DNC, but that their "sponsors" had compounded the fiasco by failing to make timely deliveries of support money.

> The Watergate bugging is only one of a number of highly illegal conspiracies engaged in by one or more of the defendants at the behest of senior White House officials. These as yet undisclosed crimes can be proved....
>
> The defendants have followed all instructions meticulously, keeping their part of the bargain by maintaining silence....
>
> The Administration, however, remains deficient in living up to its commitments. These commitments were and are:
>
> 1. Financial support.
> 2. Legal defense fees.
> 3. Pardons.
> 4. Rehabilitation.

Having recovered from post-election euphoria, the Administration should now attach high priority to keeping its commitments and taking affirmative action in behalf of the defendants. . . .

The foregoing should not be misinterpreted as a threat. It is, among other things, a reminder that loyalty has always been a two-way street.

A more succinct statement of our theory of the Watergate cover-up could hardly be imagined. And Bittman had been sitting on this memo for two years!

Bittman launched into a convoluted explanation in which he claimed that he had kept the memo sealed and unread in a file cabinet until he first read it in April 1973; that he did not divulge it thereafter because of the attorney-client privilege; that he had removed the memo from the Hogan and Hartson files because Hunt wanted him to do so. Hunt had testified, to the contrary, that Bittman read the memo in his presence and that Hunt never told Bittman to remove it from the file. The time records maintained by Hogan and Hartson showed that on November 14, 1972, Bittman's law partner spent half an hour with Bittman, which he charged to Hunt's account for "reviewing memorandum."

Despite all this, Frates took it into his mind to have Judge Sirica call Bittman during Ehrlichman's defense, albeit as a court witness. This was only one of several instances where Frates inexplicably called a witness to the stand who, after providing little or no solace for Frates's client, then proceeded to roll about on the courtroom deck like a loose cannon firing off salvos at Ehrlichman and the other defendants to boot. Jacob Stein even complained to Judge Sirica at one point about Frates's penchant for calling "fairly uncontrollable people" to the witness stand to give seemingly irrelevant testimony. Bittman, of course, had little useful testimony to give in favor of Ehrlichman but a considerable amount of information potentially harmful to Parkinson and to the other defendants.

The prospect of Bittman's appearance naturally caused a great deal of emotional consternation for Jim Neal. Frates foolishly tried to stir Neal up by suggesting that Bittman should have been called in our case and would have been but for his friendship with Neal. "He's Mr. Neal's friend, he's not Mr. Ehrlichman's friend," said Frates, smirking with delight like a bad schoolboy.

The courtroom was hushed by the grossness of Frates's taunt, but

Neal responded with grave reserve. "Yes, he's my friend," said Neal in measured tones, "and I think he did wrong. But a man can do wrong and still be my friend. I don't let him hang and twist slowly, slowly in the wind." *

SEVERAL DAYS OF technical evidence were necessary to have the tapes of conversations in which no government witness had participated admitted into evidence. After this interlude, we moved on to proof of the misuse of the CIA and the FBI. First to the stand was the portly but light-footed General Vernon A. Walters, number-two man at the CIA. After Walters testified about White House pressure we played the June 23 tapes to show the motives of Haldeman and Nixon in calling on the CIA for help in the cover-up. Finally, Walters testified, he tired of White House attempts to use the CIA to obfuscate the Watergate investigation. On July 6 he met with Gray and told him he was the recipient of a small inheritance and would rather resign his post before he would let "those kids over at the White House" misuse the Agency. While this testimony was being elicited from the witness stand, the sound of snickering could be heard from the defense tables. Laconic, as usual, John Mitchell had circulated a note which read "WALTERS + INHERITANCE = HONEST MAN."

Our second witness to the abuse of the intelligence community by Nixon and his henchmen was L. Patrick Gray, retired Navy captain and acting director of the FBI following the death of J. Edgar Hoover. The muscularly trim, balding Gray was one of the many shipwrecks of Watergate. A patriotic man of basic integrity, he was unable to navigate the treacherous shoals on which he found himself in the summer of 1972 as chief of the FBI, responsible for the investigation of Watergate. On the one hand he was surrounded by powerful Hoover-era executives at the FBI, who were wary of the "outsider" appointed as their chief and who distrusted virtually anyone in government but the FBI itself. On the other hand, it was clear that his sponsors in the Administration preferred that the investigation of Watergate be less than thorough. Gray had displayed the correct instincts but had been unable to follow them through. Early on he had screwed up his courage and telephoned Clark MacGregor, Nixon's

---

* Neal's reference was to a suggestion Ehrlichman had made as to how L. Patrick Gray should be treated when Gray's nomination to be permanent director of the FBI was thrown into doubt by Watergate revelations.

campaign chairman after Mitchell's resignation, and told him that Nixon's assistants were "mortally wounding" the President by trying to embroil the CIA and the FBI in Watergate matters. A few minutes later the President telephoned Gray, ostensibly to congratulate him on the effective handling of an airplane hijacking. Gray repeated to his Commander in Chief what he had just told MacGregor. There was a noticeable pause, after which the President said, "Pat, just keep on with your vigorous investigation." The real message was implicit.

The final segment of our case concerned the details of raising and distributing almost half a million dollars in hush money. Questioned by Jim Neal, Herbert Kalmbach detailed how he had told his friend John Ehrlichman how uncomfortable he felt raising funds for the burglars. "I told him the secrecy, the 007 aspect to it, and how disquieting it was to me, and I remember with absolute clarity saying to Mr. Ehrlichman, I said, 'John, I am looking you right in the eye. You know Barbara and my family and I know Jean and your family and you have got to tell me now, here and now, that this is something that is proper and that I am to go forward on.' "

Ehrlichman replied, "Herb, you are to go forward on this." But Ehrlichman also warned him that if the operation were not kept secret, "they'll have our heads in their laps."

Next to take the stand was the Runyonesque Tony Ulasewicz, portly and well scrubbed, in a narrow-lapel brown sharkskin suit, white shirt and narrow dark tie. He could have been the detective on the stand in "Part 30, Manhattan Supreme" testifying as to how "the perpetrator exited his vehicle, at which time I gave chase on foot." Ulasewicz detailed the elaborate system he devised for making anonymous drops of cash and how he had insisted that all communication be made by pay phone. The voracious coin telephones required so much change that in order to keep his pocket linings intact Ulasewicz bought a bus driver's coin changer. Ben-Veniste offered it into evidence.

It was Ulasewicz, quick to smell a rat, who had been instrumental in terminating Kalmbach's role in the cover-up. Despite the fact that the two men were "worlds apart . . . I mean me being a policeman from New York and him the President's attorney," the savvy cop sat the President's lawyer down for a Dutch uncle's talk. "You know, something here is not kosher," said Tony. Kalmbach didn't understand the meaning of the word "kosher." Tony tried again. Finally both Kalmbach and Ulasewicz withdrew from the conspiracy, leaving in charge Mitchell's close friend Fred LaRue.

Despite LaRue's obvious discomfiture at testifying against his old friend Mitchell, we did make one notable inroad in "refreshing his recollection" as to how he had been able to raise a particular $25,000 hunk of cash for distribution to the burglars. LaRue's answer was devastating: Mitchell had sent him to Key Biscayne, where he was to receive $50,000 in cash from the *éminence grise* of the Nixon inner circle, Bebe Rebozo. Mitchell directed LaRue to deliver $25,000 to the Kentucky senatorial campaign of Louis B. Nunn and to keep the balance for his Watergate fund.

We followed the details of the delivery of the hush money with a playing of the rest of the tapes.

First there was a never-before-disclosed tape of Charles Colson discussing with Nixon on January 8, 1973, a plan to grant clemency to Howard Hunt. Colson reminded the President that Hunt was the only one of the burglars in a "very desperate . . . sensitive" position. "Hunt's is a simple case," Nixon declared. He suggested it would be easy to generate public sympathy for Hunt based on his family's problems; perhaps conservative columnist William F. Buckley could be enlisted in the campaign. "We'll build that son of a bitch up like nobody's business," the President predicted confidently, and clemency could easily follow.

Then came several tapes bracketing the crucial date of March 21, 1973. On these tapes the President still seemed confident, aggressive—he was only beginning to have real worries.

However, as the Watergate web began to ensnare the President more tightly, the tapes of his conversations with Haldeman and Ehrlichman in mid- and late April 1973 revealed a more desperate and less coherent President. Over and over he questioned his aides about details and vulnerabilities in the cover-up, never seeming to get the story straight. He would announce a decision about strategy to his assistants, then abruptly back away from it when one or the other suggested that that might not be the best way to go.

On one tape the President assured Haldeman and Ehrlichman of his intention to grant "full pardons" to various participants in Watergate before he left office. Learning that Magruder was about to go to the prosecutors, Nixon instructed Ehrlichman to hold out the prospect of clemency to the former CRP aide by telling him of the President's "great affection" for Magruder and his family. "That's the way the clemency's got to be handled. Do you see, John?" A similar ploy would be used with Mitchell. Ehrlichman reported back after his conversation with Magruder that it had been a success and assured the President that he had mentioned the President's "affection." "He got that, huh?" Nixon replied. Later, when Ehrlichman told Nixon he was going to try to "get Dean around," the President warned that that might be difficult. A better approach, he suggested, was to let Dean know that only through a pardon could Dean be restored to the practice of law if he were convicted.

One of the greatest concerns of the President and his top aides had been to develop a cover story to explain their understanding of the hush-money payments—which Ehrlichman acknowledged were intended to keep the burglars "on the reservation." As for the men directly involved in the payoffs, Nixon was adamant that they had to "stick to their line" that they were not seeking to obstruct justice. "I know if they could get together on the strategy, it would be pretty good for them." Later, he reiterated that they "gotta have a straight damn line that, of course we raised money . . . but, uh, we raised the money for a purpose that we thought was perfectly proper . . . Right?" "Right," Ehrlichman replied.

A few days after these conversations Nixon was still urging Haldeman and Ehrlichman to "do some hard thinking about what kind of strategy you are going to have with the money." Ehrlichman suggested that he might say he was simply trying to keep the burglars from telling what they knew to the press, but he noted that he wanted to talk to an attorney before he "got too far out on that."

By late April the President had also begun to worry about his March 21 conversation with Dean and the final payment of hush money to Howard Hunt that the President had advocated in that meeting. Ehrlichman warned him that if Dean got "totally out of control and if matters were not handled adroitly . . . you could get a resolution of impeachment." Panicking, the President asked Haldeman to review the March 21 tape. When Haldeman reported back just how damaging that conversation might be ("That's a real time bomb, isn't it?") Nixon told his associates anxiously, "Let me say it's got to be you

[Haldeman], Ehrlichman and I have got to put the wagons around the President on this particular conversation."

Haldeman tried to spin out an exculpatory explanation. Nixon, he said, was just "drawing Dean out." But the President realized it would never sell: "It's not a good story. I said . . . 'We gotta keep the cap on. We can get the money . . .' I said, 'a million dollars.' . . . That's an incriminating thing. His, his word against the President's."

Then Nixon seemed to become obsessed by the possibility that Dean had been bugging *him,* carrying a concealed tape recorder. In a strange, halting late-night telephone conversation with Haldeman (the tapes of phone conversations were invariably the most distinct of all) the jury heard Nixon, an undertone of desperation in his voice, press Haldeman to find out if Dean could have been carrying a Dictaphone in a shoulder holster. Haldeman reassured his boss sleepily that such a possibility was "almost inconceivable." Mulling that over, the President gave a long sigh and answered with an observation that could well serve as an epitaph for Watergate: "In this matter, nothing is beyond the realm of possibility."

As THE GOVERNMENT's direct case drew near conclusion, events outside our control seemed to be resolving the role Nixon would play at the trial. In late October he had suddenly reentered Long Beach Hospital, near San Clemente, and undergone emergency surgery to isolate a blood clot in his left thigh that doctors feared might break loose and carom through his bloodstream. Six hours after the operation he went into shock from severe internal bleeding, and he remained on the critical list for days. At our suggestion Judge Sirica appointed a panel of three nationally respected cardiovascular specialists. After examining the former President upon his release from the hospital in late November, the doctors reported that Nixon would be unable to travel to Washington to testify before mid-February 1975, even if his recovery proceeded well. He might, however, be able to give a deposition in his home beginning as early as January 6, but only for an hour or two a day lest he get overly exhausted by prolonged interrogation.

Judge Sirica ruled that there would be no long interruption of the trial in order to explore getting a deposition from the former President. A review of the testimony the defendants were seeking from Nixon, he ruled, "reveals that, in large measure at least, the testimony they desire him to give could be, and in many instances has been elicited from other witnesses." Moreover, there had been no showing whatever that Nixon would in fact "testify along the lines the defendants have predicted."

In the end, the pardoned President escaped not only the pain of prosecution but the humiliation of public cross-examination.* In the context of our overall focus on the five defendants in the courtroom, we were not unhappy that he never appeared to testify. But psychologically we were sorry to have missed the opportunity to subject Richard Nixon, himself a lawyer, to the rules of a courtroom.

THE LAST MAJOR WITNESS to take the stand in the prosecution's case was Egil "Bud" Krogh, Jr., the former assistant to Ehrlichman in the White House Plumbers unit. Krogh resembled a Boy Scout leader without a troop. Young, good-looking and intense, Krogh had made his break with the Nixon White House when in acknowledging his guilt in the Fielding break-in he disavowed the "national-security" defense. He had just completed a term of four months' imprisonment at the Allenwood Federal Correctional Institution.

Frates got a bit tangled up trying to exclude Krogh's damaging testimony about Ehrlichman. Among other things, Frates tried to argue that Ehrlichman had not approved breaking into Daniel Ellsberg's psychiatrist's office, but only a "covert operation." This was a distinction Frates had tried to capitalize on, unsuccessfully, during Ehrlichman's earlier trial for conspiring to violate Ellsberg's psychiatrist's civil rights. This time around, Frates did worse:

> THE COURT: What is a covert operation? A secret operation. A secret operation.
> FRATES: Your honor, a covert operation is if I walk back into your office, went out of this door and walked back into your office, secretly without you knowing it, that would be a covert operation.
> THE COURT: That would be also housebreaking, too, wouldn't it?
> FRATES: No, sir, I think this courthouse belongs to the people.

* Not until late spring of 1975 did the ex-President appear in any forum to give sworn testimony about Watergate. Then, just a few weeks before the disbanding of the final grand jury looking into aspects of the cover-up, he was interrogated by members of our office in a federal building near San Clemente. The foreman of the grand jury was present, the testimony was recorded, and the questions and answers were later read to the entire grand jury in Washington. By this time, six months after the end of the trial, Nixon's testimony (which is still secret) apparently added nothing to what was already known and could not realistically contribute to any further action by the grand jurors.

THE COURT: I don't think it gives you a right to go into my office if I don't consent to it.

FRATES: Your honor, I don't want to get off on that. Judge, I am trying to get back to Florida this afternoon. That is my main problem, and I know Your Honor is trying to get away. . . .

The prosecution was happy to concede that what Ehrlichman had had in mind was similar to someone sneaking into a federal judge's private chambers and examining his private papers. Krogh's testimony was received into evidence without further analogies.

We completed our case with a summary of all the hush-money payments in the form of a large chart. Anthony Passaretti, a seasoned accountant and investigator on loan from the U.S. Attorney's office in New York, had prepared it by sifting through all the testimony and documents in evidence at the trial. The defense camp did not like this eloquent statement of the guts of our case one bit, but in attempting to nit-pick at Passaretti's work on cross-examination they only made matters worse. Without a moment's hesitation the meticulously prepared accountant could point to the precise page number of the trial transcript supporting each transfer of money illustrated by the chart. It sailed easily into evidence.

PREPARATIONS WERE NOW UNDER WAY for the jury's Thanksgiving dinner. The jurors had so far stoically endured the sacrifices inherent in sequestration—monitored TV-viewing, censored newspapers, no respite from the communal existence of the same faces day in and day out at the Mid-Town Motor Inn at Twelfth and K Streets, N.W. It is a strange irony that America in the electronic age has chosen to lock up its jurors and let its defendants out on bail. But there were some benefits in jury service: the jurors ate well at good restaurants, a former hotel maid had her own bed linen changed by others, the marshals were solicitous and Sunday excursions were planned by the former park policeman, juror John Hoffar. So far the jurors had visited George Washington's home at Mount Vernon, the Naval Academy at Annapolis, historic Harpers Ferry, West Virginia, and the Amish country near Lancaster, Pennsylvania. The line had been drawn at tickets to a Washington Redskins football game. Saturdays were reserved for personal chores, visits to barbershops, hairdressers and doctors, always in the company of a deputy marshal—even next to the dentist chair.

Thanksgiving was to provide the jurors' first reunion with their families in the forty-two days since they swore their oath of office. There would be a full-course banquet for seventy-six persons with all the trimmings at the plush Shoreham Hotel. Unfortunately for the jurors and their families, seventeen of those reservations were for deputy U.S. marshals who would sit in with each family group to insure that nothing about Watergate was discussed.

From time to time in the presence of the jury Judge Sirica had expressed his hope that the case would be finished by Christmas so that the jurors could spend the holiday at home with their families. At one point the judge suggested that he was considering convening court on Saturdays in order to accomplish this goal. In a perceptive and articulate letter to the judge the jury put us all to shame for placing so high a premium on extraneous matters. The jurors informed the judge that being home for Christmas was not an "overriding concern" on their part. Citing the time and effort that had already been expended on the trial, they concluded that they were "united in thinking that in fairness to all concerned the trial should proceed at a pace consistent with fairness and justice."

Needless to say, the prosecution team was delighted with the letter, not only because of the jurors' evident seriousness of purpose but also because of their apparent oneness of mind about extending their stay together. The communication provided some concrete evidence that the jurors were getting along well personally with one another, reducing the likelihood that a personality clash or an irrationally stubborn juror might eventually produce a hung jury. We were also relieved not to be faced with the possibility of a Christmas Eve verdict, the hope of every defense lawyer.

NOW IT WAS THE DEFENSE'S TURN to put on a case. We could stop walking on eggs trying to defend the credibility of the defendants' former associates and co-conspirators. This would be our chance to raise some hell.

In his opening statement for John Mitchell, William Hundley expostulated for nearly an hour on the contention that Mitchell had never approved the Watergate break-in and therefore had no motive to participate in any subsequent cover-up. Hundley thus conveniently avoided addressing himself to any of the evidence in the case. When time came for a lunch recess, Hundley asked Frampton, "How am I doing?" "Well, Bill," Frampton replied, "you're going good. In fact, if I were you I'd stop right now while you're ahead. No point in moving on to the facts; that's going to be a little sticky."

Mitchell was the first of the five defendants to take the stand in his own behalf. Up to this point Mitchell's attorneys, Hundley and Plato Cacheris, had pursued the seemingly impossible task of making their client appear to be a sympathetic character—the hapless victim of a cunning White House conspiracy to throw all the blame for Watergate onto his shoulders. While the taciturn, gloomy Mitchell brooded behind the defense table farthest from the jury box day after day, his counsel had smiled amiably out on the courtroom, unfailingly addressing the judge and questioning the witnesses in polite, deferential tones. Perhaps Mitchell's best tactical approach would have been to forgo testifying. In the jury's mind, the relaxed, genial personality of his counsel might have obscured the desperate substance of his case.

Neal's hammering cross-examination of Mitchell blotted out for good any glimmer of a hope that Mitchell might be able to escape conviction. In the bargain, courtroom observers were treated to an illuminating demonstration of the ingredients that make cross-examination a successful enterprise for the prosecution. Some think the object of cross-examining a defendant who takes the stand is to wrench a dramatic confession from him, *à la* Perry Mason. Nothing of the kind can ordinarily be expected when a sophisticated, intelligent defendant takes the stand. Indeed, Mitchell heatedly denied almost everything Neal threw at him; it was Mitchell's very denials that did him in. Good trial lawyers know that the best thing you can do on cross is to get the witness to argue, evade and deny.

Mitchell unwittingly cooperated in Neal's effort by issuing blatant and aggressive denials, quibbling over semantics, and even refusing to own up to sworn admissions he had made in the past. Mitchell's hard-line attitude instantly destroyed any reservoir of sympathy he might have built up with the jury.

Appropriately enough, Neal closed by asking Mitchell if he recalled the former President's giving him an instruction to "stonewall it" in Watergate.

"I remember it very well," said the former Attorney General.

"And you have stonewalled it, haven't you, Mr. Mitchell?" Neal asked softly.

The jury could supply the answer. As Mitchell left the stand, even his own lawyers were downcast at how devastating Neal's attack had been.

Mitchell's own testimony constituted his entire defense case with the exception of two "character witnesses." When the credibility of a defendant who takes the stand is attacked by the prosecution (as it invariably is), the defense may then call witnesses to blunt the attack by testifying to the defendant's "reputation in the community for truthfulness and veracity." The device permits the defendant in a white-collar case to bring before the jury—subject to reasonable limitation set by the trial judge—a small parade of prominent citizens and old friends who can vouch for his uprightness and good character.

In the cover-up case, the complete absence of such people willing to speak up for the three major defendants was painfully obvious. In fact, one of Mitchell's two witnesses, a black woman who had worked in his household as a maid, clearly hurt him more than she helped—it was more than obvious that she did not move in the same "community" as her former employer. Calling her at all was on Mitchell's part an act of either incredible insensitivity or surpassing defiance. Neither Haldeman's nor Ehrlichman's few character witnesses offered them much more support, though a pleasant and determined woman named Toberman, a longtime friend of the Haldeman family, provided some levity when she testified solemnly that she had talked to more than three hundred people about Haldeman's reputation just in the past two weeks and that everyone she talked to had declared it to be excellent. If we doubted her word, she even offered to provide a list of her interviewees!

Both Haldeman and Ehrlichman called young aides in their twenties to testify to their reputation in the community. The quality of such testimony was questionable at best; it did not help matters that both young men conceded they had obtained their positions through the coincidence of their parents' friendship with either Haldeman or Ehrlichman.

To make matters worse for the Big Three, the impressive array of prominent citizens called by Mardian and Parkinson stood in sharp contrast to the feeble effort mounted by Mitchell, Haldeman and Ehrlichman. Both of Arizona's senators appeared to testify to Mardian's character, as did the chief justices of the Arizona and California Supreme Courts and black civil-rights leader James Farmer. Kenneth Parkinson followed with an even longer string. Although none of

Parkinson's witnesses was as well-known nationally as Goldwater, they may have made more impact on the jury because all were active in local civic affairs; many were prominent Washington, D.C., lawyers or judges. Since most were colleagues of Parkinson's in community, fraternal or charitable organizations, they were able to inform the jury at length about the defendant's numerous good works in the community.

Many of Parkinson's witnesses proudly proclaimed membership in the Kiwanis Club of Washington. Eventually, Jacob Stein got around to asking one of them to explain what the Kiwanis Club was. "It is a group composed of approximately 300 prominent businessmen," announced the witness proudly. After a pause the ever iconoclastic Stein rejoined, "If they do say so themselves."

Of all the defendants, Harry Robbins Haldeman most appreciated the fact that it was the *jury* that held his fate in their hands. The man who had sold soap flakes to millions of housewives on daytime TV seemed determined, with his friendly demeanor and new hair style, to come off the best of the lot in jury appeal. From our standpoint, Haldeman's decision to follow John Mitchell to the witness stand presented us the opportunity on cross-examination to marshal the most damaging admissions Haldeman had made on the tapes in order to demonstrate to the jury how empty his defense really was.

When cross-examination began, Ben-Veniste went immediately to the taped conversation of March 21, 1973, in which President Nixon had instructed Haldeman on how to avoid being pinned down under questioning before a grand jury. He hoped that Nixon's advice—"you just say, 'I don't remember, I can't recall,' "—would stick in the jury's mind throughout the cross-examination to point up Haldeman's expected evasiveness. Haldeman could not have risen better to the bait: he professed that he "could not recall" any such instruction by Nixon!

The first afternoon of cross-examination ended on a dramatic note. Haldeman had made a slip-up during Wilson's direct examination. Denying that he ever told Gordon Strachan to destroy documents, Haldeman had testified that three days after the Watergate arrests he had instructed Strachan to go through his files to see "whether any result of bugging the Democratic National Committee had been provided to us." But at that time only the burglars and their bosses knew there had been an earlier *successful* bugging that had produced any such "results." On cross-examination, Ben-Veniste honed in on Haldeman's unfortunate admission, despite John Wilson's attempt to buy time for his client to recover his wits on the stand by making pointless procedural requests for delay. Finally Haldeman had to admit that he simply made a mistake in his earlier testimony—an "error in over-amplification," as he put it.

The second day of cross was equally tense. The pleasant, earnest demeanor exhibited by Haldeman on direct examination quickly became inoperative as he shot back his answers with an icy glare fixed on Ben-Veniste. Haldeman's attention was directed to the June 23 tape. How would Haldeman explain the instructions he had given to CIA officials to curtail the "Mexican money chain" aspect of the FBI's investigation?

It is extremely rare for a defendant in any type of case to confess guilt under cross-examination. Haldeman did no less than that. Part of the conspiracy charged in the indictment was the defrauding of the United States through the misuse of the CIA and the FBI. In defending his actions, Haldeman admitted that he had sought to manipulate the CIA for "political" reasons (to avoid embarrassment to secret CRP financial contributors, he claimed) in the same breath in which he denied manipulating the CIA to cover up responsibility for the Watergate bugging. However dubious was this explanation, Haldeman could not escape the fact that he *was* admitting to obstruction of justice.

Next, Haldeman was forced to admit that he could not explain why cash had been paid to the Watergate burglars (with his knowledge). Finally, to highlight to the jury the enormous amount of money spent to keep the burglars silent, Ben-Veniste resorted to humor. Haldeman was asked about the secret $350,000 White House cash fund that had been kept in a safe-deposit box under "cover" of a friend of a Haldeman assistant. Why wasn't that money just put into a regular savings account?

> BEN-VENISTE: Do you know how much interest you get if you put $350,000 in the bank for six months?
>
> HALDEMAN: I know you get a lot more today than you would have then. . . .
>
> BEN-VENISTE: At six percent interest in six months, you would get $10,500 just in interest, not to mention a toaster for opening the account.

From the response in the courtroom, it was clear the point had been made.

John Ehrlichman's testimony in his own behalf fell far short of the accusations his counsel had flung at Richard Nixon in his opening statement. On only one matter, the offer of clemency to Howard Hunt, did Ehrlichman claim the former President had deceived him. Ehrlichman's defense was premised on his claim that he had always urged Nixon to "get the whole truth out." Toward the end of his direct testimony Ehrlichman broke down and cried describing his last request of President Nixon: that Nixon someday tell Ehrlichman's children why the President had requested Ehrlichman's resignation. John Wilson, under his breath, muttered, "What a bunch of bullshit." *His* client hadn't behaved in this manner.

Jim Neal then rose to begin a relentless cross-examination with rapid-fire attacks on Ehrlichman's credibility, his attempt to place the blame entirely on Nixon, and his assertion that he had always wanted the entire truth out. On the second day of cross-examination Ehrlichman was even forced to admit that a part of his testimony of the previous day had been a "mistake." Ehrlichman had testified that he knew nothing of a secret hush-money payment made at a phone booth in July 1972 through the efforts of Herbert Kalmbach. The next morning he conceded that Kalmbach had told him about it.

"Did you intend to correct that mistake [for the jury] before I asked you about it?" Neal asked.

"Yes, I did, and then I forgot about it," Ehrlichman insisted. The jury wasn't buying it.

Time after time Neal threw Ehrlichman's taped statements back in his face. The struggle between the two men became bitter, but Neal stayed after his prey. Finally he accused Ehrlichman of laying out his cover-up strategy more than a year before in a (taped) conversation with Nixon about John Dean. "If I were Dean," Ehrlichman had told the former President on April 15, 1973, "I would develop a defense that I was being manipulated by people who had a corrupt motive."

Ehrlichman left the stand bloodied, but haughty as ever.

Among the many surprising things that William Frates did during the Watergate trial, calling Charles Colson to the stand to testify in Ehrlichman's defense took the cake. The other defense counsel viewed Colson's imminent appearance with unmitigated horror. Particularly stricken was William Hundley. Taking advantage of Colson's popular reputation ("I'd walk over my grandmother for Nixon") as the worst in the Nixon Administration's arsenal of villains, Hundley had pinned much of Mitchell's defense strategy on convincing the jury that Colson was the sinister force somehow responsible for all of Watergate. Now the shadowy figure of evil about whom Hundley had been regaling the jurors was going to be replaced with a flesh-and-blood human being.

The best *we* could hope for from Colson's testimony was a standoff with the defense. His sudden conversion to proselytizing Christianity notwithstanding, Colson's responses to our queries *after* his plea bargain in June were just as vague and unsatisfactory as they had been before. It seemed obvious that he still was not leveling with us. But we did see a different side of the enigmatic former Nixon aide, a more humorous side than that portrayed by published reports about him.

Colson had already begun to serve his one- to three-year sentence, and he enlightened us on his reaction to prison life. By and large, he was accepted by the other inmates as a stand-up guy—not quite a Gordon Liddy, but not a squealer either. His evangelism gave him something to occupy his time. It had only one disadvantage, Colson had told Ben-Veniste: a remarkably negative effect on a certain fellow prisoner. One particular inmate, a dwarf, invariably regarded Colson with an alarming scowl and voluble mutterings, especially when Colson was preaching to other prisoners. Upon investigation it turned out that the dwarf had been part of a clever scheme to relieve the Brinks Company of a large amount of currency shipped by commercial airplane, a caper in which the dwarf would be crated up and shipped on the same airplane in order to gain access to the money. One of the dwarf's partners, however, had attended a Southern religious festival and, taken by the spirit, turned in the entire gang. The dwarf did not look kindly upon religious proselytizers, it seemed, no matter how pure their motives.

When the time came for Colson to appear at trial he had little to say in Ehrlichman's defense. After a few questions, Frates sat down and turned "his witness" over to Hundley.

Unfortunately for Hundley, there was just something about Charles Colson that made his blood boil. A transformation in Hundley's demeanor took place that must have shocked the jurors. His warm good humor and friendly politeness put aside, his carefully developed strategy of trying to "out-nice" everyone else in the courtroom shucked off like a disguise, Hundley suddenly became the merciless prosecutor of his younger days.

Hundley started right off with some of his heaviest ammunition: Wasn't it a fact that Colson and Nixon had talked about how to grant executive clemency to Howard Hunt in early January of 1973? Colson replied that he could not recall any such conversation. Couldn't recall it! Why, the jury had heard the tape of it not two weeks before. Hundley demanded that Colson listen to the tape himself to see if it would "refresh his recollection." While the jury and the spectators looked on and waited in silence, Colson donned a headset and with knitted brow listened to the tape of his January 8, 1973, conversation with Nixon. Well, he told Hundley when he had finished listening, the voices certainly were his and Nixon's, but he still didn't recall having had the conversation—the tape just didn't refresh his recollection!

This was truly an unprecedented display of brass. Hundley was beside himself with rage. Directing Colson's attention to various passages on the tape, Hundley asked in a loud voice what Colson had meant by those statements. Colson responded that he couldn't answer that question, because he didn't remember having made the statements. Well, Hundley continued exasperatedly, Colson had heard himself saying them on tape, hadn't he? "I heard my voice, yes," Colson replied. Well, what did "the Colson voice" mean? Hundley shot back. His questions dripping with sarcasm, Hundley continued to refer to the witness in front of him as "the Colson voice," to no avail. Then he began to taunt Colson about his duplicity in tape-recording one of his own conversations with Howard Hunt—Colson's "super patriot, super friend, super-duper everything." Hundley was like a man possessed.

During afternoon recess Colson beckoned for Ben-Veniste to join him in a small office off the corridor. "What is Hundley trying to do to me?" he asked. "You know, Mitchell's looking for trouble."

"I wouldn't take it personally, Chuck," said Ben-Veniste, "but Mitchell may not like you very much. I think Hundley's defense has something to do with your being the cause of original sin. But what do you mean, 'Mitchell is looking for trouble'?"

"Well, Rick, I don't think I mentioned this to you before," said the tall former Marine slowly, "but a few days before the Watergate break-in Mitchell made a very interesting remark to me. It was in the context of my speculating on what strategy Hubert Humphrey was cooking up with his supporters at the Waldorf-Astoria in New York. Mitchell said to me, 'Tell me what room they are in and I will tell you everything that is said in the room.'"

"No, Chuck, I don't think you mentioned this one to us before," said Ben-Veniste, trying to minimize the sarcasm in his voice. "But the way Hundley is going, you may get the opportunity to remind Mitchell of this little incident."

When court resumed, Hundley was on Colson again in a flash, this time badgering him about his back-stabbing efforts to have Nixon throw total responsibility for Watergate onto Mitchell. Carried away with the progress he was making with this line of questioning, Hundley then made a classic mistake: he asked the kind of open-ended question the careful interrogator never puts to a hostile witness on cross-examination. "Well, what evidence did you have? You are a lawyer. What evidence did you have that you could pin on Mr. Mitchell?"

Colson paused, glanced at Ben-Veniste, and launched into a narrative of why he personally thought Mitchell was the real sponsor of Watergate, beginning with the damaging remark about the Waldorf-Astoria, following it with several other juicy tidbits, and concluding with Hunt's comment to Colson that Mitchell had perjured himself. Hundley, having asked the question, couldn't turn Colson off.

Under questioning by Ben-Veniste, Colson fired off at least one big round against each of the major defendants. Mitchell was saying he could bug Humphrey's Waldorf room, wasn't he? Ben-Veniste asked Colson. Colson waffled: Mitchell never actually *said* he could bug it. "You didn't draw the impression that Mr. Mitchell was going to hide in the closet, did you?" Ben-Veniste retorted. "No," said Colson.

Haldeman was Colson's next target. The former White House chief of staff had asked Colson in March of 1973 how bad it would be if Hunt were to "blow." "Very bad," Colson had told him. "Then we can't let that happen," was Haldeman's conclusion.

Ehrlichman (who, according to Jacob Stein's side-bar observation, had "projected this unidentified flying object into the trial") was not spared, either. Colson related that Ehrlichman was the one who persuaded him to meet with Hunt's lawyer Bittman in January 1973 and assure Bittman that Colson would do everything he could for Hunt;

after the meeting, Ehrlichman had voiced his elation at the progress made in keeping Hunt happy.

FOLLOWING THE CONCLUSION of Ehrlichman's case, Robert Mardian was up at bat. Mardian was nobody's favorite defendant. An ultra-right-wing Arizona lawyer whose family owned a lucrative construction business in Phoenix, Mardian had been a campaign coordinator for Goldwater in 1964 and for Nixon in 1968. In 1969 he was installed as general counsel of the Department of Health, Education and Welfare—an agency charged with administration of many federal anti-discrimination programs—to oversee that arm of the Nixon-Mitchell "Southern strategy."

By the lights of the Nixon Administration, Mardian had performed admirably. In 1970 he was rewarded with an appointment as Assistant Attorney General in charge of the Justice Department's almost extinct Internal Security Division. Under Mardian, the division was revived, expanded and made over into the vanguard of the Nixon Administration's repressive law enforcement policies. Freewheeling grand-jury probes were conducted into left-wing organizations in dozens of cities throughout the country, often with little regard for the rights of witnesses. Loosely constructed conspiracy prosecutions were conducted against the entire gamut of draft resisters, antiwar sympathizers and leftist leaders—cases that not only were regarded by many of the career prosecutors in the Justice Department as unprofessional, politically motivated and just plain stupid, but were also in the main unsuccessful.

It was fitting that as his first witness Mardian called to the stand his longtime friend Richard Kleindienst, a man who (like Mardian himself) represented to the young attorneys on the prosecution team the worst element of the Nixon-Mitchell administration of justice. A back-slapping politico, Kleindienst had demonstrated a remarkable insensitivity (at best) to the obligations the law imposes on every citizen, not to speak of those that devolved upon him as a lawyer, as second-in-command of the Justice Department and later as Attorney General.

In March and April of 1972 Kleindienst had repeatedly lied under oath in answering questions about the ITT affair put to him by the Senate Judiciary Committee during his own confirmation hearings. He went out of his way during the hearings to deny that any White House pressure had been brought on the Justice Department to drop its appeal of a pending ITT antitrust case. The truth was otherwise. In fact, Kleindienst had been given direct orders, first by John Ehrlichman and then by President Nixon, that the Justice Department should drop the appeal in the Supreme Court, orders Kleindienst managed to avoid by threatening to resign.

Had Kleindienst been prosecuted for perjury, each count on which he was convicted would have subjected him to up to five years in prison; loss of his license to practice law would have been almost automatic. Instead, Leon Jaworski permitted him to plead guilty in May 1974 to one misdemeanor charge of "contempt of Congress," a disposition that prompted public criticism and resulted in the entire ITT Task Force in our office resigning in protest.*

Kleindienst's contribution to the investigation of the Watergate case had been of a kind with his conduct in the ITT affair. On June 17, 1972, the day the Watergate burglars were arrested, Kleindienst had been playing golf at the plush Burning Tree Country Club in suburban Maryland where he was a member. Sometime in the early afternoon, he had been confronted in the clubhouse by a nervous Gordon Liddy and CRP press aide Powell Moore. Liddy maneuvered Kleindienst into a back corner of the men's locker room (dubbed "Fairyland" by club members) and there told him anxiously that some of the men arrested in the Watergate office building the night before were employees of CRP and the White House. Liddy went on to say that he had come out to Burning Tree on the instructions of John Mitchell to seek Kleindienst's help in getting the burglars out of jail.

Kleindienst had turned Liddy down, but never told anyone at the Justice Department about Liddy's visit or his claim that he was bearing a request from Mitchell. He just kept it to himself, even when Liddy soon became a target of the investigation and Kleindienst knew that his own investigators were spending thousands of man-hours building a case against Liddy and probing for any Watergate ties between Liddy and higher-ups at CRP. Had Kleindienst informed the original prosecutors in the summer of 1972 about Liddy's request from

---

* To make matters worse, when Kleindienst had appeared for sentencing before Chief Judge Hart he had not even received a ritual slap on the wrist. The judge imposed a $100 fine and the minimum sentence permissible under the law, thirty days, and suspended both. Then he praised Kleindienst as a man "of the highest integrity and loyalty . . . universally respected and admired." Later that summer, despite a recommendation from the District of Columbia bar that Kleindienst's law license be suspended for a year, the D.C. Court of Appeals suspended Kleindienst from practice for only one month.

Mitchell, the Watergate investigation might have taken a profoundly different turn and the cover-up might never have succeeded.

When the original prosecutors finally learned about the Burning Tree incident from Dean and Magruder in April 1973, Kleindienst admitted that Liddy had approached him on June 17, but left out the guts of what Liddy had said. Liddy just came to Burning Tree to "inform" him that one of the arrested men was an employee of CRP, Kleindienst claimed; nothing about getting the men out of jail, nothing about John Mitchell.

Now Kleindienst turned up at the cover-up trial as an alibi witness for Mardian ("one of the closest personal friends I have ever had in my life") to give testimony that turned upon Kleindienst's precise recollection of the time of day that he had been approached by Liddy at Burning Tree nearly two and a half years before. Mardian was trying to show, through Kleindienst and others, that the time sequence of events on that day precluded the possibility that *he* had had anything to do with Liddy's going to Burning Tree. Could Kleindienst, with his vaunted memory, help out on this issue by establishing that Liddy definitely appeared at Burning Tree *before* 1 P.M. on June 17, not after that time?

To no one's surprise, he could. Under questioning by Thomas Green, Kleindienst recalled that on June 17 he had begun his golf round in a club tournament about 8:30 A.M., finished at best estimate between 12 and 12:15, turned in his score, washed up, and begun lunch, so that Liddy to the best of his recollection would have appeared between 12:30 and 1 P.M.

Then Ben-Veniste took over on cross-examination. Did Kleindienst actually recall being in the clubhouse by 12:15 P.M. that day, or was this a reconstruction? Well, "my best recollection is that I was." Was his recollection a good recollection? No, Kleindienst answered. Ben-Veniste then pointed out that over a year before, Kleindienst had told the Watergate Task Force (and testified before the Ervin Committee under oath) that he recalled playing golf on June 17, 1972, *in the afternoon*, not in the morning. Kleindienst had even said that he had a "vivid recollection" of having lunch that day, and that he had played poorly in the afternoon because he was worried about Liddy's approach to him. How could Kleindienst explain this discrepancy? "I was wrong." Subsequently, he had checked the tournament records with the club golf pro (records subpoenaed by the prosecution). Could it have been *after* 1 P.M. when Liddy came to Burning Tree? "It could have been, sure."

The day after Kleindienst's appearance his wife was called to the stand again, to corroborate Mardian's Burning Tree alibi. If any one isolated incident epitomized the distance between the mind-set of the defendants on trial and that of the jurors they hoped to convince of their innocence, it was when Mrs. Kleindienst was asked how she happened to remember the time of day on June 17, 1972, when Gordon Liddy phoned her to locate her husband. The phone call stuck in her mind, she answered, as being "curious." One thing that was especially unusual was that Mr. Liddy actually didn't know how to get to Burning Tree Country Club—playing ground of Presidents, Cabinet members and powerful Washington lawyers. Mrs. Kleindienst had to give him directions. She concluded that "Mr. Liddy must be someone from out of town." We wondered how many jurors would also be "out-of-towners" by Mrs. Kleindienst's criterion.

During the trial, Mardian himself had made no secret of his intense scorn for the prosecution team and for some of the government's witnesses, even in front of the jury. He was constantly scowling, grimacing and making indignant faces.

While Mardian was testifying on direct examination a minor legal issue arose that permitted Jill Volner to ask him several questions with the jury temporarily out of the courtroom. Mardian promptly excoriated Volner in a most demeaning fashion. At the next recess, the other defense lawyers were observed trundling Mardian off for a talking-to. "Jee-eesus," said one, "if he acts like that in front of the jury he's going to kill himself."

When cross-examination began, however, the calming ministrations of counsel proved to be of no avail. In response to Volner's level-voiced questions, Mardian alternately sneered, barked and heaped sarcasm on her.

Technically, the cross-examination went poorly. Mardian's unrestrained hostility prevented the effective use of some of our ammunition. When Volner sat down, she was discouraged. But it was clear to objective observers that Mardian had alienated the jury through his terrible demeanor.

Parkinson's defense, like that of Mitchell and Haldeman, rested solely on character witnesses and his own testimony. Under questioning by Stein, Parkinson admitted that Jeb Magruder had confessed to him the true story of the Watergate break-in in July 1972. But Parkinson said that Mitchell (whom he termed a man "at the pinnacle of the legal profession") persuaded him that Magruder's story was untrue. The gist of Parkinson's defense was that he had been duped, not only by Mitchell but also by Mardian.

On cross, Jill Volner brought out admissions from the sometimes testy lawyer that he had shredded his notes of Magruder's confession ("a very serious mistake in judgment on my part"), that he had passed along numerous messages about "commitments" from Bittman to Mitchell and others, and that he had conveyed an assurance to Bittman on Dean's urging that the commitments would be honored. But he continued to deny any personal wrongdoing.

Parkinson's examination concluded the defense case. Before the trial ended, though, we produced two unexpected rebuttal witnesses who thoroughly demolished Mardian's alibi defense. One, a telephone company supervisor from California, was able to rebut Mardian's testimony that no private phone had been available on June 17, 1972, for him to call Gordon Liddy. Telephone records were produced showing that indeed a private phone, installed in Mitchell's suite, had been used to place a call to Liddy's CRP office that same morning. The second witness, a former CRP aide, placed Mardian at breakfast on the morning of June 17 in California when other aides were discussing an urgent telephone call from Jeb Magruder. Pressed on cross-examination by Mardian's counsel to recount the conversation that morning, our witness related that another aide had leaned over to him conspiratorially and spoken just one word in his ear, in a hushed whisper: "Liddy!" Mardian's alibi was a shambles.

JIM NEAL HAD been preparing his summation to the jury since the day John Dean left the witness stand, building up a little box of file cards listing the most important testimony and choice quotations from the tapes he wanted to cite to the jury. A bundle of energy as the time came nearer, he paced around his office thinking about how to organize his remarks. Frampton and others collected tape transcripts and marked passages to be used. With glee, Neal tried out his ideas on us every evening and we suggested others.

When the time came, he was magnificent. His summation, everyone agreed, was the high point of the trial. He pulled out all the stops, his voice rising from a whisper to a crescendo and falling back again.

After reading from the testimony and the tapes in a rapid-fire staccato, he would pause, push his glasses up on his forehead, and tell the jury that the question they had to ask themselves was *why* over four hundred thousand dollars in cash was delivered clandestinely to the burglars. Only the way he said it, his rich Southern drawl turned harsh, giving the word a screeching sound. "*Whaay?*" he asked rhetorically, again and again, his barrel chest pressed tensely against the podium as he leaned forward over it to bray at the jurors. Neal scoffed at the notion that the money had been paid for "humanitarian motives," out of mere "compassion."

Throughout the trial, in our offices, we had heard Neal's booming voice greet John Dean affectionately on Dean's frequent visits as "mean John Dean." Now Neal told the jurors that during Dean's faithful work on the cover-up he had been "nice John Dean" to the White House. Neal made the motion of patting a small boy on the head. But when Dean defected, Neal told the jurors, he was "mean John Dean," the man everyone in the White House wanted to blame for the cover-up.

After the shouting, the sarcasm, the heaping on of the evidence, Neal's voice turned low and emotional as he reached the tapes. Addressing a hushed courtroom, he said, "Members of the jury, tragically these conspiratorial conversations have happened in the hallowed halls of the White House of the United States, where once strode such giants as Jefferson, Jackson, Lincoln, the two Roosevelts, Eisenhower, Kennedy. Can you compare the White House, perhaps, when Jefferson was drafting his second inaugural, or Lincoln was writing 'With malice toward none, charity for all,' with the tapes you've heard in this courtroom? Or Roosevelt saying, 'We have nothing to fear but fear itself' with the statement 'Give 'em an hors d'oeuvre and maybe they won't come back for the main dish'?" Finally Neal closed by asking the jurors "to decide this case without prejudice, without sympathy—without sympathy to either side—but solely on the evidence."

The defense lawyers' summations were anticlimactic after the testimony of their clients on the stand. By far the most effective was that of Jacob Stein on behalf of Kenneth Parkinson. Quietly reasoning with the jury at the outset of his argument, Stein stressed Parkinson's nonpolitical background and his role as retained attorney for CRP, brought in solely in a technical, nonpolitical capacity. Meticulously Stein picked away at the weakest points in the government's case.

Growing more emotional as he proceeded into his argument, Stein contrasted Parkinson's reputation, his long record of community service and his standing in the Washington legal community with the character of the witnesses who had testified against him, principally Jeb Magruder. In the end, Stein told the jury, becoming so emotional he began dabbing at his eyes with a handkerchief and choking back sobs, it was Parkinson's own character that they had to judge. Making the most of the long string of character witnesses who had spoken up for his client (and no doubt reminding the jury of the paucity of such witnesses produced by the three major defendants), Stein asked, "What is good character worth? Is it to be redeemed in a moment of crisis or is it to be thrown away and tossed out cynically in favor of the testimony of confessed perjurers and ambitious people who seek Cabinet-level posts, knowing they are thieves and liars?"

It was a masterful summation. If Parkinson were acquitted, we told each other, a large part of the credit would be due to Stein's argument.

On Friday afternoon, December 27, we had the final opportunity to address the jury and to rebut the nearly fifteen hours of defense lawyers' summations. After Ben-Veniste refuted Haldeman's contention that he had never intended to obstruct justice in Watergate, Neal told the jurors that the only real excuse advanced at the trial by the five defendants was to lay the blame for "this whole massive cover-up" on their subordinates. High officials of the land, he said, may make mistakes, but they must not be allowed to "assault the temples of justice" in an effort to cover up those mistakes. He concluded by telling jurors that when such a thing happens, "society must call those responsible to account. You, as the representatives of a free people, are the ones who, through your verdict based solely on the evidence, must now balance the account and close the ledger . . . on Watergate."

The following Monday morning Judge Sirica instructed the jury in the law, reading—as is customary—from both "standard" jury instructions and his own instructions prepared with the help of suggestions submitted by counsel. After giving them a final warning to ignore the pardon of former President Nixon and concentrate on the evidence against the defendants, the judge sent the jurors to begin their deliberations.

Their first act was to choose as a jury foreman John Hoffar, the retired park police officer (and one of two registered Republicans on the jury) whom John Mitchell's lawyers had been especially eager to get on the jury panel three months before. We worried that Hoffar might be chosen but hoped that Ruth Gould or Marjorie Milbourn would get the nod instead; it was not a good omen for the prosecution.

After months of total absorption in trial preparation and courtroom proceedings, there was now absolutely nothing for the lawyers to do. Each mistake or omission made was magnified as the hours ticked by. Neal and Ben-Veniste were consumed in a head-on game of gin rummy, the stakes designed to keep them from brooding about the jury. Others sat around and read or chatted quietly. Downstairs in the defense camp an air of bravado disguised the pervasive anxiety.

In many ways the concept of judgment by a random selection of ordinary men and women is primitive. Among its many imperfections is the inherent imperfection of its chief ingredient—the ordinary, fallible, emotional human being. Yet in this weakness also lies its strength. It is the community that is vindicated by enforcement of the criminal law. Experience has shown that the interests of justice and of the criminal defendant are best served when the judgment is made by a small cross section of that community, applying everyday common sense and ordinary logic to the issue. Obviously, jury verdicts are seldom arrived at as "scientifically" as is presupposed by the complicated explanation of law given to the jury by the judge. But that does not make the jury's decision any less just. The system is designed to resolve doubts in favor of the accused. Despite the imperfections of the jury system, we have discovered no better alternative.

A note from the jury late Monday afternoon suggested that it was deliberating at a slow, measured pace. The next morning, December 31, more notes were received asking to listen to certain tapes. That afternoon, in an empty courtroom closed to spectators and press, the jury, the defendants, the lawyers and the judge listened again to the four most damaging tapes in the entire trial: three from June 23, 1972, and Dean's "cancer on the Presidency" meeting with Nixon and Haldeman on March 21, 1973. As many times as we had heard the March 21 tape during the investigation, it had never lost its impact. Now, even with all the evidence in, it still had the power to shock—what it showed was unmistakable, undeniable. It was a fitting climax to the trial.

When we trudged to our courthouse offices on Wednesday, New Year's Day, it seemed unlikely that the jury would reach a verdict for at least another day or two. Our expectations were reinforced when the jurors asked first for a complete summary of the judge's legal instructions on the law of perjury and then, in midafternoon, for a complete list of all the physical evidence admitted into evidence during the trial. The jurors, it appeared, were still working away on the fundamentals.

Not an hour later U.S. Marshal George McKinney burst into our cluttered sixth-floor offices with the announcement "The jury has a verdict." Hastily we straightened our ties, abandoned our card games and prepared ourselves for the trip downstairs.

The courtroom was absolutely still as the defendants filed in grimly with their lawyers. The wives of four of the defendants sat tightly together in the second row of spectator benches. The jurors, led by Foreman Hoffar, marched in and took their seats. None smiled. All avoided looking at either the prosecution or the defense, staring straight ahead at the far wall of the courtroom. This was the first sign of a guilty verdict. Jurors like to be able to acquit if they can, to avoid participation in the solemn ritual of punishment. A smiling jury usually has a verdict the defendant can smile about.

Judge Sirica's gray-haired clerk ceremoniously asked Hoffar whether the jury had agreed on a verdict.

"Yes, they have," said Hoffar in a small voice. He handed Capitanio a sealed envelope.

The clerk handed the envelope to Judge Sirica, who opened it and pored over its contents silently for what seemed like hours; then he handed the contents back to Capitanio. "The defendants will rise," the judge intoned.

All five stood, now alone on their feet in the tensed courtroom, without the protective shield of their lawyers, ready to receive the jury's judgment.

His voice quavering, it took Capitanio only a little over sixty seconds to read the verdicts, defendant by defendant, starting with Mitchell. "Count One—guilty. Count Two—guilty. Count Four—guilty. Count Five—guilty. Count Six—guilty." Mitchell did not flinch. Then Haldeman. Guilty on all counts. Ehrlichman. The same. Mardian, charged only with conspiracy in Count One: guilty. Kenneth Parkinson—*not* guilty on both counts charged. Jacob Stein pounded his client on the back. Mitchell smiled and mouthed his congratulations to Parkinson, while Mrs. Haldeman, who had shut her eyes when her own husband's verdict was rendered, congratulated Mrs. Parkinson. Mardian paled, shocked. His wife stuck out her tongue at the jurors and gave them a noisy Bronx cheer. Mardian sank into his chair, where he would remain staring straight ahead almost until the courtroom had completely emptied.

Thanking the jurors for their service, Judge Sirica told them that he could not stop them from talking to the press but strongly advised them not to do so, saying it might detract from the confidentiality and dignity of the proceedings. Then he excused them, telling them they had "made a valuable contribution to the efficient administration of justice." After formally vacating his "gag order" forbidding the attorneys to make public comments on the case, the judge adjourned court at 5.03 P.M.

The courtroom exploded, reporters running for the phones. The prosecution team pushed its way as quickly as possible out a side door to return to our offices. Mrs. Mardian went to her husband's defense table and bent over him, trying unsuccessfully to console him. The other defendants, silent, grim but composed, filed out.

Outside, an afternoon that had begun sunny and pleasant inexplicably turned threatening. Dark storm clouds raced low across the sky, the sun disappeared, and great gusts of wind began to blow. It was as though the maelstrom had struck, darkening the earth on Judgment Day.

On leaving the courthouse Neal told the press that he was resigning immediately and going back to his law practice in Tennessee. "I really don't have anything to say," Neal said. "It's not a happy feeling. We prosecuted as vigorously as we could." Ben-Veniste said only, "I think we had a fair trial and we got a fair verdict."

When the defendants emerged one by one through the front door of the courthouse into the wind and rain, they were besieged by the media. Each maintained his innocence. Mitchell said with a wry smile, when asked if he planned to take a vacation, "I'm going to the moon, I think; that's the best place." Haldeman said he would move ahead with the process of appeal. "There's only one human being in the world who knows with absolute moral certainty the truth concerning the charges against me," he said, speaking of himself. "I am totally innocent." After calling their children in Seattle the Ehrlichmans walked into the second-floor press room, where the former domestic adviser expressed confidence that his conviction would be overturned on appeal because of the extensive pretrial publicity in the

District of Columbia and his failure to obtain Mr. Nixon's testimony at trial, which he called "the turning point" of his case. Parkinson, beaming, told reporters happily, "I feel great. A new lease on life, back from the dead. I've always had great faith and trust, and it worked out." When the Parkinsons reached their suburban home that evening they found that neighbors had organized an impromptu welcome: a large banner hung across the front of the house reading, "KENNY, WE LOVE YOU." It was illuminated by a string of Christmas-tree lights.

In San Clemente, Richard Nixon had no comment on the verdicts. An anonymous associate said he was "deeply anguished" by the denouement of the Watergate process that he had been so instrumental in putting into motion.

Epilogue

ON FEBRUARY 21 the four convicted defendants came before Judge Sirica for the last time. Flanked by their lawyers, they stood in a loose semicircle before the bench. We sat quietly at the same table we had occupied during the trial. Our speculation as to the length of the sentences to be imposed had recently been revised downward after Dean's and Magruder's terms had been reduced by Judge Sirica. But we were there solely as spectators—the decision had been made long before that we would make no recommendation to the court with regard to sentencing. The courtroom was packed; those determined enough to get a seat had waited in line throughout the night in the thirty-degree cold outside the courthouse.

The sentencing proceeding was brief and somber. Judge Sirica had already sent a message to Mrs. Mardian through her husband's lawyer that this time there would be no demonstration in the courtroom from her.

Ritually, the judge asked each defendant in turn whether he or his attorney had anything to say before sentence was imposed.

Mitchell had nothing.

John Wilson told the judge, "I hope that Your Honor considers whatever Bob Haldeman did, he did not for himself but for the President of the United States; that the virtue of loyalty is not to be forgotten."

Judge Sirica nodded slightly, his face impassive.

A local lawyer known for his interest in radical causes and hired specially by John Ehrlichman for the sentencing launched into a long plea for an "alternative sentence" for his client. The long-haired, bearded lawyer asked that instead of being sent to jail Ehrlichman be ordered to provide free legal assistance to six thousand Pueblo Indians living near Espinola, New Mexico. Ehrlichman had recently met one of the Pueblo chieftains and learned that the tribes needed help. Ehrlichman wanted to do what he could to "comport with the old Hasidic command of a good deed for a bad."

The judge seemed restless. Perhaps he was reflecting that the spirit of Talmudic justice had come to John Ehrlichman a little too late.

In an unfortunate turn of phrase, Ehrlichman's new lawyer observed that while the Pueblos could hire a big-city law firm "it is not the same as being on the reservation." There was snickering from the spectators. Evidently the lawyer was the only one in the courtroom unaware that Ehrlichman had repeatedly been confronted during the trial with his own taped admission to Nixon that the Watergate burglars were paid to keep them "on the reservation." It seemed ironic to us to hear such an intelligent statement of the abstract virtues of "alternative sentencing" in a case where the countervailing arguments for imprisonment appeared overwhelming.

Then the judge. "This court has for many days now given careful and serious thought to what the proper sentences to impose in this case should be."

Mitchell: "Not less than thirty months nor more than eight years."

Haldeman: the same.

Ehrlichman: the same.

Mardian: ten months to three years.

Theoretically Haldeman and Mitchell faced a maximum of twenty-five years (five each for conspiracy, obstruction of justice, and three counts of perjury), Ehrlichman twenty, Mardian five. But the sentences imposed were stiff ones judged by the customary punishment inflicted on first offenders in white-collar criminal cases.

Federal prisoners are ordinarily eligible for parole after serving one third of the maximum sentence, less if the judge prescribes. The three major defendants would each spend at least two and a half years in jail before being eligible for release.

ONCE THE government's written brief in the cover-up appeal was filed in October 1975, the Watergate Special Prosecution Force went out of business—in everything but name. Special Prosecutor Henry Ruth was eager to disband the Force. The few minor matters remaining on the agenda, including prosecuting further appeals, could easily be handled by the Justice Department. Ruth had already prepared, in accordance with the charter mandate requiring him to "submit a final report to the appropriate persons or entities of Congress," a 277-page tome summarizing all the work of the office since its inception. The Force had served its purpose. Terminating its existence promptly, rather than letting it die a slow death as just another drain on the public budget, would reaffirm the "special" quality of the office and the professionalism with which it had carried out its duties.

But Attorney General Edward H. Levi refused to post the death notice. In an election year, he didn't want to get stuck with any politically sensitive decisions that might land on his desk in the fallout from Watergate. So the Force was denied an honorable burial. Ruth and the few remaining senior people resigned. The "Final Report," its printed soft-back cover hastily reprinted to read *Report: October 1975*, was issued anyhow. A skeleton staff, headed by a part-time Special Prosecutor, Charles Ruff (who had served on the Campaign Financing Task Force), moved into a depressing little suite with bilious-green walls in a dusty Justice Department office building across the street from the FBI's imposing new J. Edgar Hoover Building. Nine tenths of the space was occupied by file cabinets.

The venture that had begun with such energy and excitement two and a half years before seemed destined to come to a close in the style befitting the federal bureaucracy.

Before its final demise, though, the office was once again back in the headlines, this time with an investigation of allegations that Gerald Ford, while a congressman, had converted campaign contributions to his personal use. Coming smack in the middle of the 1976 Presidential race, the investigation quickly became a significant campaign issue for the Democrats.

Near the end of the campaign, the United States Court of Appeals for the District of Columbia, sitting *en banc,* affirmed the convictions of Haldeman, Ehrlichman and Mitchell. The court ordered a new trial for Robert Mardian, saying that his case should have been severed from those of his co-defendants early in the trial when his original chief lawyer, David Bress, was unable to continue.

DESPITE ITS BULK, the Special Prosecutor's report of October 1975 had little to say. It revealed no facts not already public. Discussion of how and why decisions had been made was limited to generalities.

A few critics were unhappy. They pointed out that Archibald Cox had promised a fuller and more detailed account of the Special

Prosecutor's work, which would include an explanation of why certain persons were *not* indicted. Some members of Congress and the press complained that in light of President Ford's pardon the Special Prosecutor had a "special" obligation to make public all the evidence gathered against Richard Nixon. But at least in Nixon's case the dispute was pointless. All of our evidence of his role in Watergate was already in the public domain—the prosecution team at the cover-up trial had made sure of that.

The report recommended against a permanent Special Prosecutor. Yet it acknowledged the inherent conflicts of interest involved in federal law enforcement and the need for new vitality in this area. What the report suggested was, indeed, a virtual equivalent: a new division of the Justice Department under a new Assistant Attorney General to investigate and prosecute political corruption, a division that in significant respects would be isolated from the normal lines of accountability to the Attorney General and the White House.

The first three Watergate Special Prosecutors, at one time or another, all took public stands against the institution of a permanent Special Prosecutor. But to many, the surfacing of allegations against President Ford during the 1976 Presidential campaign demonstrated precisely why it was important to have in existence some independent prosecutorial office that could be counted upon to investigate such charges thoroughly in a politically charged atmosphere, without interference from the President and his agents.

"THE SYSTEM WORKED." To many people, this was the ultimate lesson of Watergate. The resignation of President Nixon in the face of certain impeachment and the convictions of his associates in the cover-up, many said, proved it. Despite an unprecedented usurpation of executive power, our institutions—the press, the Congress, the criminal-justice system, the judiciary—responded to restore a proper, lawful balance.

To this list of our "institutions" the Special Prosecutor's report added another: an aroused citizenry. "When vigilance erupted," the report concluded, "institutions responded."

The truth is, however, that Watergate was a very close call. A more accurate lesson might be: "The system nearly *didn't* work."

In the first place, only through the criminal-justice process was it possible to extract the evidence needed to get out the truth. Time and again, Congress proved unable on its own to secure information from the Executive vital to the entire story. Only after repeated court victories by the Special Prosecutor and action by the grand jury did the House Judiciary Committee get the evidence required to build a meaningful case for impeachment of the President. Without our judicially backed trial subpoena, the White House could have defied the Judiciary Committee's demands for more tapes and documents, refused to supply transcripts, and perhaps still have defeated the move for impeachment within the committee. It was the legitimate demand of the criminal process for evidence that forced President Nixon to publish the transcripts on which the committee's eventual vote for impeachment was premised. It was the Supreme Court's affirmation of our right to get that same evidence that exposed the June 23 "resignation" tapes.

In fact, in the final analysis, throughout Watergate the most troublesome factor the President had to contend with was not the threat of Congress but the extraordinary power of a single federal trial judge. It was Judge Sirica's (sometimes criticized) use of his sentencing authority over the Watergate burglars that was instrumental in exposing the cover-up; his right to hold public hearings in open court that revealed the shocking details of missing and erased tapes, and seriously damaged White House credibility; and his power to demand production of evidence on pain of punishment for contempt of court that forced President Nixon to reverse his position after the Saturday Night Massacre, and then later to produce a second batch of tapes that cost him the Presidency.

Yet the criminal-justice system itself almost didn't work. For over nine months it was successfully obstructed by the White House and the Nixon campaign committee. Supervision of the case then had to be taken out of "the system" and put into the hands of a Special Prosecutor who wielded unusual independence and occupied an unfamiliar position of institutional limbo. Even then, the autonomy supposedly guaranteed the Special Prosecutor did not deter, as it should have, constant pressure from the White House, culminating in the eventual firing of Archibald Cox. That act, if handled more skillfully, might well have succeeded in terminating a thorough, uninhibited criminal investigation. Finally, the criminal-justice process was abruptly cut off in one important respect by the pardon granted to Richard Nixon by the man he had personally elevated to the Presidency. The system did not permit a final resolution of Nixon's guilt. The opportunity was enhanced for Nixon and those who served him at the end to put their own, self-serving "revisionist" interpretation on the history of Watergate.

Insofar as the criminal-justice process did succeed, it was mainly because of Richard Nixon's ineptness, revealed in a series of miscalculations and mistakes by the President and his cohorts. What if Nixon had destroyed his tapes in July 1973? Without Nixon's extraordinary bungling, without an extraordinary display of public outrage when the President sought to defy a clear court order, without the courage of a few judges and legislators, it might all have turned out differently.

Did the system work? True, the nationally televised debate and vote on articles of impeachment was a shining hour for the House Judiciary Committee. But all in all, the total course of the committee's investigation exposed the extreme political nature of impeachment. The cumbersomeness of the process, its politicization and the unwillingness of so many in Congress to recognize objectively the stark facts of criminal wrongdoing that were put in front of them make the Nixon impeachment case an unpromising precedent. Next time, might it not be a potent defense for a President charged with wrongdoing to argue that his conduct, however improper, fell short of the spectacularly widespread abuses of the Nixon Administration? If Watergate, or more, is what it takes to galvanize the impeachment mechanism, can we really rely on it to protect us in the future against gross Executive wrongdoing?

It is perhaps prudent to remember, too, that it was the "system's" failure to work that allowed Watergate and related abuses to happen in the first place. Congress long ago abdicated its responsibility to serve as an effective check on the Executive. The press, which in large part had become lazy in its coverage of national government, was alternately cowed and cajoled into submissiveness by the Nixon White House. Law enforcement was politicized at its highest levels. Public vigilance did not rise up to meet the rampant growth of unwarranted secrecy in government or question the spreading use of "national security" for political reasons—though common sense alone should have told us that these justifications more often than not are used to hide personal embarrassment, incompetence or venality rather than to serve any legitimate public interest.

What has been done to change these conditions? Very little. Neither

Congress nor the Executive has shown much interest in acting upon the recommendations made by the Ervin Committee, the Special Prosecutor or others who have studied Watergate closely. Congressional attempts to reduce the corrupting role of money in politics by legislating campaign-financing reform have been wrapped up in the members' narrow self-interest as much as the interest of our public weal. As the sensationalized probes of lawlessness by our intelligence agencies have amply proved, we are far better at exposing the errors of the past than at working meaningful changes in the system to insure that the same wrongs do not recur.

Another lesson of Watergate is that the system doesn't work by itself. When Archibald Cox was fired on the night of October 19, 1973, his one-sentence statement posed the question "whether ours shall continue to be a government of laws, not of men." Watergate—indeed Cox himself—proved that whether we care to admit it or not ours must be a government of laws *and* men.

There is nothing automatic, for example, about the criminal-justice process. Prosecution isn't a series of foregone legal maneuvers each of which follows inevitably from the one before. Criminal investigation and prosecution continually require the making of difficult value judgments. The abilities, personalities and biases of the prosecutors play an important and sometimes determinative role in the outcome. With respect to many of the choices facing us during the Watergate case there was not clear consensus of "right" or "wrong" at the time a decision had to be made. Yet even a single decision that in hindsight turned out to have been a misstep could have prejudiced the success of the entire effort.

The independence of the Watergate Special Prosecution Force and the vitality of the criminal-justice system would have been for naught without the political accident that yoked President Nixon's fortunes in May of 1973 to a man of integrity and independence like Cox. It was Cox's resolve to mount a truly thorough investigation that made the system work, not the charter insisted upon by the Senate Judiciary Committee. Had Cox been less adamant about assembling a highly professional staff, and we less intent upon using our power cautiously and responsibly, the effectiveness of our investigation could have been undercut by a political backlash long before any indictments were returned. Had Nixon not misjudged Leon Jaworski, a man who, once convinced by the evidence, was determined to see the criminal investigation through to a proper conclusion and the President removed from office, he might have served out his term of office to the end.

In the same vein, it was two aggressive young reporters and a handful of supportive editors—hardly representative of the national media establishment—who first bombarded Congress and the public with the possibility of cover-up in Watergate, insuring that it became a national issue that would have to be investigated by Congress. It was the unique talents of a former government civil-rights lawyer, John Doar, and a Congressman from Newark, New Jersey, Peter Rodino, that breathed life into the impeachment inquiry. It was a seventy-two-year-old Republican federal judge who in the twilight of his career decided that the President of the United States, like any other citizen, was obliged to obey the law and provide criminal evidence—and was in the end backed up by a unanimous Supreme Court, including four justices appointed by Richard Nixon.

Without all of these men, we might not have had a "government of laws."

Index